THE GREAT WORKS OF GOD:

When I started [my seven volume history of preaching] I had no idea of the treasury I was entering. Surely among the greatest riches in this homiletical storehouse were the sermons of German Protestant Orthodoxy. The story I had gotten in seminary was that Protestant Orthodoxy was dead and dry—not worth looking at. The sermons of Valerius Herberger proved that judgment more than faulty. Herberger's sermons are full of life and vitality. They show us Protestant spirituality at its most profound.

In our day so starved for a religion of the heart, Herberger opens up the contemplative study of the Word of God so that it becomes for us a word of life. He preached in an age full of change and trouble, an age that yearned for something more than the power of positive thinking. . . . The Christian Church has had a lot of great preaching— the sort of preaching that is indeed a means of grace.

—H. O. Old, PhD
John H. Leith Professor of Reformed Theology and Worship
Dean of the Institute for Reformed Worship
Erskine Theological Seminary, South Carolina

The Lutheran pastor and hymn-writer Valerius Herberger was known as the "Jesus Preacher" in his day, and this focus is quite evident in his very readable commentary on Genesis. Divided into 188 Meditations, each headed "Jesus. . .", it combines thorough familiarity with the Hebrew language and Bible history with practical applications filled with a warm awareness of the Savior's presence in the Christian's life. Along with abundant connections between Genesis and other passages, there is a ceaseless flow of reflections on Biblical references and Old Testament Messianic hope.

[Herberger] was also called "the Little Luther," and one is indeed reminded of the Reformer's lively style in the warnings, comforts, anecdotes, humor, and Old Testament Christocentricity, while the interspersed petitions bring to mind Bengel's *Gnomen*. The translator has shed much light on Herberger's thinking and allusions in his renditions and annotations. It will be found a rich and delightful resource for sermons and Bible classes as well as private devotions.

—Thomas Manteufel, PhD
Professor Emeritus of Systematic Theology
Concordia Seminary, St. Louis, MO
Chairman of the C. F. W. Walther Round Table

In this clearly translated and helpfully annotated edition, Matthew Carver provides the contemporary reader with a central work by the sadly long-neglected Lutheran pastor and scholar, Valerius Herberger. Described by his opponents as "the little Luther," Herberger's "Great Works of God" remains a remarkably inspiring work for Christians of all communions, offering the general reader and scholar alike striking insights into the dynamic religious thought of the Lutheran world just prior to the devastation of the Thirty Years War, and reflecting the finest linkage of firm piety and close scholarly attention, a heritage ever serviceable in Herberger's age and our own.

—Peter C. Erb, PhD
Associate Director, Schwenkfelder Library, Pennsburg, PA
Professor Emeritus, Wilfrid Laurier University, Waterloo, Ont.

Matthew Carver has produced a splendid, readable translation of this devotional study of Genesis by Valerius Herberger. This translation has made it possible for Herberger to speak to the heart of American Christians as he did to the German Lutherans of the past. As an outstanding example of devotional literature it is filled with comfort, giving needed consolation. Many typological and devotional themes are employed which are lacking in modern literature. For example, in one of its many prayers Herberger has Jesus encourage Christians to find rest in His wounded side (179). Herberger reminds us of the significance of the first Gospel promise (Genesis 3:15) when he asserts that all the writings of the prophets are simply postils on the text (195). *The Great Works of God* is edifying devotional literature for every need.

—Gaylin R. Schmeling, STM
President, Bethany Lutheran Theological Seminary

THE GREAT WORKS OF GOD

VALERIUS HERBERGER

1562–1627

THE GREAT WORKS OF GOD

or

JESUS,

The Heart and Center of Scripture

*Parts One and Two: The Mysteries of Christ
in the Book of Genesis, Chapters 1–15*

BY VALERIUS HERBERGER
PASTOR OF FRAUSTADT, POLAND

FROM THE FIFTH GERMAN EDITION
TRANSLATED BY MATTHEW CARVER

Peer Reviewed

FIRST ENGLISH EDITION

CONCORDIA PUBLISHING HOUSE • SAINT LOUIS

Concordia
Publishing House

Peer Reviewed

Published by Concordia Publishing House
3558 S. Jefferson Ave., St. Louis, MO 63118-3968
1-800-325-3040 · www.cph.org

Originally published as Magnalia Dei: de Jesu Christo, Scripturae nucleo et medullae, Fifth edition: Gleditsch; Leipzig, 1700.

Cover artwork: The Creation of Light by Gustave Doré (1832–1883). Reproduced with permission from The Doré Bible Illustrations [New York: Dover, 1974].

Manufactured in the United States of America

9 10 11 12 13 14 15 16 17 18   31 30 29 28 27 26 25 24 23 22

CONTENTS

Translator's Preface   xiii

General Abbreviations   xvii

Bibliographic Abbreviations   xviii

THE GREAT WORKS OF GOD

Author's Preface   3

Introduction to the Fifth Edition (1700)   5

PART ONE (GENESIS 1–3)

Dedication of Part One (1601)   13

I. JESUS, the heart and center of the writings of Moses and the prophets, from the verse, "Moses wrote of Me" (John 5:46).   15

II. JESUS in the beginning, the Beginning of our consolation, the Beginning of all that I say (Gen. 1:1).   27

III. JESUS creates heaven and earth and so displays His wisdom, omnipotence, and divinity (Gen. 1:1).   37

IV. JESUS, God, the Almighty Elohim, our Protector (Gen.1:1).   44

V. JESUS "said," and is therefore called "the Word," "our Advocate" (Gen. 1:1; John 1:1; 1 John 2:1).   52

VI. JESUS, the Light of the world, the Craftsman of light, the Light and Joy of our heart (Gen. 1:3–4; John 8:11–12).   59

VII. JESUS, the Firmament and Basis of our salvation,
the Craftsman of the firmament, or heavenly fastness
(Gen. 1:6–7).   67

VIII. JESUS, the Creator of the earth, sea, vegetation, plants,
and trees; our Friend (Gen.1:11).   75

IX. JESUS, the Sun of righteousness, the bright Morning Star,
the Craftsman of the sun, moon, and stars (Gen.1:16;
Mal. 4:2; 2 Peter 1:19).   84

X. JESUS, the Creator of the fish and birds,
our Provider (Gen. 1:21).   93

XI. JESUS, the Creator of the livestock, creeping things,
and beasts of the earth, and comfortingly depicted
in them (Gen. 1:24).   102

XII. JESUS, the Creator of man, the Lord of our body and soul
(Gen. 1:27; 2:22).   113

XIII. JESUS rests on the seventh day, keeps and hallows
the sabbath, and obtains eternal rest for us in heaven
by the unrest of His suffering (Gen. 2:2).   125

XIV. JESUS, the Paradise and Pleasure Garden of our souls,
the Creator of Paradise (Gen. 2:8).   136

XV. JESUS, the succulent, green Tree of Life (Gen. 2:9).   146

XVI. JESUS, the great River of Paradise, the River of life, which
waters and irrigates the whole garden of Christendom
and all believing hearts (Gen. 2:10).   152

XVII. JESUS, the Second Adam by way of comparison
(Gen. 2:21; 3:6).   159

XVIII. JESUS, the Second Adam by way of contrast (Gen. 2:21; 3:6).   167

XIX. JESUS joins Adam and Eve in holy matrimony, honors
the first marriage on earth with His presence, and appoints
the eternal marriage in heaven (Gen. 2:22).   171

XX. JESUS, the Second Adam, falls asleep on the cross, just as the first Adam falls asleep in Paradise; His heart's dearest bride is formed from His opened side (Gen. 2[:21–23]).   175

XXI. JESUS, the oldest, first, best, and noblest Preacher of evangelical comfort, the sweet Comforter of our heart (Gen. 3:15).   185

XXII. JESUS, the woman's Seed, shall trample the serpent's head: the First Gospel, which vividly and clearly describes Jesus Christ's person, work, and merit (Gen. 3:15).   192

XXIII. JESUS restores everything that Adam and Eve ruined in the fall (Gen. 3:15; Luke 1:31–32).   200

XXIV. JESUS clothes Adam, Eve, and all repentant hearts with the garments of His righteousness and lambskins of His innocence (Gen. 3:21).   208

PART TWO (GENESIS 4–15)

Dedication of Part Two (1602)   219

I. JESUS, the richest Treasure of our heart, the hereditary Lord of all that Eve has in her heart, mind, and mouth during the birth of Cain (Gen. 4[:1]).   225

II. JESUS, the noble Man whom Eve confidently expects in childbirth (Gen. 4[:1]).   229

III. JESUS, the Lord, *Jehovah*, of whom Eve speaks in childbirth, and by whom she overcomes her anguish (Gen. 4[:1]).   233

IV. JESUS, the Lamb of God, depicted in Abel's sacrificial lamb (Gen. 4[:4]).   240

V. JESUS CHRIST'S heaven-crying blood speaks far better than Abel's (Gen. 4[:10]; Heb. 12:24]).   245

VI. JESUS, the true Seth, or, immovable, firmly established
Rock of our salvation (Gen. 4[:25]).   252

VII. JESUS, the true Enosh, or, Man of Sorrows, and the Lord
whose name men began to preach in the days of Enosh
(Gen. 4:26).   256

VIII. JESUS and His triumphant ascension, depicted for our
comfort in the ascension of the pious patriarch Enoch
(Gen. 5[:24]; Heb. 11[:5]).   259

IX. JESUS, the true Methuselah, the mighty Conqueror of
death and Captain of Life (Gen. 5[:27]).   268

X. JESUS, the comforting Noah, who brings us relief from our
work and toil upon the ground which the Lord cursed
(Gen. 5:29; Matt. 11:28).   274

XI. JESUS places Shem above his brothers, and honors
us Christians above all unbelievers (Gen. 5[:32]).   279

XII. JESUS takes counsel concerning the flood, and as soon as
it is settled upon, He kindly and faithfully warns the pious
Noah of the coming disaster; and Noah finds grace because
of Jesus Christ (Gen. 6[:8, 13]).   285

XIII. JESUS commands Noah to enter the newly built ark
eight days before the flood; and when Noah is inside,
the Lord Jesus shuts the door behind him (Gen. 7[:1, 16]).   291

XIV. JESUS, Noah's vessel of grace, the mighty Fortress and Ark
in which we escape the flood of God's wrath (Gen. 7[:7]).   295

XV. JESUS is the noble balsam shrub; His benefits are the
healing leaves of ointment which God's Spirit, the Holy
Dove of Pentecost, ushers into Noah's spiritual ark, that is,
into Noah's heart and ours (Gen. 8[:11]).   300

XVI. JESUS speaks to Noah, saying, "Go out from the ark."
Noah's joy, as of one risen from the dead and come out of
the tomb, foreshadows the paschal joy that our heart
will have on the Last Day (Gen. 8[:16]).   308

XVII. JESUS, the Altar of Christendom, depicted in the first and oldest altar, and in Noah's burnt offering (Gen. 8[:20]). 314

XVIII. JESUS, the heavenly Father's Heart, with whom the heavenly Father decides that a flood shall no more go over the earth (Gen. 8[:21]). 317

XIX. JESUS, the blessed Man for whose sake God the Father will never again curse the ground (Gen. 8:21). 320

XX. JESUS pronounces His blessing upon Noah and his children, reminding them in a veiled way that life is found in His blood (Gen. 9[:1–4]). 322

XXI. JESUS, the beautiful Rainbow, the true witness of God's grace (Gen. 9[:8–17]). 327

XXII. JESUS, the noblest Vine in Noah's vineyard and in the garden of every pious Christian's heart (Gen. 9[:20]). 335

XXIII. JESUS, Shem's most blessed Lord and God, in whom Japheth's children, the vast mass of heathendom, will also have a share (Gen. 9[:27]). 340

XXIV. JESUS and His sibling Christians hold the highest place in the eyes of God the heavenly Father, but are always counted last in the eyes of the world (Gen. 10). 345

XXV. JESUS, the only Heavenly Tower in which we are safe from all calamity, contemplated in the tower of Babel (Gen. 11[:1–9]). 350

XXVI. JESUS makes an eternal and noble name for Shem, Arpachshad, Salah, Eber, Peleg, Reu, Serug, Nahor, Terah, Abraham, and all His family (Gen. 11[:10–26]). 355

XXVII. JESUS, the Seed of Abraham in which all the families on earth shall be blessed (Gen. 12). 359

XXVIII. JESUS, the Lord whom Abraham preached (Gen. 12[:8]). 363

XXIX. JESUS is never let out of Abraham's heart (Gen. 13). 368

XXX. JESUS, the King of righteousness, the Priest after the order
of Melchizedek, Instituter of the Holy Supper (Gen. 14).   371

XXXI. JESUS tells the greatly troubled, melancholy Abraham,
"Fear not, Abraham, I am your shield and your very
great reward" (Gen. 15:1).   382

XXXII. JESUS counts to Abraham as righteousness Abraham's
faith in Him (Gen. 15[:6]).   392

XXXIII. JESUS fills Abraham's ears with a comforting promise and
sets before his eyes a blessed token of grace, thus assuring
his heart by Word and Sacrament that his children shall
inherit the Promised Land (Gen. 15[:7–21]).   397

Most English-speakers who know about Valerius Herberger today know him as the writer of the hymn "Valet will ich dir geben" (or, "Farewell I Gladly Bid Thee," as Catherine Winkworth rendered it), which he called his "Final farewell to the world, given in the autumn of 1613, when, seeing death before him at every turn, he was nevertheless graciously preserved, as wondrously as the three young men in the Babylonian furnace." In this hymn we see a microcosm of Herberger's faith and devotion which in the pages of the present book is unfolded like a many-petaled rose with Christ crucified at the center.

Valerius Herberger, who was a humble and untiring minister of God's church, was born in Fraustadt (now Wschowa), Poland, in a city of old German heritage, on April 21, 1562. His father, Martin, a furrier by trade, died in 1571 and Valerius was sent to live with his aunt. Intending to take up his foster-father's trade as a shoemaker, his course was averted at the last minute by his godfather (a pastor), who urged him to follow his father's wishes and become a pastor himself. Thus he went off to study in Frankfurt-an-der-Oder and Leipzig, and in due time was called back to Fraustadt to fill a teaching position. He was eventually called as deacon to Fraustadt's parish church, St. Mary's, in 1590, and as pastor in 1599, where he was happy to remain with his storm-tossed congregation for the rest of his days, turning down respectable calls to other cities and faithfully tending his flock through fire, pestilence, and the persecutions of the Counter-Reformation. The congregation was famously ousted from St. Mary's in 1604 when the property was ceded by royal decree to a handful of Roman Catholics (who already had a cloister church). The congregation raised money and bought two houses by the city gate which they finished turning into a proper church building just before Christmas Eve. This is when Herberger suggested its famous name, "Christ's Manger," saying that "if there is no room for Christ in the inn, at least there is room for Him in His manger."

Throughout eastern Germany, Silesia, and the German-speaking areas of Poland, Herberger was widely known for his homiletic skill, and that mainly through his written sermons which were printed often during his liftetime. The Lutheran Princess Anna of Sweden (1568–1625) was an ardent supporter and admirer of Herberger's works. One of the most popular and most exhaustive of these is the one that Herberger called *Magnalia Dei,* that is, *the Great Works of God,* which is an ambitious edifice of devout meditations on the Scriptures as "those that bear witness about Christ." These he regarded rather like the linen cloths that wrapped the infant Jesus in the manger, and traced his Lord in every little wrinkle. It is difficult to imagine how big this enormous tome would have been if finished; he only got as far as Ruth. Though Herberger was miraculously preserved by God's hand, the cares of multiple plagues and the labor of committing half a city to its earthly slumber meant there was little time left over for writing. What we are left with is therefore as astounding as it is eminently edifying. Herberger was eventually forced into the retirement of blessed sleep on May 15, 1627, a few weeks after suffering a stroke while in the pulpit. According to his wishes, he was laid to await the Lord's coming not in the stony floor of a church but in a cemetary plot among his faithful, slumbering sheep.

The Great Works of God, by far Herberger's greatest work in terms of size and scope, was printed in twelve parts from 1601 to 1618 at Schürer's press in Leipzig, and reprinted numerous times during and after that in several editions. Among his other works which have enjoyed a wide readership in German-speaking countries are *Evangelische Hertz-Postilla,* sermons on the Gospels of the Church Year; *Trauerbinden,* a seven-volume collection of funeral sermons; *Psalter-Paradiß,* an exposition of the Psalter up to Psalm 23 (prepared posthumously by his son Zacharias); *Das Himmlische Jerusalem,* an exposition of Revelation 21 & 22; and *Passion-Zeiger,* a collection of homilies on the Passion.[1]

---

1   For more information about Herberger in English, there are unfortunately few places to turn. The interested reader will want to start with H.O. Old, *The Reading*

In translating *The Great Works of God*, I have tried to use clear but not overly colloquial English, which I think best reflects Herberger's style. My concern has been to communicate the sense of the early modern German, not improve it or make it more appealing, nor to make it sound archaic. Nevertheless, Herberger's ubiquitous use of narrative present-tense, which sounds odd to most readers of modern English, has been generally changed to a narrative past-tense following common English usage. Likewise, Bible verses are rendered from the text (i.e., the Luther Bible), but borrow as much as possible from the English Standard Version or King James, so that they "sound like the Bible" to the modern ear. It would perhaps be impossible to cite every allusion to Scripture, every little bit of borrowed wording that Herberger used, as may well be expected of a man so thoroughly immersed in the study of Holy Scripture. But where unreferenced verses are given at length or in detectable paraphrase, they have been provided with a reference in brackets. Latin and Greek quotations have been moved to footnotes; where a form of the Greek seemed helpful in the body, I have transliterated it there and included the original in a footnote as well. Several Latin or German-Latin hybrid terms have been silently translated, largely made up of those for which there were in Herberger's day no vernacular alternates in common usage, such as distinguished offices (*praeceptor, refendarius*) or grammatical terms (*plurale, signis distinctionarum*). I have generally translated the glosses as they are given in the textual edition, translating from the Latin

and *Preaching of the Scriptures in the Worship of the Church*, vol. 4 (Wm. B. Eerdmans Publ. Co., Grand Rapids / Cambridge, 2002), pp. 373–382. There are also brief articles in *Lutheran Cyclopedia* (H.E. Jacobs, 1899), *The Dictionary of Hymnology* (John Julian, 1907), and *The Handbook to the Lutheran Hymnal* (CPH, 1942). Those able to read German may refer to Ilse Buchholz, *Valerius Herberger: Prediger am "Kripplein Christi" zu Fraustadt in Polen* (Evangelische Verlagsanstalt, Berlin, 1965). There are a number of older German biographies, esp. from the 19th century, including: S.L. Lauterbach, *Vita, fama et fata Valerii Herbergeri. Das merkwürdige Leben Valerii Herbergers*, 2 parts (1708, 1711); K.F. Ledderhose, *Leben Valerius Herbergers, Predigers am Kripplein Christi zu Fraustadt*, Bielefeld (1851); G.A. Pfeiffer, *Das Leben des Valerius Herberger, weiland Pastors am Kripplein Christi zu Fraustadt*, Eisleben and Leipzig (1877); F.W. Bautz, *Von Gott will ich nicht lassen: Kreuzträger unter den Liederdichtern* (1938).

or Greek only when their tendency toward flowery and loose paraphrase obscured the sense of the original, or focused it too narrowly.

Though this book is not designed as a critical edition of the text, it is hoped that it will prove useful to historians and students of homiletics as well as serve as an edifying resource for Bible study and devotion. Some care has been taken to note original citations and provide brief notes on other things that might be of interest to scholars without access to or ability to read the original. While I have not attempted to make any apologies for any peculiar or obviously erroneous statements representative of learning in Herberger's day, I have made some notes to serve to the casual reader. It is hoped that every reader, thus forewarned, will enjoy the authentic picture of the period which such details help to provide without being distracted from the central argument.

I would be a worse translator than I am if I did not learn from Herberger's example; so my first and greatest debt of thanks is owed to the almighty, everlasting God, Father, Son, and Holy Spirit, revealed in my Lord and Savior Jesus Christ, whose grace I can never begin to repay; after whom I am most especially indebted to the patience and support of my beloved, talented wife Amanda (who also designed this book), and to Rev. Dr. Benjamin Mayes for the initial suggestion, and for his kind help and counsel along the way. This book would not have been possible without the generosity of Mr. Joshua Hayes who supplied me with photographs of the original codex, nor without the selfless attention and honest criticisms of its reviewers, Dr. Thomas Manteufel of Concordia Seminary, St. Louis, and Rev. Todd Peperkorn, for whose labors I am immeasureably grateful. Special thanks must also be given to all those others who in one form or another have contributed to any aspect of this book that is good, especially Barbara Dillenburger, Joseph Nolan, Brian Westgate, Rev. Dr. Francis C. Rossow, Dr. Stephen G. Burnett, Mark Preus, and Rev. Dr. Dan Harmelink. Finally, I would also like to thank the senior editor for professional and academic books, Rev. Ed Engelbrecht, for his support and guidance.

Matthew Carver,
On the anniversary of Herberger's death,
15 May 2010

GENERAL ABBREVIATIONS

AD	Anno Domini	Lat.	Latin
ascr.	ascribed to	lit.	literally
attr.	attributed to	p(p).	page(s)
BC	Before Christ	pag.	page
bk.	book	par.	and parallel passages
c.	century	paraph.	paraphrased
ca.	circa	prob.	probably
cf.	compare	resp.	respectively
ch.	chapter(s)	spec.	specifically
corr.	corrected	st.	stanza
d.	died	tr.	translated, translator
e.g.	for example	ultim.	ultimately
ed.	edition(s)	v(v).	verse(s)
esp.	especially	vol.	volume
etc.	and so on		
f(f).	and following		
fl.	flourished		
fol(s).	folio(s)		
fragm.	fragment(s)		
Germ.	German		
Gk.	Greek		
Heb.	Hebrew		
i.e.	that is		
ibid.	from the same source		
KJV	King James Version		

BIBLIOGRAPHIC ABBREVIATIONS

Aelian.   Claudius Aelianus
          De nat. anim.   *On the Nature of Animals*
          Var. Hist.   *Various History*

Ambr.   Ambrose of Milan
          Apost. Const.   *Apostolic Constitutions*
          In Luc.   *Commentary on Luke*
          Serm. de grano sinap.   *Sermon on the Mustard Seed*

Aesop.   Aesop[ius]

Arist.   Aristotle
          Hist. an.   *History of Animals*

August.   Augustine of Hippo
          Conf.   *Confessions*
          Contr. Faust. Manich.   *Against Faustus the Manichean*
          De civ. Dei   *The City of God*
          De Gen. ad litt.   *On the Literal Meaning of Genesis*
          Enarr. in Ps.   *Commentary on Psalms*
          Epist.   *Letters*
          Quaest. in Exod.   *Questions on Exodus*

Bacch.   Bacchides

Basil   Basil of Caesarea
          Hom.   *Homilies*
          Hom. exeg. in Ps.   *Exegetical Homilies on Psalms*

Ber. Rab.   Bereshith Rabbah

Bern.   Bernard of Clairvaux
          In Annunc. sermo   *Sermon on the Annunciation*
          In nat. Dom. sermo   *Sermon on the Nativity*
          Serm. de divers.   *Miscellaneous Sermons*
          Serm. in Cantic.   *Sermon on Song of Solomon*

Bonav.   Bonaventure
          Solil.   *Soliliquy*

Cl. Mar. Vict.   Claudius Marius Victor

Clem. Alex.   Clement of Alexandria

Chrys.   Chrysostom
         In Epist. ad Coloss. Hom.   *Homilies on Colossians*

Diod. Sic.   Diodorus Siculus
         Bibl. hist.   *Historical Library*

DWB   Jakob and Wilhelm Grimm, *Deutsches Wörterbuch.*
         S. Hirzel, 1838–1961.

Epict.   Epictetus
         Fragm.   *Fragments*

Euseb.   Eusebius of Caesarea
         Eccles. Hist.   *Church History*

Guillel.   Guillelmus Abbas
         Vita Bern.   *Life of St. Bernard*

Hier.   Jerome
         Ep. ad Damasum   *Letter to Damasus*
         Epist. ad Heliod.   *Epistle to Heliodorus*
         Hist. de omn. goth.   *History of All the Kings of the Goths and Swedes*
         Vita S. Hilarion.   *Life of St. Hilarion*

Hilar.   Hilary of Poitiers
         De Trin   *On the Trinity*

Ignat.   Ignatius of Antioch
         Phil.   *Epistle to the Philadelphians*
         Rom.   *Epistle to the Romans*

Iren.   Irenaeus
         Adv. Haeres.   *Against Heresies*

Isid.   Isidore of Seville
         Etym.   *Etymologies*

Josep.   Josephus
         Antiq.   *Antiquities*

Lact.   Lactantius
         De ira Dei   *On the Wrath of God*

LB   Luther Bible (1545)

LS   H.G. Liddell, R. Scott, et al. *A Greek-English Lexicon,* Oxford, 1996.

LSB   *Lutheran Service Book.* Concordia, 2006.

Mills   H.G. Mills, tr. *Horae Germanicae.* H & J.C. Ivison, 1856.

Nic. Selneccer   Nicolaus Selneccer
         Instit. Christian. Relig.   *Institutes of Christian Religion*

Niceph. Call.   Nicephorus Callistus
         Hist. Eccles.   *History of the Church*

Ovid
         Pont.   *Letters from the Black Sea*

Paulin.   Paulinus of Nola
         Contra Felicem   *Against Felix*
         Poem.   *Poems*

Paus.   Pausanias

Plin.   Pliny the Elder
         NH   *Natural History*

Ryan   W.G. Ryan, tr., ed. *The Golden Legend: Readings on the Saints.* Princeton, 1993. (Two volumes.)

Sanh.   *Babylonian Talmud: Sanhedrin*

Shabb.   *Babylonian Talmud: Shabbath*

Sir.   Sirach (Ecclesiasticus)

Sozom.   Sozomen

Suet.   Suetonius
         Dom.   *On Domitian*

Tertul.   Tertullian

Theod.   Theodoret

Thom. Aqu.   Thomas Aquinas
         In Symb. Apost.   *On the Apostles' Creed*

Val. Max.   Valerius Maximilianus

Wisd.   Book of Wisdom

THE GREAT WORKS OF GOD

AUTHOR'S PREFACE

To the Christian Reader:

Those who heard the apostles on Pentecost said of the new Pentecost-preaching, "We hear them preaching in our own tongues the great works of God" [Acts 2:11]. At this one should ask, "So what did the apostles preach?" I humbly give this answer: They publicly testified that Jesus Christ is the Savior of the world, apart from whom no man can be saved. This they proved from Moses, the Prophets, and the Psalms, establishing on the clear basis of the Old Testament how from the beginning God extolled this Son of His as the only choice and tried cornerstone of salvation for all believing hearts. That this is so this work will make manifestly clear, so read it earnestly. Consider and meditate on the *great works of God*. For "whoever studies them finds pure pleasure in them" (Ps. 111:2).

VALERIUS HERBERGER

INTRODUCTION TO THE FIFTH EDITION (1700)

A new introduction for the earnest Christian reader of spiritual writings, in particular of the blessed Valerius Herberger's The Great Works of God.

No man, I doubt not, can sufficiently express and perfectly describe the great works of God—for whoever would undertake such a thing would fare no better than *Simonides*, who is said to have asked King Hieron,[1] "What is God?" The King asked for a day's time to consider; when this was up, he asked for two; these also having passed, he asked for four; finally he said, "The more I consider the matter, the less I understand." Or take St. Augustine, who, seeking to comprehend the mystery of the Holy Trinity, went out all alone to the sea-shore where he encountered a boy who had made a little hole next to the sea and was trying to scoop the sea into it using a little shell. When Augustine said, "Dear child, you will never finish," he replied, "Why, then, do you try to fathom with your human mind the unfathomable mystery of the Holy Trinity in the true Godhead?"[2] It would be equally vain to trouble oneself with a comprehensive expression and worthy description of the great works of God, for in this part of our story "our knowledge is in part, and our prophesying is in part" (1 Cor. 13:9). For even though one can indeed say of the great work of creation that God created heaven and earth in six days, no man can tell how it was created out of nothing. "Do not inquire after the material from which the world was created, for there was none."[3] It is enough that we creatures see

---

1   Simonides of Ceos (556–568 BC), a Greek lyric poet.

2   A traditional legend; orig. from a letter attributed to Augustine.

3   "Materiam noli quaerere; nulla fuit" (Ovid *Pont.* 4.3.18).

with our eyes, and that the Lord says, "My hand has made all that is" (Is. 66:2; Acts 7:50). Now we can surely say that God has nourished and kept all creation, from the greatest to the least; for we not only read in Holy Scripture that the Lord "gives them their food at the proper time," and that "He opens His hand and satisfies the desires of every living thing" (Ps. 145:15–16), but we also see it daily before our eyes. For "in Him we live, move, and have our being" (Acts 17:28). "The holy and most blessed God sits in heaven and nourishes the world, from the [horn of the] great rhinoceros all the way down to—begging your pardon—the egg of the louse,"[4] say the Rabbis. But who can rightly describe and comprehensively discuss such divine providence? All reason must especially stagger and be silent when we recall the great works of God in the effecting of our salvation, when the eternal Son of God was conceived in His mother's womb, born a true human being, wrapped in swaddling-clothes, and laid in a manger. For even if it is hard to believe what Cornelius à Lapide[5] asserts about Luke 1:38, although he himself does not require it as an article of faith—that when the angel Gabriel announced to the Virgin Mary that she would be with child by the Holy Spirit and bear a son, he stood completely astounded and dumbfounded for nine whole hours and marveled, partly at her virtue, partly at the mystery of God incarnate and manifested in the flesh—still, it is certain that even holy angels could hardly marvel enough at this work, since "they long to look" into this mystery (1 Peter 1:12). And St. Paul says, "Great indeed is the divine mystery: God was manifested in the flesh" (1 Tim. 3:16). "One could see Him with one's eyes," says the blessed Dannhauer[6] (in his *Catechism Milk,* part 5, p. 908), "the height of beauty,[7] of all new things the newest, and therefore greatly to be wondered at,"[8] as the dear old man loved to say, "God manifest in flesh, the

---

4   "Sanctus Benedictus sedet et alit mundum, a cornibus unicornuum usque ad ova pediculorum." *Shabb.* 107b.

5   Cornelius Cornelii à Lapide (1567–1637), a Jesuit priest and Bible commentator.

6   Dr. Johann Conrad Dannhauer (1603–1666), a professor of philosophy and linguistics.

7   "summum pulchrum"

8   "παντῶν καὶ νῶν καὶ νότατον"

Creator in His creation, the ageless Word, the Incomprehensible in a little body, the Son of a Virgin, such as never was known." Nor is it any different with the other great works of God[9] visible in the suffering and death of Jesus Christ, when God shed His own blood and thereby purchased His Church (Acts 20:28), or when the Prince of Life was killed (3:15), and the Lord of Glory crucified (1 Cor. 2:8), or when Jesus rose again from the dead on the third day, or when the Son of Man who is in heaven ascended into heaven (John 3:13; 6:62), or when He seated Himself at the right hand of God, etc. These are all such works as no human tongue can express, much less intelligibly describe. "Who can utter the mighty deeds of the Lord? Who can declare all His praiseworthy works?" (Ps. 106:2). "Though we speak much, we cannot reach the end." (Sir. 43:27).

Nevertheless, pious Christians may still speak as much about it as has been revealed to them in God's Word, and take devout, sincere pleasure and joy in doing so, as King David does when he says, "I will remember the works of the Lord, and call to mind Your wonders of old. I will meditate also on all Your work, and talk of Your doings" (Ps. 77:11–12). "O Lord my God, great are Your wondrous deeds and Your thoughts which You show us. There is none like You. I will proclaim and tell of them, yet they cannot be numbered" (Ps. 40:5). Finally, since the Scriptures bear witness about Christ and His great works (John 5:39), and since He is the chief end[10] toward which everything in Holy Scripture moves, inasmuch as "all the prophets bear witness" (Acts 10:43) to this Christ, devout hearts should not only read Scripture carefully, but as true friends of their dearest Jesus, also appropriate all His testimonies in true faith and have great delight in them "as much as in all riches" (Ps. 119:14). To this end they are depicted in all manner of beautiful, spiritual writings, of which the prize-holder is this splendid book of the late reverend pastor of Christ's Manger church[11] in Fraustadt, Poland—titled *Magnalia Dei; or, the Great Works of*

---

9   "Magnalia Dei"

10   "Τέλος σκοπιμώτατον"

11   "Kripplein Christi." (The name for the new Lutheran church in Fraustadt, suggested by Herberger himself during his first sermon in it, delivered on Christmas, 1604, a day after the parish church had been ceded to the Catholics.)

God, wherein it is masterfully shown that "Jesus is the Heart, Kernel, Core, Essence, Substance, Object, End, Purpose, Jewel, and Sanctuary of Holy Scripture," and how this may all be employed to the wholesome improvement and edification of the Christian Church.

It is precisely this extraordinary book, first issued by its blessed author himself in 1601 at the beginning of the century now running to its end, which now at the conclusion of the seventeenth century has been revised for a fifth edition, yet much improved in many points, viz.:

1. All older editions were diligently consulted, and all the printing mistakes found in the latest one—which were not few—were fixed.
2. Biblical quotations and German translations of Latin texts have been printed with Schwabacher type[12] for the benefit of the common man.
3. Since in previous editions major errors often crept into the punctuation, at times altering the sense of the text, great care has been taken to sift through the entire work more closely so that it is much clearer to the casual reader than before.
4. In previous editions the title at the top of the page was the same through the whole book. Here, however, it will always indicate the subject of the selection beneath it.
5. The four parts of the *Psalter-Paradise*,[13] which were previously printed in a separate volume, are appended here at the request of its many admirers. In this especially there has been much improvement. The shorter Latin quotations and axioms had been replaced with German in previous editions, but here both are placed together. Likewise, verse references have been added which for the most part were lacking from the biblical quotations.

---

12   This appears in the original text as a bold style typeface. The distinction has for the most part been carried over into the present in the form of quotation marks. I have employed an italic typeface in some passages where Schwabacher is used for emphasis rather than to indicate a quotation. Italic is also used in some cases for Latin text, and in the transliteration of Hebrew and Greek.

13   Not included in this volume.

6. The divided indices of *The Great Works of God*[14] have been collated and remarkably improved; and references have been included to all noteworthy passages in the *Psalter-Paradise*.

By this it should be sufficiently demonstrated that this edition is far superior to all the others, to which end this foreword has been provided to the interested Christian reader, who is hereby heartily commended to the grace of our Lord Jesus Christ!

J.F. GLEDITSCH
Editor of the 5th edition

LEIPZIG, Easter Mass, 1700

14 "Magnalia Dei"

Part One: Genesis 1-3

DEDICATION OF PART ONE (1601)

To God, the Eternal King, the Incorruptible, Invisible, and Only Wise, be praise and worship forever.

Almighty, Everlasting God, most beloved and faithful Father, great Friend of mankind! You gave Your only-begotten Son, that whoever believes in Him should not perish, but have eternal life [John 3:16]. I thank You for revealing Your dear Son Jesus Christ to me. And inasmuch as I have learned from the books of Moses (in which I have here sought out Your Son) that You desire for Your own the first of all firstfruits (Ex. 23:19), the firstborn of man and beast (Ex. 34:19), the first boughs of the orchard (Lev. 23:40), the first of all grain, wine, oil, and fleece (Deut. 18:4), yea, the first of all the fruit of the ground (Deut. 26:2), therefore do I intend with childlike humility to obey Your earnest desire by presenting and gracing You with this the firstfruits of my labor. I pray You that this heartfelt devotion of mine may be well pleasing to You for the sake of Your beloved Son Jesus Christ, the Firstborn of all creation, the First-fruits from the dead.

Forever Your dutiful servant,
VALERIUS HERBERGER

FRAUSTADT, 1601.

I. JESUS,

The Heart and Center of the Writings of Moses and of Prophets,
from the Verse, "Moses Wrote of Me" (John 5:46).

May the Lord Jesus Christ, the Joy and Treasure of our heart, the Honor and Crown of our soul, the Alpha and Omega, the Beginning, Middle, and End of our highest concerns, the Center, Object, Purpose, Substance, and Essence of all Holy Scripture, be praised and adored by all pious hearts forever! Amen.

Dearest Reader! Since "no one can call Jesus 'Lord' except in the Holy Spirit" (1 Cor. 12:3), and since no one can say, write, or think anything beneficial, comforting, or noteworthy about Jesus without God's Spirit, and since the Holy Spirit's particular work of grace is to reveal Jesus Christ to our heart and to make Him known: therefore may you first begin by appealing to God the Father in the name of our sweet Lord and Savior Jesus Christ for the light and grace of the Holy Spirit, that you may be able to read this beneficial, comforting work profitably, piously, and to your betterment. To this end, let your first words and deepest desire be as follows: O God, let Your grace and truth be great toward me in the power of the Holy Spirit; through Jesus Christ. Amen.

Our dearest brother and blood-relative Jesus Christ says, "This is eternal life, that they know You who are the only true God, and Jesus Christ whom You have sent" (John 17[:3]). St. Peter learned this from his instructor Christ Jesus, about whom he says, "This is the stone which was rejected by you, the builders, which has become the cornerstone. And there is salvation in no one else, nor is there any other name under heaven given to men by which we must be saved" (Acts 4:11[–12]). St. Paul also agrees with this: "No other foundation can any man lay than that which is laid, which is Jesus Christ" (1 Cor. 3:11); and in the last chapter: "If anyone has no love for the Lord Jesus Christ, let him be accursed" [16:22]. All this shows that Jesus Christ alone is the rock of our salvation, as Isaiah 28:16 also testifies.

Accordingly, just as Jesus is the cornerstone of our salvation, He is also the cornerstone of all Holy Scripture, and it all rests upon Him. Indeed, He is the object, purpose, marrow, nectar, quintessence, extract,[15] ruler, and center of the Old and New Testament. Everything unanimously points to Him, and absolutely nothing is said in the New Testament that is not in every last detail founded on the Old. Indeed, nearly every deed, word, step, and gesture of the Old Testament centers on Christ so that the world might not be mistaken about the Messiah but all the better learn about this most blessed person in whom all our salvation lies. This is why the evangelists so often append the words, "that the Scriptures might be fulfilled," "that what was spoken by the prophets might be fulfilled," etc.

Furthermore, that you may understand me even better, know this: Christ and all His works are found in three places in the Bible: first in Moses;[16] second in the Prophets and Psalms (which are merely postils on Moses); and third in the New Testament.

In Moses, the Prophets, and the Psalms, He may either appear in broad daylight, clearly identified; or He may be somewhat hidden, in the event that He wishes to be looked for carefully; or else in beautiful similes, as will be shown hereafter in the proper place.

Since I have discussed this thesis with many scholars, both orally and in writing, and for many years thought about how the course of Christ's life is discernible in the Old Testament—in the Law first, and also in the Prophets—just as perfectly as in the New Testament in every detail, God has granted me not only the desire to write this book, but also the accomplishment of doing so. Therefore "I will praise the LORD as long as I live; I will sing praises to my God as long as I am here" (Ps. 146:2). "If I have but You, [Lord Jesus,] I ask for nothing in heaven and earth" (Ps. 73:25). May God grant you, pious reader, such a heart as I have to love Jesus and what is said of Him to His praise: "Lord Jesus, You know that I love You" [John 21:15]. May these words continually be on my mouth and on yours.

---

15   "quinta Essentia, Extract"

16   I.e., the Pentateuch (so henceforth).

But in order that each pious heart may see that this labor of diligently examining and searching Holy Scripture is truly pleasing to our Lord Jesus, consider the testimony of the Lord Jesus Christ from John 5 referenced in the chapter title and heading, "Search the Scriptures, for you think that you have eternal life in them; and it is they that bear witness of Me" [v. 39]; and soon thereafter, "If you had believed Moses, you would believe Me; for he wrote of Me" [v. 46].

Notice four things in this passage:

I. What the best book in the whole world is; namely, the Holy Bible.
II. How the Bible should be handled.
III. What things in it should receive the most attention.
IV. What can be expected from such labor.

Jesus had to contend with the stiff-necked Jews because they refused to let Him make Himself out to be the Savior of the world. But Jesus clearly admitted as much, said so freely, and did not mince His words. Rather, He testified to the fact that He is the Son of God and the Savior, appealing to (1) the witness of John, the great man whose mouth and hand point to Him; (2) His own unprecedented miracles, a tangible witness of the Messiah; (3) His heavenly Father's words at the Jordan where, in front of the whole world, God gave Him His stamp and seal of approval, saying, "This is My beloved Son, with whom I am well pleased" [Matt. 3:17; 2 Peter 1:17]; and (4) finally, to the great, unanimous testimony[17] of all Holy Scripture, which describes and declares Him from beginning to end.

I. Here observe what the best book in the world is.
Christ refers to the Scriptures, and with them, Moses, the earliest and oldest writer of scripture. Therefore the Holy Bible is the best book in the world. Christ does not point us to Plato, nor to Aristotle (as some years ago a doctor from Rome did when he came to Tübingen saying that he considered it very peculiar that the university taught young students the Bible, which any farmer could understand, and that one should read Aristotle's Metaphysics, which is learning about learning). Christ does not

---

17   "Formula Concordiae"

direct us to old legends and the tellers of fairy-tales. He does not call us to read the Jew's enormous Talmud, which can scarcely be purchased for less than twenty-two ducats,[18] and which, the Jews say, God Himself reads for the first four hours of every day; and when the Temple in Jerusalem was destroyed, a space of about four cubits[19] remained where God sat, reading the Talmud. Fie upon such gross blindness. Christ does not direct us to our own deluded minds and curious dreams, as though we should specu-late as we please and say with that Anabaptist, "Even if all the Bibles were piled up in a heap, I would not give one farthing for the lot." Needless to say, He does not direct us to books of jokes, buffoonery, or bawdiness, nor to profitless pasquilles[20] or libelous broadsides. Rather, He points us to the Holy Bible, which is the best book and by itself worth more than all the postils in the whole world. Every housefather ought to have his own Bible, and he can easily afford one if he learns to keep his house in an orderly way, for thus "the rooms are filled," as the wise man says (Prov. 24:4). Thus Chrysostom says, "Get yourself the Books, for they are the medicine of the soul. For not to know or understand the Holy Scriptures is the source of all evil."[21] On this, Sirach 24:23 says, "This is the book of the covenant made with the Most High God, even the law which God[22] commanded for a heritage to the congregations of Jacob," and, "from which wisdom has flowed" [v. 25]; and from the same passage, "He is not come to be who knows it perfectly; and nevermore shall he be who might find it out. For its thoughts are richer than the sea, and its counsel profounder than the great deep" [vv. 28–29]. Thomas Aquinas read many other books and studied the great literature of the world, but when he was deathly ill, he could find no book of knowledge with the power to put his heart at ease. Finally he seized the Bible and said, "I believe everything that is written

18 About a hundred dollars.

19 I.e., a fathom, or about 6 feet.

20 Popular satires formerly posted or distributed publicly.

21 "Biblia comparate, quae Medicina animae sunt, omnium enim malorum causa est, ignorare scripturas"; Chrys. *in Epist. ad Coloss. Hom. 9*.

22 LB has "Moses" here.

in this Book,"[23] which is able to give comfort and strength; and with that he recovered.

II. How should this precious Book be handled?

Christ says, "'Seek,' search out."[24] It really means "hunt, sniff out," in the way that bloodhounds, sensing wild game among the brambles, will tear through and pull it out no matter how much flesh and blood it costs them. Holy Scripture is like a thick shrub filled with all kinds of twigs and branches. The prized trophy is Jesus, the Captain of Life. Seek Him out. Let no difficulty deter you. Though flesh should bleed, keep on. If at first you fail, try again. You will not have labored in vain, for He Himself says, "I love those who love Me, and those who seek me early find Me" (Prov. 8:17). Here you see that the Bible does not belong on a stand, in an ornately latticed repository, under a bench, or on the table simply to be shown off, but in the hand, in the eye, in the mind, and in the heart. It is to be read diligently.

King Alfonso of Spain and Naples has been highly praised for having read the Bible fourteen times. Augustus, the Elector of Saxony, is justly renowned for having read through the whole Bible within four weeks shortly before his death. Emperor Theodosius used to have a mechanical lamp that would automatically draw oil so that he could read the Bible alone at night unhindered without having to disturb his servants.[25] Marulus says that St. Cecilia used to keep the New Testament at her side even when she had to do something. And everyone knows of the eunuch from Ethiopia (Acts 8:28) who read the prophet Isaiah while traveling. The people of Berea (Acts 17:11) were commended for examining the Scriptures to see whether things were as St. Paul had preached. Zenocarus, in describing the princely gifts bestowed on Emperor Charles at his Baptism, reports that the abbots had a beautiful Old and New Testament bound

---

23   "Credo quicquid in hoc libro scriptum est"; see Nic. Selneccer *Instit. Christian. Relig.* 2.25.

24   "ἐρευνᾶτε, scrutamini"

25   Niceph. Call. *Hist. Eccles.* 14.3.

together for him, and the words "SEARCH THE SCRIPTURES"[26] printed on it, to remind him that he should hold the Bible dear and read it often if he wished to become a wise and goodly ruler.

In addition to this, the Bible should not only be read through as nuns mumble through the psalter or geese gobble their oats, but also meditated on—not judged, not subjected to reason, not twisted or embellished with one's private notions—but every word weighed on the scale, following the example of Luther, who says, "The Bible is like a great, dense forest where there is no tree that I have come up against and not asked, 'What is it?'" This[27] is what the Israelites asked regarding the bread of heaven. We too should say the same thing about every word of the Bible, where the true Bread of Heaven, Jesus Christ, is presented. Thus the Hebrews call the Bible *Torah,* from [the root meaning] "to investigate." For "when the Holy Bible is diligently read and contemplated, every day brings something new," says Dr. Pommer.[28]

Gregory called the Bible God's letter to men, His sons, written for their journey in this world. For this is the whole thing summed up: Dear children, here is My faithful, fatherly heart! Dear children, take care on the journey of your life. Let My Spirit govern you. Learn to know My Son Jesus, your Lord and Savior, and believe in Him, and someday I will take you home with a blessed death and give you eternal life in heaven, where you will have a generous father in Me. Take care!

Therefore, as pious sons let us esteem this letter of our dear Father highly. Let us store it in the travel-bag of our memory, read it over frequently and studiously, find all our joy and pleasure in it, and thus pass the long duration of our journey and pilgrimage.

The letters of great lords should be read thrice over, for they speak little but mean much. The letter of our Lord God, however, should be read more than thrice 100,000 times, for He speaks little, but what He tells us in a quarter of an hour is more than we could grasp or comprehend in a hundred years. Indeed, as far as concerns our own understanding, it is

---

26 "SCRUTAMINI SCRIPTURAS"

27 "Quid est hoc?"

28 Johannes Bugenhagen (1485–1558), Pomeranian "pastor of the Reformation."

in part, pieces, patchwork, and beggary. Yet we must equip and prepare ourselves in the research school of this life for the higher institute of the salvation to come, where we shall know all things perfectly. So one must not look at Scripture as a cow looks at a new fence, but ponder it with great diligence. Basil says, "Not one syllable in the Bible has been put there in vain."[29]

Ezra is supposed to have known every last letter of the Bible by heart, as Eusebius reports. That is no mean praise indeed! Marulus wrote that Servulus earned so much money by begging that he was able to buy himself a Bible. After this, he gave it to students to read it aloud from time to time. He paid such close attention during those times that he soon came to comprehend it, memorize it, and was then able to preach to others. This is justly recorded to his honor.

Sabellicus[30] describes how once, the abbot Hilarion,[31] after praying fervently, read the Bible as though God Himself were his listener, and said, "This is the book of the Holy Spirit! The prophets and apostles only lent their hand, ink, paper, pen, and stroke to it, reporting in writing whatever the Holy Spirit dictated." Thus its words should be read, heard, and meditated on with great reverence. Primarily, however, it is the purpose, the main kernel[32] of Scripture—its founding pillars—to which attention must be paid. For when these are known, everything is grasped all the better. Otherwise, your knowledge will be like a house fallen in on itself.

III. What things in the Bible should receive the most attention?

Our Lord Jesus says Himself, "The Scriptures bear witness about Me" [John 5:39], and "Moses wrote of Me" [John 5:46]. Here you have the best summary of the whole Bible. Sure, there are fine stories in the Bible about Adam, Eve, Abel, Noah, Abraham, etc.—many fine instructions and rules for life. But these are only the peels and rinds. Jesus is the core and the flesh. One must learn to remove the peel and squeeze out the pulp. Thus

---

29   "Nulla syllaba in verbis divinitus inspiratis est otiosa"; Basil *Hexaem.* 6.11.

30   M.A.C. Sabellicus (1436–1506), a Venetian historian.

31   St. Hilarion (291 – 371), a Palestinian anchorite and ascetic.

32   "scopus, nucleus"

Luther once wrote on his good friend's Bible, "The Word became flesh, that is, God became man.[33] This wonderful and extraordinary event, to wit, that God became man, is what the whole of that single book, and none other, teaches. For if you do not seek the Word Become Flesh[34] in that book, then you had better read a volume of Marcolphus or Eulenspiegel[35]. Everything that was done and written about [in the Bible] has to do with this Word.[36] He is the Lord who lies in the manger and in the arms of Mary. This Book is of no use, etc., for anyone who does not believe this." Luther demonstrated this very truth on August 5, 1545 in an important sermon in Halle. (See *Luther's Works*, Jena ed., vol. 8, *fol.* 185. He also gave a lovely speech on this same topic in the prior vol., *fol.* 364.)

The Bible is thus a Book about Christ. Jesus is the end, purpose, marrow, kernel, and jewel of the Bible, shining out of it like the sun in the heavens. Moreover, Christ's life is recounted three times in it: first in Moses, second in the Prophets, and third in the New Testament. Our Lord Jesus Himself said as much: "Behold, I come; in the book it is written of Me" (Ps. 40:7). And as He walked with the two disciples to Emmaus, He first talked of Moses, and then of the Prophets. He furthermore called the scribe who can use both the Old and New Testaments "a wise man fit to further the kingdom of heaven" (Matt. 13:52).

In same way, St. Peter says, "To Him all the prophets bear witness that everyone who believes in Him receives forgiveness of sins through His name" (Acts 10:43). And at the First Council (Acts 15:11) he tied the Old and New Testaments together, saying, "We believe that we will be saved through the grace of Jesus Christ just as they," our fathers. St. Paul also says that "Christ is the end of the law" (Rom. 10:4); and in Acts 26:22, he protests and demonstrates publicly that he preached nothing but what was found in Moses and the Prophets. Thus Irenaeus writes, "Diligently

---

33   "Verbum caro factum est, hoc est, Deus homo factus est"; cf. Paulin. *Contra Felicem* 1.34.

34   "Verbum caro factum est"

35   Marcolphus, from *The Dialogue of Solomon & Marcolphus*, was a figure of ridicule appearing in series of popular medieval legends. Till Eulenspiegel was a fictional character who committed pranks and follies.

36   "Verbum"

read the Gospel which the apostles have given us, and diligently read the Prophets. In these you will find recounted all that our Lord Christ did, taught, and suffered."[37] Likewise Augustine says, "Christ came into the world not to restore what was lacking in Scripture, but that what was written therein should come to pass and be fulfilled";[38] and again, "The New lies in the Old concealed, the Old is in the New revealed."[39] And Jerome says, "That which we read in the Old Testament we also find in the Gospel; and that which is read in the Gospel has been taken from the Old Testament."[40] Also, Paulinus, "In the Old is the New and in the New is the Old."[41] Every person, place, name, timeframe, word-order, and number must therefore be carefully heeded, especially in the New Testament, for it is all full of utter mystery. And I say *mystery* with special emphasis. For you should not imagine that I will show you Christ in common, everyday allegories (contrived explanations and propositions)[42] devised by human reason, as Origen did. For the easier something is to build up, the easier it is to tear down. Rather, I will tell you about Jesus our Redeemer in beautiful and memorable mysteries not based on human wisdom but on the clear testimony of the Holy Spirit in Scripture. Outside of Scripture, all kinds of allegories, or artificial and allusive explanations, are sure to be found also. But the mysteries[43] discussed here are not to be met with anywhere but in the Bible. Allegories are all fine, lovely constructions in which something of note is conveyed to us, even though they do not all speak about Christ, and even though they do not all have a clear basis in

---

37 "Legite diligentius id, quod ab apostolis Evangelium est nobis datum, et legite diligentius Prophetas, et invenietis universam actionem, et omnem doctrinam et omnem passionem Domini nostri praedicatam in ipsis"; Iren. *Adv. Haeres.* 4.34.

38 "Venit Christus non ut adderentur, quae deerant, sed ut fierent et implerentur quae scripta sunt"; August. *Contra Faust. Manich.* 17.6.

39 "Novum in veteri latet; Vetus in novo patet. Item: Vetus Testamentum est occultatio novi; Novum est revelatio veteris"; August. *Quaest. in Exod.* 73; *De Civ. Dei* 16.26.

40 "Quicquid in veteri Testamento legimus, hoc idem in Evangelio reperimus, et quod in Evangelio fuerit lectitatum, hoc ex veteris Testamenti autoritate deducitur"; Hier. *Ep.* 18 *ad Damasum,* §7.

41 "In veteri novitas, et in novitate vetustas"; Paulin. *Poem* 28.

42 "allegoriae"

43 "mysteria"

Scripture—just as long as they do not conflict with any clear verse. But these mysteries[44] are only taken from Scripture and only speak about Christ alone, or His Church, and they have a clear, express foundation, established from Holy Scripture. Some allegories are flimsy, ridiculous jokes, as Augustine confirms. But these mysteries are nothing other than words of life drawn from the sure foundation of the Bible.

For example, the sun presents Jesus Christ to us in a mystery, as Malachi 4:2 clearly demonstrates. The copper serpent of Moses points to the Lamb of God, the crucified Jesus, by way of a mystery. Jesus Himself demonstrates this in John 3:14–15. The mercy-seat in the tabernacle is a mystery of the Mediator, Jesus Christ, which St. Paul clearly demonstrates in Romans 3:25. Regarding these images revealed to us by the Holy Spirit Himself, Luther says (in his *Commentary on Genesis*),[45] "They not only ornament the doctrine, but also comfort consciences."[46] And again, "They not only agree well with the matter, but also instruct us in the faith and comfort consciences."[47] In common allegories there is only the vegetables and sauce, but in these mysteries the meat, vegetables, and sauce are served at once. And Holy Scripture uses this honorific word in reference to Christ, His Church, and His Gospel: "To you is given to know the mystery of the kingdom of God" (Mark 4:11; cf. Matt. 13:14; Luke 8:18). St. Paul calls the Gospel "mysterious" (1 Cor. 2:7), and the minister a "steward of the mysteries of God" (1 Cor. 4:1); "In the Spirit he utters the mysteries" (1 Cor. 14:2), and: "Pray also for us, that God may open to us the door of the word, to utter the mystery of Christ" (Col. 4:3). Likewise, the meaning of the stars and the lampstands in Revelation 1:20 is called a mystery. And St. Andrew (in *The Golden Legend*)[48] called the cross of Jesus Christ a mystery when it appeared strange to a heathen.

Many years ago I read that, in his old age, not long before His blessed

---

44 "mysteria"

45 "*In Genesi, in mihi fol.* 119," i.e., *In Genesi* 9.

46 "Non solum ornant doctrinam: sed etiam consolantur conscientias"; ibid.

47 "Non solum bene consentiunt cum re, sed etiam docent animos de fide et sunt utiles conscientiis"; ibid.

48 "Lomb. Hist."; see Ryan I 16–17.

death, Luther said (in *Luther's Life*),[49] "The best exposition of Moses, the Prophets, and the Psalms is the New Testament, for so the Old Testament is the foundation of the New Testament. If I were younger, I would search out all the words of the New Testament in Moses and the Prophets. When the languages and texts are compared side by side, it provides a great and marvelous explanation of Scripture." To tell the truth, these words have inspired me in my endeavor.

We also have fine depictions in the Bible of how the Old and New Testament both have in view a common object. For instance, there is the mercy-seat (Ex. 25:17) upon which two angel-heads with wings face each other, viewing the mercy-seat and touching each other's wings. The true mercy-seat is Jesus Christ (Rom. 3:25). The two cherubim (i.e., angel-heads with wings) are the Old and New Testament which stand directly facing each other, one prophesying, the other fulfilling, and both looking at Jesus Christ and embracing each other so that the whole world might know the Mercy-Seat, Jesus Christ.

In Numbers 13, two men carry a red cluster of grapes on a stick, one leading, the other following. Jesus is the blood-red, succulent cluster of grapes on the tree of the cross "from whose fullness we have all received" (John 1[:16]). He is carried by the Old and New Testament. The Old leads in hope, the New follows after with joy and thanksgiving, and together they carry Jesus in their heart,[50] and are saved by Him. As Christ was going to Jerusalem (Matt. 21:9), a great crowd of people went before Him, Christ rode in the middle, and a great crowd followed after Him. The people going before depict the Old Testament; those following, the New Testament. Surely this is the one Christian Church, for they all walk together in a single confession and in unison cry, "Hosanna to the Son of David! Blessed be the great Captain of Life! May all that He undertakes for our salvation prosper!" These are also the swaddling cloths (Luke 2:7) in which the infant Jesus was wrapped. Paper is made from linen rags. The little infant Jesus is swaddled in the paper of the Bible, and there He must be sought.

49   "Vita Lutheri."

50   Or, "in their midst, or between them."

IV. What profit is gained from seeking Jesus diligently in Holy Scripture?
First, it confirms us in our faith and makes us certain and confident so
that we are anchored, secured, shielded, bastioned, and preserved against
all heresies. Not many years ago, a fine, learned man died in whom the
arrows of the Samosatenes had sliced so many venomous wounds that he
often used to become despondent regarding the article of the true divinity
of Jesus Christ. When he heard these mysteries being discussed, he said,
"Oh, my God! How sweet and powerful it is, how greatly it strengthens
my faith! There has to be something about Christ that is greater than any
other common man. Since the beginning of the world God has made such
a powerful display of His Son, there must be something great invested in
Him. He must be superior to any common man."

Second, it is thus that we achieve the most certain knowledge, the
highest wisdom of all. For "in Christ are hidden all the treasures of wisdom," as St. Paul says (Col. 2[:2–3]). "Christ…was made to us wisdom from
God, and righteousness and sanctification and redemption" (1 Cor. 1:30).

> If Christ be known aright, there is naught else to know;
> If Christ be not in sight, all else is empty show.[51]

Third, this is how we come to everlasting life, as Jesus Himself testifies
here in John 5:26. For our light and life are in Jesus (John 1:4), and whoever believes in Him has eternal life (3:16). Accordingly, since Jesus, the
Fountain of life, is revealed to us in the Bible—for which reason it is called
the "Book of Life" (Sir. 24:23)—it is clear and obvious that whoever reads
the Bible earnestly, meditates on it devoutly, searches it for the Lord Jesus,
takes comfort in His benefits, and lays claim to Him with a living faith has
eternal life. "Blessed are all who trust in Him!" (Ps. 2:12).

O most beloved Lord Jesus, You are the Heart and Center of the Bible.
My heart will seek You in the Scriptures. Let me find You to my comfort
there, that through You I may be bold and consoled in my faith, wise in
my mind, holy in my life, and blessed in my death. Amen!

---

51   "Si Christum bene scis: satis est, si caetera nescis. / Si Christum nescis: nihil est, quod
     caetera discis"; motto of Johann Bugenhagen; ultim. from Ludolph of Saxony, 14th c.

II. JESUS

In the Beginning, the Beginning of Our Consolation, the Beginning of All That I Say (Gen. 1:1).

Genesis the true primer, history-book, and textbook. Everything lovely, profitable, and comforting that can be said of God is found in Genesis. Blessed is the man who can seek, discover, and avail himself of such precious pearls and treasures.

At the start of chapter 1, Moses demonstrates that there truly is a God and that this God is not simply an idea invented by the fanciful mind—as in 1 Corinthians 8:4, where St. Paul says that the heathen gods are nothing—but that our God is a true Being, existing and living and working powerfully, able to command and create. He also shows there is only one God, for He says, "God created." He speaks of one Being, contrary to the heathen masses who have fabricated thirty thousand idols and three hundred other chief gods. Furthermore, he shows that there are three independent and distinct persons in this single divine Being, listing them by name: first "God," second "Said," and third, "the Spirit…hovered over the waters." And he inserts this mystery secretly into the word *Elohim* (which is plural) saying, "In the beginning, the 'Gods' created." He actually speaks of one and yet more than one so that we might know that there is, to be sure, only one God in essence and yet more than one person, namely, three: (1) "Father," (2) "Son," and (3) "Holy Spirit" (1 John 5:7). The ancient cabalists also cunningly prove this from the word "created," which in Hebrew is written with the three letters *B R A*[52] and they explain these letters as follows: B = *Ben* ("Son"); R = *Ruach* ("Spirit");[53] A = *Abba*

---

52 "A" here stands for 'Aleph.

53 "Spiritus"

("Father").[54] This can be read about in Reuchlin's[55] book, *The Wonder-Working Word*.[56]

Next, Moses testifies that this God of ours created heaven and earth. The world has not existed from eternity as Aristotle dreamed. It was not thrown together from a little speck of the Sun as Epicurus foolishly proposed. Rather, it was artfully framed and molded by our God 5,570 years ago (counting from AD 1600).[57] Moses furthermore says that this God is almighty because He created all things from absolutely nothing, simply by His powerful Word, and because He existed before all creatures, that is, from eternity. For there was nothing before the creation of the world but pure eternity.

Here already in the first few words we find our Lord Jesus. This is He who in the beginning with God the heavenly Father and the Holy Spirit created heaven and earth.

That our Lord Jesus is already visible in the first few words, however, I will not prove by subtle sophistry. For *bereshith* ("in the beginning") can also be correctly translated and rendered in German as "by means of the beginning." For the prefix *be-* is often used as the ablative of instrument, with the meaning "through" or "by means of." *Reshith* means "beginning." Now, in the first and last chapters of Revelation, our Lord Jesus calls Himself the beginning. And John says that "all things were made through Him" (John 1:2). St. Paul says, "through Him...are all things" (Rom. 11:36).

---

54 "Pater"

55 Johannes Reuchlin (1455–1522), *alias* Capnion, a German humanist and scholar of Hebrew.

56 "De verbo mirifico."

57 The chronology that Herberger uses is similar to that of the chronologist Elias Reusner, who estimated the first year of the world at 3970 BC. Following the analogy of the days of creation held by Africanus, Augustine, and others, he saw the world consisting of six ages of a thousand years each, with a seventh, non-literal millennium fulfilled in the Last Day and eternity. These in turn were related into three eras of two millennia each, according to the understanding of the school of Elijah. He placed the date of creation on the first day of his year, March 25, the Annunciation on the same day, year 3970 (= AD 1); Our Lord's Baptism on the same day in the year 4000 (= AD 30); and the year of his writing 5670, as stated above. Hence according to Herberger's scheme, if meant literally, the world would end on the last day of the year 6999 (= March 24, AD 3029).

Now I am aware that the cabalists read the word as *bar-shith*, "I will give My Son."[58] And using their methods, the letters are supposed to add up to 4,000. Counting from the beginning of the world, this would be the year of Jesus Christ's Baptism, where, before the whole world, the heavenly Father made known with His own voice that He had given us His Son, saying, "This is My beloved Son, with whom I am well pleased" [Matt. 3:17, par.]. I will refrain from making such arguments, and will instead use plain, clear texts to prove that one ought to look for and locate Jesus Christ here in the beginning.

In Proverbs, the Lord Jesus, who "was made to us wisdom from God" (1 Cor. 1:30), says, "The LORD possessed Me in the beginning of His ways; before He made anything, I was there" (Prov. 8:22). Arius read the verse thus: "The LORD *created* Me in the beginning." But in the Hebrew it reads "possessed Me." The same word was also used when Eve said, "I have begotten the Man, the LORD" (Gen. 4:1). It means "The LORD possessed—or brought out, begot, and bore—Me," like a chick or a hen-chick. The origin of this error lies in the fact that in the Septuagint some of the writing has been corrupted, and instead of *ektêse* ("possessed")[59] it reads *ektise* ("created").[60] Likewise the Jerusalemite Targum also has "In wisdom God created heaven and earth."[61] Thus at the very beginning of his books, John directs us with his sharp eagle-eyes to this very Beginning, saying, "In the beginning was the Word" [John 1:1], and, "That which was from the beginning," etc. [1 John 1:1]. Here a studious eye and heart should ask, All right, my friend, if you wish to connect these verses, why then does it say *At* the beginning" in Genesis but "*In* the beginning" in John[62] (as well as in Proverbs 8:22)? So hear the answer: It is all one whether it says "at" or "in." Yet with great zeal Luther purposefully put an A at the beginning of the Bible, for just as A is the first letter in every language's alphabet, so all

---

58   "dabo filium"

59   "ἔκτησε, possedit"

60   "ἔκτισε, creavit"

61   "In sapientia creavit Deus caelum et terram."

62   LB, Gen. 1:1 reads *Am anfang*, lit., "At the beginning;" and John 1:1, *Im anfang*, lit. "In the beginning."

the letters of Holy Scripture proceed from this uppercase A in *Am* ["At the"] and lowercase a in *"anfang"*[63] ["beginning"]. For the Bible is the true book of ABCs[64] which Christians must wrack their brains over all the days of their lives and thus learn to pray the Canonical Hours.[65] Furthermore, Jesus Christ Himself appears to us in the first letter A, for in John's Revelation He expressly calls Himself "the Alpha and Omega,"[66] (Rev. 1:8; 21:6; 22:13). A Christian heart, then, should not disregard what is done to the glory of Christ.

In their Bibles, the Hebrews always turn the first phrase *Bereshith*, that is, "In the beginning," into the title. Thus they call Genesis *"Bereshith."* In this way, the Hebrew Bible's title and first letters summarize all Holy Scripture; for Jesus remains the Bible's heart and center. Let us then gladly grant our Lord Jesus the privilege and honor of being cleverly placed in the first words and even in the first letters of both the German and the Hebrew Bible. And let us also grant that henceforth the first letter ("B" in the Hebrew Bible and "A" in the German Bible)[67] is the synopsis of all Holy Scripture. Thus Jerome also sees the words of Psalm 40:7 here: "In the head of the book it is written of Me."[68] For he translates *rosh* "head."[69]

From this we learn that Jesus already existed in the beginning when God created heaven and earth, that in fact He existed before the beginning of all creation, that is, from eternity. This is not only found in Moses, but also in the Prophets and the New Testament. Isaiah calls Him "Everlasting Father" (Is. 9:6). The prophet Micah says that His "goings forth" (plural in the Hebrew) are first, "from the beginning," and second,

---

63 Especially noteworthy, since nouns are normally capitalized in German orthography.

64 Elementary textbooks on writing used the series Aa, Bb, Cc, etc., to teach uppercase and lowercase letters.

65 "horas Canonicas," i.e., the traditional daily order of singing psalms and praying; here figuratively, following the metaphor of the school primer.

66 "A *und* O" (from LB).

67 "Biblia"

68 "In capite libri scriptum est de me."

69 "caput."

"from eternity" (Micah 5:2). One Jewish rabbi presses this, saying, "The Messiah has a twofold going forth: one from the beginning of time, another from eternity." How could a Christian have put it more strongly? The scribes in Matthew 2:5–6 omit these words. This is a mystery. The Jews have always been enemies of the doctrine of Christ's divinity, and wish to omit it and blot it out. In the New Testament, the Lord Jesus Himself says, "Glorify Me, Father, in Your own presence with the glory that I had with You before the world was" (John 17:5).

Behold, Jesus here confirms that He did not exist at the decree[70] of God, as Samosatenes[71] suppose, but in essential glory. Thus St. Paul says to the Colossians, "He is before all things, and in Him all things hold together" (Col. 1:17). This must be confessed in opposition to Samosaten,[72] who says, "Jesus did not come into being until He was carried beneath the chaste heart of Mary, and He was not God until 4,000 years after the creation of the world when at the Jordan river the heavenly Father called Him His Son." A very notable man once listened to a Samosatene preacher; and when he was asked what he thought of him, he said, "He may be a learned, eloquent man, but this alone cannot reconcile him to my liking, for John solidly demonstrates from Genesis that Jesus was already there from the beginning, and this man is trying to convince others that Jesus did not exist until He was in the manger at Bethlehem."[73] One must also take note of this to oppose Arius, who was a crafty, wily wolf. For as soon as he saw that Samosaten had perverted the doctrine, and that Scripture was too clear, he made Jesus the origin of other creatures, saying, "God created His Son first, (for which Prov. 8:22 from the corrupted Septuagint served his purposes) and then through this created Son He fashioned the other creatures." This is all refuted on the same grounds. Moreover, Moses clearly places Jesus in eternity and maintains

---

70 "in decreto"

71 Followers of Samosaten; see following note.

72 Paul of Samosata (A.D. 200–275), bishop of Antioch who taught the heresy that the Son was not from eternity.

73 "quem Johannes ex Mose probat, fuisse in principio, cum ipse probare conabatur, fuisse primum in praesepio."

that He was not created but is Himself the Creator of all creatures. Thus, in Hebrews 1:6 He is called the "First-Begotten," not the "First-Created," which fact it is very well to keep in mind.

Now from this flow great benefit, strength, and power.

That our Lord Jesus appears right at the beginning of the Bible is lovely beyond measure. Of course, He does not only appear at the beginning, but also in the middle—everything moves toward Him—and with Him the Bible also concludes. For these are its final words: "Yea, come, Lord Jesus. The grace of our Lord Jesus Christ be with you all. Amen" [Rev. 22:20–21].

This really is a demonstration and beautiful reminder that the Bible chiefly talks about Jesus. And if it has made this Lord known to us, then it has accomplished its task. Accordingly, since Scripture has its beginning, middle, and end in Jesus, our concerns also should have their beginning, middle, and end in Jesus. All our thoughts and utterances should commence, continue, and conclude with Jesus. Blessed is the man who begins with Jesus in his youth by swearing all loyalty to Him in Baptism; then continues His life with Jesus by worshiping, loving, honoring, and praising Him; and finally concludes his life with Jesus, following the example of Stephen.[74]

Just as Moses put Jesus before all else, so the angel in Matthew 2:13 put Him before all else, saying, "Take the Child and His mother." And these words are often repeated there in this order, which Chrysostom in particular commends to our attention.

This gives us a good rule of faith and life:

Light of my faith, prince of my heart
May Jesus Christ be from the start.[75]

Therefore, whenever I am told much about good works and the merits of saints, let me answer, "In the beginning Jesus." O Lord Jesus, You are the foundation of my blessedness. May You be its continuance, may You be its

---

74 I.e., by commending his spirit into God's hands.

75 "Sit mihi Lux fidei, Dux vitae, ante omnia Jesus / O fidei et vitae regula sancta mea!"

end, for then I will have comfort, strength, and power in life and death.

When I pray, I will say, "In the beginning Jesus, may You be the foundation of my prayer. Dear Lord Jesus, help me to strengthen my prayer. Put in a good word for me with Your heavenly Father. O God the heavenly Father, if You refuse to hear my prayer because I am such a great sinner, at least hear me for the sake of Your dearest Son whom I set at the beginning of my prayer. Do not give me anything on account of my worthiness, nor withhold anything from me on account of my unworthiness. Rather, in the beginning, first regard Christ on whose worthiness I rely." This prayer will pierce the clouds and attain much with God the Father.

When all kinds of cross and trouble oppress me and poverty gnaws at me, when my heart cries nothing but blood and my heartache throbs without ceasing, then I will say, "Why are you downcast, my heart? If in the beginning you count your troubles, you will find no comfort. Think of Jesus in the beginning. Put Him before everything. See how He sanctified and hallowed your grief by His own misery and hardship. See how He won eternal salvation which you can confidently expect after this present poverty." Then my misery will be filled with such sweetness that I will have patience and be able to forget my grief.

In heavy spiritual attacks, when the evil one thrusts the ledger of my sins in my face and deals me sharp blows, let this be my breastplate: "In the beginning Jesus," with all His benefits. Soon all attacks will vanish, just as when that troubled man asked to have these words placed on the ledger of his sins: "The Virgin's Son will crush the head of the serpent."[76]

In dangerous quarrels over religious doctrines, when one party asks this and the other that, these will be my words: "In the beginning Jesus." What does He say about it? His Word will be my foundation. Thus Ignatius said, "My Lord Jesus is more to me than all antiquity and all the Fathers. Whoever refuses to hear Him must perish."[77]

I will never forget the beautiful words of Dr. Staupitz, Luther's professor, when he said, "If you would speak comfortingly about eternal

---

76 "Semen mulieris conteret caput serpentis."

77 "Mihi antiquitas Jesus Christus est, quem nolle audire manifestum exitium est." Ignat. *Phil.* 8.

predestination, begin with Jesus Christ and His wounds,"[78] yea, and with His blood and benefits, and let this be an account of your righteousness before God and your provision for eternal life. Then this teaching will not terrify, but make you the more joyful in your heart, for "whoever believes in Him will not be put to shame" (Rom. 9:33).

So when the day is about to break, this will be the first thing that I say: "At the beginning of this day, may Jesus be my comfort, helper, blessing, and stay, and guard me and my family from all trouble." If I begin with Jesus in all my dealings and doings, in all my works, all will go well; as when in Jesus' name the apostles threw out their nets and caught an unimaginably large haul of fish.

Someday when I must die, and the throes of death press upon me, then may You, O Jesus, be at the beginning of my inmost thoughts. Depart neither from my heart nor my mouth, and I shall not taste death, but in Your comfort drift into blessed sleep and abide with You forever.

Besides this, let my heart also take note of this powerful, beautiful comfort here. O Lord Jesus, just as You led the charge in Scripture, You will also lead the charge before us in every distress, as You promised Joshua (ch. 5)[79] that You would lead the charge before him against the heathen in Canaan. In the same way, You also led Your people in the wilderness (Ex. 12, 23, 33; 1 Cor. 10). Therefore I will pray with Moses (Ex. 33:13ff), "Oh Lord Jesus, be our captain! Clear the path for us. Lead us in the right way. If You go not before us, let us not go of our own accord. When I pray, take the lead. Clear for my prayer a path to the heart of Your Father. When I must die, take up my soul and clear for it the heavenly path to eternal life. On the Last Day, I will follow You joyfully with body and soul as You go before all Your faithful Christians, leading them into eternal glory. When I undertake some task in this world, lead the charge as You did for King David (2. Sam. 5) when he was to fight the Philistines, so that all my deeds and endeavors may redound to the praise and honor of Your name."

---

78   "Disputaturus de praedestinatione incipe a vulneribus Christi"; see Luther *Tischreden*, I. 1017.

79   Perhaps Joshua 1:5; but Joshua 5:1 is an example of this promise fulfilled.

O Lord Jesus, the fact that You have existed not merely for 1,600 years[80] but from eternity fills my mouth with joy once more. What then shall I say? In You, Lord Jesus, we have an aged and experienced Master indeed! You have many solutions of which we know nothing. When we cannot figure out what course to take, You will know. You are an old, practiced Counselor (Is. 9[:6]). I will store You in the chamber of my heart as my richest Treasure, and always follow Your wise and prudent counsel. Oh, if only Rehoboam had followed his old counselors (1 Kings 12[:6–7]), how well he would have fared! He who follows the Lord Jesus is blessed forever and ever. When no one in the world can think of a way to help us in our trouble, You can. No woe is so great that is surpasses Your wisdom. You are an old, seasoned Physician of bodies and souls. You have no need of new graveyards. A veteran fencer always has a move that he has not yet taught his student. O Lord Jesus, since we are young and ignorant, Your ancient and most wise counsel will be for our good. You are old and clever enough.

Here one may rightly ask whether we should think of God and Christ as an old, frail, gray man that is always aging and growing weaker. Painters depict God the Father as an old, white-haired man, and they get this from Daniel 7:9. But you, dear heart, should know that Scripture takes into consideration the limitations of our minds. For when we hear of a hundred-year-old man, we can think of nothing else than a gray-headed Leontius.[81] By such language, Scripture only indicates that, while God is older than the heavens and the earth, yet He does not age, He does not turn gray, nor does He have bodily limbs such as we have—as the monk Audaeus[82] raved and as Serapion once imagined.[83] For He is spirit (John 4:24). He does not grow weak, old, tired, or faint, but is just as stout, healthy, hale, and all-powerful at any given moment as He was 5,000 years

---

80 I.e., until the year of our author's writing (AD 1600), according to the heresy of the Samosatenes.

81 Leontius (348–357), bishop of Antioch.

82 Fourth century Mesopotamian monk who taught that God resembled a man physically.

83 I.e., before he was corrected.

ago and has been from eternity. We have this to take comfort in and rely on each and every moment.

O Lord Jesus, You were in the beginning, in fact, You are the beginning of time. You are the beginning of my welfare; may You also be the beginning of my cares, my comfort, and my joy!

III. JESUS
Creates Heaven and Earth and So Displays His Wisdom, Omnipotence, and Divinity (Gen. 1:1).

Luther, a well-read man, often said, "There's no finer book in the world than Genesis."[84] This is certainly true, for all its words are as heavy as a hundredweight and worth pure gold, and require diligent, devout contemplation. Hence Jerome writes that the Jews used to permit no one under thirty years of age to interpret this book. For it calls for an adult, and for the devotion and wisdom of an adult.

Having now weighed the first few words, let us also put the next one on the scale and turn our attention to the word "created." Luther translated it "created," not "has created," because of the following *Elohim*. Let us listen to the proofs that Jesus, along with the heavenly Father and the Holy Spirit, truly was the Creator of heaven and earth. And let no one stumble upon seeing that the creation of heaven and earth in the Apostles' Creed is only attributed to God the Father. For the apostles did this to show that it was through the creation of heaven and earth that God the Father began to reveal Himself to man.

Now God the Father was (as Basil says) the initiator, predicator, and instigator of the creation of heaven and earth, while the Lord Jesus was the craftsman of creation, and the Holy Spirit was the finisher, polisher, and preparer, and made everything beautiful and pleasant to look at. Thus all three persons were active in this work. For now, let me confine myself to discussing the Lord Jesus and locating the evidence that He had a considerable role in creation here, and that He is to be regarded in this word "created." As mentioned above, this will not be established by subtlety—as was done with *Bereshith* and proven from the letters *B R A* according to

---

84   "Nil pulchrius Genesi."

the cabalists' method—but will be established from text as clear as day, so that it may be seen with the eyes and taken hold of with the fists.

It is not only found here in Genesis in the phrase "God said," but also in the Prophets and the New Testament; he who has ears to hear, let him hear! [Matt. 13:9, 43]. "I am the first, and also the last" (this is the Lord Jesus, cf. Rev. 1:17; 22:13) "My hand laid the foundation of the earth, and My right hand spread out the heavens" (Is. 48:12[–13]).[85] "By the word of the LORD the heavens were made, and all their host by the spirit of His mouth" (Ps. 33:6). In Proverbs, Jesus, our Wisdom, says, "When He (My Father) marked out the foundations of the earth, then I was the Craftsman with Him" (Prov. 8:[29–]30). Likewise, "all things were made through the Same Word, and without the Same was nothing made" (John 1:3). "By Him all things were created that are in heaven and on earth, visible and invisible, be they thrones or dominions or principalities or authorities—all things were created through Him and for Him. And He is before all things, and in Him all things hold together" (Col. 1[:16–17]). "Through whom (i.e., His Son) He also made the world" (Heb. 1[:2]). St. Paul says, "Who created all things through Jesus Christ" (Eph. 3[:9]).

Moreover, the Holy Spirit depicts the Lord Jesus to us robed in His creation like a great King in kingly raiment, so that by such robes we are led to consider the eminent majesty of our great, rich, and mighty Lord. He says, "The heavens are the work of Your hands; they will perish, but You will remain. And they will all grow old like a garment, and like a robe You will roll them up, and they will be changed" (Heb. 1:10[–12]; Ps. 102:26). In other words, if you wish to behold the majestic might and wonderful wealth of the Lord Jesus, simply look at the robes in which He has cloaked Himself. How handsomely heaven and earth sparkle! And these are only His everyday garments which He grants us to see Him wearing in this life. What beauty, then, will enlighten our heart in eternal life when He will dress all things in their Sunday-clothes and make a new heaven and earth! King Demetrius of Macedonia once caused the heavenly constellations to be woven into his royal robe. For this hubris, however, He was thrust from His throne before the robe was ever finished. After him,

85   Corr. for "Is. 49:1."

no king was audacious enough to don the garment, for they all thought it too splendid for a man (see Caelius bk. 16, ch. 9). Our Lord Jesus, the King of glory, has a far more skillful garment which He is able to wear with honor [or glory]. It is not too big, but all things are too little for it. Yet it does us great good, for by examining it, we learn of His wisdom, goodness, and omnipotence. Heaven is His throne, and the earth His footstool (Is. 66:1; Matt. 5:34).

At this point some ask, "So where was Jesus before He created heaven and earth with God the Father and the Holy Spirit? The Turks say, "God dwelt in a white cloud," from the Qur'an.[86] This contradicts Genesis, for there were no clouds yet. Augustine tells us of a person who answered thus: "God prepared Hell for those who ask such idle questions."[87] But he himself adds, "To ridicule a question and to answer a question are two different things," and concludes, "I will not hesitate to confess that I cannot tell anyone what I do not know."[88] Luther once said to a similar questioner, "Listen, fellow, He sat behind a birch tree making a sharp switch to whip you senseless for your question." Our dear forefathers spoke aptly. God was in Himself; He was in His own being, where He was, where He still is, for He still is not restricted in any way. God the Father was in Himself, Jesus in the Father, the Holy Spirit in the Father and the Son, and so it remains from everlasting to everlasting. So what was God doing in this everlasting? I answer from St. Paul: "God chose us through Jesus Christ before the world was founded" (Eph. 1:4). In His omniscience, God beheld as in a glass all things that were to be, and even then provided for our salvation. Here my heart deduces a blessed comfort: Ah, my God! If You cared for me before even a speck of myself or my ancestors existed, how much more will You care for me now since You have given me body and soul, and since Jesus has shed His blood for me and carried my flesh and blood to the right hand of God and seated Himself next to Your heart?

---

86 Precisely, a hadith attr. to Abu Razin al 'Aqili, prob. as commentary on Qur. 11:7.

87 August. *Conf.* 11.12.

88 "Nescio quod nescio"; *loc. cit.*

Since we have been informed by such solid reasons that Jesus, along with God the Father and the Holy Spirit, is the Creator of all things, let us contemplate creation at every passing moment and get to know the Master from His work. For this is why He created heaven and earth, that we might learn of His goodness, omnipotence, and wisdom from two books, as it were: first from the Bible, second from creation. Thus when St. Anthony was asked where he had acquired his great wisdom, he said, "I have no more than two books. One is in my cell: an old, worn Bible that I have gotten to know very well and every word of which I have weighed with special care; the other is too big to fit in my cell." At this, he led his guest outside into the open, indicated the entire world, and said, "Behold, this is my second textbook, the great *cosmography*, which has only two pages. The first is heaven, wherein the capital 'A' is the Sun, and the lowercase 'a,' the moon. And then come the other stars, which to me are nothing less than letters that I read thus: My God! how rich You are; how manifold is Your creation! My God, how mighty You are; who can do what You can? My God, how wise You are; how orderly and skillfully everything is arranged! O my God, what a great friend of mankind You must be; for all these things have been made to benefit me and my neighbor with their light, movement, and power! The second page is the earth's foundation, its sphere, and all that is on and above it. There in the clouds gliding over the earth I read how God is almighty, for He can hold the water over our heads and it does not drown me. There in all the streams and in all the birds, in all the trees and sprouting plants, in all the little leaves I read how God is my Father and Provider, for He has given me all this as furnishings for my home. In short, the Bible is where I read how God gave me His Son; creation is where I read how God honored me with all that I need for this temporal life."

Therefore, when I look at all created things in heaven and earth, it seems that all the stars, trees, birds, plants, flowers, and grasses joyfully proclaim the words of Psalm 100:3 to the glory of the Lord Jesus: "He made us, and not we ourselves." We are every one of us a masterpiece of our Lord Jesus. I am skillful and wonderful, but He, far more beautiful and wonderful. If the heathen had had such thoughts, they would not have invented so many idols, nor given created things the glory which is due God.

Augustine says, "I asked the world, 'Are You my God?' and it answered with a strong, unanimous voice, 'No, I am not your God, but the creature of God, whom you seek in and with me; He created you and me. If you wish to find Him, seek above and beyond me.'"[89] Since, then, all creation recognizes Jesus as its Creator, let every pious heart also do as it ought and say in true humility, "He made us"[90] (Ps. 100:3). "But we Your people, and the sheep of Your pasture, will give thanks to You forever, and recount Your praise from generation to generation" (Ps. 79:13). All of Psalm 139 is relevant here, too, as is the explanation of the First Article in the Small Catechism.

This will give a devout heart comfort to the full. O Lord Jesus Christ, if I am the work of Your hands, how can You not know me? How can a blacksmith not know his own knife? Does he not stamp it with his own mark? How can a master not know his own work? O Lord Jesus, how can You not know me? Before I was in my parents' hands, I was in Yours. You knew me before I or anyone else in the world knew me. You gave me my body and soul and all that I have. It all comes from You. Rejoice in your Creator, dear heart. Do not be so sad and gloomy. You are the work and creation of a great Lord.

O Lord Jesus, if I am Your creation, if You know me, oh, then You will not despise me! O Lord Jesus, You will not forsake Your handiwork. You gave me life, and You uphold it. "You who created the day shall also provide me with all that I need for each day."[91] You are not only the Creator of the world, but also its Caretaker, Custodian, Ruler, and Steward. You did not make things and leave them like an earthly carpenter, for You did not begin this work for the sake of money or gratification, but out of pure, abiding love, favor, and grace which continue and remain forever on me and all creation.

---

89 "Interrogavi molem mundi: Dic mihi, esne Tu Deus meus? Et respondit voce forti: Non sum Deus tuus. Sed per ipsum ego sum, quem quaeris in me. Ipse fecit te et me. Et eum quaere supra te et me." August. *Conf.* 10.6.9.

90 "Ipse fecit nos."

91 "Qui diem dedisti, dabis etiam in diem necessaria." Clem. Alex.

So even if all manner of cross and trouble come, I will confidently declare from these words: Take courage! We are not distressed, for we have a mighty Maker whose own we are [Ps. 100:3]. He can and will come to our aid. All creation bears witness to this. When I look at the heavens arching so high above, my heart says, O dearest Lord Jesus, how mighty Your hand must be! If You were so mightily able to construct this edifice, how can Your reach ever be prevented from helping me now in so little and petty a woe? As soon as I see the stars, my heart says, Dear Lord Jesus, how lovely the works of Your hands are! You must be far more beautiful in Your glory! Oh, how beautiful Your redeemed in heaven will be, for it was for us that You shed Your blood, not for the stars. We too are Your creatures, no less than the stars, and yet You have loved us a thousand times more than the stars; in this I take comfort. Though diseases may waste me and wither me, yet eternal bliss will make everything beautiful and rosy again. Then I shall shine like the stars, yea, like the angels! (Dan. 12:3; Matt. 22:30).

When I look at the earth and see how everything wiggles and wriggles, my heart thinks, Oh my Lord Jesus, how rich You must be! Every corner of the earth is full of Your treasures. If I am poor, yet You are rich. Let Your riches help me in my poverty, that I not perish!

When I look at the air and the water, these thoughts soon appear: Dear Lord Jesus, how deeply You must love me and all men! All that I see before my eyes was created by You for the comfort, service, and support of us men. When You command, all created things must don their armor and do your bidding.

When I look at the movement of creation, the goodly revolution of time and year, O Lord Jesus, I confess Your unspeakable wisdom. Wholly unsearchable is Your wisdom. I will never meet a misery so great that You cannot by Your wisdom deliver me from it.

O wealthy man, when you survey your fields, houses, gardens, meadows, etc., turn your heart to the Lord Jesus and say: Oh my Lord Jesus, how much good You grant me, Your creature, when I am only sinful and grossly provoke Your wrath at every passing moment! How much, then, You will make of me in eternal life when I shall serve You in eternal, perpetual innocence as Your own possession! Oh, help me not to forfeit this great inheritance by despising Your Word! This observation should inspire and drive us to lead a God-pleasing life. We are creatures of our Lord Jesus, so it is fitting that we should also serve Him and not be led astray by the evil one, lest, as we find written in the prophet Isaiah, the Lord Jesus should lament concerning us, "I reared children and brought them up, and they have fallen away from Me. The ox knows its master, and the donkey its master's crib, but Israel does not know" (Is. 1:2–3).

So let your heart speak thus: O Lord Jesus, Comfort of my heart, I promise You as Your creature and handiwork to remain faithful in due and willing service to You. By Your Holy Spirit, grant to my desire the ability to carry it out, that I, as Your beloved creature, may in the beholding of Your noble creation, heaven and earth, always and forever stand in awe of Your power, wisdom, and goodness, and in such devotion be well-pleasing to you. Amen.

IV. JESUS,

God, the Almighty Elohim, Our Protector (Gen. 1:1).

In the name of Jesus, we now come to the fourth word in Genesis: "God." In the original language it reads *Elohim*. Behold, in this word the Lord Jesus is once again presented to our heart with clear and evident proofs. For our Lord Jesus plainly wishes to be called *Elohim* even when He is specifically referring to Himself, as in Exodus 3:6: "I am the God of your father, the God of Abraham, the God of Isaac, and the God of Jacob. And Moses hid his face, for he was afraid to look at God." In the Hebrew, *Elohim* occurs in every instance here. But as for the angel who spoke from the bush, all the devout fathers understood him to be our Lord Jesus, which is also obvious from the verse itself as will be shown at the proper place. Thus Psalm 45:7 reads, "Therefore God, Your God, has anointed You with the oil of gladness more than Your companions." Here these words are attributed to both God the Father and the Lord Jesus. In the New Testament, John 1:1 says, "And the Word was God." Here we understand *Elohim,* for Luther always rendered *Jehovah* as "Lord," written with uppercase letters, but *Elohim* as "God." You will find an example in Deuteronomy 6:4,[92] and again in Psalm 7:3.

Second, the word *Elohim* also makes us contemplate the Lord Jesus in a mystery, for *Elohim* is plural in number and properly means "the Gods." Moses states "[He] created" as though only one did it, saying "the Gods," as though more than one did it. For there is surely only one God (Deut. 6:4) but more than one person, namely (1) God the Father, (2) Jesus, and (3) the Holy Spirit. They are all at work in this passage. Relevant here are the words of St. Athanasius: "The Father is God, the Son is God, and the

---

92   Corr. for "Deut. 6:6."

Holy Spirit is God, and yet there are not three Gods, but one God."[93]

Third, the activity itself proves that the Lord Jesus also belongs to *Elohim,* for the Lord Jesus is Creator of heaven and earth, too, as shown in the words that follow it.

Fourth, John demonstrates it in chapter 1 of his Gospel by the order of his words.[94] For John puts "the Word" in exactly the same place that Moses puts "God." Simply count it on your fingers. Moses said, "(1) In the (2) beginning (3) created (4) God."[95] Likewise John says, "(1) In the (2) beginning (3) was (4) the Word." John, moreover, shows that he means to teach this when he says "and the Word was God" [John 1:1]; as if he meant, "The Word is the very same *Elohim* and God that Moses says created heaven and earth." And lest this word-order be confused, Luther used the imperfect tense "created" rather than the perfect tense; for otherwise he would have had to say, "In the beginning, God has created the heaven and the earth." Here the similarity is kept between the order of Moses' and John's words, and the veil is lifted from the beautiful mystery. Therefore, O my most beloved Lord Jesus, I can rightfully join Thomas in calling You my *Jehovah* and my *Elohim,* "My LORD and my God" [John 20:28]; *Jehovah Elohai,* "LORD my God" (Ps. 7:3); *Jehovah Elohenu,* "LORD our God" (Deut. 6:4)." Now, O Lord Jesus, let me consider the word *Elohim,* that from it I may learn to know You rightly.

When *Elohim* is added to a verb of singular number[96] it can refer to no one else than the true God, as is clearly shown by the Hebrew Bible. Therefore, O Lord Jesus, You are not some created god, as the Samosatenes rave, but the one true God. This is not simply Your honorific title but a name of power and of truth. I hear it from Your own mouth in Isaiah 44:6: "Thus says the LORD, the King of Israel and His Redeemer, the LORD of Sabaoth: I am the first and I am the last, and beside Me there is no God." In the New Testament, furthermore, 1 John 5:20 adds, "This (Jesus) is the true God and eternal life." O Lord Jesus, You are true God in essence, and

---

93 From the Athanasian Creed. See *LSB* 319, vv. 15-16.

94 "ipso situ et ipsa constructione vocum"

95 This is the order in the German.

96 "Quando additur verbum singularis numeri, *als* creavit Elohim"

true in all Your words. Therefore I will receive Your words as though they were sworn with a thousand oaths.

Second, the word *Elohim* means "a God that is great and mighty," which is why Aquila always rendered the word "The Strong One," "the Mighty One," And Jerome says that Aquila sought to interpret word-origins[97] precisely. O Lord Jesus, it is yet again a mighty consolation that You are a great and mighty God and Deliverer, just as in Isaiah 9:6, You are clearly called "Mighty God,"[98] our Power. Furthermore, Lord Jesus, You Yourself say, "I am the Alpha and Omega, the beginning and the ending, who is and who was and who is to come, the Almighty" (Rev. 1:8). O most mighty Lord Jesus, the Christian Church finds its protection in You, as You Yourself say, "The gates of hell shall not prevail against it" [Matt. 16:18]. Note here: The devil will suppress the Christian Church but not subdue it.[99] The most mighty power of Jesus Christ consumes all the might of the whole world. Oh, then, let all might of the whole world assemble into one host and throng! With You, the almighty Lord Jesus *Elohim,* on our side, nothing can destroy us. O Lord Jesus, let Your almighty power be revealed in my powerlessness; let Your power be mighty in my weakness [2 Cor. 12:9]. Amen.

Third, the word *Elohim* means "a Lord that is omnipresent, from whom nothing is hidden, who has His eyes everywhere and pays close attention to every secret place."[100] The same thing is also proclaimed of *Elohim* and our Lord Jesus in Psalm 139:7–9: "Where shall I go from Your Spirit, and where shall I flee from Your face? If I ascend to heaven, You are there. If I make my bed in hell, behold, You are there also. If I take the wings of the dawn, and dwell on the farthest sea, even there Your hand will lead me, and Your right hand hold me." Likewise, O Lord Jesus, You personally assure us of Your presence in the last words of Matthew's Gospel, the evangelist's last will and testament: "Behold, I am with you every day until the end of the world." This is a great comfort. Even if I

---

97 "etymologiae vocum"

98 "Deus fortis"

99 "Valebunt sed non praevalebunt." See Thom. Aquin. *In Symb. Apost. Art. 9.*

100 "qui omnibus adest, cui omnia adsunt"

were stuck thirty miles beneath the earth or in the deepest ocean, or lost in a wild forest, or in a swamp where no one could reach me, even there, Lord Jesus, You would be with me. But since You are present everywhere, grant grace that I too may be faithful everywhere and never anger You, lest You should complain of me, "If am God (*Elohim*),[101] where does one fear Me?" (Mal. 1:6).

Fourth, *Elohim* means "a gracious, merciful God"—which is why the Greeks used it and turned it into their *eleêmôn*.[102] O Lord Jesus, how lovely it is to hear this of You! This is also testified of You by Psalm 145:8: "Gracious and merciful is the LORD, patient and of great goodness." And Isaiah 42:3 says of You, "A bruised reed He will not break, and a glowing wick He will not quench." John uses this in his Gospel, calling You a fountain of mercy, "full of grace and truth" (John 1:14). Dear Lord Jesus, every word, glance, step, and gesture that You have made testifies to Your merciful nature. You brought Your mercy from heaven. Every drop of Your blood is a witness to Your mercy. For this I must give You eternal praise.

Fifth, *Elohim* means "a sworn God," from [Hebrew] *alah*-. For our God swore Himself to us in Ezekiel 33:11, "As truly as I live…I have no pleasure in the death of the ungodly, but that the ungodly turn from his way and live." O Lord Jesus, here we see another of Your mighty honorific titles, for You are sworn to us, sworn even with the very first oath that God swore the Bible: "By Myself I have sworn…through Your seed shall all the nations on earth be blessed" (Gen. 22:16[, 18]). Likewise Psalm 110:4 says of You, "The LORD has sworn and will not change His mind, You are a priest forever after the order of Melchizedek." Dr. Luther held this to be the most important verse in the Bible. Dr. Cruciger[103] once asked him, "My good Doctor, what is the most beautiful verse in the Bible? Luther thought for a moment and said, "For me, let it be this one verse: "(1) The LORD (2) has sworn (3) and will not change His mind, (4) You are a priest (5) forever (6) after the order of Melchizedek."

---

101 Lit., "God." LB has HERR ("LORD").

102 "ἐλεήμων." Actually, from ἔλεος. See entry in LS.

103 Dr. Caspar Kreuziger (*or* Creutziger) the elder (1504–1548), Lutheran scholar and preacher.

Here we are instantly reminded of Hebrews 6:13 and 7:20[–21], which say that it was all for our comfort, for we were to find a mighty consolation in two things: first in God's clear Word, and second in His divine oath; these provide us with a sure and steady anchor; for "it is impossible for God to lie" (Heb. 6:18). This was the basis on which our dear forefathers said, "All things are possible for God; but one thing is not, namely, to condemn a man who repents and believes in the Lord Jesus." For it is impossible for God to change His mind and prove His own words false. Accordingly, God has clearly pledged His grace and abundantly sworn it to all believers on many occasions. Besides this, all God's words have the force of an oath; or as Philo says, "Every word of God is an oath."[104] Nevertheless, He swears His oaths again and again to excess so that we are not without perfect consolation in every spiritual attack.

O Lord Jesus, You swore a similar oath to us in the New Testament when You said, "Truly, truly, I say to you, if a man keeps My word, he will never see death" (John 8:51). Here, Lord Jesus, You pledged salvation to us by a double oath. In our Baptism we too swear to be faithful to You. A soldier is not trusted unless he has pledged allegiance to the standard. O Lord Jesus, You will not confide in us, either, if we refuse to swear to You. It is this sworn oath that we baptized Christians are to hold in our heart at every passing moment lest we do any evil. In the world, once a sworn man becomes a deserter, he is no longer held to be trustworthy; he is immediately branded a rogue. So those of us who desert You, O Lord Jesus, will be put to shame on the Last Day. All baptized Christians should be mindful of this, that they may guard themselves from an unchristian life. So, too, Ambrose calls those who willfully spurn the Holy Supper "false, faithless people who have deserted their Lord Jesus and turned rogues."[105] Dear Lord Jesus, help me remain true to You to the end. You shall not break Your sworn pledge; help me not to waver or withdraw my hand from You first. Even this, O Lord Jesus, is my sweet comfort, that I am sworn to You. For I am Yours in body and soul; I am

---

104 "Omnia verba Dei sunt juramenta."

105 "perfidos desertores castrorum Domini apud Deum castrorum desertor"; Ambr. *Serm.* 1 *de grano sinap.*

Your possession. No evil spirit will wrest this comfort from my heart.

Here I must relate a beautiful, noteworthy story: There was once a woman who was very sick and commended herself to the devil for a cure. Eventually regretting this dealing, she fell into a fearful worry. Luther came to see her and asked why she was so full of grief, whereupon she said, "Oh, good Doctor, I have forsaken God and commended myself to the devil. Oh, what have I done?" Luther said, "Dear Elsa, that sin is nothing. Have you done nothing worse?" Then she answered, "Oh, good Doctor, how could I ever commit a worse sin?" Luther repeated, "I will tell you again and again, that is nothing. The worst sin would be if you had wished to leave this life in such a foolish state. Dear Elsa, are you able to give away Mr. Fröschel's[106] book or my coat?" Then the woman said, "No, I can't, for they aren't mine." Luther continued, "Who redeemed you?" She answered, "Jesus Christ." Then Luther concluded, "That is what I wanted to hear. You have spoken rightly. Jesus Christ has redeemed you, so you are His possession. You are the Lord Christ's in body and soul. This was your oath and pledge in Baptism, so you cannot commend your body and soul to the devil. You cannot remove one finger of your Lord Christ. You are not in control of yourself. Remind the devil of this purchase and say, 'Listen, devil, if you want me, go on up to Jesus Christ and ask Him yourself. He'll give us both what's good for us. He'll give you a knock on the skull, and He won't let me be plucked from His hand.'" The woman took the good advice and instantly recovered. This is a masterpiece in Luther, and it shows what kind of comfort is ours for having been sworn to the Lord Christ in Baptism.

Accordingly, our Lord Jesus, with God the Father and the Holy Spirit, is the only Lord to whom we should swear; from which it follows that He must be a Knower of hearts. Oh, this is comforting beyond all measure! O sweet Lord Jesus, even if I fell into such a swoon that I could speak no word, yet You know my inmost thoughts, for such is often told of You in the events of the New Testament. If ever it be Your will that I should lose my faculty of speech, this will be my rock-solid comfort. In the same way,

---

106 Sebastian Fröschel (1497–1570), Lutheran theologian and deacon of the city church of Wittenberg.

You were fully aware of Moses' thoughts and worries at the Red Sea even though he did not say a thing.

Let every one else also see to it that he is true of heart if he would serve our Lord Jesus, for the Lord will not be dispelled and dismissed with slick words as is the world's custom. Rather, He desires a true heart. He was well aware of the secret plots of the Jews even though no one leaked them. Guard yourself therefore, lest your secret wickedness be brought into daylight by this Knower of hearts.

O most beloved Savior, Lord Jesus, Your honorific title *Elohim* is like a living fountain filled with beautiful, unmingled comfort. It teaches me that You are (1) the true God, (2) the great and mighty, omnipotent, and powerful Master to help, (3) an omnipresent God, (4) a gracious and merciful God, (5) a sworn and most assured Savior to whom we are bound by sworn oaths, and who is a Knower of hearts and an omniscient Lord.

Here, dear heart, consider the reasons for which our Messiah and Savior had to be such a great and mighty Lord and God:

1. He was to baffle mankind's every foe, far greater in strength than you or I. Therefore, He had to be such a great and mighty Lord.
2. He was to be both King and High Priest; these great offices would have been far too heavy for a mere man to bear.
3. He was to pay a great debt. Therefore He had to be wealthier than men.
4. He was to give all men everything that they needed. From His fullness we were all to receive [John 1:16]. Therefore He had to be true God, not lacking in any way.
5. God's grace and love were to be undoubtable. Therefore the mediator between God and man had to be God Himself.
6. He was to lift a heavy burden—He was to bear the sin of the whole world, and this calls for broad shoulders and strong legs. What he bore would have dragged us down to hell. Therefore He had to have superhuman strength.
7. He was to be the foundation, pillar, and rock of our salvation. Therefore He had to be the great and mighty God, or the rock of our salvation would not stand firm. Let us therefore be wary of

the holes which the devil tries to cut by way of the Samosatenes.[107] He wants dig out from under us the comforting knowledge that our happiness is certain, and in his bitterness cast doubt on it. For if Jesus is not God, one might doubt whether His merit were overwhelmingly and perfectly sufficient. But since He is God, our happiness stands strong and fast, built on the foundation of Jesus Christ's merit.

8. Furthermore, the Savior of the world was to give us life. Therefore He Himself had to be the source of life, and the living God.

9. The perpetual, eternal, incomprehensible God was stirred to wrath by the sin of Adam and Eve. Therefore the ransom that was to free us from God's wrath also had to be an eternal, perpetual, and incomprehensible good.

O Lord Jesus, Great and Mighty *Elohim*, help me to hold Your divine omnipotence as my strongest fortress, highest comfort, greatest joy, and most beautiful treasure and glory during this frail human existence, to lead my life in a Christlike manner in the safe escort of Your invincible strength, and to conclude it blessedly! Amen!

---

107 I.e., by the heretical teaching that Christ had a beginning, is not supreme God, etc.

V. JESUS

"Said," and Is Therefore Called "The Word," "Our Advocate"
(Gen. 1:1; John 1:1; 1 John 2:1).

Moses now proceeds to give a thorough account of the daily tasks in the creation of heaven and earth, saying that on Sunday, as evening began, God created a large storehouse for His marvelous project, just as a builder brings out his lumber, stone, lime, and clay. But everything was mixed up, having no form or shape. At the break of the following dawn He commanded light to shine out of darkness (2 Cor. 4:6).

On Monday He enclosed the whole world in a circular barrier. Like some kind of miraculous carpenter, He began with the roof, making a vault for the firmament and putting His word under the clouds like a pillar to keep them from falling.

On Tuesday God paved the floors of the house, swept the parlor, dug ditches, channeled the water in like a gardener who has an irrigated garden, and trimmed the new manor with blossoms, wildflowers, and trees.

On Wednesday God put lamps up in the heavens, much as a rich man hangs brass lamps in the middle of his parlor; and made the hour-marker, the Sun, the half-hour-marker, the Moon, and the little quarter-hour-markers, the stars.

On Thursday God populated the bird sanctuaries and built the fish reefs, making a market for wild game.

On Friday God filled the forests with wild game, made the tame beasts, and finally concluded with His dearest pup of the litter, man.

On Saturday God took a holiday and rested from His works. God could have made everything in one moment, but He did not wish to. He wanted us to perceive not only His omnipotence but also His wisdom and thoughtfulness, so that we might say with Psalm 104:24, "O LORD, how great and manifold are Your works! You have ordered them all with wisdom, and the earth is full of Your riches."

For each day's task, Moses uses the phrase "God said." Here we have the Lord Jesus, the heavenly Father's essential Word, as established by Psalm 33:6: "By the word of the LORD the heavens were made, and all their host by the Spirit of His mouth." And John says of this Word, "All things were made through the Same" (John 1:3), and Hebrews 1:3, "He upholds all things by His mighty Word." Hence we have learned to understand the Word of the Lord as Jesus, the Word of Life (John 1:1). "And there are three that testify in heaven: the Father, the Word, and the Holy Spirit" (1 John 5:7).

Luther omitted this verse from the German Bible because it is also absent from many Greek exemplars; nor did Œcumenius, Cyril, Augustine, or Bede find it in the books of their time. It may therefore be supposed that the Arians erased and concealed it. Yet we quarrel with no one, for even without this testimony we are satisfied that Jesus is the Word. Moreover, there is no doubt that John learned such a teaching from the schools of the Jews, for it is here in Genesis 3:8: "They heard the voice of the LORD God walking in the garden." Here the Chaldean translator has rendered it thus: "They heard the voice of the Word of the LORD." Accordingly, when John calls Jesus the Word, he points us to the word "said" in Genesis, testifying that our Lord Jesus Himself is the same Spokesman—the eternal Father's Lord High Chancellor and Privy Counselor[108] through whom He enunciated all things, and arranged and appointed the order of creation.

.This brings us to the question, Why is the Lord Jesus set forth for us to contemplate in the verb "said" and in the noun "Word"?

First, because Jesus, the heavenly Father's essential Word, was begotten of the Father's heart from eternity, as the Church sings, "Of the Father's heart begotten."[109] For the word flows from the heart, is an image of the heart,[110] as we say, "Whereof the heart is full, the mouth overflows"

---

108 "secretarius"

109 "Corde natus ex parentis" (Prudentius, d. 413) st. 1, line 1, and its German paraphrase, "Herr Gott, der einig Gotts Sohn" (E. Cruciger, 1524), st. 1, line 3; for English versions, see *LSB* 384, 402 resp.

110 "[oratio] est character animi."

[Matt. 12:34]. "It springs forth as a word in the mind," says Basil.[111] Cyril, Augustine, and Luther (in his *Commentary on Genesis*) agree. Therefore He is called "the radiance of His glory and the exact image of His being" (Heb. 1:3), and "the image of the invisible God" (Col. 1:15).

His begetting from the Father is incomprehensible, for He was carried *within* the heart, not *under* the heart, as Mary carried Him in His incarnation. He is a part of the heavenly Father's heart, of the same substance, of the same power and glory. And just as we know how our neighbor feels about us through his words, so we know what God the Father thinks of us through Christ.

My Lord Jesus, how can You not know Your Father's heart and its pledge of love toward us? (John 3:16). Are You not a part of His heart? Oh, how unspeakable the love of God Your Father is, that He has shared His heart with us, and sent us its most beautiful part from heaven!

The Lord Jesus is also rightly called the Word because He is the person with whom the Father has always conversed from eternity, deliberating how to save man (Eph. 1:4), and by what means everything should be made, as God says, "Let *Us* make man." Here God the Father conferred with His Son, and the Holy Spirit took part in the conference, too. In his old age, Dr. Pommer said, "Dear sons, being a man of seventy years, I could perhaps say why the Son of God is called the Word, but I must hold my tongue. It is too profound." Yet one thing has occurred to me lately: The reason He is called the Word is that He has held a private conversation with the Father from eternity. God the Father conversed with this Person. Another reason why He is called the Word is that He conveys His Father's words and speaks them to mankind. Thus it says, "The only-begotten Son who is in the bosom of the Father, He has made Him known to us" (John 1:18). He reveals to us the Father's secret thoughts about our salvation: "God (My Father) so loved the world, that He gave His only-begotten Son, that whoever believes in Him should not perish but have eternal life" (John 3:16). Thus when He was asked "Who are You?" (John 8:25), He said, "He who spoke to you from the beginning"—I am the oldest Speaker, the first Preacher in the world, who always made Himself known to the patriarchs.

---

111   "Gignitur ut verbum in mente" (see. Basil. *Hom.* 16.)

Furthermore, He is also called the Word because He is such an expressive, eloquent Lord. He is very kind when He speaks, and is furthermore very eager to do so—a great, wealthy Lord, speaking eagerly, speaking kind words to the poor, and worthy of more praise than possible. This is the kind of lord we have in the Lord Jesus. He is the richest, the most powerful, and yet at the same time the kindliest also. Thus He says in Isaiah 50:4, "The LORD has given Me a learned tongue, that I should know how to speak to the weary." And in Psalm 45:2, it says of the Lord Jesus, "You are the most handsome of the children of men: full of grace are Your lips." And in Luke 4:18, the Lord personally relates the words of Isaiah 61:1 to Himself, saying that He was sent "to preach to the poor, to bind up the brokenhearted, to proclaim liberty to the captives, and to those who are bound, that it may be opened to them; to proclaim a gracious year of the Lord." In Nazareth, moreover, His countrymen "marveled at the gracious words that were coming from His mouth" [Luke 4:22]. There, too, His teaching was said to be full of authority [Matt. 7:29]. Thus Micah 5:1[112] calls Him *Moshel,* which not only signifies "a very powerful Lord," but also "a Master of speech who speaks with authority"[113]—who speaks weighty words that should be heard by all the world, and who propounds nothing but *mashal* ("enigmas, very deep matters")[114] which penetrate with great force. Truly, the Lord Jesus surpasses all the orators in the whole world. St. Paul can also speak well, St. Peter, too, etc. But when Jesus speaks, the brilliant sun shines. The others are but starlight compared with this Light of noon. The highest prize remains with Jesus. He knows the heart-rending words that get through God the Father's heart and man's heart, too. And if anyone is to win the hearts of others, this Speaker must Himself put the words on his lips as He did for St. Peter on Pentecost (Acts. 2:14). Our Lord Jesus is the true sweet *Chrysostom* ("Mouth of gold"), and Mouth of delight, and Mouth of victory. He does not say "Cursed be,"[115] etc., as

---

112 Corr. for "Micah 7:7."

113 "doctorem authenticum" (*Moshel* may be translated "ruler" as well as "one who declares wisely").

114 "Magnalia Dei" (*Mashal* may be translated "dominion" or "wise saying").

115 "maledictus"; see esp. Deut. 27:16–26.

Moses does, but rather He pronounces the blessing. Even His last work on Ascension Day was a blessing, that we might know for certain that He does nothing in heaven but pronounce blessing after blessing upon His believers. How comfortingly He beckons us with His voice! "Come to Me, all who are weary and heavy laden; I will refresh you" (Matt. 11:28). "Whoever comes to Me I will not cast out" (John 6:37). And in John 8:[10–]11, He says to the worried harlot, "Has no one condemned you? …Neither do I condemn You." Oh Lord Jesus, do not leave me, "if I have but You, I ask for nothing in heaven and earth" (Ps. 73:25). For You are able to speak such masterful comforts, and what is more, You speak gladly. "Though my body and soul should faint, yet You, O God, are forever my heart's ease and my portion" [v. 26].

Finally, He is called the Word because He speaks to the heavenly Father in our need. He is our advocate, assistant, custodian, and spokesman, as clearly stated in Romans 8:34: He "is at the right hand of God… interceding for us"; and in 1 John 2:1–2: "If anyone does sin, we have an advocate with the Father, Jesus Christ, who is righteous. And He is the propitiation for our sins, yet not for ours only, but also for those of the whole world."

Our great rulers employ reporters,[116] learned, eloquent, and courtly men who listen to civic delegates and report and relay their messages to their sovereign lordships.

In the same way, our Lord Jesus is the Reporter of the heavenly Father and of all mankind. He graciously and gladly receives our words and reports them, faithfully and diligently putting them before the heavenly Father. He does not let this faithfulness and humility toward us tarnish His divine majesty. We cannot plate our Spokesman's hand with gold or silver.[117] He does everything freely out of sheer love and favor. Neither should we allow this consolation to be cast into doubt by the enemies of the Gospel, for it is founded on God's Word, and was also taught by the ancient doctors of the Church: Cyprian, Eusebius, Nazianzen, Cyril, and Augustine. This brings our heart yet another great benefit.

---

116   Lit., "refendaries."

117   I.e., we cannot bribe Him.

My dear heart, who would not listen devoutly to this Speaker? "Therefore we ought to pay much closer attention to the Word that we hear" (Heb. 2:1). The heavenly Father Himself says, "Hear Him" (Matt. 17:5), and, "to Him you shall listen" (Deut. 18:15). Again, the Father reiterates, "Whoever will not listen to My words that He shall speak in My name, I will require it of him" [v. 19].

O Lord Jesus, if I cannot defend my cause in a wise and prudent manner, I will confer with You. You are a Master to speak. You can put words in mouths, as You have plentifully demonstrated in the martyrs who spoke the truth of the Gospel so eloquently in the midst of their agonies. O Lord Jesus, if You did not put the words in my mouth, my prayer would lapse into silence.

O Lord Jesus, keep me company when I must deal and speak with Your Father. I long to be heard, I long to be free of my sins and sorrows; but I am too stupid, yea, and rough of speech besides. I do not know how to the win the heart of Your Father. Speak the words for me. You speak with power. Wherever Your speech is heard, all creation is forced to stand at attention. I have learned this from Genesis. For the sake of my comfort, make Your words resound once more in the ears of Your Father, that my misery may vanish and my happiness be secured by Your word of power. You can weave words far more skillfully than I. Now I have a certain means whereby the words of my prayer shall pierce the clouds of heaven. O great Orator, Jesus Christ, I will make my prayer from the words which You gave me in the Our Father and recorded elsewhere in the evangelists. I build on these words with strong faith and say, Dear Father, hear the words of Your dearest Child, the renowned heavenly Orator—words that are aimed at Your heart, heart-piercing words. Let these words avail when mine are too simple and crude. I am poor in the world and have many burdens. Dear Lord Jesus, if You would speak the word for me, then I would be helped. I know that You will do it, for You are my Spokesman and Advocate. Among men, I have none who can comfort me with a good word, none who defend my cause. For he who has not a cent cannot fix what is bent. But I have learned that You are a communicative, eloquent Lord, and You do not honor bribes. Do not abandon me! Comfort my soul. Speak but a word and my misery will vanish, my heart be avenged, and my burden made bearable. Rebuke my foes with Your solemn words and they will all be silenced. Command my foes with Your mighty word and they must all become friends; yea, they themselves will speak Your word to me.

Often in the meditation and contemplation of his sins, a man is made wholly and utterly speechless, like the man who was found without a wedding garment [Matt. 22:12]. If this should ever happen to me, help me not to forget You, but to say, O Lord Jesus, dearest Orator, I have need of You now. I must be silent and confess that I am guilty of sin. If You would but begin to tell me of Your blood and death, I would be pulled out of my anguish. My conscience speaks words that terrify and condemn me. O Lord Jesus, speak Your customary words of sweetness which comfort, absolve, and bless me.

If I am wrapt in sickness and the anguish of death, if language escapes me and my lips cannot speak, nevertheless I will groan in my heart, O Lord Jesus, essential Word of the heavenly Father! You are all-knowing; my heart is familiar to You. Though my mouth can utter no words, and though my mind is repeatedly obscured and eclipsed by clouds of fever, nevertheless my heart sends sighs up to You. Prove now that You are my Spokesman, my Advocate, and my Reporter. Speak the words to Your heavenly Father in my behalf, and I will be free of my sins, and assured of heaven, and able with gladness to bid the world farewell at any hour, and through the blessed sleep of death pass into eternal life. Amen.

The Light of the World, the Craftsman of Light, the Light and Joy of Our Heart (Gen. 1:3–4; John 8:11–12).

In describing God's task for Sunday, Moses says that "God commanded light to shine forth out of darkness" (2 Cor. 4:6). His first stroke was an instant masterpiece. God gave light the first place and primacy, and with the light He began the work of clarifying creation—for important reasons.

For "God is light, and in Him is no darkness" (1 John 1:5). God is eternal, unbounded, uncreated, unfathomable Light and "dwells in a light which none can approach" (1 Tim. 6:16). Light is furthermore the noblest created thing, for without it nothing in the whole world would be beautiful. Likewise, light is the most precious thing among men, for light is life and life is light.

Now of this gift of light our Lord Jesus was yet again the Craftsman (Prov. 8:30), which fact is demonstrated by the words "God said," as sufficiently discussed before. Rabbi Moses Hadarshan also understands this to be the Messiah here.

In this noble creature of light we should also see our Lord Jesus' noble estate which He presents in it for our consideration, as also Psalm 104:2 teaches: "Light is the garment with which You cover Yourself." As a nobleman is known by his regalia, so our Lord Jesus is known by this noble light.

First, according to His divine nature, the Lord Jesus is the heavenly Father's "Light of Light,"[118] as the Church sings in the Nicene Creed; "the reflection of eternal light" (Wisd. 7:26); "the image of the invisible God" (Col. 1:15); and "the radiance of His glory and the exact image of His being" (Heb. 1:3). Of this we also sing:

---

118   "Lumen de lumine"

> O Christ, the very light and day,
> Naught hides, O Lord, before Your ray,
> O Radiance of the Father's light,
> Teach us the way to truth aright.[119]

And also:

> O Christ, You are the Day so bright,
> Before You fly the shades of night,
> You to the Father light our way,
> The word of light You do convey.[120]

Accordingly, He is also our light, the light of our heart, and the blessed light of the souls of all believers. Of this Ambrose sings:

> Kind Maker of the stars of night,
> Believers' everlasting Light,
> O Christ, Redeemer of us all,
> Receive the pray'rs of those who call.[121]

He has enlightened our eyes just as He enlightened the eyes of Bartimaeus (Mark 10:46) and the man who was blind from birth (John 9:1). He has enlightened our inmost heart and mind, that we might put one another in a beautiful light and behold the bright light of understanding. And even greater than this, He brings us the light of the Gospel from the bosom of the heavenly Father, setting the heart of His Father in the bright light of noon for us to behold. Thus He says, "I am the light of the world: whoever follows Me will not walk in darkness, but will have the light of life" (John 8:12); "As long as I am in the world, I am the light of the world" (John 9:5). John says, "That was the true Light which enlightens all men who come into this world" (John 1:9). So, too, the aged Simeon says of our Lord Jesus, "A light to enlighten the heathens, and for the praise of

---

119   From the hymn "Christe, der du bist Tag und Licht," st. 1; for a translation of the Latin original, see *LSB* 882:1.

120   From the hymn "Christ, der du bist der helle Tag," st. 1, lines 1–4.

121   "Conditor alme siderum, / aeterna lux credentium / Christe, Redemptor omnium, / Exaudi preces supplicum"; from the Latin hymn for vespers in Advent; cf. *LSB* 359:1.

Your people Israel" (Luke 2:32). And Isaiah says, "The people who walk in darkness see a great light, and on those who dwell in a dark land it shines brightly" (Is. 9:2); and, "The heathen shall walk in Your Light, and kings in the brightness that rises above You" (Is. 60:3). And the Father says to the Son, "It is too light a thing that You should be My servant to raise up the tribes of Jacob and to bring back the preserved of Israel; rather, I have also made You as the light of the heathen" (Is. 49:6).

Yet the Lord Jesus not only gives us the light of His Gospel, but He also presents us with the light of the Holy Spirit, of whom we sing "O most precious Light," etc.,[122] so that the fine and lovely light of true faith may also be kindled in our heart and so produce good works, a bright radiance, in accordance with the rule of Christ the Lord, "You are the light of the world" (Matt. 5:14) and, "Let your light shine before men, so that they may see your good works and give glory to your Father who is in heaven" [v. 16]. And this is precisely what is meant by the brightly burning lamps of the wise virgins (25:4). It is of course grace above all graces that in this world God "has qualified us for the inheritance of the saints in light" (Col. 1:12). Yet far greater is it still that in the end our Lord Jesus will transport us from this temporal light to the eternal light of heaven, and we will see God face to face in His light, and glorify Him in the everlasting light and radiance of heaven.

I exhort you to keep this in mind whenever the daylight arises: O Lord Jesus, let the blessed, eternal light of heaven which You won for us with Your blood arise at last, and help us, that we may be enabled to receive it with joy.

Dear pious heart, contemplate the nature and properties of light, and so call to mind the Light of Your heart, Jesus Christ. Daylight lets its beams and brightness fall in every place. A lamp gives light to all in the house (Matt. 5:15) with equal brightness, to rich and poor, great and small, lofty and low. O Lord Jesus, You do so, too. You make the light of Your comfort fall wherever it is wanted. The poorest man is as dear to You as the richest. There is no respecting of persons with You [Eph. 6:9, et al.].

---

122 From the hymn "Nun bitten wir den heiligen Geist" (Luther, 1525), st. 2, line 1; see *LSB* 768:2.

Light is the most beautiful created thing. Dear Lord Jesus, "You are the most handsome of the children of men" (Ps. 45:2). "Christ is handsome in the womb of His mother, handsome in the manger, handsome in the world, handsome in the garden, handsome in the religious court, handsome in the Praetorium, handsome on the cross, handsome in the tomb, handsome in heaven," says Augustine.[123] Even soaked in blood, You are still handsome to our heart, for thus You cleansed us handsomely, that we might be well pleasing to Your Father forever.

Without light, nothing in the whole world would be beautiful. Likewise, without You, no idea, no expression, no sermon, and no speech is beautiful. I would rather not live than not know You, O Lord Jesus. It were better for those who do not know You never to have been born.

In the light, one feels good. How happy a traveler becomes when the daylight breaks upon him after he has been stumbling around in the dark forest! All the birds begin to flutter and sing for joy; flowers lift their little heads. Often, the sick find strength and recover. The dark night is friend of none, but daylight brings a gleam to every eye. In the same way, Lord Jesus, our hearts are happiest with You. How glad they become after a severe spiritual attack when You behold them with Your comforting light! Then we begin to sing, "My soul now praise your Maker; let all within me bless His name" (Ps. 103:1).[124] O Lord Jesus, what a comfort You are to the sick! In short, You are the gleam in the eye of every believing heart.

In the dark, one's hair stands on end; but in the light, all fear dissolves. Without You, O Lord Christ, our heart stands in fear of hell; but with You, our heart is enlarged and we are happy.

In the light, one can see things. O Jesus Christ, in the light of Your comfort, we can see how the heavenly Father's heart burns with love for us poor sinners (John 3:16).

In the light, one does not stumble (John 11:9). O Lord Christ, whoever has You in his heart escapes many a great calamity. Therefore, O

---

123 "Pulcher in matris utero, pulcher in praesepio, pulcher in mundo, pulcher in horto, pulcher in consistorio, pulcher in praetorio, pulcher in patibulo, pulcher in sepulchro, pulcher in caelo" (cf. August. *Enarr. In Ps.* 44.3).

124 I.e., as paraphrased in the hymn "Nun lob, mein Seel, den Herren" (J. Graumann, 1525); see *LSB* 820.

my bright Light, I will put You in the lantern of my heart and surround You with earnest devotion and prayer, and a sober life and God-pleasing existence lest the stormy winds of the evil one blow You out. Whenever I then go out to fulfill my calling, I will carry my Lord Jesus at the forefront of my heart, that my way may be blessed and all my enterprises prosper.

In the light, one can find the right path from which one has strayed. Indeed, if there is light, one may take a street that would have otherwise been unsafe. Likewise, O Lord Jesus, in You I can find the right way to heaven and to the heart of Your dear Father. For truly, You are Yourself "the way and the truth and the life" [John 14:6]. With You I can take the dark, dangerous road through death and come unhindered to eternal life.

In the light, one does not fall as easily as in the dark. O Lord Jesus, whoever has You in his heart will not fall into the snares of sin as easily as he who does not heed You. "Whoever walks in the night stumbles, because there is no light in him" (John 11:10).

In the light, all that was hidden in the dark is disclosed. Likewise, O Lord Jesus, on the Last Day You shall reveal all things and disclose what was hidden in this world. This should make all the shameless and secret sinners uneasy. You see into every hidden place. "Even the darkness is not dark to You, but the night shines like the day; darkness is as light to You." (Ps. 139:12).

Dear pious heart, never forget this all the days of your life.

In the evening say: The daylight is vanishing. O Lord Jesus, blessed light of every believing heart, do not leave me, but shine on me day and night, and when my eyes must grow dim, shine on me and light my way to eternal life.

When the morning dawns, speak thus: The beloved light of day fills all creation with joy. O Lord Jesus, You also are light, Light of the heavenly Father's light. You are the light of the world; You keep the light of the Gospel among us, and by the light of the Holy Spirit You work the light of a strong, true faith in my heart. "You are my light and my salvation; whom should I fear?" [Ps. 27:1]. You are my Light and my Life—the two words in which John encapsulates his whole Gospel. O Lord Jesus, be my Light and my Life, that I may be instructed, comforted, and saved by You.

O Lord Jesus, because You are our Light, I will therefore confess and glorify You. Because You cause the light of Your Word to shine on us, I will humbly and gratefully make use of it:

"We are all children of light, children of the day. We are not of the night or of the darkness" (1 Thess. 5:5).

"Believe in the light while you have it, that you may be children of the light" (John 12:36).

"At one time you were darkness, but now you are light in the Lord. Walk as children of light" (Eph. 5:8).

"Arise, shine, for your light has come, and the glory of the LORD has risen upon you. For behold, darkness covers the earth, and thick darkness the peoples; but the LORD arises upon you, and His glory is seen upon you" (Is. 60:1–2).

"The darkness is passing away and the true light is already shining. Whoever says he is in the light and hates his brother is still in darkness. He who loves his brother abides in the light, and there is no offense in him. But whoever hates his brother is in the darkness and walks in the darkness, and does not know where he is going, because the darkness has blinded his eyes" (1 John 2:8–11).

"This is the judgment, that the light has come into the world, and men loved the darkness rather than light because their works were evil," laments the Lord Jesus (John 3:19).

When the light of evening fills the rooms of the house, join our forefathers in saying: O most beloved Lord Jesus, blessed Light of the world, grant me after this light the light everlasting. Help me to live in the light of Your Word, to serve You in the light of Your Spirit, and to inherit the eternal light of salvation.

In reference to consecrated candles, simple folk used tell those who were dying, "Receive this candle in your hand, and pass into your fatherland." This is childish babbling. I prefer to tell the Christians dying in my care, "Like Simeon, receive the light of Jesus in faith's hand, and enter by a blessed death into your blessed fatherland." With this, no one is deluded.

When I make a spark with a hard piece of flint, I think to myself, What a great a work of art it is that we should be able to get light from a rock! But the only reason this was shown to us is so that we would seek our soul's true light in Jesus Christ, the rock of our salvation. Jesus Christ, our rock upon which our salvation is built, is the one who gives us the light of consolation, as suggested by Gideon's rock from which fire and light sprang (Judges 6[:21]).

Let my daily morning-blessing, then, be as follows: Dear Lord Jesus, be my Light. Shine in my heart, that I may pray devoutly, soften Your Father's heart, and serve You worthily throughout this day.

Should I fall into depression, and a pitch-black night descend upon on my heart, I will say: O Lord Jesus, blessed Light, now I have need of Your brightness. Let the rays of Your comforting light fall upon my heart, and I will be healed.

Should it come to the last and most dire distress, and I must die, this shall be my sigh: Dear Lord Jesus, many times in my life Your light has filled my heart with joy and driven away all the gloomy clouds of my grief. I pray You once again to let Your light shine upon me that I might not shiver at the dark sight of death but confidently pass through and find the road to eternal life where You dwell.

Ammianus Marcellinus once tricked some foes pursuing him at night by tying a lamp to a horse and making it run another way (see Fulgentius I, 7.6.4). Friderus did likewise, as did Marabottus also. In the same way, if anyone takes hold of Jesus, the Light of the world, with true faith, and protects himself with this Light in the midst of his spiritual attack, no devil can pluck him away, but all the enemies of our salvation will be put to shame.

Finally, I see the Lord Jesus' profound love for us in His immediate creation of light on the first day for the great benefit of man. What miserable creatures we would be in the dark, tumbling over each other like worms! Think what great misery befell the land of Egypt when "no one saw another, nor rose from the place where he was for three days" (Ex. 10:21–23). Thus by His sorrowful sweating of blood on that dark night in Gethsemane the Lord Jesus graciously redeemed us from the thickest darkness where there is howling and gnashing of teeth. O dearest Lord Jesus, help us to contemplate Your love at every passing moment, living meetly in this world as in broad daylight, that we may never pull the wool over another man's eyes as hypocrites do, and that we may behold the eternal light of heaven won for us by Your dark and doleful matins.[125]

In Rome, there was was once a noble citizen named Julius Drusus who had an awful house full of holes. A skilled architect said to him, "Sir, you are a man of means. It is a wonder that you should live in such a decrepit house into which all manner of men may peer. For five thousand florins, I will renovate it for you from the ground up." The noble Drusus said, "My good man, I do not care one whit if anyone can look into my house. I will give you ten thousand florins if you make it entirely transparent. For I, my wife, and my children live in such a way that everyone is welcome to watch. No one will see anything unbefitting, nor find anything befitting reproach." That is what you call walking in the light. Dear Lord Jesus, if a heathen who did not know You could live in such an honest way, oh, then, direct my heart by Your Spirit, that I may be incited not to let any heathen and unchristian man surpass me in piety in my Christian walk.

Venomous bats cannot stand the light. They only come out of their caves by dark of night. Likewise, whoever shuns the light and crawls toward the works of darkness is not good and Christian. This is not the character of the children of light, but of the coveys and kindreds of venomous bats. O Lord Jesus, deliver me from sin! Grant me to live as a child of the light and blessedly to inherit the light everlasting! Amen.

---

125 Dark matins: a form of matins used during Holy Week in which candles are not used; here meaning Jesus' prayer in Gethsemane.

VII. JESUS,
The Firmament and Basis of Our Salvation, the Craftsman of the Firmament, or Heavenly Fastness (Gen. 1:6–7).

Moses goes on to describe God's task for Monday, saying that God "spread out" the heavens, much like a peacock's tail. For so in the Hebrew text, firmament derives its name from "spread out"; and Jeremiah says that He "stretched out the heavens by His word"[126] (Jer. 10:12). But God made the heavens from water, as the Hebrew word for "heavens" shows; and Psalm 104:3 explains, "You make a vault over it with water." Moreover, God established the heavens between two waters. For there are waters above it, too, as Psalm 148:4 also testifies: "Praise Him, you heavens in every place, and you waters above the heavens!" Here the Hebrew text says, "beyond the heavens."[127] Below the firmament are the clouds that we see quite often. As to what purpose waters above the heavens should serve, we will let God worry about that. We will just have to see when we get there. Meanwhile we must simply believe Moses. Let us also leave others' opinions in peace.

In addition, God wound and wrapped the heavens around the earth and thereby enclosed the whole earth as in a circular city-wall. But it is called firmament or "fastness" by Moses because God made it fast and firm so that it might not be weakened by any tempest, storm, or earthquake. Thus firmly He anchored, secured, and enclosed it by His powerful word, and thus tightly and securely He fastened it together. A spider's web is also subtle but not firm. A swallow's nest is also skillful but not fixed. God builds things skillfully, neatly, gracefully, subtly, and firmly. This is a masterpiece.

---

126 LB: "by His understanding"

127 "supra caelos"

Here again our Lord Jesus is the Craftsman (Prov. 8:30), being referred to by name, (1) in "said"; and (2) in "let there be."[128] On the word "said," you have a detailed account above. As for "let there be," Chrysostom refers to this when he discusses the Gospel reading about the Canaanite woman, saying, "When no one would help the grieving Canaanite woman in her great distress, the Lord Jesus helped her by speaking these words: 'Let it be done (or happen) for you as you desire' [Matt. 15:28],[129] that our heart might see that He is the selfsame LORD who in Genesis [1:6] said, "Let there be a firmament."[130] From this we can palpably perceive and discern His almighty power, and say from Psalm 19:1, "The heavens declare the glory of God (our Lord Jesus), and the firmament proclaims His handiwork." That the heavens are such a noble work also shows what kind of lord our Lord Jesus must be. And so that even simple folk might know that the Lord Jesus is the true architect of it all, it wondrously behooved God the heavenly Father for a period of time in the New Testament to be taken for and called the son of a carpenter (Mark 6:3). And in His early years, as the ancient doctors of the Church write, our Lord Jesus carried a carpenter's axe so that all the world would affirm, Yes, yes, this man is a carpenter—indeed, the oldest carpenter of all, who built, erected, and furnished the heavens, and furthermore established the heavenly Jerusalem through His blood, and who now builds the Christian Church, yea, and daily chips away at our heart with His Word, Sacraments, and the cooperating power of the Holy Spirit so that we are made into God's temple. In fact, He is the carpenter and appointed architect of the poor. He is building for many paupers such mansions as they never dreamed of in all their life. He protects the poor man's dwelling. He inspects it and finds where it is leaking and squeaking and falling apart. He shores it up with joists and bundles. Indeed, if He were not so careful, all its beams would have long since been cast in a heap by the devil's cunning. If you want to build a house, hire this Carpenter Jesus with a humble prayer, or all will be in vain: "Unless the LORD (Jesus) builds the house, those who build it labor

---

128 "fiat"

129 "Fiat tibi, sicut vis."

130 "Fiat firmamentum."

in vain" (Ps. 127:1). This Carpenter is also fashioning a casket for many an ungodly mocking-bird and persecutor of the Christian church. So Libanius' pious tutor, having been mockingly asked what it was that this carpenter-boy Christ was carpentering, replied, "He is making your prince Julian[131] a coffin." After a few days, the news was received that the devil had snatched Julian away.[132]

On the other hand, for pious, believing Christians, this faithful Lord Jesus is fashioning heavenly chariots, like the prophet Elijah's, whereby their souls will be snatched from death to eternal life.

My faithful reader, consider here the traces of Jesus Christ's profound wisdom. He could have, with His heavenly Father and the Holy Spirit, made everything all at once, or at least all on the first day, but He did not wish to. He took His time. On Sunday He made the light, on Monday the heavens, and so forth. He did so with great prudence, with great purpose, for the work was to be durable and last a long time. "That which springs up quickly also withers swiftly and soon."[133] You should do things the same way. Don't travel too swiftly. Don't ride too fast. Don't be so hot in the head. Think first, avoid the worst. Good things come to those who wait. He who rides slowly breaks no wheel and still makes it to the inn.

Oh, contemplate Jesus' unspeakable omnipotence here! He made everything so exceedingly high, and yet so enduring. He put the heavens above *and* below the waters. All that He put under the heavens was a word, and it held it fast like a pillar and column. It is a daily wonder that the clouds do not fall down and drown us. That the waters of the Red Sea stood up like walls is considered miraculous, but no one pays any attention to the fact that the waters float over us in clouds and do not fall; and yet one miracle is as great the other. Regarding this great miracle, Luther wrote from his "Patmos" in 1521, saying, "During severe storms, heat rips through the clouds with great force, making a crackling noise, and rattling the earth; yet the clouds do not fall. Is this not a great miracle?" Some of

---

131 Julian the Apostate, fourth century Roman emperor.

132 Sozom. 6.2.

133 "Quod cito fit, cito perit: cito nata non durant"

them float a half mile up, some over nine miles up. The pillar that holds all things is the powerful decree of Jesus Christ, as Psalm 148:5–6[134] says, "He commanded and they were created. He holds them forever and ever." He "upholds all things by His mighty word" (Heb. 1:3). And Philo, the Jewish scholar who wrote the Book of Wisdom under Solomon's name, called the Law God's eternal "foundation of the world."[135] So when Jesus snatches away His Word on the Last Day, everything will fall to pieces, just like when Samson knocked down the pillars of the temple of Dagon the bread idol (Judges 16:29). Hydraulic systems are considered marvelous. My friend, do you not marvel at the hydraulic power of Jesus Christ who summons the rain-clouds and thus waters the earth? Jesus needs no pulley, no bucket, no ropes, no chains, etc. At His command, it all goes perfectly.

But consider to the glory of the Lord Jesus what an unusual master builder He is! He started the cosmic house on top of the roof and in the vaulting. Where have you ever heard of such a thing all the days of your life? Normally, the joists have to be laid first, then the walls raised, and after that the gable and roof put on. What is to be said? O Lord Jesus, You are the Master of Your craft. I would not have given You such advice, yet in times of anguish my heart always tries to advise You how and when to help me. Oh, let me not forget that You are the Master of Your works, and that You remain the Master to help[136]—that when no other creature can find a solution, You can.

Also consider here the Lord Jesus' great love for mankind. Dear Lord Jesus, how dearly You must love us men! For You did not create heaven for Yourself alone but also for us. And if Adam and Eve had not sinned, we would have lived awhile on earth, and then You would have taken us to heaven like Enoch and Elijah. But since we lost the right to heaven through sin, You gave every drop of Your blood so that we might have new hope.

As certainly as we believe in You now under the heavens, so shall we be blessed forever above the heavens. Yea, out of overflowing love You

---

134   Corr. for "Ps. 148:15."

135   "basis mundi"

136   From Is. 63:1; cf. KJV: "mighty to save."

have written our names in the heavens so that Your heavenly Father always sees them. You write them so high that the goats of hell cannot scratch them out, and You say, "Rejoice that your names are written in heaven" (Luke 10:20). This is the true form of canonization, by which our names are placed with all the saints in the Book of Life with the red ink of Jesus Christ's blood.[137]

So when you look at the heavens, do not look at them as a cow does a new fence, but think like a rational man and remember your Craftsman Jesus Christ.

Oh, how wonderfully beautiful the heavens are! How lovely they are to behold!

A happy conscience views the heavens with pleasure and says, Oh how beautiful heaven is from the outside! How much more beautiful will it be from the inside? Praise God! I not only get to see heaven from without, but also from within—and on top of this all, it was built and bought by Jesus. O Jesus, if heaven is so beautiful, how beautiful You must be Yourself! For the master is always nobler than his craft.

When you contemplate the height of the heavens, think in your heart: Dear Lord Jesus, how staggering its height is! Astronomers estimate it at 65,237,500 miles. Oh Lord Jesus, now I am reminded of the words in Psalm 103:11: "As high as heaven is above the earth, so great is His mercy toward those who fear Him"; and when Psalm 57:10 says, "Your mercy is as high as the heavens," the Hebrew reads, "beyond the heavens."[138] You gave the heavens such a vault that I might have an image of Your unfathomable love and mercy. Your grace is not merely as high as the heavens, but higher than the heavens. You are pure love, as John says: "God is love" [1 John 4:8]; and: "Your mercy is as great as You Yourself are" (Sir. 2:18).

Further: How delightful the heavens are! How delightful and noble You must be, Lord Jesus, since you have mastered the heavens! Therefore, "If I have but You, I ask for nothing in heaven and earth" (Ps. 73:25).

---

137 "canonisatio sanctorum in rubrica sanguinis Jesu Christi" (cf. the Roman Catholic doctrine of canonization).

138 "supra caelos"

O Lord Jesus, You are my heaven, I Your star; let me be your star, and twinkle and shine in You.[139]

How firm the heavens are! They have stood all this time, yet not one brick has fallen down. Nothing is firm on earth. What the hands of men establish, the hands of men can destroy:

> We build our buildings firm and fast
> And yet our visit will not last;
> And there where we should ever be
> Is where we build infrequently.[140]

Dear Lord Jesus, here we have no firm, lasting city (Heb. 13:14). But in Your Father's house are many dwellings, that is, firm, sturdy houses, or as it says in the Greek, "mansions"[141] (John 14:2). Help us ever to build firmly in heaven with a firm faith, to trust firmly in You, to rely firmly and steadfastly on You, our mighty Fortress, and to dwell in the heavenly firmament firmly and forever.

How orderly the heavens are made! Psalm 136:5 says, "Who by great orderliness made the heavens, for His goodness endures forever." You are a lover of order. Help us also to serve You in an orderly fashion, to admire order and to learn good order from You, for "by orderly housekeeping the rooms are filled," says Solomon (Prov. 24:4).

When you say, "Our Father who art in heaven," think to yourself: Oh my God, heaven is the masterpiece of Your powerful word! Your almighty power is visible in the heavens; therefore I will pray boldly, knowing that You can give me whatever I ask of You.

When you are on your sickbed, do not just stare off into the corner. Open your window, look up at the heavens and say: Not to worry! In heaven it will all be better, for heaven was built and bought for me by the Lord Jesus. Only below the heavens do we find cross and misery. Above the heavens there is nothing but joy and good health. Under the heavens

---

139 "Christe, mihi caelum es, sim tibi stella micans"

140 "Noch baun wir alle feste / und sind doch frembde Gäste / und da wir ewig sollen seyn / da bauen wir gar selten ein."

141 "mansiones," i.e., via the Latin.

all is vanity of vanities; above the heavens there is nothing but Song of Songs.[142] So St. Martin had the habit of gazing up at the heavens and would never stop, even when several men mocked him for it.

When Philipp Melanchthon was asked on his sickbed if he wanted anything, he answered, "Heaven."[143] This is comforting for those who are sick and sorrowful. If the evil one afflicts you and tries to cast you into doubt or sin, say: O Lord Jesus, when at the creation of heaven You said, "Let there be a firmament,"[144] it had to be. When to the Canaanite woman You said, "Let it be for you as you desire,"[145] the evil one had to vanish that very second. Repeat in my anguish, "Let it be[146] for you as you desire," and my troubles will be forced to flee, and my foes defied to hurt or harm one hair of my head.

If for the sake of the Gospel you are hunted from place to place, and even mocked, "Where will you dwell?" then say: I will dwell under the heavens and above the heavens,[147] for there is plenty of room there. I will dwell "under the shield and shelter of the Most High" (Ps. 91:1) as long as it pleases my Lord Jesus. When I have no more room below the heavens, I will dwell above the heavens.[148] Heaven was built for me, too.

In 1582, a pious lady who was near death said, "Those who are dying have no more beautiful comfort for their eyes than heaven, which is the straightest road." Since those around her did not understand, she raised her arms and said, "To heaven, to heaven. The Lord Jesus paved this straight road in His ascension."

On his deathbed, Titus Vespasian ordered that he be allowed to look at the heavens, and said that he could think of no contemptible undertaking in his whole life except one thing. Some believe that it was the destruction

---

142 "vanitas vanitatum" and "Cantica Canticorum," a play on the books of Ecclesiastes and Song of Solomon, resp.

143 "Caelum."

144 "Fiat firmamentum."

145 "Fiat tibi, sicut vis."

146 "Fiat."

147 "Sub caelo et supra caelum"

148 "Si terra non capit, caelum capiet."

of the Temple in Jerusalem that he had in mind.

When Amatricianus grew fearful in his affliction, his very own mother said to him, "Dear son, look at the heavens. There is the castle that you shall enter very soon." At these words he found fresh courage.

Therefore in the hour of your death speak thus: Dear Lord Jesus, I must depart from this world, even if I live a long time. But from heaven I will never depart, for that is my firm and lasting city, my eternal dwelling. As certainly as I see this firmament from the outside, so certainly will I also see it from the inside, and rejoice forever. Good night, O wretched shelter of the world! In God's name I greet you, O new heavenly house, built and bought for me by Christ. To Him be praise and glory forever for this grace! Amen.

For good measure, it may be asked here, If heaven is a masterpiece, why does it not say here, "And the LORD saw the firmament, that is was good"? Some ancient writers say that it was withheld because of the fall of the wicked angels who betrayed God on that day, having been created with the light the day before, as inferred from Psalm 104[:4].

But in regard to such matters I am very fond of the saying by John Mauburnus,[149] "Whoever does not wish to burn his tongue should not go too far in discussing these things"[150] (in his *Rosary*).[151]

In any event, what is passed over here is addressed on the third day, and established on the fourth day, and demonstrated even more clearly on the sixth day: "And God saw everything that He had made, and behold, it was all very good" [Gen. 1:31].

O Lord Jesus, Firmament of my salvation, stand by me firmly in every need. Help me to put my trust firmly in You, to be firmly defended in this way against all adversity, to serve You in peace beneath the heavenly fastness here in time, and then to worship You above the heavenly fastness forever! Amen.

---

149 Johannes Mombaer (ca. 1460–1502), alias John of Brussels, ascetic monk and writer.

150 "Qui errare nolit, nil temere de his afferat."

151 "Rosetum" = *Rosetum exercitorium spiritualium et sacrarum meditationum* (1474).

VIII. JESUS,

The Creator of the Earth, Sea, Vegetation, Plants, and Trees;
Our Friend (Gen. 1:11).

Moses goes on to write of God's task for Tuesday, describing how God enclosed the earth's circumference within the borders of the waters, 5,400 miles around. Man was not to live like nixies in puddles and noxious lagoons. Therefore God did what a man does when he irrigates his garden. He dug the Oder, Elbe, Weichsel, Bartsch, Warthe, Donau, the natural channels,[152] etc. Like a cunning Dutchman, He contrived a system of waterworks that made the waters subside and the ground appear, dry and good for life. Around the newly manifested ocean (which was higher than the land) God set a boundary that it could not pass (Ps. 104:9): "Here shall your proud waves be stayed" (Job 38:11). He used His sounding-line to measure how deep it should be in this or that place, and put "the deeps in the hidden places" (Ps. 33:7).

Next, He lifted up the rocky ground by the force of His almighty power and made it float on the water.[153] Islands were formed here and there, some of which[154] were not discovered until our times, e.g., in 1492 by Christopher Columbus. Indeed, all of the dry land on earth is an island, bounded on every side by flowing waters. If God's word did not uphold it, we would be drowned in an instant.

At the same time, God tilled the garden, ridding it of rocks and weeds, paved Adam's parlors, and trimmed them with beautiful wildflowers. For there was to be a wedding soon, and God refused to spare any expense in its honor. God made the grass of the field so that Abel could have his

---

152 Rivers familiar to Herberger's original audience in Poland.

153 On this formerly held theory, connected to that of continental drift, see Abraham Ortelius (1527–1598), *Thesaurus Geographicus.*

154 The Bahamas, etc.

rural pastures and sheep-farms. God made the plants, that is, all of man's food: herbs, grains, and vegetables. He set the table and quickly served up one course after another. (Adam was to have a cozy kitchen.) God saw to it that Adam had a place to find goodly medicinal herbs. He made a large pharmacy for him. For every plant that is in the world there is a curative potion waiting to be found. God made the trees with their beauty and pleasure and adorned them with blossoms, leaves, and fruit. He furthermore gave all the vegetation, plants, and trees their own seeds.

Is this not a miracle? You take a handful of different seeds and scatter them around on the same patch of soil where they get the same kind of nourishment, moisture, and attention, yet they never get confused. Rather, each one brings forth its own kind: one white, the other yellow. Up they spring, sweet and sour, brown and black, red and green, perfumed and putrid, lofty and lowly. Similarly, though we may be buried like seeds in God's field, we will not be confused with one another on the Last Day, but each man shall come out in his own flesh, albeit incorruptible (Job 19:26; 1 Cor. 15:38).

God saw this and thought it all very good. This is stated twice during this day's work and not once during Monday's work, and many have butted heads about this fact, as we were informed above. Some see this as proof that God's concern was not so much for His own habitation as for ours.

In the task for Tuesday our Lord Jesus is also the Craftsman (Prov. 8:30), as the phrase "God said" twice in a row indicates. This was discussed above.

Likewise, we also hear in the New Testament that the Lord Jesus preached to earth and water, walked on earth and water, performed wonders on earth and water, and even exhibited His power by turning water into wine. Indeed, He talked about earth and water, and about vegetation, plants, and trees, so that our heart would understand that He is the same Man of Wonders who mightily reveals Himself in earth and water, and in vegetation, plants, and trees as found in Genesis. Therefore, my pious heart, do not neglect the Lord Jesus in these created things.

When you look at the water, say: Dear Lord Jesus, all the dry land floats upon the waters by Your will, command, and ordaining. Oh, how powerful You are! How can Your almighty power not be my comfort and joy?

The waters are higher than the earth,[155] yet do not drown us. His command makes it so. O Lord Jesus, may you be praised forever for this good work!

The pious brother Hilarion understood this, for on July 21, AD 369, when the earth shook and the sea drowned the Epidaurians, he went to the shore, drew three crosses in the sand, lifted up his hands, and prayed in the name of Jesus. Then the ocean waves stood like towers and fell backwards.[156] O Lord Jesus, it was not the drawings of crosses that performed this miracle, but You repeated the old miracle from Genesis.

Dear Lord Jesus, how deeply You must favor us, since You created the noble waters for our great good! What unspeakable benefit we get from them in turning mills, washing, cooking, and bathing! You serve us refreshing drinks of "goose-wine," spring-water, finely filtered through the sand as through cheesecloth so that it does us no harm.

If we should ever have to pay for water, as Jeremiah groaned (Lam. 5:4), if we should have to measure it for each other like the citizens of Bethulia (Judith 7:21), if everything should go dry like the brook Cherith (1 Kings 17:7), then we would realize what a great treasure water is. But because we can guzzle it, splash it, and scoop it up to our heart's content, we do not think about it. Oh Lord Jesus, pardon my carelessness. Surely, You are the noblest Water. You wash me white as snow. You cool and refresh my soul. I will never be unmindful of You whenever I am dealing with water.

When you look at the dry land, think: Lord Jesus, I could not stay here if You had not prepared this dwelling. I am Your tenant; I dwell on Your ground floor. Oh, help me to serve You there, and be devoted entirely to You, and daily offer You the true tribute of the genuine fear of God.

What exceedingly tall mountains, castles, and towers the earth supports, and yet it does not collapse, even though heavy storms shake it to the foundations. This is the work of Your ancient, almighty, miraculous power.

---

155 E.g., at the coastline.
156 See Hier. *Vit. S. Hilarion.* 40.

On St. Andrew's Eve, 528, there was such a disastrous earthquake in Antioch, where the name Christian was first applied (Acts 11:26), that as many as 4,870 people were struck down when the houses collapsed. Then the citizens came out of the gates barefoot, crying, "Lord, have mercy, Christ have mercy upon us!"[157] It was then revealed to a pious man that they should return and write over the doors of the remaining houses: "Christ is with us, stand firm."[158] This was done and the disaster instantly subsided. Here we see that the Lord Jesus is easily able to hold the earth still—a feat impossible for all other created things.

But who can speak of the riches that You, Lord Jesus, have buried in the earth, from which Your inscrutable wealth can be measured? Is it not a marvelous thing that *terra sigillata*[159] (or "sealed earth") can also be used against poison? O Lord Jesus, what is there then to fear? You are my best *terra sigillata*. You can deliver me in every need and from every poison, even when nothing else can help.

When you are walking in the field and you look at the grass and herbs, think at once of our Lord Jesus: Each and every herb shows that Jesus is present there and a skilled Craftsman.[160] Dear Lord Jesus, here again I see Your presence. Without You, everything would be bare—all hot, parched sand or scorched earth. "You crown the year with Your bounty" (Ps. 65:11). You sow one little seed after the other, like a maiden making her little wreath. You give us grass, flowers, foliage, fruit, seeds, wheat, and all that we need. Your word of command has given this power to the dry land.

O Lord Jesus, You are the true Mary's-grass.[161] In Your green, gentle appearance, my eyes view their comfort, pleasure, and strength.

When I survey the whole world, it seems to me like a rich pharmacy built and supplied by You. I am merely to be the shopkeeper.[162] There is

---

157 "Kyrie eleison, Christe eleison"
158 "Christ[us] nobiscum; state"
159 A type of clay-based rock once thought to have medicinal properties.
160 "Praesentem und artificem Jesum quaelibet herba docet"
161 An aromatic herb used chiefly in brewing and medicine.
162 "provisor"

not one sickness to be found in this world that cannot be reversed if only we knew our own remedy. But because of sin, we poor souls are in such a woeful state that we often unwittingly trample our own doctor underfoot and run over the medicine that could cure us.

In Caeserea Philippi, the woman with the flow of blood (Matt. 9:20) was supposed to have set up a statue of Christ cast from molten ore. If a plant growing next to the statue were to touch the seam of the cloak, that plant would have power to cure all diseases (in Eusebius' *Church History*).[163] My pious heart, do you not believe that in this world there are many plants which hold great miraculous power even without having to grow next to some metal statue? Nevertheless there is nothing that can aid against death. Therefore we must stick to our Lord Jesus. Dear Lord Christ, You are the true Herb that can help me in every need. Many God-pleasing hearts attest to having experienced this. Your benefits shall be my pharmacy when I find no other help.

When you go for a walk in your garden, say: On these little flowers the name of my glorious King Jesus Christ is written.[164] They are all little masterpieces of His hands.

O Lord Jesus, You are also a flower according to Your divine nature: You are a bud from the heart of the heavenly Father. Moreover, according to Your human nature, You are "from the root of Jesse," as Isaiah 11:1 says. With the hand faith I will pluck You from the ground of the Christian Church where You bloom, and put You in the garden of my heart. I will bottle You for the winter so that You can give me strength and refreshment. You are the true counterdeath flower.[165] You were cut down with many agonies, You were macerated and infused in my misery, dropped into the boiling pots of Gethsemane, the Praetorium, and the cross, and cast into the kiln of the heavenly Father's wrath at the highest degree,[166] and You give us true, living water (John 4:11; 7:38). You were cooled off in

---

163 Euseb. *Eccles. Hist.* 7. 1.

164 "Hic flores inscripti nomina Regis"; cf. Verg. *Ecl.* 3, lines 106–7.

165 Germ. *Widertod.*

166 "ad quintam essentiam"

the hollow[167] of the tomb. Now I will let my heart be the little vessel and vial in which the drops of Your merit are preserved with the tight cork of careful remembrance. This will strengthen my soul for eternal life.

In short, there is nothing of beauty in the whole world that has not portrayed our Lord Jesus to us. Just look at the lonely blue violet for an example of how God's works should be meditated upon.

The beloved violet comes unexpectedly. It may not be dug up or re-planted, and it suffers great pain. Dear Lord Jesus, Creator of the violet, You also came to us unexpected and unsought, and took on all our misery from the very beginning. How can we thank You for this unexpected, unsought, and unsolicited love?

The violet is the loveliest flower. O Lord Jesus, I regard You as the loveliest flower in the whole world. I count You as "the most handsome of the children of men" (Ps. 45:2).

The violet is shaped like a wide-brimmed rain-hat. Oh Lord Jesus, You are my rain-hat. You shelter me so that the deluge of God's wrath does not drown me.

The violet has five petals. O Lord Jesus, You have five holy wounds, which are my petals of comfort. In these I will wrap myself. In these I will live out my Christian life and die a blessed death.

The violet's color is the blue of heaven and the purple of scars. In its center it has a gold head. Dear Lord Jesus, how purple You were in the Praetorium, how purple You were on the cross with Your streams of blood! By Your purple scars I am healed. You came from the azure heavens to us on earth. You are true man and God, and the golden head of Your divine nature (1 Cor. 2:8) strengthened You so that all that You did had to prosper.

The violet is very effective at strengthening the heart, and it cools a high fever, and can be used against epilepsy. O Lord Jesus, You are the greatest strengthening for my heart, the best cordial. You cool me in the fever of spiritual attack, and keep me from falling into eternal death and perishing.

---

167 Germ. *Röhrlein,* "small reed," perhaps from an apothecary's practice; or else for Germ. *Rohlein,* "linen."

The violet does no harm to the sick. O Lord Jesus, You are not harmful in the least. You are good for young and old, great and small, sick and healthy alike. Blessed is he who carries You in his heart.

The violet is tender; it withers easily, it is trampled on everywhere. O Lord Jesus, so it was with You in the world. You were denied, trampled on everywhere, and at last You were made to wither on the cross so that we could flourish in eternity.

Violets come up early in the year; they are the most fervent flowers of all. Dear Lord Jesus, You also came up early in Paradise to herald the plan of our salvation. You are the "hind of the dawn" (Ps. 22:1).[168] You still come up today, fervent to help us. You never once come too slowly. You omit nothing, and You yield all the more splendid returns.

Violets are the first up in our gardens after the cold winter here in the countryside. O Lord Jesus, You are the Firstfruits from the dead. And just as after the beloved violet the whole world comes to bloom, so by Your rising You obtained a joyous rising and summertime for us. On the Last Day, the whole world shall bloom, all Your Christians shall come back to life; then we will all heartily rejoice.

Violets have a scent that is lovely beyond all measure. O Lord Jesus, You also "were made a sweet-smelling fragrance" (Eph. 5:2) on the cross, and You fill our heart with unspeakably lovely incense through the words of the Holy Gospel, as we hear every day in church.

The violet is a humble shrub. It grows by fences in lowly patches, not on high mountains. It bows its head to the ground; it creeps along the earth. Oh Lord Jesus, here I see an image of Your profound humility. You offered Yourself to lowly, humble, and sad hearts, and by Your patient humility atoned for our arrogance and pride.

The violet turns three petals toward the earth but directs and raises two up over itself toward heaven. Likewise, Lord Jesus, in Your humiliation and the anguish of Your heart, You never neglected to pray.[169] You entered Your afflictions with prayer, and as the mortal agonies of death drew closer, You prayed the more urgently. Indeed, on the cross You

---

168 I.e., "Aijeleth Shahar" from the title.

169 Herberger likens the two upper petals to hands raised in prayer.

concluded Your life with prayer, and constantly amid the distresses of body and soul made the petals of Your sighs ascend to heaven. Oh, grant that I may learn from this in my adversity, and look to God in heaven when misery presses me to the earth.

The violet has very deep roots; under small shrubs I have found roots over a span in length. O Lord Jesus, You have deep roots, the might that You concealed. "Your throne stands firm" (Ps. 93:2), and therefore the evil one himself could not uproot or harm You.

This is how you should survey the world and learn to contemplate the Master from His works. But if I were to go through the entire natural world, it would take a whole book.

Besides this, when you look at the herbs and flowers your heart should say: Dear Lord Jesus, You care for the herbs and flowers all year round. You clothe and adorn them as You Yourself preached. Will You not then care far more for me? I am far more precious to You than the flowers. For it was for my sake that You created all the flowers, and for my sake You also take care of them year by year. Therefore I will say with joy, "The Lord (Jesus) is mindful of us and blesses us" (Ps. 115:12).

Likewise, when you look at trees in gardens and forests, say: O Lord Jesus, this too is a masterpiece. Without You, not one leaf would be here. In every leaf I have another testament of Your wisdom and almighty power. You not only give us the apple trees and pear trees, but firewood and lumber as well. You also give us birch trees so that naughty boys can be whipped. Blessed be Your wisdom! We too are trees on Your soil and earth. Help us to glorify You as we grow, to take the whips of true repentance, to weed out all bad habits, to bring forth the fruits of good works, and not to be chopped up like fruitless trees by the axe of Your wrath and turned into kindling for hell.

Finally, when you go out to sow your seed, say: O Lord Jesus, You too are a seed, the promised Seed of the woman, the blessed Seed of Abraham. You alone bore the fruit that saves us. I will scatter You in the precious seed-grains of Your Gospel on the soil of my heart so that it becomes a green meadow in which Your Father may take eternal pleasure.

In Matthew 13:31, You compare Yourself to a grain of mustard seed, which has a lowly reputation. Who would think that something big could come from it? You were likewise counted lowly and of little value in the world. Your Gospel did not have a high reputation among the children of the world. But just as the tiny mustard seed turns into a tree and shrub of such size that even the birds can make their nests in it, so we have the highest, greatest, most enduring, most precious comfort in You. Under You we find shade, as did the beasts under the king's great tree (Dan. 4:12). Our sad souls nestle and dwell under Your branches and wings, finding their most exquisite comfort and joy in You.

The mustard seed makes coral-beads red.[170] O Lord Jesus, You make our heart red in the power of Your blood, and when we blush with shame in the contemplation of our sins, You deliver us so that we do not despair.

The mustard seed, when smoked over coals, repels snakes. O Lord Jesus, when You were placed as an offering on the coals of Your Father's wrath, You repelled all the forces of the serpent. That is what You meant when You said, "It is finished."

The mustard seed strengthens the brain, warms the belly, dispels fever, and makes men light-hearted. O Lord Jesus, You help me when I am weak and You make my heart happy.

Taking two mustard seeds on an empty stomach every morning will guard against stroke[171] during the day. O Lord Jesus, whoever in true faith takes comfort in Your benefits each day is safe from the hand of God's wrath, for You took our strokes, that we might be spared forever.

The mustard seed, when ingested, strengthens and sharpens language and speech. O Lord Jesus, You make us keen and bold so that in our prayer we may call on Your Father with a loud voice and be heard.

Mustard seed juice makes the eyes clear because it etches and eats away at small obscurities. Oh Lord Jesus, You make the eyes of our heart clear by Your bright Gospel, that we may know the heart of Your Father in bright light and know how we should serve Him rightly and pleasingly. For this we must praise You with glad hearts and sweet-sounding voices forever.

---

170 Germ. *Das Senffkörnlein machet die Corallichen roth.*

171 Germ. *der Schlag,* "apoplexy."

IX. JESUS,

The Sun of Righteousness, the Bright Morning Star, the Craftsman of the Sun, Moon, and Stars (Gen. 1:16; Mal. 4:2; 2 Peter 1:19).

We now come to the task for Wednesday. Here God made the lights that were to be lamps and lanterns for the light that God had created on the first day. God had built a big, beautiful house, so now he hung up big, gleaming lamps in the middle of the parlor—great illuminating lanterns, as Basil says. Thus Nazianzen also called these lamps the first carriages of light. God put these lamps right up on the firmament so that our heart would think, If heaven is so beautiful on the outside, oh, how beautiful it must be on the inside! (cf. Is. 64:4; 1 Cor. 2:9). Oh, help us to behold it from the inside someday! And help us to think thus: What a fine, beautiful house; it must be a wealthy Lord who lives there! Truly, God is wealthy. The more He gives, the more he has to give. Blessed be His rich generosity!

Now the purpose of these lamps was to divide the day and night. In other words, the sun was to mark off the beginning and end of the day, like a town crier, or those drummers in Leipzig. When man has worked himself to exhaustion, the sun puts away its light for the evening like a mother draping the window when she lays her child to sleep—so that we are the better enabled to rest through the night. Thus Moses says, "to govern the day"; and Psalm 136[:8], "to rule over." For the light of the first day is clearly called "day," so the sun added no new light. Next, they were "to be for signs," that is, to serve as the world's calendar, dividing and changing the seasons and weather so that everything in heaven and earth would move in an orderly fashion. Oh, what a powerful and wise and benevolent Lord our God is! These lamps furthermore tell the years, days, and hours by their movements. Thus they are the world's clock-hands and gears. The hour-hand is the sun, which finishes its circuit in 365 days and

6 hours. The minute-hand is the moon, which finishes its circuit in four weeks. The stars are the small quarterly markers. Who can say how many there are? The ancients counted 1,022 of them; our contemporaries have observed 300 more than that. But God alone knows their true number (Ps. 147:4).

God wished to reveal Himself to mankind at various seasons, and man should accordingly remember Him in due season. Oh, with what little diligence we crude men examine these profound matters! We ought to consider for what purpose God has given us our minds.

Now, once again, our Lord Jesus is the Craftsman of these noble creations, as illustrated by the word "said" in Genesis 1:3, and by Proverbs 8:30 and John 1:1. Therefore it fitting that we should learn to contemplate in these works their Master and Craftsman. Also, Malachi clearly points us to the Lord Jesus in the image of the sun (Mal. 4:2): "But for you who fear My name, the sun of righteousness shall rise, and salvation under its wings" (which are the Word and Sacraments) "and you shall go out and come in, leaping like fatted calves."

Psalm 19:5–6 similarly represents Jesus in the sun. As the sun is led around earth's bounds, so in the Gospels, Jesus leads the twelve apostles around the world. As the sun leaps boldly with its light, so Jesus reveals Himself boldly with His light to all men. As no man can hinder the course of the sun, neither can any tyrant or heretic stay or hinder the course of the Gospel. In the New Testament (Luke 1:78) Zechariah calls the Lord Jesus "the rising from on high." Jesus shines "like the sun" in Matthew 17:2. Likewise see Revelation 1:16, which demonstrates that He is the true Sun of righteousness. Revelation 22:5 further says that the city of the heavenly Jerusalem will need no sun or moon to shine in her, for the glory of the Lord will be her lamp, and the Lamb her light. Thus Luther sings:

> Christ is Himself the joy of all,
> The sun that warms and lights us.
> Now His grace to us imparts
> Eternal sunshine to our hearts.[172]

---

172 From the hymn "Christ lag in Todesbanden" (Luther, 1524), st. 6, lines 3–6; tr. *LSB* 458:6.

Dear Lord Jesus, I thank You for revealing Yourself to my heart in this noble creature of Yours. I promise to study the Book of the Sun every day. Whenever the sun rises and sets, I will turn my thoughts to You and say, Just as I would not be able to see the sun in heaven if it did not announce and manifest itself to me by its light, so I would not be able to know You were it not that You have manifested Yourself by the light of Your Word. Oh, shine on me by the brightness of Your Gospel, that I might perceive You rightly, and in the knowledge of You be saved.

Dear Lord and God, how quickly the sun runs its course! If it ran along the earth, it would travel over two hundred miles an hour. It runs faster than Hercules did when he had to run a race.[173]

Dear Lord Jesus, Your word runs far more swiftly (Ps. 147:15). When You spoke Your word of grace to the chief steward, its power was felt at the very same moment many miles away (Matt. 8:13). I will take comfort in this in my every sadness.

The sun scatters vapors, clouds, mist, and water. O Lord Jesus, You scatter and turn into "a quickly passing mist"[174] the black storm-clouds of the fierce tyrant who, like Julian, seeks to drown Your church. You scatter the flood of God's wrath merited by the flood of our sins. You dispel the sad vapors of our misery, tribulation, and cross, and usher the fair weather of comfort into our heart.

The sun begins the day and ends it, and yet exists before the day and endures after it. O Lord Jesus, You began our salvation in Paradise, you carried it through the high noon of the scorching cross, and You shall end it on the Last Day, in the evening of the world, and on the day of the restoration of all things[175] You shall summon us to gladness. You are before all ages from eternity, and You endure forever.

The sun is often eclipsed, sending deadly plagues and other calamities to earth. O Lord Jesus, Your Gospel is often eclipsed by the vanity of men, which brings people the plague of despair over sin,[176] death, perdition, and

---

173 See Paus. 5.7.6–10.

174 "nubeculae cito transiturae" Theod. 3.5.

175 "in die restitutionis omnium" (Acts 3:21).

176 "pestem desperationis"

lack of consolation. But just as the eclipse of the sun is not seen at the same time in every land, neither is the knowledge of Jesus darkened in the whole world and in all hearts. There are always those who adore, honor, praise, and confess our Lord Jesus, see Him in the true light, and are blessed by Him.

The sun fills gardens with beautiful flowers. O Lord Jesus, You fill the little garden of my heart with the flowers of virtue, with the beautiful buds of the Paradise Rose, which in turn yield Trinity-flowers,[177] and praise-glory,[178] and keys-of-heaven,[179] and blue-sorrows,[180] and the-longer-the-loveliers,[181] and peace-lilies,[182] etc.; that is to say: the confession of the most blessed Trinity, thanksgiving, prayer, heavenly sorrow, faith, unity, hope, etc.

The sun makes the earth fertile; wherever it is kept from shining nothing will grow. O Lord Jesus, make my heart fertile so that everything in it may grow to Your praise.

The sun makes men happy; when a storm fills the sky, men are gloomy and sad. Dear Lord Jesus, You are my heart's comfort and my gladness. Without You, my life would never be happy.

There is only one sun in the heavens; "mock suns" are mere foolishness. Therefore I have only one Mediator and Savior (1 Tim 2:5). The suggestion that there are helpers is idle nonsense from which I will guard myself.

The sun's heat both softens and hardens. O Lord Jesus, with Your comfort You soften the pious whose hearts are of flesh, not hard and thick-skinned. But whatever is earthly-minded You give over to be hardened in its thinking. Oh, how righteous Your judgment is! Grant that my heart may be good. Let it be soft, not hardened in carnal wickedness

---

177 Germ. *Dreifaltigkeitsblümlein,* "Trinity-flower." Here and following, Herberger chooses flowers primarly for their names.

178 Germ. *Ehrenpreis.*

179 Germ. *Himmelschlüssel.*

180 Germ. *Blausorgen.*

181 Germ. *Jelänger Jelieber.*

182 Germ. *Einblatt.*

like Pharaoh's heart. O Lord Jesus, You are gentle toward all timid and humble hearts, but You are angry and fearsome toward all prideful, shameless sinners.

The sun is the king of the heavenly lamps; all stars ride behind it as their emperor. They all follow its course. O Lord Jesus, You are the King of the Christian Church. To You all the prophets bear witness (Acts 10:43), as do all the apostles (Acts 15:11). May we all desire to follow You also, and find the way to salvation.

The sun is the light of the world; it shines over the whole earth. O Lord Jesus, You are the light of the world, "which enlightens all men who come into this world" (John 1:9). Oh, shine in me always, that I might never have to cry with the condemned, "The light of righteousness did not shine on us, the sun did not rise for us" (Wisd. 5:6).

The sun overshadows all the stars. O Lord Jesus, Your merit overshadows the good works of all the saints as well as my own. Therefore I will rely on You alone.

The sun must give its light to the moon, otherwise the moon would have no light. Dear Lord Jesus, my heart is Your moon; without You, it has no comfort. As the moon has more light at certain times and less at others, so is it with our heart: "The sweet hours of consolation come but seldom, nor do they last for long."[183] One moment we have a whole heart full of the light of comfort; and quicker than the flick of a wrist, all is extinguished. Oh dearest Lord Jesus, shine upon the full moon of my heart, lest in the night of temporal death my courage should wane and I despair.

The sun's circumference is 166 times greater than that of the earth.[184] O Lord Jesus, You are not only greater than earth, You are greater and higher than heaven and earth combined (Ps. 73:25). You are more excellent than the angels (Heb. 1:4). You are greater than all creation, for You Yourself are great. You are true God and true man. Your office is greater than that of all the prophets, for no man was permitted to undertake it, and Your benefits are greater than we can even begin to dream of. Who, then, would not regard You more highly than his own life and limb?

---

183 "rara hora, brevis mora (consolationis)"
184 Based on ancient estimates.

There is nothing in the world more useful to men then sun and salt. Likewise, O Lord Jesus, when I am under spiritual attack, there is nothing in the world more useful to me than You and Your most holy merit.

There is nothing more beautiful in heaven than the sun. Dear Lord Jesus, You are the most beautiful in the kingdom of heaven, "the most handsome of the children of men" (Ps. 45:2).

The sun rises and sets; if it is red when it sets, fair and friendly weather is expected. It then keeps moving, beaming, and shining beneath our horizon. Finally, it returns and fills the earth with gladness. Dear Lord Jesus, You appeared in the manger at Bethlehem. Then You climbed into the great noon-day heat of God's wrath on the cross and bore the burden of Good Friday. Finally, You set, blood-red, hung on the tree like Moses' red, copper serpent. This was the token of the fair, clement weather of Your Father's grace and mercy obtained by Your bloody death. You then descended into the nether places of the earth. You scoured hell and returned on Easter Day, and with the words "Peace be with you"[185] [John 20:21] made the dawning rays of Your comfort fall on the earthly-minded hearts of the apostles, and climbed again into the high noon, and set Yourself in great majesty at the right hand of the heavenly Father. And now in Your unsurpassed brightness and mighty rule You are our King and High Priest eternally, never to die again.

The closer the sun gets to the horizon, the more faintly it shows its power; but the higher it is, the more strongly its heat is felt, as winter and summer prove. Dear Lord Jesus, so it was with You also. When You visibly walked around in the land of the Jews, You wore the wretched form of servant, enduring our misery and neediness. But now that You have been exalted to the right hand of Your Father's majesty, You manifest Yourself with great and mighty omnipotence, power, and splendor.

When the sun rises, the sick recover. Dear Lord Jesus, when You rise in my heart, I recover. No other comfort affects my heart. Yet as soon as I take hold of You, nothing but light and life ensue. For every drop of Your blood confirms how kindly You are disposed toward us.

---

185 "Pax vobis"

The sun melts the snow in deep valleys far more quickly than on high mountains. O Lord Jesus, the lowly and humble are always Your most beloved. You are seated on high, but You look far down on the humble (Ps. 113:[5–]6), saying, "I look on the miserable and contrite in spirit" (Is. 66:2).

The sun stopped when Joshua prayed (Joshua 10:13). It went back when Hezekiah prayed (Is. 38:8). O Lord Jesus, You also stopped when Bartimaeus prayed (Luke 18:40). You also went back at the humble urging of the disciples who walked to Emmaus (Luke 24:29), and at the persistent petition of the Canaanite woman (Matt. 15:28).

Oh Lord Jesus, I too will cry to You in my need. Oh, do not pass by, but stop for me. Be my Good Samaritan and do not forsake me!

The higher the sun gets, the more slowly it travels. O Lord Jesus, the higher You are seated, the gentler, friendlier, more amiable, and more gracious You are.

The sun gives life to all that died in the winter. Dear Lord Jesus, on the Last Day You too shall give life to all those who trust in You, and awaken what was dead (Job 19:25). I will take this comfort with me to my grave.

The sun warms all things. O Lord Jesus, You warm us with Your Spirit so that we do not end up chattering [or gnashing] our teeth, cold as death, and trembling and travailing forever.

Even If every forest were set afire, it would not give off as much heat as the sun. Even if every torch were kindled, it would not give off as much light as the sun. Likewise, O Lord Jesus, even if all knowledge and learning were compiled, there would still not flow from it the comfort that we have from You. (For more, read *Treasury of the Saints,* sermons 18, 15 & 19.)[186]

So what is there to fear? I will clothe myself from head to toe in the Sun of righteousness, as written of the woman in Revelation 12:1. I will put on my Lord Jesus. I will wrap and wind myself in His benefits, bright as the sun, and know for certain that I too will shine like the sun in heaven, as Daniel, Christ, and St. Paul inform us (Dan. 12:3; Matt. 13:43; 1 Cor. 15:41).

I will have the eyes of an eagle to behold the noble Sun, Jesus, with unaverted gaze in my every need, for "this is the will of Him who sent

186   "Si vis plura, lege Thesaurum de sanctis, Sermon," etc.

Me, that everyone who looks on the Son and believes in Him should have eternal life" (John 6:40).

Eaglets that cannot look at the sun are not of good eagle stock. Whoever refuses to look at Jesus with pleasure, joy, and gladness is not the of true Christian stock. He will be cast out of the nest of the Christian communion of the saints.

O Lord Jesus, shine in my heart, mind, words, and actions. I do not want to obstruct the window of my devotion willfully.

Dearest Lord Jesus, let my heart flourish with sunflowers and way-white[187] blossoms that face and turn toward the sun. Let my heart face You at every moment.

In the morning when the sun rises, let this be my request: O Lord Jesus, arise in my heart also, that I may walk in the daylight; govern the day of my life. When the sun is at its peak: O Lord Jesus, stand over my body and soul also, and fill me with warmth, lest I despair. When the sun goes down: O Lord Jesus, do not set for me. The evening falls; O Lord, abide; let not Your light from us subside. Oh Lord Jesus Christ, "stay with us, for it is toward evening" [Luke 24:29]. On March 10, 1600, a pious old lady died with these same words upon her lips. When I pray: O Lord Jesus Christ, Beloved Sun, shine for me, that my petition may be received. When I bear some cross: O Lord Jesus, shine for me, lest I despair. When I am pent in by anguish and spiritual warfare: O Lord Jesus, shine for me and scatter the gloomy storm-clouds of my depression. In my whole life: O Lord Jesus, shine for me, lest I take the path of transgression. When I must die, shine for me and light me through death's dark road to eternal life.

Now, just as Jesus is depicted in the sun, He is also depicted in the stars: "A star shall arise out of Jacob" (Num. 24:17). And Jesus pledges to make those who confess Him shine as brightly as stars (Dan. 12:3). Peter refers to Jesus as the bright morning star (2 Peter 1:19), as we sing:

He is the Star of Morning,
No star so brightly burning,[188]

---

187 Germ. *Sonnenwendel*, "sun-turning"; Germ. *Wegweiße*, "way-white."

188 From the hymn "Herr Christ, der einig' Gotts Sohn" (E. Cruciger), st. 1, lines 5–6; see *LSB* 402.

Make use of this as follows: I have a lucky star in the heavens; my star is Jesus Christ. He stands next to the heart of the heavenly Father, enlightening, gladdening, and blessing me, and exalting me so that I too shall shine like the stars in heaven with a brightness relative to my having exercised my faith in good works (1 Cor. 15:41), not to my having been rich or poor, as Pliny fancies.

O Lord Jesus, beautiful and most blessed Star, I will put You on the shield and coat-of-arms of my heart, for then I will be noble indeed, though poor by birth. Help me in this world to imitate the nature of a star, and to sustain my light, brightness, and orderly course: to keep the light of true faith, to let the glow of good works be seen, to conduct my vocation in an orderly fashion, to pursue unity, not to step on others or get in their way, but like the people in John 6:10, to behave and be seated according to Your will. Help me by such a Christian way of life to be well pleasing to You, and as Your star in heaven to sparkle and gleam forever in ceaseless and everlasting glory. Amen.

X. JESUS,
The Creator of the Fish and Birds, Our Provider (Gen. 1:21).

Moses informs us that God created the fish and birds on Thursday, and put the fish in their habitation in the waters, and the birds on the earth and in the air. God miraculously made all these creatures from the earth, as it says below in Genesis 2:19, and from the waters. One sign of this in nature can be noted in the way that swallows hibernate underwater.[189] O my God, what a Craftsman You are! How wonderful all Your works are! Let Your skillful Master's hand be my comfort, help, and stay in every need!

In this way, God stocked the fish-stores and fish-beds for the good of us men before we were even created. Now that is an attentive and loving God! Natural scientists count 153 kinds of fish, as Lyra[190] also confirms. Yet Moses is not only thinking of the small, everyday fish that we eat, but also of the great whale in which God's omnipotence is especially discernible, as in the events of Job 41. Surely the fish that swallowed Jonah could not have been a small creature (Jonah 1).

Lyra writes that a whale was cast ashore in Portugal the tongue of which would have required twenty-four mules to be carried. In August, 1532, the English sea cast up an enormous beast one single fin of which ten oxen were barely able to haul away, as Olaus Magnus attests.[191] In arctic territories, a whale's hide will often clothe forty men. Its ribcages are propped up and whole houses are built from them; whoever sleeps beneath them constantly dreams that he is traveling at sea. God created this great wonder of the waters, and Moses says this so that no one might

---

189 A theory proposed by Olaus Magnus (see below).

190 Nicholas of Lyra (ca. 1270–1349) Franciscan monk and Bible commentator.

191 Olaus Magnus (1490–1558), Swedish Romanist, author of the fanciful *History of the Northern Peoples* (1555).

think that it was a phantom. Finally [God also created] the birds, so great in number that they cannot be counted.[192] In addition, He spoke a powerful blessing on both fish and birds so that they would multiply and be fruitful. Birds are frequently caught by snares, and fish are caught every day. Vast numbers are cut down when they are swarming, yet still there is no lack of the creatures. The pike devours other fish all day, engorging itself, and yet it is unable to eat them all up. It would be no miracle at all if all fish and birds were chased away, but the fact that they never disappear is a result of this powerful blessing. Here then our Lord Jesus is the Craftsman once again, as the words "God said" explicitly prove, and as explained by Psalm 8:6–8 and John 1:3. Therefore Jesus is also Lord of all the fish and birds. Notice how Psalm 8:6–8 clearly says of Christ that all things were "put under His feet...the birds of the heavens, and the fish of the sea." In the desert, Jesus was even able command the quail to flock into the camp of the Israelites. At a word from our Lord Jesus, fish instantly swarmed together and swam into a net (Luke 5:6). At Christ's command, 153 fish entered a net (John 21:11), testifying that He is the Lord who created the 153 species of fish. Indeed, Jesus even prepared the broiled fish on the shore when the disciples were working [v. 9].

Fish know their Creator and are obedient to Him. Oh Lord Jesus, help me also to know You rightly and always to be found obedient to You. A fish was once made to obey Christ and bring Him a gold half-dollar[193] for the temple tax (Matt. 17:27).

This gives us good table-talk. Dear Lord Jesus, what diverse and delicious fish You created for our good! You really must love us deeply. Oh, how mighty, how skillful You are! How wealthy and generous You are! If You did not bid these creatures of Yours to swim into our net, we wouldn't have one fish-bone in our pantry. You created the fish. You commanded them to swim into the net. Blessed be Your goodness forever! Continue to be our Master Chef and Cellarer, and provide for us and our children.

---

192 Here Herberger may also be thinking of other flying animals and insects not normally classed with birds. See below.

193 Germ. *einen halben Güldenthaler.*

Jesus Christ is Himself depicted in many fish. In the old days when we were children, our parents used to show us how the whole Passion and its instruments were marked on the pike's head.[194] Such table-talk is truly more beneficial than other idle chatter.

The echeneis[195] is a small fish and stops a great ship at full sail and full speed. O Lord Jesus, You are the smallest in the kingdom of heaven, and You even call Yourself as much [Matt. 11:11]. To the world You and Your Gospel seem small, yet You demonstrate the greatest power in that You are able stop and hinder all our foes in their fiercest assault. A few years ago outside Danzig, a man with a specially equipped vessel tore down the bridge that the enemy had built over the water. Our Lord Jesus has also built a bridge over the water of our sins and eternal death. The devil often seeks to tear this down with all his might and pluck from our heart the hope of eternal salvation. In such times, our Lord Jesus Himself hinders the infernal sailor in his wiles so that he cannot cause us hurt or harm.

Likewise, let us not be unmindful of our Lord Jesus when we watch birds fly through the sky. Dear Lord Jesus, every bird that exists is a masterpiece of Your divine, wonder-working power right before our eyes. You gave us game-birds for dainty dishes and siskins[196] and nightingales for lutists and musicians. Without You, not one bird would boast either wing or feather. What a mighty, wealthy Lord You are! Long ago, monks said that when He was young the Lord Jesus would play with the neighbors' children and make little birds out of mud or earth which immediately flew from His hands. There is no need for such trifles. For truly, Jesus created all birds and gave them flight—not in His childhood in land of the Jews, but right at the beginning of the world on the Fifth Day.

---

194 "A pike's head has all the parts of the crucifixion of Christ. There are the cross, three nails, and a sword distinctly recognizable. The German tradition is that when Christ was crucified, all fishes dived under the waters in terror, except the pike, which, out of curiosity, lifted up its head and beheld the whole scene"; *Dictionary of Phrase and Fable,* E.C. Brewer, 1894.

195 See Plin. *NH* 9.41.

196 Meaning the common or Eurasian siskin (Carduelis spinus), a small songbird of northern Europe.

What is more, He still cares for birds today (Matt. 6:26), even for the useless raven (Ps. 147:9), and miraculously feeds them with worms that crawl right up into their beaks. Here your heart should say: Dear Lord Jesus, how then will You not care far more for me? For am I not, like the birds, also one of Your creatures, in fact, Your dearest and noblest creature after the holy angels? Indeed, You shed Your blood for me and not for the birds, so You must care far more for me than for them. Oh, help me in my times of sorrow never to forget this!

Also remember the words of Jesus Christ, "The birds of the air have nests, but the Son of Man has nowhere to lay His head" (Matt. 8:20). Dear Lord Jesus, for my sake You were made far poorer than a bird. The birds have their nests, but You did not own so much as a place where You might happily lay Your head [Matt. 8:20; Luke 9:58]. Blessed be Your most holy poverty by which You make me wealthy in heaven. "Christ's poverty is my patrimony"[197] I say with St. Ambrose. Dear Lord Jesus, You want us to be constant students of Your creation. Thus You said that from the birds of the air we should learn to trust Your Father in every need (Matt. 6:26). No one has ever known a bird to cry itself to death, hang itself in desperation, or drown itself. Oh, help us never to forget Your faithful warning, but to trust You confidently and to leave You to care for us little birds of the forest!

You have given us far better portraits to meditate on in the kingdom of the birds.

The stork nurtures its old parents. How much more we ought to do so as Your children!

The rooster rises, looks at the heavens, and chants the Canonical Hours[198] as regularly as the devout canon of a cathedral. So, too, we should always turn our heart toward heaven and never once sleep through our hours of prayer.

The cuckoo, by contrast, gobbles up his mother after she hatches him, and is therefore a monster warning us to oppose such ingratitude.

---

197 "Paupertas Jesu meum patrimonium"; Ambr. *In Luc.* 2.

198 "horas canonicas"

The raven abandons its young and has thus earned a bad name, teaching us diligently to guard ourselves from mercilessness and disloyalty.

The peacock is arrogant, and struts and swaggers with his beautiful, reflective feathers. But as soon as he catches a glimpse of his black feet, he is horrified and his proud heart falls flat. Should we not do the same who are by nature inclined to arrogance? Should we not continually keep our earthly origin in sight and our mortality in mind, that we might accustom ourselves to the most blessed state of humility?

O Lord Jesus, in the time of Moses, You also depicted Yourself and Your merit in doves and other clean birds, as we shall frequently find below at the proper place in the writings of Moses.

Now I turn my thoughts to that lovely little flier, the gentle honeybee. O Lord Jesus, this is a delightful picture in which I find the comfort of beholding and contemplating You.

Green meadows and flowing waters are the best and most pleasant places for the honeybee. O Lord Jesus, You are present in Your Christian Church, where the green pastures of the divine Word and fresh waters of the Holy Gospel (Ps. 23:2) are found. You are with us until the end of the world [Matt. 28:20].

The honeybee is a clean animal; it cannot stand any impurity. O Lord Jesus, You are wholly pure, without any sin or indecency, neither can You endure anything impure in us. You gave every drop of Your blood so that we might be cleansed and purified of our sins.

The honeybee has terrible fury. I know a story about some Spaniards who were plundering a certain town. A miller who lived nearby learned of this and thought, They'll do the same to me. So he locked all his family together in a room and asked them to pray. But he went out into the garden where many bees had been breeding, guarded himself with a beekeeper's hat, took a hoe, knocked over the hive, dashed out the honey, and went away. When the Spaniards came and, according to their custom, wished to explore what they thought was a water-mill, the bees fell in a great swarm upon the horses so that they were driven into a frenzy, tumbled, and fell over. Behold, what terrible fury the bee has! O Lord Jesus, You also have terrible fury toward the devil, death, sin, and hell. But as great as Your fury is, Your love toward those who believe in

You is still greater. Oh Lord Jesus, what terrible fury You will display on the Last Day toward all the accursed and condemned! Yet what great love and kindness You will show Your elect!

The honeybee does very heavy and bitter toil in the summer. O Lord Jesus, You also toiled bitterly and bloodily in order to take away my sins, of which You Yourself say, "Yea…you have made toil for Me with your iniquities" (Is. 43:24). Oh, how bitterly You toiled in the Garden of Gethsemane when You sweated blood! How bitterly You toiled in the Praetorium when You were scourged! How bloodily and bitterly You toiled upon the cross so that Your eyes were darkened! You worked Yourself to death. The prophet Isaiah also has Your holy labors in view when he says, "Because His soul has toiled, He shall see His pleasure and be satisfied" (Is. 53:11).

The honeybee stores up the sweetest and most beloved fruit, honey, even though it is "a small bird" (Sir. 11:3). O Lord Jesus, You seem so small and insignificant to the world with Your Gospel, and yet our heart does not find such honey-sweet consolation anywhere else but in You alone. Oh, how honey-sweet Your words are! How honey-sweet Your benefits are! Oh, let our heart be the blessed cell and consecrated comb in which the sweet honey of Your merit is safely stored.

The honeybee does not harm the flower on which it lands. O Lord Jesus, You bring no man to harm. Although we often think that we will only receive harm for our piety—which concern also weighs on Psalm 73:13, "Shall it be in vain that my heart lives innocently?"—yet let us remember, as much as we may lose in temporal things by serving You, so richly shall we gain in eternal things. You do not bring us to harm but to eternal good.

The honeybee does not fly silently but hums along as it goes. Likewise, O Lord Jesus, You make the hum of Your voice resound by the Holy Gospel in every land, revealing Yourself and assuring us of the comfort that we find in You.

The honeybee has no father but is begotten by its mother in miraculous chastity. O Lord Jesus, You had no father according to Your human nature but were born to a chaste Virgin.

Nevertheless, the honeybee has a powerful sting to defend itself. O Lord Jesus, You used Your almighty divinity to arm Yourself and valiantly crush and conquer all the foes of our salvation.

In Psalm 102:6, we find the word "bittern."[199] Jerome and the Septuagint read it as "pelican." This is yet another mighty, beautiful portrait of the Lord Jesus Christ.

The serpent kills the pelican's young. The elder pelican mourns for three days and pecks at its breast in anguish. As soon as the young are sprinkled with its blood, they come back to life. Dear Lord Jesus, the serpent poisoned us to death. You came and took up our cause. You bewailed our sorrow and injury, and rested in the grave until the third day. You gave up Your precious blood for us. You spattered blood all over Yourself (Is. 63:3). You allowed Your side to be opened, by Your blood gave us the eternal life that we had lost, and healed all our injuries. In 1598 my dear old professor Valentin Florian[200] wrote of this as follows:

> Thy blood, O Jesus Christ, doth all Thy children quicken
> Who by the serpent's lies were stricken unto death,
> And as the pelican doth give its brood, thus stricken,
> New life by its own blood: So Thou restor'st our breath.[201]

Now, O Lord Jesus, I remember how You said, "O Jerusalem, Jerusalem...how often would I have gathered your children together as a hen gathers her brood under her wings" (Matt. 23:37). Here You depict Yourself in Your creature, submitting Yourself for our heart's consideration in the image of a broody hen. Thank You, O Lord Jesus, for this comforting comparison.

The broody hen suffers bitterly to hatch her chicks from their shells. Dear Lord Jesus, how bitterly You suffered on the cross and in Gethsemane to hatch me from the hard shell of sin and make me a newborn infant of God [1 Peter 2:2].

---

199 Germ. *Rohrdommel* (LB).

200 Rector at the school in Fraustadt who taught Herberger the ancient languages.

201 The meter and rhyme follow that of Herberger's gloss. Florian's original Latin is quoted as follows: "Christe tuus sanguis / Mortem quibus intulit anguis / Dat vitam pullis, / Dum noxia crimina tollis. / Suscitat ut stratos / Pelicanus sanguine natos: / Participes lucis / Sic nos ex morte reducis." There is a syllable missing in the third line; one should perhaps read *Dedit* or *Dabat* for "Dat."

The broody hen's voice changes; she grows hoarse, she crows very sadly and clucks pitifully. Oh Lord Jesus, how woeful Your words in Gethsemane were! "My soul is aggrieved to the point of death" [Matt. 26:38, par.]; and on the cross: "My God, my God, how You have forsaken Me!" [Matt. 27:46, par.; cf. Ps. 22:1]. You did this to bring us to eternal joy.

The broody hen calls to her chicks. Oh my Lord Jesus, how gently You call to our hearts throughout the year with so many friendly evangelical sermons! You Yourself say, "Come to Me, all who are weary and heavy-laden" [Matt. 11:28]. Oh, help us to hear Your soft voice and follow it willingly!

The broody hen loves her chicks dearly; she lets them crawl over and under her. Oh, Lord Jesus, how great Your love is for us! "No one has greater love than this, that he lay down his life for another" [John 15:13]. Likewise, You gave up life and limb, possessions and blood for us, that we might be saved.

The broody hen finds food for her chicks. She pecks for grain, not eating it herself but chewing it up for her chicks. O Lord Jesus, You are just as caring toward us, feeding us in body and soul. You were able to forget Yourself in Your Passion; but You could not let mournful Peter out of Your heart, mind, and thoughts. You could not leave him disconsolate. When You could not comfort him with words, You did so with a friendly, tender glance.

The broody hen takes care of her chicks with true loyalty. She fights with the chicken-hawk until her blood runs and her feathers fly. She leaps in front of him and defends her young. O Lord Jesus, You took care of us with Your right hand. When the devil attacked us, you fought with him until Your blood ran, until Your power slipped away. You pecked out the eyes of everlasting death and mightily defended us from all the forces of the gates of hell.

The broody hen covers her chicks with her wings; she spreads her wings out for the good of her chicks, warming them, keeping them safe from rain and other mishaps. O Lord Jesus, You spread out Your two wings, Your Word and Sacraments. You spread out both Your arms on the cross, wishing to draw us all to You, wishing to warm and shelter us from the beating rain of Your Father's wrath and from all our foes. You will cover me with Your pinions; my refuge will be under Your wings; Your truth is a shield and buckler (Ps. 91:4).

Oh, how chicks peep and chirp for their mother hen! How happy they are beneath her warm wings! How pleasantly they begin to sing and twitter as if they were nothing but robins or finches. Likewise, O Lord Jesus, our hearts are also happy in You. Oh, how warm we are beneath Your merit! Oh, how dry we stay in Your grace! There we begin to pray comfortingly, to praise God, to sound our beautiful songs of praise. Help us at all times to follow You, to call on You, to keep ourselves under Your wings, and not to run away from You, so that under Your protection, shelter, and shadow, we may be safe from hell's hawk, and well provided for in all our human misery. Amen!

XI. JESUS,

The Creator of the Livestock, Creeping Things, and Beasts of the Earth;
And Comfortingly Depicted in Them (Gen. 1:24).

Now we proceed to God's task for Friday. But let us at this time restrict ourselves to God's creation of the tame livestock. Sheep, cattle, goats, etc., were to serve for man's livelihood. Next, horses were to be the appointed laborers, serfs, and footmen for man. Dogs were to be man's watchmen, bodyguards, and protectors. Indeed, just as great lords have their zoological gardens in which they amuse themselves with pleasant diversions, man was also to have his own park and animals in which he was not only to find all sorts of pleasures, but from which he was also to derive much benefit, yea, and at every passing moment even to find in them manifest sermons on beneficial matters.

Truly, the Canaanite woman makes very skillful use of the dog in Matthew 15:27: "O my Lord Jesus, thank You for what You have said, calling me a dog. Dogs get the scraps. If I cannot get a large helping of Your favor and grace, then allot me but a small scrap of Your love and mercy, and I am already saved. I have followed Your scent like a dog. I will not leave You unless You bless me [Gen. 32:26]. What is more, dogs get a place in the house. Oh, grant me also a little plot in Your house, in Your kingdom of grace, under Your table of mercy which You have decked with Your love and filled with great wonders. Dogs may eat of the crumbs that the children drop [Mark 7:28]. O dear Lord Christ, Your children[202] dropped the scraps. They hounded and chased You away. Oh, let me but partake of that remedy which Your thankless children have now thrown away! Dogs paw at their masters and whine for food. I too now scratch at You with the paw of my prayer: Oh Lord, help me! Many a country squire would practically

---

202 I.e., those Jews who rejected Christ.

lay down his life for his hound. O Lord Christ, You are a great squire of city and country. Let me have as much kindness from You as a dog has from his squire. I will trot behind You as behind my squire. I will not leave Your heel. Yes, Lord, it is true, I am Your dog. Oh, how You have cut me to the heart! I have been a snapper, a barker, and a tattle-tale. I have often promised You piety and yet returned to lick up what I had vomited. Like a dog I have been openly obscene. Yes, Lord, it is true. Yet I console myself in Your good heart. You came to save sinners [1 Tim. 1:15]. I do not want to be like this anymore. I want to be faithful to You, like a dog to its master. I want to be awake and aware, to watch and pray [Matt. 26:41; Mark 14:38]. I want to serve every man henceforth with a wholesome tongue, hating that wolf, the devil, and every sin along with him. Even if You strike me, I will run back to You like a faithful dog, and in humility huddle and cuddle up next to You." This[203] pleased the Lord Jesus so much that He promised to give the woman more than she had asked of Him.

Next, God created the creeping things. Here everyone might think it was all for nothing—that in fact there is no use to be had from creeping things.

But, God help us, what artistry is contained in this miniscule creation! I will speak of only one little insect so that everyone may look with the more wonder on what is bigger.

It is not for nothing that Solomon points out the little ant to house-fathers and heads of household: "Go to the ant, O sluggard; consider her ways, and learn. Although she has no chief or officer or ruler, she prepares her bread in summer and gathers her food in harvest. How long will you lie there, O sluggard?" etc. (Prov. 6:6[−9]). And again: "The ants are a weak people, yet they provide their food in the summer" (Prov. 30:25). Just see what great wisdom God has instilled in this little creature. Jerome describes how, long before, a newcomer to his country took spe-cial pleasure in this little insect and noted its industrious nature (*Lives of the Fathers*[204]). On this also read Pliny.[205]

---

203 Referring to the words of the Canaanite woman in Matt. 15:27.

204 "Vitae Patrum *fol.* 31."

205 Plin. *NH* 11.36, 65, 76.

The ant keeps track of its holidays and workdays by the cycle of the moon. Likewise, the head of household should keep track of his holidays and workdays in an accurate and orderly fashion, and not mix everything up, for "by orderly housekeeping the rooms are filled" (Prov. 24:4). Orderly housekeeping is first to seek the kingdom of God, to remember the Sabbath, and to ask for God's blessing, and after that to earn one's bread in the sweat of one's face [Gen. 3:19; Ex. 2:2–11; 20:12–17; Matt. 6:33].

The ant thinks no task too great. It avails itself of bright nights when the moon is full. Often it can be found carrying or rolling a kernel of grain greater than itself. Likewise, the head of household must not dread his tasks or be afraid of getting a few blisters on his hands, but seize the opportunity when he is young, while the moon is full and his face is rosy and plump and his muscles still strong. For a young squire makes an old beggar. Whoever earns something now in the full moon of his youth has something to expect later when his powers wane and old age bows his back.

The ant is very wise and cautious; it does not step on or touch any poisonous plant. Oh housefather, do not step on the poisonous plants of sin and scheming in your deeds and dealings, but make your living fairly and honestly, and you will have God's blessing.

The ant does not overtax itself. When a grain is too big to fit into its hole, it chews it apart and carries it down in pieces. Likewise, dear housefather, do not overload yourself. Enough is as good as a feast. Large morsels are likely murderers. Little often is better than much seldom. Be agreeable, not greedy.

When the weather has been rainy for a long time, the ant worries that the grain may become spoiled and moldy, so as soon as there is fair weather, it puts it out in the sun. Thus when travelers find such a thing in the wild, they say that there will be no rain that day. Likewise, dear housefather, do not be a "soaked sponge,"[206] observing your "weekly Shrovetide" and hanging around the tavern each day, or you may spoil all your assets. After you have had the pleasure of good friends on a day of celebration, turn right around and go back to your appointed task.

---

206 Germ. *nasser Bruder,* "wet brother."

Ants are deeply loyal to each other. They help each other to push and move the grain when it is too much for one of them. In fact, they even bury each other. Likewise, those who live in a happy house must be true to one another, come to each other's aid, and not leave everything on one man's shoulders.

Ants do not wage war amongst themselves. If confusion arises, it means great disaster for the lord of the anthill, as demonstrated in certain stories. Likewise, those who live in a happy household must not be fractious, but walk together in heart, mind, speech, and word. When discord enters a house, it means certain destruction and calamity.

The ant cleverly bites off the germ of the seed to prevent it from sprouting and growing. Every head of household should be so cunning and clever that, whatever God grants him, he knows how to keep it from sprouting and thus slipping through his fingers. He who keeps, has, and takes as he will; and he who saves wisely can also do more good.[207]

The grasshopper, children are told, once came to the ant in the winter to beg for grain. The ant offered him four kernels. The grasshopper said, "What good is this to me? How long can I live on this? The ant replied, "There are many anthills in this forest. If they all give you four kernels, you'll be as rich as I. Why did you not gather in the summer yourself?" The grasshopper answered, "Well, I did not have time. I had to sing, you see, and dress my little grasshoppers in fine garments." Then the ant said, "If you sang in the summer, then you can dance now that it is winter, and feed your young on hops!" Oh, what a good house-lesson this is for those who would but consider and heed it well! (I will not speak here of how anthills are made use of by men as curative sweat-baths.) Who then would say that these little insects were not created with great prudence and profound wisdom?

Finally on Friday, God also created the beasts of the earth, that is, all the wild animals, and gave man, His dearest pup in the litter, absolutely everything that he might desire or need.

Learn from this that beasts are not gods, as the heathens used to believe, but rather God's creations. "All the beasts of the forest are Mine," says God

---

207 "bonus servatius facit bonum bonifacium."

(Ps. 50:10). Diodorus Siculus wrote that, in Egypt, some thousand Roman soldiers were slain because of one cat that the Romans had stuck on a spear as a mockery to the idol-worshiping Egyptians.[208] Oh, what great blindness this was! Thanks be to You, O Lord Jesus, for graciously delivering us from such heathen blindness and bringing us into the bright light of the knowledge of the truth.

Our Lord Jesus is again the Craftsman of this part of creation, as Moses shows by the word "said," and as clarified by Psalm 33:6, and as seen in Proverbs 8:30 and John 1:1 as well. Therefore, whenever you look at or contemplate the animals, insects, or wild beasts, remember their Craftsman, Jesus Christ.

Dear Lord Jesus, how much You must love us! For in the creation of the beasts You put a large sum of laborers, serfs, and servants under us as though we were great lords. Oh, how rich You are! How immeasurable is all that You have given and granted us!

Oh, how wise You are, not only in providing us with great benefit in these creatures, but also in setting before us at every passing moment visible lessons, sermons, and admonitions through them. Help us to keep Your wisdom, gracious love, and great power in our heart and before our eyes, and to rejoice in them.

All animals were put under Your feet (Ps. 8:6–7). Besides this, O Lord Jesus, You also skillfully fitted these creatures so that they comfortingly depict You to us, that we may know the Master by His work. I will not speak at this time about the beasts that depict Christ in Moses' writings, with which we shall deal expressly later, but rather restrict myself to considering those beasts in the Prophets and the New Testament presented to us as portraits of the Lord Jesus.

Psalm 22 is a prophecy of Jesus' Passion; the title reads "Of the Hunted Hind." Here our Lord Jesus, who was sniffed out and set upon early by that bloodhound Caiaphas, is likened to a young female deer. This is worthy of consideration.

The deer is light and quick on its feet, an agile leaper. O Lord Jesus, You are swift and agile in all Your works. "Your word runs very swiftly"

---

208 Diod. Sic. *Bibl. hist.* 1.41; 1.83, adapt.

(Ps. 147:15). You are *Jeduthun,* the true Leaper,[209] as the sequence for the Feast of the Ascension goes: "From heaven He made a leap..."[210] etc. You made a graceful leap from the heart of Your heavenly Father to beneath the chaste heart of Mary. You were born true man. You made a graceful leap from Mary into the manger in Bethlehem, a mighty leap into Egypt, again a leap to Nazareth, another leap to the Jordan, from thence into the wilderness, and back again to the land of the Jews, where You filled everything with lovely, comforting, evangelical sermons and mighty wonders. You made a leap to Gethsemane into the fire of the wrath of Your heavenly Father, and sweated blood. You made a leap from judge to judge, letting Yourself be bound, flogged, and reviled. You made a mighty leap on the cross to atone for our sins. You made a mighty leap in the tomb and buried our sins inside. You made a mighty leap into hell and crushed the serpent's head, curbed the power of death and, like Samson, stormed the temple of the devil Dagon. You made a mighty leap back to life. You rose from the dead and brought us the forgiveness of sins, the hope of the resurrection of our body, and the life everlasting. You made a triumphant leap to the right hand of God's majesty, and now stand as our Mediator with God and our most mighty Protector in every need. Even now You leap with Your Gospel across the world, from heart to heart (Ps. 19[:4]).

The deer is the arch-enemy of the serpent. When it notices one in a hole, it runs toward it, draws it out with its mighty lungs, and crushes it with its hooves.[211] But in so doing it acquires such a great thirst that it has to run for fresh water, as seen in Psalm 42:1. Likewise, O Lord Jesus, You are the arch-enemy of the devil, who once disguised himself as a serpent. And because he deceived Your dearest creature, You earnestly attacked him, forcibly pulled him from his cavernous stronghold, and trampled his head with Your unbroken legs. In so doing You acquired such a thirst that You cried out in pain, "I thirst!" [John 19:28].

---

209 Lat. "Idithum," from the beginning of Pss. 39, 62, 77.

210 "Saltum de caelo dedit"; from "Summi triumphum Regis," Notker's sequence for Ascension.

211 See Aelian. *De nat. anim.* 9.20.

The deer is hunted, baited, and set upon with hounds and nets. In its anguish, it trembles and travails, many times running of its own accord into the hands of men, as it were to seek help and protection with them, only to end up a nobleman's quarry. Dear Lord Jesus, You were assailed by great anguish in the garden, where You began to tremble and travail. You ran to Your disciples hoping to find comfort in them, only to end up the quarry of the spiritual and worldly noblemen of Jerusalem and fall right into their hands. By this anguish You redeemed us from the eternal anguish of hell.

The deer, if it is left in the wild, lives a long life beyond all measure, as also natural scientists attest from some accounts. Dear Lord Jesus, since You died for our sins once and rose again for our righteousness, You will not die again [Rom. 6:9] but live forever, and we will also live with You perpetually.

Now the hind, that is, the female deer, is mentioned chiefly because it does not struggle as violently as the male. Likewise, O Lord Jesus Christ, You did not struggle in Your afflictions but kept Yourself quietly obedient on Quiet Friday[212] so that the long-fought battle between God and mankind would be given a peaceful conclusion.

In the profound Song of Solomon, the Church says to Jesus, the Bridegroom of her heart, "My beloved is like a roe or a young stag" (Song of Sol. 2:9).

Much can be said of the sharp eyes of the roe-deer. O Lord Jesus, here Your clear vision is accurately portrayed for me, for "Your eyes are brighter than the sun, seeing every hidden place" [Sir. 23:19]. This gives me living consolation. You see me in my misery wherever I am. Help me also to stand in awe of Your bright eyes and to live all the more carefully.

In Psalm 22:6, our Lord Jesus says, "I am a worm and no man; a reproach of the people, and the nation's contempt." The Messiah is saying, "I will let Myself be so punished for Your salvation that I will look more like a squashed, bloody little worm than a man." The word used here is *tolah,* that is, a little blood-colored worm [*or* bug] from which crimson

---

212   I.e., Good Friday.

cloth is made.[213] Dear Lord Jesus, You are the innocent crimson worm. You yield the good red ink by which our names are written in the book of life and in heaven.[214] Just as the names of the chief saints are indicated by red ink on the calendar, so our names are written with Your blood in the Book of Life and included in the register of the elect children of God. On this, Luke 10:20 says, "Rejoice that your names are written in heaven."

Now, following the instruction of our devout forefathers, let me briefly contemplate the blessed earthworm.

When spring comes and the birds of summer appear, the earthworm also comes into sight. Likewise, when the spring of the New Testament commenced, and the angel Gabriel, the true bird of summer from the warm summery fields of heaven, appeared, You, the Christ Child, first came into sight like a lowly earthworm in Your manger at Bethlehem.

The earthworm has neither father nor mother, but miraculously arises from the earth.[215] Dear Lord Jesus, You have no mother according to Your divine nature, but are begotten from the heart of Your heavenly Father in an indiscernible way. Neither do You have a father according to Your human nature, but were conceived under the heart of a chaste Virgin by the overshadowing of the Holy Spirit.

The earthworm grows in rich, warm earth and soil. O Lord Jesus, You entered our flesh and blood at Bethlehem ("Bread Home"), the fat of the land of the Jews.

The earthworm is weak and despised. It is easily wounded. It is pushed about and turned out everywhere. In this I see Your sufferings, O dearest Lord Jesus. You felt our weakness and pains. You were pushed about everywhere, oppressed and afflicted, and finally turned out at the gate of Jerusalem and led away. And there on mount Calvary, where all the refuse was thrown, You were crushed like a worm and died on the cross.

The earthworm is stuck on a barbed hook and used to lure the great, ravenous pike. Likewise, O Lord Jesus, You so beguiled eternal death with

---

213   I.e., kermes vermilio.

214   "ad canonisationem sanctorum"

215   On this idea, see Arist. *Hist. an.* 570 A 16–23.

Your simple form of a servant that he devoured You to death and was destroyed along with all his dominion.

The earthworm keeps its mouth on the ground and pulls itself along from place to place. If its way is blocked, it changes direction. Likewise, Lord Jesus, You keep Your evangelical mouthpieces on the earth, winding with Your Gospel through the whole world. But where Your road has been blocked and You find only ingratitude, You take up Your travel-bag again and seek another people and another nation. Grant grace that, holding You dear, we may leave the road to our heart standing free and open to You at every passing moment!

The earthworm does not seek vengeance. It does not bluster about. It bunches itself up and quickly crawls away. Dear Lord Jesus, You are mild and gentle. You do not rumble or grumble at the pious and humble. You are the very essence of humility and meekness. You receive sinners. You purge them with ardent words. You make no one depart from you desolate.

The earthworm has sharp teeth nevertheless. It can even turn hard wood into sawdust. O Lord, You also are amiable and gentle toward repentant hearts, and sharp and stern toward those who do not accept Your Gospel. On the Last Day all unbelievers will come to know the irreparable harm of Your sharp teeth and Your zealous, righteous anger.

If an earthworm [Regenwurm] is put on that kind of wound which is often called a "worm,"[216] the worm itself will be killed and the wound healed. O dear Lord Jesus, if I bind You with the bandage of faith onto the worm of my wounded conscience, I will be made whole. The worm will die—the anguish of my conscience will cease—and my wounds will be healed.

In Revelation it says, "Behold, the Lion of the tribe of Judah, the Root of David, has conquered" (Rev. 5:5). Here, Lord Jesus, You are clearly compared to a lion.

The lion is the king and lord of the animals. Lord Jesus, You are the King of the Jews and the Lord Protector of all Christendom. Your kingly heart, Your kingly pledge is my heart's greatest joy in every sorrow.

216 Prob. whitlow or some herpetic inflammation of the skin; see DWB "Wurm," V. §3.

The lion takes a young lion under its strong protection (Is. 31:4). I can say the same of You, O Lord Jesus. I experience it daily.

The lion has such a great ferocity that it rumbles with its fierce breath as if it were no different from gurgling water—as it can be seen to do toward chickens which are thrown to it. Yet it does not use its wrath and strength against humble buildings of wood. O Lord Jesus, You are surely a wrathful and zealous Lord against those who revile You, but You are also very gentle and mild toward those who in humility and true faith look to You for every good thing. You will not break a bruised, trampled reed, and a glowing wick You will not quench (Is. 42:3).

The lion does not devour everything but lets other smaller animals join in the feast. Likewise, O Lord Jesus, You do not chiefly seek what is of use to You but what is for our eternal good.

The lion is the most courageous animal on the earth. O dear Lord Jesus, You have the courage of a true, mighty Prince (Is. 9:6) and lion in respect to all our foes. You will also grant us this princely courage in great persecution whenever we have need of it.

Although the lion is stout of courage, it trembles when it sees a fire in front of it. You are a stouthearted Captain, O Lord Jesus, yet when You were in Gethsemane and saw the fiery wrath of Your Father before You, You began to tremble and travail so that we would not have to tremble and travail in torment forever.

The lion is subject to many diseases. It is often sorely plagued by the four-day fever. Truly, O Lord Jesus, You also bore our diseases and took upon Yourself our afflictions [Is. 53:4]. In You we have a High Priest who was tempted in every respect as we are [Heb. 4:15]. You know very well how fearful, sick and depressed people's hearts can be. You were broken by affliction, for which reason we can expect all the more faithfulness, assistance, love, and kindness from You.

When the young lion is born, it is blind for three days and sleeps, but on the third day it awakes with a cry and stands up. O Lord Jesus, You slept in Your grave, but on the third day You woke Your own body with great honor and glory.

To conclude, I would like to look at one more creature. When the crocodile has eaten its fill, it lays itself out in the sun and spreads its jaws as wide as it can. The birds pick out what is left stuck between its teeth while it sleeps. When a certain little animal called the *ichneumon*[217] learns of this fact, it rolls itself in the mud to cover itself, slips into the crocodile's throat and bites a hole in its belly, killing it. Dear Lord Jesus, how beautifully You are portrayed here! That predator of man, eternal death, once sat on his throne and tyrannized mankind. What did You do? You armed Yourself in the suit of our flesh and blood, took on the form of a servant, encountered the jaws of death, died, and were buried. Then You entered the belly of the earth, descended into the kingdom of hell, and pierced a hole in it so that neither death nor hell could keep any believer captive. Now there is nothing condemnable in those who believe in You [Rom. 8:1]. For this benefit be blessed and adored henceforth and forevermore! Amen.

---

217   A fabulous beast, prob. based on the mongoose; see Plin. *NH* 8.35–37.

XII. JESUS,
The Creator of Man, the Lord of Our Body and Soul (Gen. 1:27; 2:22).

After God created the livestock, the creeping things, and the wild beasts, He prepared for His holiday and at last created man, the dearest pup of His litter, the noblest and most skillfully made of His creatures. From this God's profound love for men can be appreciated yet again.

He had no desire to set man inside a big, bare house with no furniture, but first filled the house with cabinets, chests, cellars, and attics, and fitted it out with all everything needed to run a farm. Now man would be king of his castle and have absolutely everything that he would want, need, or enjoy. The ordering of creation proves this, for after everything was ready it was cleaned up for man and stocked for his lodging. The whole world together with all creation was to serve men, but man was to be devoted to God alone. In addition, man was created last of all so that he could consider, contemplate, and marvel at all creation, and thus get to know God's almighty power, unsearchable wisdom, and unfathomable love for all mankind.

Now devoutly consider the great ceremony with which God made His preparations. God did not say as above, "Let there be man," etc., or, "Let the waters swarm" or "the earth bring forth," etc. Rather, He called a solemn council: "Let Us make man." For man was to be God's master-piece and work of art. He wanted to end His work well by taking every wonderful thing in the whole world and wrapping it up in man like a little bundle[218] so that man would be a microcosm, as philosophers say.

Simply look at the world for a moment: God has His imperial throne in heaven's height where the firmament moves and stirs. Beneath it lies

218 "compendiosè"

the earth's sphere where the winds blow, where the waters flow, where the hard cliffs of rock are found. In the same way, man has the royal seat of his spirit and mind in his brain and from thence directs all his members what to do or do not. There the mind, like the firmament in the heavens of man, never rests an hour or moment, working, stirring, and moving even in slumber, as can be detected in dreams. After this, we have the earthly masses of our body where the winds of our breath blow, where our veins and capillaries flow with blood, where our hard bones are found. In short, everything artful in the world finds a mirror in man.

Next, Moses says that God skillfully molded a lump of earth and artistically proportioned it so that all its parts were useful and graceful. If even one thing in the lump had been misshapen or awry, it would have resulted in a crippled man.

After this, God blew and breathed a spirit and breath of life into the nostrils of this lump of earth, and "man became a living soul" [Gen. 2:7], and began to live and move. Paul carefully alludes to this in 1 Thessalonians 5:23 when he counts three parts in man: body, spirit, and soul.

Simply think of this, dear man: you not only possess body and being, as do the senseless beasts, but also divine breath. You are divine offspring (Acts 17:29). You have a bit of God's breath.[219] Heaven and earth are united and joined together in you, for you were not only meant to dwell on earth but in heaven as well.

Consider your humble origin according to your physical birth. You are a handful of soil: "How can wretched dust and ashes be proud?" (Sir. 10:9).

Be humble and gentle, for dust you are and to dust you shall return [Gen. 3:19]. Prester John[220] always had to have a golden coffer carried before him filled with earth and adorned with a cross, for even when great lords were being married or honored, they were never to forget the cross of Jesus Christ and their lowly origin from this earth. Indeed, St. Willigis, the archbishop of Mainz, refused ever to forget that he was the son of a poor cartwright, so he had a cartwheel painted on the wall with

219 "Divinae particulam aurae"
220 "Praetus Johann," a legendary Christian patriarch.

the words: "Willigis, Willigis, do not forget your humble beginnings on this earth."[221]

At the same time, you should always remember your lofty pedigree from heaven, for you received your spirit and soul from God. This ought to give you great courage and steadfast comfort. Thus Basil says, "Man is nothing, and yet something great. He is nothing, a lowly creature by virtue of his arising from a piece of earth; but he is something great by virtue of his Creator and because he received his spirit from divine breath."[222]

Moses further testifies that man was created in the image of God. No one should understand this to mean that our God also has physical members as we have, for God is a spiritual being. But the meaning is this: just as God is a righteous, holy being, so man, too, was full of the holiness and righteousness that avails before God [Rom. 1:17]. Just as God is the omniscient Lord and very Truth Himself, so man was full of wisdom and understanding. Nothing at all was hidden from him. He could speak exhaustively and judiciously of all matters as they are in truth. Just as God is a being of free will, so man was truly a free lord. He had a free will to do or do not.

Likewise, St. Paul himself explains, "But be renewed in the spirit of your mind, and put on the new man, created after the image of God in perfect righteousness and holiness" (Eph. 4:23[–24]).

Behold, what a noble creature man was before the fall! For by sin everything was ruined, defiled, and darkened. Nevertheless, there are some vestiges of this treasure in man remaining, and yet it is only in part, in pieces and scraps [1 Cor. 13:12].

But in order that we might regain this former perfection, the Lord Jesus, the exact image of God the Father (Col 1:15; Heb. 1:3), offered up His own blood. In this life, however, we only have the beginning. In heaven, the image of God will shine and shimmer in us perfectly without any blemish. For "Eternal life is perfect obedience,"[223] says Philipp Melanchthon.

---

221 "Willigis, Willigis, recole, unde veneris"

222 See Basil. *Hom. exeg. in ps.* 19.8.

223 "vita aeterna est integra obedientia."

And "To see God will be no less than to learn all things at once,"[224] say our dear forefathers. There our mind shall know God in clear light. There our heart shall trust in God with deepest love. There our will shall honor and serve God with the most beautiful enthusiasm.

You should consider this at every passing moment and thank God that He did not make you a senseless beast but created you in His image. Plato said that he could never thank God (the Lord)[225] enough for three things: first, that he was a man; second, that he was a Greek and not an uncouth barbarian (for the Greeks were a brave, learned, experienced, and refined people); and third, that by God's special providence Socrates had been his instructor and trained him up from early youth to every good thing. The wise king Alfonso likewise said that he thanked God every day and every hour: first, for making him a reasonable man and not a wild beast; second, for bringing him into the Church and not leaving him in heathen blindness; and third, for blessing him with much land and property in this world and promising him far more blessings in heaven. Such godly men should always serve as models for imitation.

Luther, in his explanation of the Third Commandment, and again in his exposition of Mary's hymn of praise [Luke 1:46–55], recounts a fine story that took place around the time of the Council of Constance[226] when Jan Hus was burned to death: Two cardinals were riding in the field when they saw a shepherd standing and weeping. The first cardinal, a compassionate man, refused to pass by, but wished to console the man. So he rode over to him and asked him the cause of his affliction. The shepherd was so sorrowful that for a long time he could not speak a word. Finally, he looked up, pointed at an ugly toad, and said, "I am weeping because God did not make me as ugly as this creature,[227] and because I never realized it, much less thanked and praised Him for it." The cardinal, startled

---

224 "Deum vidisse erit omnia semel didicisse" (see Bonav. *Solil.* 4.5).

225 Plato was thought by some to have been a kind of pious gentile, or honorary "Christian before Christ."

226 AD 1414–1418.

227 Lit., "worm."

at these words, fainted and fell off of his mule so that he had to be carried back to town, whereupon he cried, "O St. Augustine! how true it was when you said, 'We learned men wallow in our flesh and blood while the uninstructed come and pull heaven out from under our noses.'"[228]

Now Moses further says that God spoke a mighty blessing upon our first parents. This still holds to the present day, and will continue to do so until the end of the world. If this blessing from God did not remain in effect always, no mother anywhere would be able to have a child. It is by virtue of this blessing that all of us came into the world. Whoever does not reflect on this profound miraculous work with amazement and speak about it in pure, virtuous words is not worthy of having been born to pious parents. In Psalm 139:17, King David meditates on this great work of grace, saying, "How precious are Your thoughts toward me, O God! How great is their sum!" Dear, old, pious Christians used to say that as soon as a child is born, it should be kissed as an honor to God's hands, which are there being held in that very act. For if God did not lay His miraculous hand of grace upon every child, not one could be brought alive and healthy into the world. But "since such miracles happen often, they are not counted as anything special,"[229] says Augustine. If only one child were born every thousand years, the whole world would report it with amazement. All the chronicles would have to know of it. But let us not be so dull and lazy in the contemplation of divine matters.

Finally, God crowned man with an imperial crown, styled him lord of all creation, gave him a rich, warm, well-stocked kitchen, and set him inside his newly built house. Here you see that we are all God's tenants. He rents us the earth and asks no other mortgage than godly fear and piety. So behave like an honorable housemate. Do not defile and besmirch the house of the Lord God your landlord by sinning. Do not turn it into a stinking sty by acting shamefully. Rather, be devout, pure, and upright, and in the end He will take you from your earthly house and relocate you to your heavenly mansion, which will be far more beautiful and delightful.

228 See August. *Conf.*, 8.8.19.
229 "miracula Dei assiduitate vilescunt"; August. *De civ. Dei*, 21.4.

Our Lord Jesus Christ is once again the Craftsman in this creation of man. This is explicit in the word "said," as demonstrated above. Next, we read in this passage "Let Us make man." Here God the Father confers with the Lord Jesus and the Holy Spirit. Therefore, whenever you look at yourself, remember the Lord Jesus and say: O my most beloved Lord Jesus, I too am Your handiwork; You have given me body and soul, all my members and my senses. These all are nothing but works of art from Your miraculous hand. You have dressed all my members for my benefit and beauty. Oh, how deeply You must love me! Oh, how wise and sagacious a Lord You must be! Oh, how profound and immeasurable Your omnipotence must be!

There are 365 parts in my body, and there are 365 days in the year. For every day in the year, for every part comprising my body, I have a witness of Your favor, love, benevolence, and grace, and I have a cause to serve You, to praise You, to love You, and to worship You. Oh my Lord Jesus, help me to serve You all my days, 365 days a year, with all 365 parts of my body; that I may not live contrary to You in the least part, but that all my veins, every drop of my blood, all my thoughts and expressions may be poured out and directed toward You with sincere and fervent love.

Alas, not everything can be done perfectly in this life; still, this is my desire. O Lord Jesus, grant the ability to carry it out. What I cannot perform in the present life will happen in the eternal, where I will forever extol You and serve You with all my senses, all my words, with every drop of my blood, indeed, with all 365 parts of my glorified body.

Go through the rest of the major parts of the body, contemplate their benefit and goodness, and stand in awe at the artistry and affection of their Craftsman, Jesus Christ.

Lactantius[230] wrote an entire book on this. Doctors, too, demonstrate their skill in this field. I only wish to discuss this in a plain and simple manner so that the common man may understand.

When you look at your body, say: Dear Lord Jesus, all that I have in and around me is Yours. Without You and Your masterful hand I would not have a single limb, nor would I be able to make the least vein move or stir.

---

230 Lucius Caelius Lactantius (ca. AD 240–ca. AD 320), early Christian rhetorician.

I will therefore be fully and completely devoted to You in all my actions.

Oh Lord Jesus, help me to serve You with all my members, to use them all for Your honor. Help me not to misuse any of them, but to look after them as a trust, to keep my body and all my members in good shape and not become their executioner or murderer through gluttony or some other wicked behavior.

Dear Lord Jesus, You put my head on top of my body. How fitting that is! What prestige does a church-tower have without a spire or dome? You had no desire to forget anything that might serve for my beauty and benefit.

You enthroned my reason in my brain like a queen, that from thence as from a royal castle it might command all my members like peasants and farmhands. Help me to act cleverly, wisely, and sensibly in all my dealings.

You covered my head with hair so that it would not be as easily damaged by the frost. You also set certain bounds to where the hair could grow. Not one little hair is permitted to trespass its bounds and disfigure our face. Oh my Lord Jesus, from this I see that it is true when You say, "The hairs of your head are all numbered" [Matt. 10:30, par.]. If You care so much for our hairs without which we would still very much able to be men, exist, serve You, and be saved—even if we had not so much as a single hair on our body—how much more will You care for the other parts of our body which are far nobler and far more necessary, and without which we could not lead and conduct our lives to any avail?

Long ago there was a tale that was told to children: God brought the newly created man to a sage and asked him if anything had been overlooked in this creature. At this the sage replied, "Man is truly a masterful work of art, but You have forgotten one thing. I see that he has a little villain hiding in his heart. ('The heart of man is a perverted thing'; Jer. 17:9.) You should have made a window in his heart so that he could see how villainous it is."

Please, there is no need for such a solution! God did not forget this window for the heart, but put it in the expressions and gestures of man's face. The heart of man cannot be concealed. It betrays itself, especially when love or hatred is hidden within. A wise man takes account of his own actions and expressions and recognizes the villain hidden in his heart.

Dear Lord Jesus, how can I repay You enough for the treasure of my eyes? What is more beautiful than the eye? Experts still cannot quite explain how it is that we can see and comprehend so exceeding many things with such a tiny little star.

You gave our body the two orbs of our eyes to lead it like two torches or lanterns going before a nobleman. You created us with two eyes, not one, so that we would always have one in case the other went out, and so that, like rich men, we would always have two lamps lit before us on our table.

How precious the eyes are, protected by eyebrows, lenses, and lids which open and close with indescribable speed. Thus the eye is kept from harm and specks prevented from falling into them at night. Likewise, the eyebrows protect them from the sweat of the brow. Oh, help our eyes always to look and turn to You in every need!

You did not position us facing the earth like mindless livestock, but upright, facing heaven. For livestock are only created to eat the mast and serve man's needs. We, on the other hand, were not made merely to graze on worldly goods but to set our heart and mind on heaven and to pay attention to You. Oh, help me to set all my thoughts on You, and not only to lift up my head but also my heart to that which is above [Col. 3:2], yea, to "seek first the kingdom of God and His righteousness" [Matt. 6:33]. "Man, you lift up your head, but you will not lift up your heart,"[231] says Bernard.

Dear Lord Jesus, how gracefully You set the tongue in the mouth and hung it in man's body just like a church-bell on top of God's church! So, too, Gellius calls the tongue the Lord's bell, saying, "This bell should never be struck and sounded unless it be tolled and set aswing by the bell-ringer of man's heart." In other words, whatever the heart knows to be good, useful, praiseworthy, and edifying is whereof the mouth should speak [Matt. 12:34] and otherwise be still.

You only gave one mouth, but two ears, for while we may see and hear a great deal, this will not bring us shame as quickly as talking a great deal.[232] Oh my Lord Jesus, help us to guard our tongues and mouths! "Oh,

---

231 "Homo sursum caput habes, et sursum cor non habes"; Bern. *Serm. de divers.* 12.2.
232 Epict. *Fragm.*

that I might set a lock upon my mouth, and press a tight seal upon my lips, that I may not fall by them, and that my tongue may not destroy me!" (Sir. 22:27).

Dear Lord Jesus, You have closed and guarded my tongue with two walls: with a fence of bone, with teeth and lips—just like a nun holed up and secured in her cloister, so that she cannot come out except with some pressing need and cause. Grant that my mouth may declare Your praise henceforth and forevermore. O Lord Jesus, You unstopped our ears and opened them wide to stand watch day and night, that we might be instantly alerted to danger even during our nightly rest. Oh, grant that my ears and my heart may stand open to Your word day and night, receive it with delight, and esteem it as the greatest treasure; for "faith comes from hearing" [Rom. 10:17]. In this life we must get by with hearing the good that You have granted us. After this life we will look and see with our eyes what we have heard and taken hold of by faith here.

My Lord Jesus, how skillfully You arrayed my teeth like a troop of soldiers in fine formation! They are my millers to grind and mill my food for me. Indeed, they even aid me in speaking and forming my words clearly and distinctly. Oh, what a great treasure this is! The ancient doctors of the Church as well as the old learned philosophers knew splendidly well how to cut through man's chatter [*Mundwerk*] with their skillful "pipe-organ" [*Orgelwerk*]. The lungs are bellows, the throat is the air-pipe and the valve, the teeth are like the organ's principal and trumpet stops, and the tongue is the swift keyboard. Man's mind should be the skilled organist who directs the music and words as fitting. Oh my Lord Jesus, help the beautiful pipe-organ of my mouth always to sing, ring, resound, and declare You and Your benefits, that it may be well pleasing to You.

Is this not a masterpiece and most mighty wonder? Whatever I carry hidden in my heart I can express with words. By this, others hear and understand what secrets are ticking in my heart. And what is even greater: the hands writes letters, a reader sees them and understands what the first man had thought in his heart. This is the pure heavenly wisdom of God shining through man.

My Lord Jesus, how skillfully You have made all parts of the body so that they can be bent, directed, and moved. How swiftly the eye can turn!

How swiftly the neck can swing the torches of the eyes back and forth! This is truly worthy of astonishment. Oh, help all my members to be as quick and eager to honor You as they are able by Your grace to turn and move!

What a miserable man I would be if I had no fingers or hands! "Knowledge is not gained by looking; a thing must be physically grasped and practiced,"[233] said Anaxagoras.[234] Indeed, the hands are the laborers, bodyguards, attendants, and caretakers of the whole body. Help me to lift up clean hands in my prayer [Ps. 24:4.], to wash my hands in innocence, to rob no one of anything, nay, to have hands generous in doing good to the poor, to hurt no one with my hand, but rather to help and be of service to everyone.

Oh my Lord Jesus, how great is Your wisdom! You knew that our inner organs, the intestines and bowels, on account of their tender nature could easily be damaged. Therefore You wrapped a strong breastplate of bone around them able to resist a blow so that harm would not so easily befall us. Help us not to injure our health willfully.

O Lord Jesus, You gave the heart constant life and movement so that it never stands still but always beat as with the ceaselessness of the second-hand, as can be clearly felt in every pulsing vein. This is so that man would not go stale in peaceful stagnation like a fetid cask of water, but rather that life would be continually refreshed. And in order that man should not faint from such heat, the lungs were made to keep pumping in fresh air like bellows and cooling the body. Oh, how can I ever marvel at Your intelligence enough? It is often supposed that spiritual things can be comprehended and outsmarted with the mind, and yet it must be confessed that this thing that we carry on top of our necks is not fit for the task. O Lord Jesus, help me in blessed awe at Your unfathomable wisdom to receive Your Word unconditionally and in true humility.

What a great treasure we have in our feet! Here God keeps two strong steeds stabled and groomed for us so that we can go for a stroll on the "apostles' horses" whenever we like. And in order that it all may proceed swiftly and nimbly, there had to be a skillfully made joint in the knee; and,

---

233 "Manus causa sapientiae"

234 Anaxagoras (ca. 500—428 BC), a pre-Socratic philosopher from Ionia.

the toes of the foot also had to be jointed to grip the earth so that man could steer himself on it while running and swiftly leap from it like a bird in the air. Is this not a wonder above all wonders? Oh Lord Jesus, help my foot not to slip, not to go down the way of sin, nor to tread the path of disgrace. Indeed, help me to be fleet of foot in following Your Word.

Is it not a noble treasure that all the members of the human body sense and instantly notice their injuries, and that each member has such a faithful, reliable, and indissoluble kinship with the others? If one meets with woe, the other mourns. If one is honored, all the members throughout the body join in its splendor. Oh Lord Jesus, help this to be for me a daily sermon on the blessed state of unity. Help us Christians also to walk together with such a kindred spirit, supporting, loving, and honoring each other to the depths of our ability.

What an acute sense of taste the tongue has! O Lord Jesus, help me to taste Your benefits and Your sweet heart when I am in anguish, and help me by the power of Your blood not to taste death, but to be able to taste the blessedness of eternal joy together with all those who believe in You.

Is it not a precious treasure that our nose can smell? Oh dear Flower of Jesse's branch, help us in every need to inhale the scent of Your virtue, and not despair.

Yet how deeply we are able to ponder all things with our minds, and not only to contemplate what is on earth but also what is in the air, in the heavens, and above the heavens, yea, in the heart of God! This is a work of art which we will discuss with one another in eternal life, God willing.

What enormous creatures, what strong animals, what swift birds, etc., there are in the world! Yet the mind of man so excels them that it brings all things under its control and subdues them. A little boy often catches the quickest bird simply by some clever trick. I need not mention other, greater works.

What depths of knowledge man's reason has plumbed, that even the motions of the heavens can be accurately comprehended and measured! To think that man's mind invented the mechanical clock and hour-hand so that steel and iron and common wood are brought to life and measure off the hours! Oh my Lord Jesus, sustain my reason, and grant that it may above all study that which is profitable for salvation!

Thus I have given you a brief set of instructions for contemplating your body, for I still have far more to say hereafter about the works of Jesus.

Ponder this last item with godly fear: O Lord Jesus, open my mind, that from Your masterpieces which I bear in my own body, I may recognize Your master's hand helping me in every need.

Finally, O Lord Jesus, it is the honor and glory of our body and our members that You clothed Yourself in our flesh and blood. You did not give such a high honor to any other created thing. Thus even the angels do not have this honor. You did not receive the angels to Yourself, but You did receive the seed of Abraham to Yourself.[235] It is our eternal renown that one Person with our blood, body, and nature is present in the solemn council of the most blessed Trinity. What kind of great honor this is for mankind we will, God willing, better ascertain in eternal life. O Lord Jesus, thanks be to You for honoring and raising our flesh and blood to such an exalted nobility in Yourself. Because of this honor, we will return honor and praise to You forever. Amen.

235   Heb. 2:16, with the earlier rendering, Germ. *an sich nehmen*; cf. John 18:3.

XIII. JESUS
Rests on the Seventh Day, Observes and Hallows the Sabbath,
and Obtains Eternal Rest for Us in Heaven
by the Unrest of His Suffering (Gen. 2:2).

After creating all things in six days with His Father and the Holy Spirit, the Lord Jesus rested on the seventh. For when a task is finished it is good to rest.

Let this not be understood to mean that God lay down to sleep and thus left the created world unattended, as a carpenter does the house that others paid him to build. Rather, God was satisfied with the aforesaid creatures and made no new ones. So as soon as man had been created there followed a blessed day of rest and feasting; for God wished from thenceforth to rest in man as in His own property, residence, and temple, to celebrate His day of joy and peace with man, to fill man's heart to the brim with His wisdom, righteousness, holiness, light, and life, and evermore find in man His rest, delight, gladness, and pleasure. Man, for his part, was simply to rest in God, to expect all good things from Him, to have his day of delight, joy, and peace in God, to find his enjoyment in God, to receive nothing from God but love and goodness in eternal peace, and to speak of God's works in constant tranquility. To sum it all up, nothing was to exist or be felt between God and man but restfulness and joy, nothing but the splendor of Sunday.

God blessed and sanctified this seventh day, the Sabbath (or "day of rest"). In other words, He set it apart for holy uses. Since God took a holiday, God's favorite pup of the litter, man, was also to take a holiday. But the holiday of the body was to be the workday of the soul. Man's heart was to concern itself with the work that God did on each of day of the week, and from these works get to know the Master and His skill. Thus the seventh day was to be mankind's school, church, jail, and mustering-house.

The Sabbath is the oldest festival in the world, the root of all feasts.[236]

For this reason, due examination was called for. It is clear that after the fall, the Sabbath was not observed again until the time of Moses, and he had much to do to persuade the Israelites to keep it (Ex. 19:15). Therefore God repeated its institution in Exodus 20[:8–11]. It suffices to gather from this that, through the wiles of the evil one, the day had come to be treated with scorn and contempt.

Of course, Adam did not neglect the Sabbath. When the seventh day of the week came, he and all his children would rest from their labors, and gather together under a green tree on that holy day; for Adam's church in Paradise was the tree of the knowledge of good and evil. There as pastor, with his vicar, mother Eve, he celebrated the divine service, and to his children seated around him he preached fine sermons: "Dearest children, today is the day when God rested. Let us also take a rest from the bitter sweat of our face. Today it is our inward spirit and soul that is to labor. Dear children, hear me, your old father.

"We did not come from the earth spontaneously like earthworms. Rather, God created me and your mother, and also the whole house that you see before your eyes. For He loves us so much that He wished to put us in a fully stocked residence and manor.

"Before the fall, I understood everything, but now, on account of my sin and anguish, I have forgotten quite a lot. Yet I wish to tell you what by God's grace I still know and understand. Receive this as divine truth.

"On Sunday, God got ready to build heaven and earth. He made a big stockpile, and finally, by way of a happy beginning, He called forth the light out of the darkness. For God Himself is Light and dwells in light. Moreover, He is the light of my heart, and will someday take me out of this misery into eternal light.

"On Monday, God made a vault for the firmament. Great wonder-worker that He is, He began with the roof, and planted His word of power under the clouds like a pillar and column to keep them from falling.

"On Tuesday, God paved, adorned, and decorated the dry land with leaves and grass, and dug the ocean, ditches, and rivers of water, and

236 "Radix omnium festorum"

commanded the waters to stay within their bounds.

"On Wednesday, He put up the lights, the sun, moon, and star-lamps, and hung a host of clock-hands and hour-pointers in the firmament.

"On Thursday, He filled the air with birds and the waters with fish.

"On Friday, He made the livestock, the creeping things, and the wild beasts, and last but not least, myself.

"God took a little lump of earth, molded it just so, and shaped it with great skill, so that every part of my body would be useful and graceful. God didn't leave one thing out.

"Finally, He breathed His divine breath into the lump of earth, and I began to live and move before Him. Oh, what unspeakable joy filled my heart! What divine light filled my mind and reason! How free of imperfection, lament, worry, sorrow, and affliction I was, without any fear or anguish at all!

"God caused me to fall into a deep sleep. He took a rib from my side, not far from my heart, and from it made your mother Eve. She is truly bone of my bones and flesh of my flesh [Gen. 2:23].

"On this day God rested, and He intended to rest in our heart forever; there was to be nothing but a day of rest and peace between God and us. But, oh God, alas! the devil would not begrudge us this rest, but came and worked unrest between us and God, disguising himself as a serpent and tricking your mother Eve, my dearest sweetheart, with treacherous, mischievous words. I also allowed myself to be coaxed by my Eve, and we transgressed God's commandment. Then all tranquility and consolation fled from my heart. When God, the Treasure of my soul, called to me in Paradise, I became afraid of Him in whom I should have rejoiced. I lost the innocence that avails before God, for which reason I am now forced to weep and lament bitterly. My eyes weep water, dear children, my heart weeps nothing but blood. Yet let us not despair, for I heard these words: 'The woman's Seed shall crush the serpent's head, and the serpent shall prick His heel' [Gen. 3:15]. The Virgin's Son shall give his blood, die, rest in the grave, and restore to us our lost day of rest. In this I take comfort, and in this comfort I will live and die. Oh God, forgive me my sins! Be gracious to me and my children for the sake of the promised Seed of the woman, for the sake of the Serpent-Trampler. I know that You shall not leave me. Just as You clothed me in the skins of a lamb, so shall You clothe me in the skins of the Lamb, the innocence of the Messiah. So, dear children, let my hope also be your hope, your joy, and your salvation. Be good and thank God for the grace which He has shown us. Oh dear children, help me pray that the blessed time may come when the Virgin's Son shall bring about what He promised in Paradise. 'Oh, that You would rend the heavens! Drop down, you heavens, from above!'"[237] [Is. 64:1; 45:8].

With such holy words Adam sanctified his day of rest. Let us do likewise on our Sundays and days of rest.

"Remember the Sabbath, to keep it holy," God says in the books of Moses [Ex. 20:8; Deut. 5:15]. To no other commandment but this one did God attach this "Remember."[238] For well He knows our carelessness and forgetfulness, as Bonaventure says.

To take a Sabbath is no art, but to begin, continue, and end the Sabbath in a holy manner is a great art indeed.

The apostles shifted the Sabbath (which was celebrated on Saturday in the Old Testament) to Sunday, as can be gathered from 1 Corinthians 16:2,[239] Revelation 1:10,[240] and Acts 20:7, to distinguish us publicly from the Jews and to give us a tangible example of Christian freedom (Col. 2:10). This, moreover, they instituted in honor of Jesus Christ's resurrection, the sending of the Holy Spirit, and the beginning of the Creation of heaven and earth, all of which fell on a Sunday.

May you therefore hold your Sunday Sabbath most dear, and following Adam and Eve's example, hallow it with holy thoughts, speech, works, and deeds.

Now who is the Lord that rested here? Moses says *Elohim*, that is, "God the Father, Son, and Holy Spirit," the eternal God, revealed in three persons, the selfsame God who was at work before this. Here we find Jesus once again. He was at rest with His heavenly Father and the Holy Spirit.

237 "Utinam dirumperes caelos! Rorate caeli desuper!" (traditional liturgical text for Ember Saturday during Advent).

238 "Memento."

239 Corr. for "1 Cor. 1."

240 Corr. for "Rev. 1:5."

Accordingly, just as the Lord Jesus rested here on the seventh day after having completed all His tasks for Friday, so after the rest between God and man had been disturbed by sin, the Lord Jesus rested yet again in the tomb, and by His resting won back that rest that man had before the fall, restoring everything that had been lost by the deceit of the evil one. Just as the Lord Jesus once completed all creation on Friday (Gen. 2:2), so the Lord Jesus completed the work of redemption on Good Friday, saying in truth, "It is finished." Just as Jesus once rested on the eve of Saturday, so after the quiet Friday in the tomb, He rested on Saturday and acquired for us the most blessed rest previously lost by Adam's fall. Here ponder, dear heart, what a great and inexpressible treasure this is. Take this comfort as your prized trophy, use it well, and say: Dear Lord Jesus, thanks be to You for Your rest in the tomb whereby You have restored to me the first rest for which man was created. By my sins the Holy Spirit was driven from me, but by virtue of Your rest the Holy Spirit is now to rest in my heart and lead me from one good deed to the next. For "all whom the Spirit of God leads are children of God" [Rom. 8:14]. Now I am to rest from sins instead of laboring in the devil's courts. I am to find rest for my soul by virtue of Your rest. When I have a restless conscience and my deepest fears are gnawing at me, I will simply recall Your merit in living faith and all the unrest of my heart is dispelled. My soul is to find in Your benefits an everlasting Sunday, an everlasting day of joy, jubilee, and pleasure. And someday, when the restless world has vexed and annoyed me enough, I will come to rest in the churchyard in my resting-chamber. There I will rest for a season, free from all sin, adversity, hunger, care, sorrow, and misery, until the bright morning of the blessed Last Day. For "Blessed are the dead who die in the Lord from now on. Yea, says the Spirit, that they may from their labors" (Rev. 14:13). And finally, O Lord Jesus, by the power of Your rest I am to have eternal rest, where there shall be nothing but Sundays "from Sabbath to Sabbath" (Is. 66:23), nothing but joy and bliss, delight, pleasure, and life. "In Your presence there is fullness of joy, and pleasures at Your right hand forevermore" (Ps. 16:11).

On Sunday we go to church in flocks, or congregations. Likewise, in eternal life we will flock together continually: "And the ransomed of the LORD shall return and come to Zion with exultation; everlasting joy shall be upon their heads; joy and delight shall they obtain, and sorrow and sighing shall flee away" (Is. 35:10). This eternal life will be a great Convention of the Converted,[241] that is, of those who believed in Jesus and fell asleep in the knowledge of Him.

On Sunday we pull out our finest clothes. Oh Lord Jesus, what fine Sunday clothes You will bestow on us in the Sabbath of eternal life! Forever we will wear the true wedding garment, the robes of salvation, the innocence that avails before God.

On Sunday we hear fine sermons preached. Dear Lord Jesus, on that eternal day of rest which You procured we will hear You Yourself speak with Your learned tongue. How You will stir our heart then! How our heart will burn, laugh, leap, and spring for joy on that day! Then we will all know perfectly what was too profound for us in this life.

On Sunday we hear beautiful music at church. First the organ plays a tone, then the choir sings, and then the whole congregation joins in. So it is in heaven among the holy angels. Oh, what beautiful music we will hear on that eternal Sunday! There we will hear the holy angels sing with one accord, then the elect children of God with their glorified, tuneful tongues, then everyone together. The joyous song[242] of Allelluia will be heard, sung by many countless thousand voices (Rev. 19:1). There we will hear the Sanctus sung: "Holy, holy, holy is our God, the LORD of Sabaoth" (Is. 6:3).

On Sunday we refrain from work. So in eternal life no ordeal shall touch us (Wisd. 3:1). No hardship will trouble us, no biting wind will blow in our face: "Our heart shall rejoice, and no man take our joy from us" (John 16:22). "No eye has seen, nor ear heard, neither can man's heart consider nor any mouth express the things which God has prepared for His children" (Isa 64:4; 1 Cor. 2:9).

On Sunday even a poor man dreams of better, daintier food, and prepares a joyous meal with his children, even if he must get by on salt and bread during the week. So we who must bake our bread of tears and butter it with our cares in this life shall sit at table with Abraham, lacking

241 "conventus conversorum"

242 "canticum laetitiae"

nothing, tasting of the joyous wine[243] of God's grace with the highest bliss, feasting forever and rejoicing. There all that we will know will be God and His abundance, without any lack of whatever might serve for our delight, benefit, comfort, and joy. We will walk, wait, live, and linger in God's sweet graces.

On Sunday offerings are brought. So on the eternal day of rest for the children of God we will bring our offerings, devoting and lifting up to God every thought, word, and deed. Our worship and praise will be the true incense with which the golden cathedral of heaven will be filled and censed to the full.

Oh Lord Jesus, You won this treasure for us. Send Your Spirit into our heart that we may not squander this great benefit through willful sin. For You Yourself say of wicked unbelievers and unrepentant people, "I swore in My wrath that they should not enter into My rest" (Ps. 95:11). Just as the grumbling Israelites who scorned the red cluster of grapes from Canaan all died within thirty-eight years and were not led by Joshua into their rest, so all who despise our succulent, red Cluster of consolation who was carried high on the stick of the cross will die and not be carried into the blessed rest of the eternal promised land. But we who believe will enter into our rest (Heb. 4[:1]).

Notice also, dear heart, a mystery concerning the time when our rest won by Jesus will draw nigh. God worked for six days and rested on the seventh. Likewise, the world, created by God in six days, is to have its continuance for six thousand years. For "a thousand years are to God as one day," says St. Peter (2 Peter 3:8). When the seventh millennium dawns, our day of rest will begin. Here you see that these days in Genesis form the basis for the prophecy of the house of Elias,[244] which says, "Six thousand years shall the world stand; for in six days it was created." But since now, for the sake of the elect, these last days are to be shortened, and we

---

243 "vinum laetitiae"

244 An extra-biblical Jewish tradition.

are already 5,648[245] years along, we may look for eternal joy at any given moment. "Watch and pray,[246] therefore, for you know neither the day nor the hour wherein the Son of Man comes" (Matt. 25:13). And notice another mystery here: In the seventh day of creation, which is a foreshadowing of our day of rest, there is no evening as with all the days before. For we are to suffer adversity for six days, but then it will all cease. On the seventh day, that is, on the Last Day, our day of rest shall come and there shall be no evening, no ceasing, no end.

From this St. Paul concludes, "I consider (*or* calculate) that the sufferings of this present time are not equal to the glory which shall be revealed in us" (Rom. 8:18). And Jesus says, "A little while, and you shall not see Me" (John 16:16). And St. Peter says, "greatly rejoice in the salvation made ready by Jesus Christ to be revealed in the last time, you who now for a season are in heaviness through manifold temptations" (1 Peter 1:5–6).

On the seventh day everything had been so prepared by God that man lacked nothing. Likewise, everything will be prepared in eternal life (Luke 14:17). We will lack nothing there. Take comfort in this, dear heart, in the midst of your great poverty. That which you have lost and been deprived of in your temporal life will be returned and restored in your eternal one. There we will find the royal Millo,[247] the "excess of everything that we desire."[248]

Therefore, to keep us constantly mindful of this, God set apart and isolated for us the seventh day of the week for such blessed contemplation, and also set this image before our eyes in many other profound mysteries.

Adam, the first man, died. All who came after him also died until the seventh, Enoch, who was taken up into heaven alive. So the world will die after six millennia, according to the sign of the first six patriarchs. But

---

245 Given the year of Herberger's writing as 1601, this number would significantly adjust his earlier estimate of the year of creation from 3970 BC to 4047 BC. See part 1, meditation 2.

246 "and pray" prob. from Luke 21:36.

247 A part of the old city of Jerusalem, according to its traditional understanding; see 1 Kings 9:24; 2 Chron. 32:4–5; 2 Sam. 5:9.

248 Indicated in the text as a gloss for Millo.

when the seventh millennium of the world begins, the resurrection of the dead will follow and the elect will be taken to heaven.

On the seventh day the walls of Jericho fell. At the seventh millennium the world's present corruptible state will cease and its eternal one begin. Then, like Rahab's house marked with the scarlet thread [Joshua 2:18–21], all those who have been marked with the scarlet blood of Jesus Christ will be preserved.

Every seventh year among God's people was a year of jubilee (Deut. 25:5). In eternal life we shall have our year of jubilee and find our seat at the table of unperturbed blessedness.

In the seventh year of jubilee, that is, in the forty-ninth year, the great year of jubilee and remission was held among the people of God, and everyone returned to his own property and people, and each man was happy and in high spirits. Eternal life shall be our year of jubilee and remission. We shall be immediately and perfectly restored to the estate that we possessed before the fall of our first parents (Lev. 25:10–11). Then we shall enter the freedom of God's children and reside like noble lords and landed gentry in heaven.

In the seventh month[249] the people of God celebrated the Feast of Trumpets; likewise, the Feast of Atonement, when God pledged to forgive all the sins of His repentant nation for the sake of the blood of Jesus Christ signified in the blood of the goat; likewise, the Feast of Tabernacles, which lasted for the whole of eight days with great rejoicing; likewise, the Feast of Binding,[250] when they sang from Psalm 118:24, "This is the day which the LORD has made; let us rejoice and be glad in it"; and again [v. 27], "Bind[251] the feast with green branches,[252] up to the horns of the altar" (Lev. 16:18; 23:27; *Calend. Ebe.* 342; Zwinger's *Theatrum*, 4029).

Likewise, when seven millennia have passed in the world, the archan-

---

249 I.e., "Tishri" (approx late September to late October).

250 Lit., "Vincite Feast." See Paul Eber's *Calendarium historicum*, p. 342 (the 24th of October): "The Jews call this day the Vincite-feast, from Psalm 118, when they have a feast and finish the leftovers from the celebration that came before."

251 "(vincite)"

252 Lit., *Meien*, "wildflowers."

gel will blow his trumpet and the true Feast of Trumpets will be celebrated, and all who sleep in the earth will be awakened and gathered. Then the Feast of Atonement will take place and we will partake of what the Lord Jesus won by His blood. Then we will be led into the inner sanctuary of heaven, enter the presence of God, and partake of His grace in body and soul. We will dwell in the tabernacles of God (Rev. 21:3)—we with God and God with us, in eternal, blissful fellowship. We will have true, congenial brotherhood to the four corners, and let our voices ring out with gladness, "This is the day which the LORD has made."

Moses, the seventh from Abraham, having received the Law from God, represents a great change. The seventy-seventh from Adam was Christ, says Basil. So on the Last Day, as the world approaches seven thousand years, a great change will take place, and all our adversity will be exchanged for eternal glory.

In order that we not forget this, God imprinted for us important changes in the seventh stage of various natural phenomena. It is seen that children lose their baby-teeth in their seventh year. Thus noteworthy changes are often to be found in the seventh year of our lives, either for better or for worse. In cases of illness, doctors pay close attention to the seventh day and seventh year; thus they call these pivotal days and years.[253] So draw this conclusion, dear heart: truly, when the seventh age of the years of the world draws nigh, everything will change, too—not for the worse, but for the better. "Our redemption draws nigh" [Luke 21:28].[254] For the unbelievers, it will be a change for the worse, because that is when their torment and anguish will first appear. God deliver us from this! In the seventh hour,[255] the son of the nobleman of Capernaum was healed (John 4:52). As in this verse it is the seventh hour when the Lord Jesus says, "Your son lives," so when it is the seventh age, all trouble will desert us and we will live.

Oh Lord Jesus, Comfort of my heart, after the task of creating everything else, You rested and created me for rest and blessedness. But when

253 "dies critici and anni climacterici"
254 "Appropinquat redemtio nostra"
255 I.e., about 1:00 PM.

the evil one brought my heart and soul to great unrest through sin, You labored once more on the cross, and rested in Your tomb on the seventh day of the week, and thereby won rest for my soul. Oh, help my body find rest from all sins and to serve You alone. Help my heart to find rest from all spiritual attack and anguish and to take comfort in Your merit. Help me meet my a blessed hour of death in goodly rest, to take a rest from all sins in my grave and bed of rest, to rest away all adversity, and on the Last Day to be removed in body and soul to Your rest. Grant me in eternal Sunday-joy and holiday-glory, beauty and blessedness, to live before You and dwell in Your mercy. Amen!

O Lord Jesus, come soon. Take us to that blessed rest. Amen!

(See Augustine's *City of God*, bk. 11, ch. 31, "On the mystery of the number seven"; Basil's *Hexameron*, homily 2, "On the Works of the Six Days"; Gellius, bk. 3, ch. 10, on Varro [*Hebdomades*], etc. But the voice of Basil (hom. 2) is pleasing: "The Church gathers not to hear wonderful and unusual things, but to learn what serves for edification.")[256]

---

256 De mysterio numeri septenarii August. *de C. Dei*, lib. 11. c. 31; Basil. *Homilia* II. de operibus sex dierum; Gellius, bk. 3, ch. 10. ex Varrone, etc. Sed placet vox Basilii, *Homil*. II: "Adest ecclesia non ut audiat mirabilia et inusitata, sed ut ea cognoscat quae ad AEDIFICATIONEM pertinent."

XIV. JESUS,

*The Paradise and Pleasure Garden of Our Souls,
the Creator of Paradise (Gen. 2:8).*

Moses goes back over the events of creation and considers certain works
which for the sake of brevity he previously passed over. He says that God,
the same Lord and Master Builder as before, built a beautiful pleasure
garden toward the east. Moses Bar Kefa the Syrian claims that it happened
on Tuesday, nor does this seem incredible, for that is when God created
the flowers, plants, and trees. This Paradise was the center and nucleus
of the whole world, a veritable land of fatness and riches where nothing
desirable, beneficial, or honorable was lacking in any way. Adam and Eve
were to have their seat in this place as in a king's or emperor's palace, and
dwell there as in a stately summer-house. And when they had lived there
long enough, they were to be taken by God into heaven, like Enoch before
the flood and Elijah after the flood. Thus Paradise was to have been the
heavenly nursery from which heaven would be populated.

Here once again our Lord Jesus is the Craftsman, for Moses is speaking of the same Lord God as before. When Adam and Eve sinned in Paradise, they and their children were evicted from the beautiful house of
pleasures and driven out. At last, all the beauty of Paradise was stripped
away by the flood. For since God intended to punish the world's sins, He
also visited His wrath mightily upon that place where the sin was conceived and brought forth. While God allowed the region to remain, and
left the foundation and soil in tact, He utterly destroyed its beautiful pleasures and splendors. For Paradise is thought to have been located where
Jerusalem is now. Many notable experts, moreover, say that the tree by
which Adam and Eve first sinned stood in the place where Christ's cross
was raised, so that sin was thus blotted out in the selfsame place where it
had come into the world.

Oh my Lord Jesus, here I see again Your love for mankind. It was not enough that You created the whole world for his good. In addition, You built him a pleasure garden and beautiful palace as for a great lord.

So since the evil one cheated us out of this through sin, You came to that same place where Adam and Eve had sinned, let Yourself be nailed to the cross, and won for us a far greater paradise than that which Adam and Eve enjoyed before the fall, namely, eternal bliss. Thus You began Your sufferings in a garden; and on the cross You told the repentant murderer, "Today you will be with me in paradise" [Luke 23:43]. You also had Yourself buried in a garden. You appeared after the resurrection in the form of a gardener to show that You would restore all that the first gardener, Adam, had lost in the pleasure garden of Paradise.

Indeed, it was all so that in Your goodness You might personally fashion my heart into a beautiful paradise and pleasure garden. In the same way, O Lord Jesus, in Sirach 24:17–19, Wisdom, which was understood by several of the ancient doctors of the Church to mean You, is also compared to a fine paradise and pleasure garden.

This gives pleasure and strength to all devout hearts, so let me persevere in this contemplation.

O Lord Jesus, You are my royal Garden (Neh. 3:15). David and Solomon found pleasure in royal gardens. My heart finds its greatest pleasure in You. As my eyes feast on an orchard, so my soul and mind are fed and refreshed on You. Though I may not have my own garden in this world, I have my own paradise and pleasure garden in You and Your benefits.

O Lord Jesus, dear Garden of my soul, You have four sides. You are presented in the books of the four holy evangelists. Your joyful benefits are shown to me in the Second Article of the Apostles' Creed.

To begin with, four fences are erected: (1) *I believe in Jesus,* my Helper and Savior; (2) *I believe in Christ,* my King under whose protection I safely dwell, my High Priest who will grant me a comforting word before His heavenly Father; (3) *I believe in God's only-begotten Son,* who has the right to heaven and the power to grant me salvation; and (4) *I believe in our Lord,* I entrust myself to my Redeemer as my Lord Protector, and am confident that He is my Savior, Blesser, and Prince of Peace, and ever shall be. My soul is secured and enclosed by these four honorific titles just as by four fences.

Yet just as a garden contains many beautiful beds, patches, and nooks filled with all kinds of pretty flowers, so in this pleasure garden of mine let us briefly examine ten beautiful patches of spice, beds of comfort, and nooks of joy, the contemplation and enjoyment of which is satisfying to my soul.

The first bed of spices and flowers is: *Jesus was conceived by the Holy Spirit.* Dear Lord Jesus, because of my conception I must perish. But through Your most holy conception, You consecrated and hallowed my sinful and unclean conception so that it is covered, forgiven, and forgotten in Your Father's sight. Oh, what a treasure this is! What joy I find in my heart because of this!

The second: *Jesus was born for my consolation.* Dear Lord Jesus, because of my birth, I am a child of wrath and kindling for hell. But because of Your birth I am made a newborn infant of God. You became a child of man, that I might be a child of God. Oh what a treasure this is!

The third: *Jesus suffered for us under Pontius Pilate.* O dearest Lord Jesus, by Your sufferings You won eternal rest and salvation for me. You suffered the punishment of my sins, and I have rest and peace. With a joyful heart I must say, What a precious gem this is!

The fourth: *Jesus was crucified for my sake.* O Lord Jesus, I was to be a curse. I was not worthy that the sun and moon should shine on me, or that the earth should bear my weight. You endured this great misery. You hung on the tree of the cross like an accursed worm so that You could bring Your eternal blessing to me. Because of Your humiliating crucifixion I am called a child of God, and will be received as one on the Last Day. Oh, what a comfort this is!

The fifth: *Jesus died for my good.* O Lord Jesus, Your death is my life; Your death transformed my death into a gentle rest and sweet slumber. I need no longer be appalled by death. By virtue of Your death it has become for me only an entrance to eternal life. Oh, what a blessed thing this is!

The sixth: *Jesus was buried for my sake.* O sweet Lord Jesus, You buried all my sins in Your tomb and filled my bed of rest with warmth. My sins are remembered no more. The holy angels, moreover, will be watchmen over my tomb. All my bones and particles will be stored up in eternal rest and kept safe. Oh what a joy this is!

The seventh: *Jesus descended into hell and destroyed it for my good. O Lord Jesus,* Your descent into hell is my ascent into heaven. I, even I, should have descended into hell. But now that You have stormed hell and crushed the head of its prince, my soul can rise from my mouth, unhindered by any evil spirits, and ascend into heaven. Oh, what a glory this is!

The eighth: *Jesus rose again from the dead for my joy.* Oh Lord Jesus, by the power of Your resurrection I too shall not remain in the tomb, but shall celebrate a joyous Easter at the end of the world. Who can praise and extol this benefit of Yours enough? What a comfort this is!

The ninth: *Jesus ascended into heaven for my greatest good.* Dear Lord Jesus, by Your majestic ascension You opened for my prayer the road to heaven and to the heart of Your Father. You cleared for my soul the way to eternal life, unlocked paradise, and gained for my body and soul a certain ascension into heaven on the Last Day. What a treasure this is! How shall I ever repay You for this grace?

The tenth: *Jesus is seated at the right hand of God for my honor; from thence He shall come to judge both the living and the dead.* O fairest Lord Jesus, You are seated at the right hand of God's omnipotence; You are my gracious Lord and King. You have set Yourself on high, but You look upon the lowly [Ps. 138:6]. You have seated Yourself next to the heart of Your heavenly Father. As my advocate You will remember me and obtain all that I need for salvation. Your last work on Ascension day was a blessing, for You do nothing else in heaven than speak one powerful blessing after the next upon Your faithful people. You sit as a judge for us. You will hear our plaints and deliver a just judgment. You sustain us as You did Stephen, and will not forsake us in any need. You are even now waiting to hasten to our side. You will be with us until the end of the world [Matt. 28:20], and at last shall come with great glory to take us to Yourself, that we may be with You. What an honor, what a salvation this is!

Here you see, dear heart, that our dear Lord with His treasures of grace is a pleasure garden. Go for a stroll in this Garden, you who are poor and have no garden in this world; survey it well with the eyes of your faith. Take from it a whole heart-full of what is pleasant, beneficial, and best for you.

If you confess that you owe ten thousand pounds because of your sins, if the devil leads you up to Mount Sinai, strikes you with one of the ten thundering words of the holy Ten Commandments, saying, "Do you not see how you have acted contrary to God, how you have lived contrary to His strict Ten Commandments? Do you not hear how God's rumbles and flashes? You shall deal with a fiery God, He shall repay you with eternal storm"—then say: I will not stay here. I can find no comfort in the ten sayings here on Mount Sinai. Here I must confess that I owe ten thousand pounds, so I will run to my soul's pleasure garden which God the Father Himself built and freely gave me in the merit of His Son. To Him alone the Holy Spirit points in the Old and New Testaments by all the faithful prophets, apostles, and evangelical preachers. There I will find rest and consolation for my soul.

Dear Lord Jesus, the ten sayings of Mount Sinai condemn me, but the ten words of Your benefits in paradise absolve me. My sins are vast and heavy, yet Your merit is far greater and weightier. One single drop of Your blood shed on the cross outweighs all my sin.

I will pay for the ten thousand pounds of my sins from the ten comforting flower-beds of the paradise of Your grace and benefits, saying, O God, heavenly Father, I owe ten thousand pounds; I have transgressed Your Ten Commandments. Do not bind me hand and foot and cast me into outer darkness [Matt. 22:13]. Have patience with me and I will repay You everything [Matt. 18:26–19]! Of course I cannot pay one farthing with my own works, so I will pay You everything with the works which I find in the pleasure garden of Jesus Christ's benefits. I will pay for my ten thousand pounds of heavy sins in true faith from Your Son's most holy benefits which far outweigh ten thousand pounds.

The first thousand I pay with *Jesus' conception,* the second thousand with *Jesus' birth,* the third thousand with *Jesus' sufferings,* the fourth with *Jesus' cross,* the fifth with *Jesus' dying and death,* the sixth with *Jesus' burial,* the seventh with *Jesus' descent into hell,* the eighth with *Jesus' resurrection,* the ninth with *Jesus' ascension into heaven,* and the tenth with *Jesus' majestic session at the right hand of Your omnipotence.* Now I have paid You all, ten thousand pounds, sum total.[257] Oh, be gracious to me for the sake of the precious merit of Jesus Christ!

257 "facit in summa"

This is enough for our discussion of the paradise and pleasure garden of all believing hearts and souls as found in Jesus Christ's sweet benefits.

Now this pleasure garden is only found in the Christian Church, and therefore Tertullian, Augustine, and others besides call the Christian Church the spiritual paradise. Just as Adam was to dwell for a season in Paradise and afterward be removed to heaven, so whoever wishes to dwell in heaven must confess the Christian Church with heart and mouth in this world. We also have a tree of the knowledge of good and evil in the Christian Church. It is the Holy Bible, in which death and life are laid out before us. We also have a tree of life: the cross of Christ with His benefits. Here also we have the great streams of the water of Baptism and the Holy Supper, the true fountain of salvation, running and flowing in the four evangelists. Jesus Christ builds this garden of the Christian Church by His Gospel, the Sacraments, and the cooperating power of the Holy Spirit.

Furthermore, our heart is also to be trimmed and adorned in Christ's honor like a beautiful garden with all kinds of virtues. Thus Jesus, the Bridegroom of souls, says of His bride, the Church, that she is "a garden locked" and her "growth is as an orchard" [Song of Sol. 4:12–13]; and "their soul shall be like a watered garden, and they shall not be grieved any more" (Jer. 31:12). Augustine also says, "A pure, happy conscience is a beautiful, exquisite garden, an everlasting life of joy"[258] and, "A pious, faithful Christian life is a beautiful paradise; the trees thereof are the lovely understanding of God's matters; its fruits are beautiful virtues, deeds, and morals; its tree of life is the high wisdom of the right knowledge of God."[259]

Oh my Lord Jesus, help my heart to be filled and adorned with beautiful flowers of the paradise of Christian virtues. Let the foundation and soil of my heart and whole life blossom and flourish with that which is pleasing to You.

Let beautiful *Trinity-flowers* grow inside me, that I may distinguish my dear God in three persons, yet one substance, and that at every

---

258 "Laetitia bonae conscientiae paradisus est"; August. *De Gen. ad litt.* 34.65.

259 "Paradisus vita beatorum, ligna eius utiles disciplinae, lignorum fructus, mores piorum, lignum vitae sapientia"; August. *De civ. Dei* 13.21.

passing moment I may keep Him in my heart, and truly honor, love, extol, and worship Him. Let true *heaven's-key-flowers* grow inside me. This prayer is the very key to heaven and to the heart of God Your Father when it is spoken in Your name. Let graceful *forget-me-nots* bloom there, lest I grow forgetful of You, of my soul, of my honor, of my death, or of Your Word and Sacraments. Let beautiful *humble-blossoms* grow in me, that in every cross I may humble myself beneath Your mighty hand until You lift me up again in due season. Let me be humble and meek toward those to whom I owe humility and obedience. Let precious *peace-lilies* grow in me, that I may take pleasure in love and unity, for unity is a foreshadow of eternal life. Let graceful *purity-flowers* also spring up in me. That is, help me to be pure of heart, to pursue purity in body and soul, and to look to You with a joyful conscience in my prayer, distress, and death. Give me true *shepherd's-purse*[260] for the little garden of my heart, that I may store and preserve whatever You grant me, that I may also diligently meditate on Your Word (since it is now so affordable) and that I may gather a supply of fine teachings and verses of consolation, so that whenever illness appears I have something to pull out of the little purse of my memory to keep myself comforted. Let beautiful *blue-sorrow flowers* bloom inside me. In other words, grant that my sorrows may be directed up to the blue of heaven, that I might seek first the kingdom of God and His righteousness, that everything else might be added to me [Matt. 6:33]. Let me not gaze too closely at the black sorrows of the earth, lest in doing so I forget the blue sorrows of heaven.

Plant beautiful *sprinkle-blossoms* in my heart. Help my heart to be sprinkled with Your blood in true faith. Let beautiful *love-measure flowers*[261] grow gracefully in me. Grant me to love You according to the measure with which You have loved me. Yea, grant me to love my neighbor according to the measure of love that You have shown me, for that is Your commandment and the true mark of those who love You sincerely.

---

260 Germ. *Täschel-Blümlein,* "pocket-flowers."
261 Germ. *Maßlieben,* "measure-loves."

Let beautiful *heart-joy*[262] flourish inside me in every cross and sadness. When I am crowned with cross-thistles (as ancient brides used to be when they were betrothed), give my heart comfort and joy. Let these flourish and increase in summer and winter like the hardy rue.

Whoever will thus amble with daily meditation through the paradise of the sweet benefits of Jesus Christ, and join himself by his confession to the spiritual paradise of the Christian Church, and to the glory of Christ trim his heart like a pleasant garden with all the flowers of Christian virtues—he shall have certain hope in the exquisite heavenly paradise of eternal life.

This paradise was opened by Jesus Christ using the lock-pick and skeleton key of His cross, for we had lost the old key in Adam's fall. Thus it was there on the cross that the Lord Jesus promised the repentant robber, "Today you will be with Me in Paradise" [Luke 23:43].

In this paradise we will hear "inexpressible words," as St. Paul says of the foretaste of eternal life that he heard (2 Cor. 12:4).

In this paradise the virgin Dorothy rejoiced even though she was mocked for doing so.

From this paradise an angel brought three apples and three roses in the name of St. Dorothy to the Lord High Chancellor Theophilus, as our dear forefathers wrote (see *The Golden Legend*).[263]

The heathen heard rumors of this paradise, but they did not all strike the same way. Thus out of the same idea they forged their Elysian fields[264] and their Isles of Fortune.[265] We, however, do not have any such uncertain dreams or notions but are assured by God's Word that we shall occupy eternal paradise by Christ's merit, and that there shall be such joy there as "no eye has seen, nor ear heard, nor man's heart been able to imagine" [1 Cor. 2:9], nor man's tongue able to express.

262 Germ. *Herzensfreude*.

263 "Hist. Lomb. *mihi fol.* 169." (Not in Ryan; see F.S. Ellis, ed., *The Golden Legend...* [1973], vol. 4, p. 47).

264 "Elysios campos"

265 "insulas fortunatas"

Beautiful *Pentecost-roses* will grow there. It will be Pentecost forever. God shall be all in all [15:28]. He will pour Himself into the hearts of all His elect by His Holy Spirit so that they will all live, delight, and rejoice in Him. Then we will praise and talk of nothing but the great works of God,[266] extolling them with new tongues and heavenly languages. Beautiful *praise-glories* will bloom there. God will be praised and glorified eternally by our heart, mouth, and song. That will be our eternal labor, and yet we will not grow tired of it. "Love shall be our law, God's Son our king, God's praise our diligent labor,"[267] said our dear forefathers. The beautiful herb *God's-grace*[268] will grow there. God's grace, love, and favor shall dwell upon our heart and soul forever. The true *tree of life* will stand there. We will be happy, hale, and hearty forever, and never grow old or die. The herb *glad-heart*[269] will abound there. Not only our mouth but our heart, too, will rejoice and be bright and merry. True *angelica* will grow there. We will be angelic, like God's angels[270] [Matt. 22:30], living without food or drink, and free from sorrow. *Longer-the-lovelier* will bloom there. Our heart will increase in love toward God and the elect of angels and men. The beautiful *ground-heal*[271] shall flourish there. All our wounds will be healed from the ground up. *Angel-sweet*[272] will be planted there. We will share in the sweet company of the angels. The sweet speech of angels shall ring in our ears. Blessed *thousand-beauties*[273] will spring up all over creation. Extraordinary gifts and extraordinary virtues will come to light.

Wonders are told of the gardens of Babylon; they were held up by high arches, and supposedly built by Semiramis, or Syrus Rex.[274] But this is like comparing the point of a needle with a great mountain.

---

266 "magnalia Dei"

267 "Charitas erit lex, filius Dei erit Rex, assidua occupatio, Dei laudatio."

268 Germ. *Gottesgnade.*

269 Germ. *Herzenfroh.*

270 "ἰσάγγελοι"

271 Germ. *Grundheil,* "complete healing or salvation (from the ground up)."

272 Germ. *Engelsüß.*

273 Germ. *Tausendschön.*

274 See Plin. *NH* 19.3 (19).

O dearest Lord Jesus, help me to refresh my soul daily in the garden of Your benefits, to visit the garden of Your Christian Church with sincere yearning, to adorn my heart in Your honor with beautiful virtues like a beautiful little paradise by the indwelling of the Holy Spirit, and finally, to possess forever with everlasting pleasure and joy the wonderful garden of heavenly paradise won by Your blood and cross. Amen!

XV. JESUS,
The Succulent, Green Tree of Life (Gen. 2:9).

Moses, describing the decoration of Paradise, tells how God filled it with exquisite fruit-bearing trees, and in the midst of it planted two trees of a magnificent and miraculous nature: the tree of life, and the tree of the knowledge of good and evil. The tree of life was to sustain Adam and Eve in everlasting vitality, youth, strength, and health. It was to cure Adam of all weariness, mightily sustain all his powers, and preserve him from gray hair, the weakness of old age, and disease. Oh, what a splendid treasure this would have been! Both the elderly, oppressed by the years, and laborers, worked nearly as hard as mules and forced to pant beneath many troubles— these can understand to some degree what a glorious thing it would be if such a refreshment were found in nature now. The tree of the knowledge of good and evil was to be Adam's church, cathedral, school, and cloister. Under its branches he would have kept his Sabbath and celebrated the divine service, praising good and dispraising evil. But only when Adam learned at his own expense and met his injury upon this tree, as Lyra believes, was it called a tree of the knowledge of good and evil, after the fact.[275]

Now, after Adam and Eve transgressed God's commandment, they were chased by God's righteous anger away from the tree of the knowledge of good and evil. The way to the tree of life was also barred, as Irenaeus says, so that Adam would not eat of it and live forever in his sorrow and misery.

So because of our sins we poor souls had no Paradise, nor a tree of life, nor a tree of the knowledge of good and evil. But the Lord Jesus went through great pains to win back Paradise for us. He had Himself lifted up

---

275 "ab eventu"

on a tree, that by His bloody death we might have a tree of life. He had His Gospel proclaimed throughout the world, that we might have a true knowledge of good and evil. For when we hear, "Whoever believes in the Son has eternal life" [John 3:36], we have knowledge of the good. But when we hear, "Whoever does not believe is condemned already" [3:18], we have knowledge of the evil. And this is the sum and substance of the whole Gospel.

Accordingly, whoever would have the tree of life must look for it in Christ, and in His cross, merit, and benefits. For this image in Genesis is explained by the Prophets and the New Testament in just this way. Solomon says, "Wisdom," that is, "Jesus Christ, who was made to us wisdom from God" (1 Cor. 1:30) "is a tree of life" (Prov. 3:18); and, "The fruit of the righteous," that is, Jesus Christ (Is. 53:11; Jer. 23:5), "is a tree of life" (Prov. 11:30). As He was being led out of Jerusalem, Christ said, "For if they do these things in the green tree, what will be done in the dry?" (Luke 23:31). Here our Lord compares Himself to the succulent, green tree of life. And that we might see this even more clearly, He had Himself stretched out on the cross like the blessed fruit of the tree of life, in the very place in which, ages before, the tree of life and the tree of death had stood, to the end that mankind's sins should be blotted out and extinguished right where they had entered the world. Luther puts Christ's cross and the tree of the knowledge of good and evil in the same place. (For what is written about Adam's skull being found there is doubtful because Adam was driven out of Paradise, and many reliable persons report that Adam's tomb was in Hebron.) In Revelation 2:7, Christ's merit is pledged to believers as follows: "To him who overcomes, I will give to eat of the tree of life, which is in the paradise of God." And again, [in Revelation 22:2], the tree of life stands on either side of the crystal-clear river, and its leaves are for healing. Here in the final chapter, the Christian's state of eternal bliss is described. And then it says, "Blessed are those who keep His commandments, so that they may have the right to the tree of life" [v. 14]. This should all be understood as meaning the benefits of Jesus Christ.

Dear Lord Jesus, You are the true succulent, green Tree of Life. Let me be grafted into You like a branch, that in life and death I may be quickened and strengthened by You. O Lord Jesus, let my heart be Your soil and foundation in which You are deeply rooted, that I may always have shade and shelter in You.

The tree of life stood in the midst of Paradise, as described by Moses. O Lord Jesus, sweet Tree and Captain of Life, You were crucified in the midst of the worldly Paradise. "You wrought healing (salvation, great good) in the navel (*or* midst) of the earth";[276] as Psalm 74:12 reads in the original Hebrew. This is why cosmographers put Jerusalem in the middle of the world. Likewise, You are also confessed in the midst of Christendom. This is what our forefathers meant to indicate by putting an image of Jesus Christ's cross in the middle of the choir-arch[277] of nearly every church. O Lord Jesus, I want You in the midst of my heart where You properly belong. When St. Elizabeth saw a beautifully painted crucifix in the cloister, she said, "O Lord Jesus, may You not refuse my poor, wretched heart!"

The tree of life had wide-spreading branches. Dear Lord Jesus, You stretched Your arms on the cross as widely as possible, like strong, fruit-bearing branches. You wished to embrace me, to hold me close and kiss me. You wished be my umbrella.[278] You wished to keep me safe from the hard, beating rain of Your Father's wrath. I can hide beneath You. You are just like the king's great, high tree that stood in the midst of the land (Dan. 4:10–12). You give nourishment, shade, and refreshment to all men in the land. You were cut down by death in the mist of Your afflictions, but now You flourish, stand, live, and bloom forever and ever.

The tree of life had beautiful, green leaves. O Lord Jesus, You have beautiful, comforting words that burst from Your holy heart and spring from Your sweet mouth. On the cross You spoke seven words of comfort. Oh, what lovely, green leaves these are! You prayed for us poor sinners. You were concerned for poor widows and orphans. You absolved repentant, confessing hearts. You groaned, wailed, and shared in our greatest afflictions. You quenched the thirst of our souls. You finished all that we need for salvation. You bound Your soul and mine together and commended

---

276 "Operatus es salutaria in umbilico vel medio terrae"; cf. Ps. 74:12; Bonav. *De Invent. S. Cruc. serm.* 1.

277 I.e., the arch over the space between the nave and the sanctuary.

278 "umbraculum"

it to Your Father. My heart cannot thank You enough for these beautiful leaves of consolation.

The tree of life has beautiful blossoms. Dear Lord Jesus, You have beautiful blood-red blossoms. What red flowers spring from Your hands! What red roses bloom from Your feet! What red buds I see in Your opened side! How beautifully all Your scars bloom! I will remember this whenever I see the red blossoms of the apple tree pushing out. Your blossoms were red because You wished to offer an antidote to the apples that Adam and Eve ate in sin. You bore apples of life against the apple of death.[279] This is why the infant Jesus used to be painted holding an apple in His tiny hand.

The tree of life had appealing fruit. O Lord Jesus, You bear the most desirable fruit. You bring us the forgiveness of sins, the hope of the resurrection of our body, and the life everlasting. You bring consolation in prayer, refreshment in cross, strength in the face of spiritual attacks, joy in the face of death. Every benefit that I extol in You is a fruit that I may account to You. For my sake You were conceived and born. For my consolation You suffered death on the cross. For my good You had Yourself buried. For my benefit You descended into hell, rose again from the dead, and ascended into heaven. For my salvation You seated Yourself at the right hand of Your Father's majesty. Oh, how beautiful, how refreshing Your fruits are!

The effect of the tree of life's leaves and fruit is eternal life, as we are informed: "lest he…eat and live forever" (Gen. 3:22). Likewise, O Lord Jesus, the effect of Your benefits is eternal life. "In Him was life" (John 1:4); "Christ is my life" (Phil. 1:21); "as Moses lifted up the serpent in the wilderness, so must the Son of Man be lifted up, that whoever believes in Him may not perish but have eternal life" (John 3:14[–15]); "Truly, truly, I say to you, if anyone keep My word, he will never see death" (John 8:51); "I am the resurrection and the life. Whoever believes in Me shall live, even though he die, and whoever lives and believes in Me shall never die" (John 11:25). O Lord Jesus, these are Your own words in which You have revealed what we can expect from You as our true, blessed Tree of Life, namely, our salvation and eternal life.

---

279 "poma vitae contra pomum mortis"

When Moses cast a tree into the bitter waters, they were made sweet (Ex. 15:25). Dear Lord Jesus, when by the hand of faith You are immersed in our bitter tears and waters of woe, we forget all our misery, and our sadness is so sweetened with delight that we are delivered from despair.

When Elijah cast a tree into the Jordan (2 Kings 6:6), the servant's iron axe head floated contrary to the laws of physics. Our hearts also have heavy iron axe heads. They want to make us sink deeper and deeper in doubt. Yet, O Savior, Tree of Life, when we take hold of You in our misery, then our heavy hearts instantly start to grow and rise up toward the heavens as we patiently yield and trust God's will.

Therefore, O Lord Jesus, green Tree of Life, I will never let You out of my mind. When I pray, my heart will flourish with the beautiful leaves of Your comforting sayings. Then I will be earnest and ardent in my prayer. When I remember the words which You pledged: "Truly, truly...whatever you ask of the Father in My name, He will give it to you" [John 16:23]—oh, how boldly and confidently my heart pours out its prayer to Him then!

When I am sick and ailing, I will lay myself at Your bosom and curl up, like John at the [Last] Supper. I will lay myself down within the wood of this tree, enclosing myself in Your benefits, and thus sweat out every adversity. You are the true healing Guaiac Tree.[280] You are the wondrous Aloe tree[281] and Paradise Tree. You heal all my wounds.

O Lord Jesus, Tree of Life, when I grow old and weak, I will break off a branch from You for a staff. I will remember Your merit, and in my weakness confidently traverse all the foul roads and wet puddles of the world. I am a guest, a stranger upon earth, as David says (Ps. 119:19). I am only a wanderer and pilgrim in this world. Therefore, O Tree of Life, give me from the riches of Your benefits a comforting walking-stick, Jacob's sturdy staff with which I may steady myself as I wander on to eternal rest in my true, heavenly fatherland.

O Lord Jesus, Tree of Life, the rods and staves of Your benefits comfort me [Ps. 23:4] so that I can fend off all the hounds of hell and overcome

---

280 "lignum guajacum *und* lignum sanctum."

281 "lignum aloës," unrelated to aloe vera; see Num. 24:6; Ps. 45:8; Prov. 7:17; Song of Sol. 4:14.

all my foes. Thus Emperor Constantine had the golden cross emblazoned on his banner with the title: "In this you shall overcome."[282]

O Jesus, Tree of Life, when I must die I will cheerfully look to You with the eyes of faith and receive eternal life, deathlessness.[283] This is that great good which King Alexander could not give his advisors on his day of triumph. Instead, he was forced to blush with shame at such a request, although he had brashly presumed that he would and could grant everyone's petition.

O Lord Jesus, in my last voyage hence, I will make a little canoe or boat from the lignum vitae ("wood of life") of Your benefits and paddle away, and float confidently over the Dead Sea. When a squirrel wants to cross the water, it cleverly takes a piece of wood, sits on it, and uses its little tail like a rudder to sail away at full speed. Should I then not also be clever enough to know how to cross the black river of death and reach the green meadows of life? I will borrow a piece of wood from You, Lord Jesus. I will make use of Your benefits. I will rely on them and paddle forth with unwavering trust, setting a firm course for the heavenly meadow of paradise, and be saved.

Wooden houses in towns and villages often burn down when someone handles fire incautiously. Dear Lord Jesus, when with true faith I build myself a house in heaven from the tree of Your cross and merit, neither temporal nor eternal fire will consume it. This will be my comfort even if my house and home in this world burn down.

In Podolia,[284] large trees are set as memorials on top of the graves of great noblemen. Dear Lord Jesus, Tree of Life, You will be set on my grave, You will be set on the burial mound of my heart. I will take You with me to the grave, and by Your grace live in hope; yea, on the Last Day I will depart by Your power to eternal life. Amen.

---

282 "In hoc vinces."

283 "immortalitas"

284 Part of what is now the Ukraine, near the border of the Dniester.

XVI. JESUS,

The Great River of Paradise, the River of Life, Which Waters and Irrigates the Whole Garden of Christendom and All Believing Hearts (Gen. 2:10).

Wherever hill and dale, meadow and stream, tree and foliage are found in one place, there is one of the most beautiful places in the world. This, moreover, is precisely how Moses depicts Paradise, not only telling of the wonderful fruit-bearing trees, but also of a mighty, rushing river and fountain flowing into Paradise from the east and dividing itself into four great streams, which were in turn filled by God with numerous treasures. These bodies of water are still there today, and are called the Ganges, the Nile, the Tigris, and the Euphrates. In the Ganges nuggets of gold can be found, as can the valuable substance gum arabic,[285] which is very useful for medicine, and also that precious stone onyx, not to mention rubies, sapphires, and emeralds. But the flood caused these rivers, which once ran close together, to be separated from each other by several hundred miles.

Our Lord Jesus is again portrayed in this great river. He is distributed in the writings of the four evangelists, in which He wells up, runs, flows, and makes Himself known throughout the world, and in this way waters, irrigates, refreshes, replenishes, and encourages the whole paradise of the Christian Church—indeed, all believing hearts. Thus, on the subject of Christ and the evangelists, the Church sings:

> See the rivers four that gladden,
> With their streams, the better Eden
> Planted by our Lord most dear;
> Christ the Fountain, these the waters;
> Drink, O Zion's sons and daughters,
> Drink, and find salvation here.

285 "gummi bdellion"

Here our souls, by Jesus sated,
More and more shall be translated
Earth's temptations far above;
Freed from sin's abhorred dominion,
Soaring on an angel pinion,
They shall reach the Source of love.[286]

Christ is the fountain; the evangelists are conduits, conveying the healing waters of His merit through their mouths and pens. Delightful, incorruptible gold, that is, such comfort as no amount of gold can buy, is found in the evangelists. There is the precious gum arabic, too; that is, the true and proven medicine for the soul. There also are found the best, priceless jewels[287] fit to adorn us for God's presence. This is so because they point us only to the benefits of our Lord Christ, in whom our healing, salvation, treasure, joy, and glory consist.

Many passages of Scripture lead us to see our Lord Jesus here. Psalm 36:8–9 says, "You give them drink from Your delights as from a river. For with You is the fountain of life." Psalm 68:26 says of the Lord Jesus, "Praise God, the LORD, in the congregations, you of Israel's fountain." Isaiah 12:3 prophesies about the New Testament period with similar words: "With joy you will draw water from the wells of salvation" (or "from the wells of the Savior,"[288] as Jerome rendered it). Zechariah 13:1 states, "In that day the house of David and the inhabitants of Jerusalem shall have a free and open fountain against sin and unrighteousness." And John 1:16 likewise says of the Lord Jesus, "And from His fullness we have all received grace for grace." Moreover, the Lord Jesus Himself told the Samaritan woman, "Whoever drinks of the water that I will give him will never thirst" (John 4:14); and in Revelation 21:6, "I am the Alpha and the Omega, the beginning and the

---

286 "Paradisus his rigatur, / viret, floret, faecundatur, / His abundat, his laetatur, / quatuor fluminibus. / Fons est Christus, hi sunt rivi: / Fons est altus, hi proclivi, / ut saporem fontis vivi / ministrent fidelibus. / Horum rivo ebriatis, / siris crescat charitatis, / ut de fonte Deitatis, / satiemur plenius. / Horum trahat nos doctrina, / vitiorum de sentina, / sicque ducat ad Divina, / ab imo superius"; The last 10 stanzas of "Iucundare, plebs fidelis," attr. Adam of St. Victor, ca. 1150; tr. R. Campbell, 1850, alt.

287 "clenodia"

288 "ex fontibus Salvatoris"

ending. To the thirsty I will give from the spring of living water without payment." And when in the final chapter John describes the heavenly joy prepared for us by the Lord Jesus, he says, "And he showed me a pure river of living water, clear as a crystal, which proceeded from the throne of God and of the Lamb, in the midst of her streets" [Rev. 22:1–2]. Furthermore, in order that the whole world might know the Lord Jesus as the fountain of life, He opened His side on the cross and let water and blood flow forth. "This is He who comes with water and blood" (1 John 5:6).

He is the sweet fountain that comforts us, the blessed river of grace that saves us, and the overflowing wellspring of power that revives and uplifts us. And He causes these benefits, merits, and gifts to be distributed in the Holy Gospel, Baptism, and the Holy Supper. These are the conduits, canals, and riverbeds by which the healing floods of Jesus Christ's treasures flow forth. Thus they are also called the "streams with which the city of God will always be glad and merry" (Ps. 46:4). And Psalm 23:2 calls them "refreshing water"[289]; likewise, Sirach 24:30. The twelve fountains of Elim (Ex. 15:27) were also understood by the early fathers to be an image of the doctrine handed down by the twelve holy apostles.

The waters of Baptism can likewise be compared to the true, miraculous pool of Bethesda (John 5:2) in which the sick were made well; and to the healing waters of the Jordan, in which Naaman washed away his leprosy (2 Kings 5:14); and to the Red Sea, in which Pharaoh drowned (Ex. 15:1); and to the true water of sprinkling (Num. 19:13). Furthermore, the holy fountain of blood in the blessed chalice of the Holy Supper meetly flows from the cleft side of Jesus Christ, the Fountain of life.

Now whoever would find the true Fountain of life and well of our salvation must by no means neglect but rather hear the Gospel and use the Sacraments. Then Jesus, the River of life, with all His gifts will be instantly poured into his heart.

Dear Lord Jesus, You are the clear, shining Fountain of life, the Pharmacy of the whole Christian Church, and the Water of life[290] that gladdens my heart. The rivers of Your grace flow out from You in all evangelical

---

289 "aquae refectionis"
290 "aqua vitae"

sermons. For this I will thank You forever. Your benefits flow into my heart by means of the Holy Spirit, the heavenly Master Plumber. Oh, how can I praise this enough? Jeremiah lamented having to pay for water (Lam. 5[:4]). O Lord Jesus, I enjoy Your favor at no cost whatsoever. I do not have to pay one penny for it (Rev. 21:6; 22:17). The water in the brook Cherith dried up for the prophet Elijah (1 Kings 17:7), but You will never dry up or ebb away for me. You flow in summer and winter. I have You to comfort and gladden me in life, death, and all eternity. You do not give Yourself stingily. Your benefits are unfathomable. The more I take from You, the more I find in You. St. Paul admonished Timothy not to drink too much water because it might upset his stomach (1 Tim. 5:23). O Lord Jesus, I can drink of You as much as I want, as long as I want. No man will be able to restrain me. I can drink till my eyes overflow with joy. It will not hurt me but support my health in body and soul. I cannot get dropsy from You. Instead, the more I consider You, take comfort in You, and speak of You, the more benefit, consolation, and good I have.

The waters of Egypt were impure and filled with frogs (Ex. 8). O Lord Jesus, Your waters of grace are all as clear as crystal (Rev. 22:1). Indeed, Your purity even removes all my impurity.

In Bethulia, water was measured out to the people (Judith 7:21). O Lord Jesus, I do not have to take You in rations and measures. Rather, I can have You in my heart all for my own. Therefore I will never forget You. In fact, whenever I do anything with water, I will remember You with adoration. What would we do if we did not have any water? Oh, what could we boast of, how could we be happy, if we did not have You, O Lord Jesus Christ, the Fountain of living water? The land-dwelling serpent must release its venom before entering the water. O Lord Jesus, You also release all the harm imposed on us by the serpent when with true faith we are immersed in Your fountain of salvation. Water takes all the uncleanness of the body away. Your blood, Lord Jesus, cleanses my soul from all sin. Oh, how relieved the perspiring farmhand is in the full heat of summer when he takes a refreshing drink of pure water! When my heart is in such great anguish that my conscience feels the heat of God's wrath, oh, how relieved it is as soon as I think of You. "If I have but You, I ask for nothing in heaven and earth. If my flesh and my heart should fail, yet You alone, O God, are forever the ease of my heart, and my portion" (Ps. 73:[25–]26).

Dear Lord Jesus Christ, the healing fountain of Your benefits has been freely given and granted to me out of the mercy of Your heavenly Father; thus I will greatly, highly, and worthily esteem this gift. Let my heart be a water pail, like Rebekah's water jar [Gen. 24:45]—a pure, clean vessel with which to draw from Your fullness and fill my heart to the brim. The childish notion of holy water is far too base for me. The "springs without water" of the heretics (2 Peter 2:17), who profess great things and yet in tribulation bring no comfort, are of no use to me. I will guard myself from all the murky mud-puddles that human cleverness can devise, lest You should lament as in Jeremiah 2:13, "My nation commits a twofold sin: they forsake Me, the living Fountain, and hew out wells for themselves here and there which nevertheless are full of holes and yield no water." I will fill my heart to the brim with You; and when my heart is full of comfort, I will share with my neighbor as well, in order to fulfill what You say in John: "Whoever believes in Me, as the Scripture says, 'Out of his body shall flow rivers of living water'" (John 7:38). Oh, help my heart to be purged and cleansed for You, by true contrition and repentance. That is, help me not to pour the pure water of Your merit into a stinking vessel, nor to make myself unworthy of this exalted treasure. Such St. Arsenius was shown in a vision regarding his worldly course, as Jerome describes in *The Lives of the Fathers*.[291] Oh Lord, guard my heart from the waters of strife,[292] the puddles of envy, and the currents of immorality. May You alone be sovereign in my heart, mind, speech, and life.

"Come, all who thirst, come to the waters (of Jesus Christ's consolation); and you who have no money, come!" (Is. 55[:1]).

If you wish to pray, then say with Psalm 42:1, "As the deer cries for fresh water, so my soul cries, O God, to You." Oh Lord Jesus, Fountain of Life, You are my cool drink and refreshment. I can refresh myself in You to my heart's content and lift my spirit. Oh, how stricken with misery my heart is! Lord, water the parched paradise of my heart with Your rivers

291 "Vitae Patrum"

292 Or, "waters of Meribah" (Num. 20:13).

of grace. Feed me, strengthen me, and refresh me. O God the Holy Spirit, be the skillful Master Plumber. Lay a conduit from the Fountain of life, Jesus Christ, into my sweltering heart. Glorify my Savior in my thoughts, that I not despair. When my eyes become "fountains of tears" (Jer. 9:1),[293] remind me of Jesus Christ's well of salvation. When the bitter waters of this world bring me anguish, make the sweet waters of Jesus Christ's merit flow into my heart!

O God the heavenly Father, rule and restrain the evil one and every heretic who would take this Fountain of grace from me and rob me of my soul's treasure, like when Sennacherib tried to take the fountains outside of Jerusalem. Hide my Fountain of life from their eyes, like the outlet of Hezekiah's water (2 Chron. 32:30), and preserve this treasure for our children. Bodily thirst afflicted the nobles of Glogau whom Duke John starved. They testified far more to their thirst than to their hunger in the account which they wrote with lampblack inside the prison-tower (see *The Annals of the Silesia, Year 1488*).[294] When spiritual thirst thus afflicts my soul, do not leave me like the rich man in hell, crying in vain for a drop of water, but refresh my heart with a droplet of Jesus Christ's sweet benefits. Those who have a high temperature think in the heat of their fever that getting a drink of water is like heaven itself. O Lord Jesus, in Your wells of salvation I have my whole heavenly kingdom. No drink of barley can cool me off as quickly. No rose-water can give me as much refreshment. No elixir of blessed thistle[295] can stifle my fever as effectively. If I have You, then heaven must be mine.

King David longed for a drink of water from the well by the gate in Bethlehem (2 Sam. 23:15). O Lord Jesus, I long for You day and night. You are the Well of grace in Bethlehem given to us in a manger.

Gideon's three hundred soldiers who scooped up the water of the Jordan and lapped it up from their hand became the knights and victors over the Midianites (Judges 7:7). A little handful won against a whole land-full. Likewise, when I scoop from the abundant Jordan of Your merit with

---

293 "fontes lachrymarum"

294 "Anno 1488. Annal. Siles. Curaei."

295 *Carduus Benedictus*, an aromatic, bitter herb with healing properties.

the hand of true faith, and gradually sip it in my need, and rejoice in its consolation, then by the cooperating power of the Holy Spirit I am filled with such a valiant courage—"as of a fire-breathing lion,"[296] to the terror of the devil himself, says Chrysostom—that I can wage war with boldness, uphold the faith and a good conscience, overcome the foes of my salvation, scatter the ranks of the world, sin, mockery, distress, and death, and obtain the glorious crown of eternal salvation.

O Lord Jesus, in church I hear You extolled as the Fountain of life. Oh, help me to love church, the place where this comfort resounds! Help me to keep the pitcher of my heart pure, to fill it to the brim from Your well of salvation, to carry it attentively at home, nor to neglect it through carelessness, but to make great use of it in my prayer, cross, affliction, distress, tribulation, and death, and to share its comfort with others also. Finally, help me in such comfort to conclude my life in this world blessedly and to inherit eternal life! Amen.

296 "quasi leo ignem spirans"

XVII. JESUS,
The Second Adam by Way of Comparison (Gen. 2:21; 3:6).

Adam was the grandfather of all mankind; all other men descended from him. Thus we are all brothers and sisters, since we all share one father on earth, namely, Adam. Indeed, we also share one Father in heaven, the Lord our God.

God Himself created our grandfather Adam in His own image and quickened him with His divine breath. Adam was God's coin,[297] as Christ suggests in Luke 15:8. God Himself was the master of the mint inside His casting furnace, skillfully stamping His deep counsel. He took a piece of earth, shaped it with skill, proportioned it gracefully in the mint of His almighty power, polished it in the forge of Paradise, and stamped His noble, exact image on Adam's heart and soul with the pile and stamp of His divine breath. This coin was to be deposited in God's treasury and beautifully sparkle and shine upon God's table of grace, but by way of a sinful deed the devil managed to have it rejected. He cast it away, and it rolled off into the crack of all calamity. He clipped it, scratched it, defaced it, and so obscured the imprint that it would have been lost forever had not our Lord Jesus kindled the light of His Gospel, sweated His blood in Gethsemane, and with the broom[298] of His cross sought the coin again. When Adam was sought for, he immediately showed himself, leapt up with true repentance, and sang a beautiful hymn of praise to God's glory.

Adam came from both earth and heaven, for he received his flesh from earth but his life, spirit, and soul from heaven. This shows that Adam was to have a right to both earth and heaven. He was to dwell for a season

---

297 Germ. *Grosche.*

298 A play on words: Germ. *Besem* can also be an instrument of punishment.

in Paradise, in heaven's nursery, as it were, and then be transported to heaven. God made him emperor, king, and sovereign lord over the whole earth, and groundskeeper of the Garden of Eden. God ordained him pope and bishop so that he would declare the great works of God. He made him a merry housefather and fashioned a bride for him out of his side. He equipped him with such a noble, beautiful, and wonderful mind that he was able to name every beast and created thing according to its innate, true nature and character.

Adam's first utterance was a prophecy; he knew what Eve had been created from without ever having seen her before. He also knew what a great throng of children would be born to her. Josephus adds that Adam knew of and spoke about the flood as well. God dressed him with great splendor, and everything in him was pure, clean, and innocent. God gave Adam a free will to worship, praise, and adore God without constraint or compulsion out of his own good pleasure, and to count this his greatest happiness. But the devil was Adam's sworn enemy and would not (and did not) rest until he brought him to disobedience, disgrace, destruction, and derision, from which our Lord Jesus graciously had to save him.

Here we will look at our Second Adam, our Lord Jesus, and following the instruction of St. Paul (1 Cor. 15:45–47; Rom. 5:14), begin by comparing the characters and similarities of the sinner Adam and the sin-bearer Jesus, and then follow this by distinguishing their differences.

Adam and Christ are the most important men in the world. Whoever knows the history of these two and understands it well is wise enough for life now and forever.

Oh my Lord Jesus, heavenly Adam, the true Sin-Canceler, give me a devout heart to ponder these lofty matters for my good.

After the first man, Adam, we are all called men and children of men; after You, Lord Jesus Christ, the Son of God, we are all called Christians and children of God. Oh, help us to be true posessors of this honor, and as truly as we are men, to be the children of God and honest Christians by Your grace!

Adam means "blood red," for among the Hebrews, *dam* means "blood" and *adam,* "a red man." Lord Jesus, You are the true King Erythraeus,[299] the true red mouth, the Lord of Rothenburg;[300] You are the man in red garments (Is. 63:2). You have washed Your clothes in the red blood of grapes, as the patriarch Jacob says in his last will and testament (Gen. 49:11). In Gethsemane I see You red. On the cross I see You holding court in such rich and lovely hues of red. Adam got his name because he was made from the red earth. It is fitting for You to have the same name because You paid for our sins with Your blood. You were made blood-red that our blood-guilt might be washed away and white as snow (Is. 1:18), for Your blood "cleanses us from all sin" (1 John 1:7).

Adam carried the image of God in his soul; but You, O Lord Jesus, are Yourself the image of God the Father, the radiance of His glory (Col. 1:15; Heb. 1:3). You also carry the beautiful image of Your Father's heart in Your words. Whoever has seen and heard You knows the Father and has learned how Your Father's heart is disposed toward us (John 1:18; 14:7).

Adam was shaped by God's hand from pure, virgin earth unsullied by the blood of man. O Lord Jesus, You were conceived by the Holy Spirit under Mary's chaste, virgin heart unmarred by impurity, unstained by the intercourse of man, that by Your holy conception my sinful conception might be sanctified.

Adam came from heaven and earth. O Lord Jesus, You also come from two origins. According to Your divine glory, You were begotten and born from the heart of Your Father from eternity; but according to Your tender human nature, You were conceived, carried, and made true man under the sacred heart of Mary by the overshadowing of the Holy Spirit, yet without sin, and were born, that You might deliver man completely, body and soul. You were to reunite heaven and earth in the bond of kinship, and this You most surely did. "For as the rational soul and flesh is one man," says Athanasius, "so God and man is one Christ."

Adam was the emperor and king of the whole world. Dear Lord Jesus, You are the King of heaven and earth. At Your command all creation

---

299   From Gk., lit., "red-hued" or "ruddy."; sometimes equated with Esau or Edom.
300   Lit., "Red City."

must stand at attention. You are "Jesus of Nazareth, King of the Jews," that is, Lord Protector of all those who love You with their heart and confess You with their mouth. Your royal heart is my comfort and confidence in every need.

Adam was the guardian of Paradise. O Lord Jesus: Guardian of Israel, Your beloved Church, You neither slumber nor sleep. Watch and preserve me from all enemies (Ps. 121:4).

Adam had all the animals at his service and command. O Lord Jesus, You have all creation, including angels and men, at Your command. You have the power to do as You will. You have the power to grant or withhold heaven from us. You have the power to incline Your heavenly Father's heart toward us. All authority in heaven and in earth has been given to You (Matt. 28:18). All things have been put under Your feet (Ps. 8:6). Therefore I can flee to You in every distress and ask for what I need.

Adam was to be prophet, patriarch, bishop, and pastor, and to proclaim the great works of God. O Lord Jesus, You are the great Prophet to whom we must listen or else forfeit salvation (Deut. 28:15, Matt. 17:5). You are the One who has forever revealed to men how God is disposed toward them (John 8:28). Oh, grant that I may receive Your Word with open ears and preserve it in a good heart.

Adam had to have a bride. O Lord Jesus, You, too, will have Your bride, that is, Your beloved Christian Church. My heart is Your most beloved bride. You will be betrothed to my heart with true love forever.

Adam was full of heavenly wisdom, discerning all the animals and their properties. Such he depicted in their names, giving them in these nothing else than memorials of their nature[301] in Hebrew. O Lord Jesus, You are wisdom itself. You were "made to us wisdom" (1 Cor. 1[:30]); in You are "hidden all the treasures of wisdom" (Col. 2:3). When no creature in Paradise could help us, Your wisdom gave us the solution. You gave counsel and brought help,[302] and You still show Your wisdom today whenever You help me and other Christians in great need when no one else can help.

---

301 "signaturae rerum"

302 "dedisti consilium et tulisti auxilium."

Adam called all the animals and gave them their own names. O Lord Jesus, You call to us wretched sinners, "Come to Me, all who are weary and heavy laden; I will refresh you" (Matt. 11:28). You also give us new names, calling us Your brothers, the friends and children of God, and heirs of eternal salvation.

Adam was completely pure without any defect, without any sin or infraction. O Lord Jesus, You also are completely pure by Your very nature and Your glory. No one could convict You of a single sin (John 8:46). You give me Your purity and innocence so that I will not perish on account of my uncleanness.

Adam had a joyful free will able to glorify God. Dear Lord Jesus, You also have a joyful free will obedient to Your Father. In the Garden of Gethsemane You placed Your will in His, and by Your willing obedience atoned and paid for our selfish will and disobedience.

Adam had a sworn enemy in the devil. O Lord Jesus, You had a sworn enemy in the evil one who would have hindered and hampered all Your benefits. But You are stronger than Adam. The devil was unable to overpower You, and You valiantly conquered and crushed him (Rev. 12:10–11).

Adam received a blessing: "Be fruitful and multiply." Lord Jesus, You also received a blessing. As the true High Priest, Your hand was filled, and from its fullness You are able to share with us abundantly, as You say, "All things have been handed over to Me by My Father" (Luke 10:22), and "You received gifts for men" (Psalm 68:18).

Adam was put in Paradise. O Lord Jesus, You also were put in the blessed land where Paradise once had been. You were sent to the people of God in the spiritual paradise of the Church, that by Your merit You might open the heavenly paradise and lead us in.

Adam was assigned a heavy task; yet before sin, such work was a great pleasure. It did not exhaust him. O Lord Jesus, You also came to do a great task. You were to remove mankind's mountain of sin. You were to exhaust Your blood. You were to work Yourself to death. Blessed be Your wonderful, masterful work! Elijah had Your holy work in view when he said, "Because His soul has toiled, He shall see His pleasure and be satisfied" (Is. 53:11).

Adam was chased out of Paradise. He did not dwell there for long. O Lord Jesus, You were not suffered to tarry long in the land of the Jews where Paradise once had been. Herod chased You out as soon as You were born. And when You returned, they still could not endure You for long. Your preaching was only tolerated for three and a half years. They led You out of Jerusalem's gate, but Your leading out is our leading in to eternal life. No one can run You out of heaven; no one can drive You out of Your Christian Church. You will abide with us until the end of the world (Matt 28[:20]), and we will abide with You forever.

Adam was made a curse, an abomination, and a monstrosity before God because of his sins. Dear Lord Jesus, You were made such a curse for us on the tree of the cross (Gal. 3:13) that the sun would not even shine on You. The earth's foundation shook for You. Thus You caused Your promised blessing to be poured out on us, body and soul.

Adam realized that he was naked. He became fearful and had to hide himself away in shame. O Lord Jesus, You were stripped bare and lifted up naked on the cross, that You might strip away the shame and fearfulness of naked Adam. The rag that was wound about You has become for us the good fig-leaves whereby our nakedness is covered. Your precious merit clothes us so that we can stand before God Your Father.

Adam put the blame on his wife and complained that the wife that God had given him had brought him to such a wretched end. But Adam spoke wrongly. O Lord Jesus, You placed the blame of Your suffering on Your bride, on us men, and in righteous, full, and accurate truth You said, "Yea, you have made work for Me with your sins, and you have made toil for Me with your iniquities; but I, even I, blot out your transgressions for My own sake, and do not remember your sins" [Is. 43:24–25; cf. Heb. 8:12; 10:17].

Adam groaned, cried, lamented, and regretted his sins for his whole life. O Lord Jesus, from Your youth up You anguished Yourself to death, making public satisfaction for our sins in place of mankind until You finished it all on the cross and paid for our sins.

Adam fathered a son after his own image, sinful and impure (Gen. 5:3). O Lord Jesus, You also father children after Your own image, holy and righteous. You have made us born again to eternal life. You were pregnant with us from Your youth up. You went into labor on the cross in the land of the Jews. The cross was Your birthing chair. Opening the sluice of Your side, You let blood and water flow out to change our hearts and make them new. You cried out in Your holy Passion, "My God, My God, how You have forsaken Me!" [Matt. 27:46; Mark 15:34]. You groaned like a mother in her birth-pains. You bore us up to heaven and said, "It is finished" [John 19:30]. Your tomb was Your holy recovery bed where You slept in complete silence and stillness. On Easter day You observed the rite of churching, and consecrated the "newborn infants"[303] of God [1 Peter 2:2]. You had twins: You fathered children of God from both Jews and heathens. Oh, thanks be to You forever and ever! Even today You scatter the imperishable seed of Your Gospel on our hearts (1 Peter 1:23) and with it send the cooperating power of the Holy Spirit, renewing our hearts and making us children of God (John 3:3; Heb. 3:7; Rom. 8:16).

Adam's children all came from the same lump of dough; they were like him. They fared no better in the world than Adam had. O Lord Jesus, we believers also have no choice but to be like You. If we would share in Your glory, we must also suffer and die with You (Rom. 8:17). On this Paul says, "The first man Adam 'became a living soul,' and the last Adam, a spirit that makes alive. But the spiritual is not first, but the natural, and afterward the spiritual. The first man is of the earth and earthly; the second man is the Lord from heaven. Such as the earthly one is, such also are those who are earthly; and such as the Heavenly One is, such also are those who are heavenly. And just as we have borne the image of the earthly, we shall also bear the image of the heavenly" (1 Cor. 15:45[–49]). Also: "For those whom He foreknew He also predestined to be like the image of his Son" (Rom. 8:29).

Adam's children scattered themselves to the four corners of the world. In Greek, the four corners of the world are written with the four letters of Adam.[304] O Lord Jesus, Your children, Your believers, brothers, sisters, and friends, also scattered themselves throughout the whole world. You have holy seeds in every land. There are in every place hearts that know and love You. You know them best of all. Your children are not bound to any certain place and station.

---

303 "Quasimodo geniti infantes" (from the Introit on the first Sunday after Easter).

304 *Anatole* ("east"), *dysis* ("west"), *arktos* ("north"), *mesembria* ("south").

Adam was not to be alone (Gen. 2:18). O Lord Jesus, You were not to be alone, either, but to have many hearts to give You glory. So You said, "Unless a grain of wheat falls into the earth and dies, it remains alone; but if it dies, it bears much fruit" (John 12:24). Here You spoke of Your death and burial, and how by these You would gather again the children of God who had been scattered (John 11:25). That is why Isaiah says, "When He shall make His soul an offering for sin, He shall have seed" (Is. 53:10).

XVIII. JESUS,
The Second Adam by Way of Contrast (Gen. 2:21, 3:6).

Observe furthermore, dear heart, following St. Paul's instruction in Romans 5:14, that the Lord Jesus is presented in the account of Adam by way of contrast. Do not let the pondering of these comforting things trouble you. For the knowledge of Adam leads us to the knowledge of our own miserable estate, but the contemplation of Christ leads us to the knowledge of our salvation. This is a Christian's most profound insight. Thus St. Augustine prays in his briefest, most beautiful little prayer, "Oh God, grant me both to know myself and to know You."[305]

Adam is the source of all men's physical life. But You, O Lord Jesus, the heavenly Adam, are the source of all believers' spiritual and eternal life. You are the Alpha and Omega, the beginning and end of our salvation [Rev. 21:6]. You are the breaker before us [Micah 2:13]. Whoever believes in You has eternal life [John 3:16].

Adam struggled with the evil one and was overcome. But You, O Lord Jesus, wrestled with the evil one in the desert and won (Matt. 4:1–11). You are mighty in battle [Ps. 24:8]. You gave the devil a foretaste of Your might, and at last by the power of Your cross crushed his head and took all his power and dominion away.

Adam transgressed God's law and fell into grievous sin. But You, O Lord Jesus, fulfilled all of God's law and gave us Your perfect obedience, that, being covered with it, we might stand in Your Father's presence.

Adam did an evil work on the first Friday whereby we were all condemned. But You, O Lord Jesus, atoning for Adam's sin, did a good work on Good Friday whereby we have all been saved and restored to the estate from which we had been banished.

---

305 "Deus, noverim me, noverim te"; August. *Confess.* 2.1.1.

Adam by his sin laid for himself and his children a road to hell. But You, O Lord Jesus, by Your merit have laid for us a road to life everlasting.

Adam was arrogant and sought to steal God's crown. He was not content with his position and wanted to be like God. But You, O Lord Jesus, "did not count it robbery to be like God"; You set aside Your divine authority, and humbled Yourself, and were "obedient to the point of death, even death on the cross" (Phil. 2:6–8). By Your profound humility You blotted out the pride and arrogance of Adam and all mankind.

Adam fell by his sin into slavery to the devil, death, and damnation. But You, O Lord Jesus, ascended on high and became the Lord of sin, the devil, death, hell, and damnation. Therefore You say, "I will redeem them from hell and rescue them from death. O death, I will be your poison; O hell, I will be your pestilence." (Hos. 13:14).

Adam was deceived by the evil one through cunning and beguiled by his beloved Eve. But You, O Lord Jesus, beguiled the evil one with profound wisdom. You walked as one despised in our flesh and misery, and let Yourself suffer an accursed death, and thus You cut down the devil and all the foes of our salvation. When a fisherman wishes to catch a large pike, he covers his barbed hook with a tiny earthworm. Likewise, You kept the hook of Your divine omnipotence secret, letting the evil one and death behold You only in the humble form of a servant, like that of a poor earthworm. Thus in Your innocent simplicity You fooled eternal death, and in You death consumed death, such that henceforth he cannot keep anyone who believes in You.

Adam, after committing sin, fled from God; he crawled into hiding and lay in fear. But You, O Lord Jesus, after atoning for our sins, returned and went straight up to heaven, right to the heart of Your Father, and won for us bold access to Your Father in our every need.

Adam, after committing sin, had no right to the tree of life. But You, O Lord Jesus, by the expiation of our guilt have given us access to the tree of life and brought us everlasting health and salvation.

Adam sinned at the tree. But You, O Lord Jesus, paid for sin at the tree of the cross.

Adam, after committing sin, was forced into misery with all his children. But You, O Lord Jesus, after making satisfaction for our sins, seated

Yourself at the right hand of God's majesty as our sovereign King and worthy High Priest, and in Your exaltation draw us after You.

For Adam's sake we are called God's enemies and sinners. But for Your sake, O Lord Jesus, we are all called God's children, saints, and heirs of eternal salvation.

Adam's guilt is passed on by the fleshly and physical birth. But Your merit, O Lord Jesus, is passed on to those whom You have chosen and regenerated unto heaven, not by physical birth but by spiritual rebirth.

Adam ate delicate foods in Paradise, and then vegetables outside of Paradise. But You, O Lord Jesus, are Yourself the Food of our souls which strengthens and sustains us unto eternal life.

In Adam, three ages and estates are observed: first, his nobility before the fall; second, his wretchedness after the fall; and third, his renewal after receiving the forgiveness of sins. Likewise, O Lord Jesus, in You we also observe three ages and estates: first, Your most mighty Lordship from eternity in the heart of Your Father: God of God, Light of Light, etc.; second, Your self-revelation in the estate of Your humiliation, when You clothed Yourself in our flesh and blood, bore the weight of our sins, and laid aside the manifestation of Your divine omnipotence; and third, Your eternal, mighty Mastery following the subjugation of all adversaries and adversities, and present reign in the glory which was Yours before the world was founded [John 17:24]!

To Adam it was said, "You are dust, and to dust you shall return" [Gen. 3:19]. But to You, O Lord Christ, it was said, "Sit at My right hand, until I make Your enemies Your footstool" (Ps. 110:1; 1 Cor. 15:25).

Adam's children are seen with physical eyes. The children of God, however, whom with Your torments, O Lord Jesus, You bore unto heaven, and whom You regenerated by Your Word and Spirit, are seen only with spiritual eyes. This requires much reflection and spiritual experience.

From Adam comes sin; from You, O Lord Jesus, righteousness. From Adam comes death; from You, life. Adam's guilt condemns us; Your merit, O Lord Jesus, absolves us. Adam's fall has filled us with terror; Your bloody death consoles us. As mighty as Adam's sin is to curse us, so mighty is Your righteousness to bless us. As mighty as Adam's guilt is to cast us down to hell, so mighty, Jesus Christ, is Your obedience to raise us up to heaven. On this St. Paul says, "If because of one man's (Adam's) sin, death reigned through that one man, much more will those who receive the abundance of grace and of the gift for righteousness reign in life through one man, Jesus Christ. Therefore, as through one man's sin condemnation came upon all men, so through one man's righteousness the justification of life came upon all men. For just as by the disobedience of one the many were made sinners, so by the obedience of one many are made righteous" (Rom. 5:17–19).

O heavenly Adam, Lord Jesus! You restored all that the first Adam corrupted. May all praise, glory, and honor be attributed, addressed, and ascribed to You forever. Amen!

XIX. JESUS

Joins Adam and Eve in Holy Matrimony, Honors the First Marriage on Earth with His Presence, and Appoints the Eternal Marriage in Heaven (Gen. 2:22).

God realized in His profound wisdom that it was not good for Adam to spend his life alone but that it would be fitting for him to have a female companion, helper, and comforter beside him.

This decision was published and announced by the Lord Jesus. This is what Moses means when he writes, "and God said." Here we see how our Lord Jesus, the lover of marriage, was already busying Himself with the first wedding.

The wedding was conducted in the Garden of Paradise under the open sky in the richest parcel of land in the whole world, where everything was godly and good, for God would not suffer any honor to be lacking. by doing so, God shows that in His eyes marriage is a true pleasure garden, yea, the nursery of heaven.

Adam and Eve's wedding took place in the state of innocence, before they had ever sinned, from which it is plain that wedlock is a holy, God-pleasing estate and that it should be kept in in a holy manner.

God the Father was the ancient Nobleman at this wedding, endowing His two children honorably and generously. Adam and Eve were fatherless and motherless. They were poor orphans. God the Father adopted them and bequeathed as dowry the emperorship of the whole world.

Our Lord Jesus was the preacher here, giving a bridal homily on the nuptial lesson: "It is not good that Adam should be alone." He addressed the bride and groom with sincere, comforting, wholesome words: "Adam, dearest Adam, discern and praise the love of My Father. When you were sleeping, He watched and cared for you. Behold, here I entrust to your hand and heart this fair virgin Eve, who was taken from beside your heart. She was taken from your side, for she is to be your companion in your life, nor stray too far from your side. She was fashioned from your rib, not from your feet, for you are not to think of her as a foot-servant, but to show her heartfelt loyalty. Ribs are not as strong and hard as the other bones in the arms and legs. Your Eve is also somewhat more fragile of nature than you, for which reason you would be wise to learn how to deal with her frailty." Adam kept this all his days. All pious husbands should still heed it today, too, for the faithful pledge is the best.

Likewise, the Lord Jesus also preached to Eve: "Eve, dear Eve, you are to be Adam's beloved, the comfort of his eyes, and the joy of his house. You were not taken from his head, for you were not meant to be his head. The headship is to remain with Adam. You were taken from his rib, from his side, where Adam supports his clothing, for you are to support Adam's heart and the livelihood of his house. You are to keep his things in good order and, just like a rib, know how to be fitted, cooperative, and yielding. Oh, make sure that this rib does not go awry! As in the body the rib covers the heart, so you should soothingly cover and keep Adam's heart. As in great distress of the heart the ribs lift to let the air in and out, so you too should soothingly lift Adam's worries with suitable words and cool off his distressed heart."

In addition to this, our Lord Jesus also spoke a powerful blessing upon Adam and Eve, and does so upon all those who enter marriage honorably and with a good conscience. This blessing's power shall be witnessed until the end of the world, and it is, furthermore, our Lord Jesus' own office to give it, for so He ascended into heaven speaking a blessing.

The Holy Spirit served as the best man and official witness at this wedding. He brought the bride and groom together. He exchanged the rings of their hearts and bound them in constant love that continued even after the fall, for nowhere do we read that Adam ever quarreled, fought with, or mistreated his Eve after the fall. Rather, they helped each other bear their crosses. When one was sad, the other spoke words of comfort, and together they made their crosses easier to bear.

Adam and Eve's wedding garments were their beautiful wisdom, innocence, and righteousness.

How happily the holy angels must have sung at this sumptuous feast, praising the Instituter of holy matrimony with a beautiful, heavenly hymn, and waiting to serve the new bridal pair as their eager wedding servants!

Oh, how lovely the beautiful fruits of Paradise must have tasted at this wedding! For surely before God cursed the earth everything was dainty and delectable.

Therefore, just as the Son of God was here troubling Himself with the arrangements for Adam's wedding, so after Adam's fall He would also be at pains to obtain Adam's salvation. Soon after Adam's wedding, things went for him as at the wedding at Cana when the bridegroom ran out of wine [John 2:1–11]. Adam fell into trouble, distress, sin, and great calamity, and had nothing but a heart full of woe and eyes full of tears. Then our Lord Jesus came, faithfully took up Adam's cause, pledged to save him from his sin, and turned the bitter tears of his eyes into the glad wine of comfort. Thus He did a far greater miracle here than at Cana of Galilee. And this is precisely how concerned our Lord Jesus still is today with the marriage of every pious, God-loving wedding couple. He supports them with advice and action. He refuses to leave them, even if they fall into such distress that nothing but a miracle would help them—as with the wedding at Cana and the one in Paradise.

For this reason, you should never forget the Lord Jesus Christ at any wedding. The bride and groom especially should carry the Lord Jesus in their hearts, saying: Dear Lord Jesus, without You there would be no wedding in the world. Without You no wedding today is happy or beautiful. Oh, adorn my wedding, too. Deign to help as You did at Adam's wedding, and at the wedding at Cana. Be my chief wedding guest, for it is Your way to eat little and honor much. I will give You the seat of honor. You have no desire to displace or make anyone move down the table, so I will show You into my heart. Oh, occupy the seat of honor in my heart. Be my witness there, grace me with Your lavish hand. Speak a blessing upon me, as You did upon Adam and Eve, and my water shall be turned to wine, and all sadness to joy and blessing!

Additionally, in this and in all other wedding feasts, be mindful of the heavenly wedding of all the elect children of God in eternal life. Concerning this, it is written in Revelation 19:7[–8]: "The marriage of the Lamb has come, and his Bride has made herself ready; and it was granted her to clothe herself in clean and beautiful silk (and the silk is the righteousness of the saints)." Jesus, the Bridegroom of our souls, shall celebrate an ever-lasting wedding feast with His believing Christians.

Oh dearest Lord Jesus, what joy and gladness You won for us in Your death! You love us as Your betrothed bride and only sweetheart. You plight Your troth and loyalty to us in Your Word. You pledge Yourself to us in the Holy Supper. You will be mine and I Yours. You will give us a splendid wedding in the high and stately hall of heaven. It will be far more beauti-ful there than in the Garden of Paradise. There will be a whole heaven full of tables filled with guests. Angelic, sweet-sounding music will be heard there. Alleluias will resound there in myriad thousands of voices, and there will be joy, pleasure, and delight. We will be given great honor there, and our endless day of glory and joy will begin. O Lord Jesus, how gently You will receive and embrace us! How graciously You will look upon us! How tenderly You will speak to us! How sweetly You will comfort us! Oh, to think that You will bring us to heaven to Your mansion, that we may sit with You forever in an undivided estate! Oh, to think that we will be given new names by You, and be called the blessed children of God!

Oh, to think that we will sit at table with Abraham and have our fill of heavenly consolation! What a great gathering of faithful hearts will be seen! What beautiful conversations will be had! All will be delight and leaping and dancing. What splendid wedding gifts will be laid before us! And all these things will last forever. There we will receive the keys to all the treasures of heaven. There we will shine and sparkle in the beautiful wedding garments of eternal, unbroken innocence, and we will know adversity and sadness no more. Oh most precious Lord Jesus, bring us soon to this blessed, heavenly wedding. Amen!

XX. JESUS,

The Second Adam, Falls Asleep on the Cross, Just as the First Adam Falls Asleep in Paradise; His Heart's Dearest Bride Is Formed from His Opened Side (Gen. 2[:21–23]).

God wanted to present Adam with a beautiful bride, so He caused him to fall into a deep sleep; for Adam was not to feel any pain when his side was being opened. In the state of innocence we would have known no days of sorrow or sadness—a blessed state that will be restored to us in eternal life. God took a rib from Adam's side and from it formed the beautiful Eve. No sooner did Adam catch sight of her than his heart burned with beautiful, bright love and kindness toward her.

Here we have yet another beautiful picture of the Lord Jesus Christ and His Christian Church.

The Lord Jesus, the Second Adam, also fell into a deep sleep of death on the cross. His side, too, was opened; and from it flowed blood and water, which, it is preached in the Gospel, are distributed in the Sacraments. Christian hearts receive this treasure by faith. Thus the Christian Church is built. Thus our hearts are brought to Christ. Thus we are washed of our sins by the Lord Jesus' true holy water, and hallowed by His blood. And just as Adam's heart poured itself out in beautiful love for Eve,[306] so the love of Jesus Christ also burns for our heart.

In the little book of Adam's heart, our Lord Jesus engraved an image of His goodwill toward our hearts. As Adam was attracted to Eve, even so, and to a far greater extent, Christ is attracted to us, and in the same way Jesus Christ is the Bridegroom of our soul, our fairest Treasure, Comfort, and Joy.

He Himself says, "And I will betroth you to Me forever; yea, I will betroth you to Me in righteousness and in judgment, in grace and in mercy. Yea, in faithfulness I will betroth you to Me, and you shall know the LORD"

---

306 Corr. for "Adam."

(Hos. 2:19–20); again, "I will say to that which was not My people, You are My people; and it shall say, You are my God" (v. 23). And so St. Paul says, "Husbands, love your wives, as Christ loved the church and gave Himself for her, that He might sanctify her, and cleanse her by the washing of water in the Word, so that He might present her to Himself as a church that is glorious, not having a spot or wrinkle or any such thing, but that she might be holy and blameless" (Eph. 5:25–27); and again, "No man ever hated his own flesh, but nourishes and cares for it, just as the Lord does the church, because we are members of His body, of His flesh, and of His bones" [vv. 29–30]; and again, "This mystery is great, but I speak concerning Christ and the church" (v. 32). And our Lord Jesus Himself portrays His heart similarly in a parable (Matt. 22:2) where He describes the wedding of the king's son.

By marriage, great wars between great lords are often reconciled and settled. Likewise, by the marriage which Jesus Christ celebrates with our hearts, the great conflict between God and mankind is brought to a harmonious end.

By marriage, a poor girl often enters into a great family and great honor. By the marriage of Jesus Christ, we enter into the family of God and of all the holy angels. We get heaven's supremely loyal allies who show us a thousand times more favor and support than all the families in the world. By this marriage we enter into eternal honor and glory.

Luther said, "They are profound, precious words whenever you hear that Jesus Christ is your Bridegroom, and your heart His bride. Yea, here are divine, unfathomable words which no human heart can grasp, and which cannot be learned well enough." Again, "The whole treasure of divine mercy could not have been depicted for us with more splendor than by the Church being called the bride of Christ. In the Old Testament, the Holy Spirit composed a beautiful song, Psalm 45, to honor the bridegroom, Christ, and His bride, the Christian Church. You might wish to read this now."

Therefore, let us also pause for a moment with this comforting thought. Oh, most beloved Treasure of my heart, Lord Jesus, what a desirable Bridegroom You are! You are noble by both Your Father and Your mother. According to Your divine nature, You are of the noblest Lord: God the

Father's very Son. According to Your human nature, You were born of the noble, royal Virgin Mary. Who would dare refuse to lift his heart up to You? You are the most faithful in heaven and on earth. "You are the most handsome of the children of men" (Ps. 45:3). You are the richest of all, for heaven and earth are Yours. All creation stands at Your bidding. You are rich in merit and benefits. You are gentle beyond all measure, and humble of heart. You are kind in every gesture and utterance. You speak nothing but words of life [John 6:63, 68]. You have a contrite spirit. You have endured great misfortune. You have risked much. You eagerly pursued great hardship. You are a well-traveled man. You traveled from heaven to earth, from thence to the cross, into the tomb, down to hell, back to life, and up to the right hand of God's majesty. This is why You know how to deal so gently with us. You are not proud and churlish, not silly and stubborn, but noble of heart. You are mighty and able to protect us and champion our cause. Praise and honor be to Your inexpressible humility! You did not seek a wife above Your station, for You have none higher than You. You did not seek a wife within Your station, either: You did not bring angelkind into Your family. Rather, You sought a wife below Your station. You took on Abraham's seed. You brought dust and ashes into Your family. Oh, how great Your humility is! We were not Your equals by any means, yet You were not ashamed of us. We were just village children, untrained in etiquette,[307] yet You did not reject us. We were unhealthy, with sore wounds in our conscience. Neither were we honorable or good. We were so abhorrent, covered in our own blood, that one is ashamed to read what is written about it in Ezekiel 16:6. Nevertheless, You came and said to me, "You shall live" [Jer. 38:17; Luke 10:28]. We were not rich, but naked, needy, and poor by birth. We were not beautiful, but disgusting and beggarly. Nevertheless, You set Your heart on us, and for Your sake Your heavenly Father is also gracious to us and loves us as a good father-in-law loves his dearest daughter-in-law. Oh, how can I ever repay You for this?

O Lord Jesus, You are portrayed in the same manner by St. Agnes, the Christian virgin, who says, "My heart loves the most ancient Lord whose mother was a Virgin, whose Father had no wife, whom angels

---

307 "mores"

serve, at whose beauty sun and moon stand in wonder, whose power never fails, who can raise the dead, heal all ailments, who has given me as a pledge the ring of His Spirit, that I am to be His own; who will be mine, who has marked my heart with His blood and made it red— the same red that rises thence to color my cheeks as a rose—who holds me in His arms, from whom I can expect eternal riches," etc. (from *The Golden Legend*).[308]

O dear Lord Jesus, how properly You go about Your works of grace! When as a sweet bridegroom You desired to betroth Yourself to our souls, though we had fallen into sin, You offered Yourself to Your Father, that You might help us and take up our cause, saying, "I will redeem them from hell and rescue them from death" (Hos. 13:14). Your Father agreed to this and said, "You are My Son, today I have begotten You. Ask of Me, and I will give You the heathen for a heritage, and the ends of the earth for a possession" (Ps. 2:7–8). For Your sake Your Father is also willing to turn His heart to us.

Next, Lord Jesus, You proceeded to sue for us in Paradise. You courted the hearts and souls of Adam and Eve in Genesis 3:15, and You continued to do so as You revealed Your heart "at many times and in many ways" [Heb. 1:1] to the pious patriarchs in the Old Testament.

At last, having donned Your human nature, You traversed the land of the Jews, speaking soothingly and tenderly to win our hearts. Then You stood on the holy cross, speaking words of nothing but comfort. You sang Your seven love-songs: one by one You spoke Your seven holy words. You flaunted Your blood-red garments of crimson. You wore Your nuptial wreath, Your crown of thorns, given You by a beloved hand (it was we who plaited it with our sins). Though it was painful to You, You gladly and willingly endured it all for our good. You wore perforated gloves. You wore an iron wedding ring of iron spikes (just as long ago, rings were made of iron to signify the durable nature of marital love). You wore slashed shoes: Your feet were pierced through. Like a generous nobleman, You poured out one crimson coin[309] after another.

---

308 "H. Lombardica"; see Ryan I 102.

309 Lit., "gulden."

You spread Your arms wide to embrace me. You inclined Your head to kiss me.

You made public appearances, that I might believe in You. You said, "'It is finished'; you will be Mine, I will be yours." Oh my Lord Jesus, help my heart to break forth and show You true love.

In addition, You sent out Your matchmakers to form in us a desire for You and Your benefits. In the Old Testament, Your matchmakers consisted of all the patriarchs and prophets. John avowed himself to be Your matchmaker, calling himself the "friend of the Bridegroom" (John 3:29). All preachers of the Gospel are Your ambassadors, as St. Paul says (2 Cor. 5:20), and he calls himself Christ's matchmaker by saying, "I betrothed you to one husband, that I may present you as a pure virgin to Christ" (2 Cor. 11:2). Accordingly, O Lord Jesus, if we pay heed to the Gospel, confess our sins, and believe in You, we are betrothed to You. Oh Lord Jesus, I pledge myself to be Your own in body and soul. Even death shall not part us.

Yet, Lord Jesus, we are betrothed to Your heart in Holy Baptism and the Holy Supper. There You vow to our heart, "Behold, dearest bride, here I give Myself wholly to be Your own. My blood shall cleanse you from all your sins. My cleft side shall be your resting place and mighty fortress in every turbulent storm. I have resolved to be faithful to you forever. Amen. This I swear to you by My divine truth. Amen." Oh Lord Jesus, I am not worthy of this great honor, yet I am needful of it, to be sure. This is a love unsought, unexpected, and undeserved. Eternal thanks be to You for Your loving heart!

O Lord Jesus, sweet Bridegroom of the soul, everything that a good, honorable bridegroom offers his bride You also offer my heart.

A proper bridegroom offers his bride pure, unfeigned, sincere love. O Lord Jesus, You also offer me pure, sublime, unmingled, divine love. All Your words testify to this. Your heart is just toward me. Thus You let Your side be pierced on the cross, that I might inspect Your heart closely and know how it was disposed toward me.

A bridegroom offers his bride all his possessions. His bride sits at his side in a house united. O Lord Jesus, You also offer us all Your possessions. As You have a right to heaven, so we have also. As You have a right to speak with Your Father, so by Your grace we too may come before Him and address Him as His children. All that is Yours, Lord Jesus, is ours as well.

A bridegroom also wants his bride to suffer hardship with him. Likewise, whenever we fall into hunger, worry, or any kind of difficulty, You want us to be content with You, following Your example, and be comforted by the fact that everything will be better one day.

A bridegroom takes his bride under his rightful protection. He will not suffer anyone to lay hands on her. O Lord Jesus, You also take us into Your protection against all the gates of hell, that they may not prevail against us. You will not suffer anyone to harm one hair of our head.

A bridegroom puts much that his bride does in a good light. He lovingly covers over a multitude of her defects and follies. O Lord Jesus, You put our great coarseness in a good light. You cover over our vast stupidity with the cloak of love and subdue it in us. In Your dealings with us You are the very Lord of tenderness and gentility.[310]

A bridegroom is faithful to his bride. He does not deceive her with empty words. His bride can boldly look to him for every good thing without any nagging doubts. O Lord Jesus, You are faithful to us forever. No deceit was found in Your mouth [Is. 53:9]. We can boldly and confidently take comfort in and rely on You. We shall not be deceived.

A bridegroom shares every occasion of joy with his bride. O Lord Jesus, You will share every occasion of joy in heaven with us. We will be with You for all time.

A bridegroom confers on his bride his own nobility; his bride immediately assumes his title. O Lord Jesus, You also confer on us Your noble status when we adopt Your royal and priestly name "Christ," and are called Christians.

A bridegroom swears fidelity to his bride. O Lord Jesus, You have also sworn fidelity to us with a twofold oath: "Truly, truly, I say to you, if a man keeps My word, he will never see death" (John 8:51).

A bridegroom clothes himself in his bride's colors. O Lord Jesus, You honored us by clothing Yourself in our flesh and blood. You also clothe us

---

310 Germ. *Lindenrode* and *Sänfftenberg*, resp., imitating names of nobility.

in Your colors, red and white. You adorn us with Your red blood, cleansing us from our sins. You clothe us in Your white innocence, initiating our godly life in this world. In the end, You will bring us to perfect righteousness in eternal life.

A bridegroom receives a glorious wedding wreath from his beloved bride. He also gives one in return. O Lord Jesus, You received from us a thorny wreath plaited with our sins, and in exchange gave us the wreath of glory, yea, the crown of eternal joy and righteousness.

A bridegroom honors his beloved bride, if she is of noble standing, with a golden necklace. O Lord Jesus, You regale us with the gifts of the Holy Spirit so that we take pleasure in pursuing works of Christian love. This gives us an adornment a thousand times more excellent than any golden necklace in the world. Indeed, if we live uprightly, we can boast of true nobility in God's sight.

A bridegroom readies a sweet-smelling bath of herbs for his bride before and after the wedding. O Lord Jesus, You prepared for us "the washing of regeneration and renewal of the Holy Spirit" [Titus 3:5], and You cleanse us with Your holy blood, making us white as snow (1 John 1:7; Eph. 5:26 [Ps. 51:7; Is. 1:18]).

A bridegroom arranges for a delicious wedding feast in honor of his bride. O Lord Jesus, You ordain the great Supper of Your Gospel and the most worthy Sacraments for our honor. You cause Your benefits to be served by the spoonful, and You are generous to our souls, that we may have refreshment and encouragement in every need.

A bridegroom has wedding servants designated to wait upon his beloved. O Lord Jesus, You also have designated wedding servants. Your holy angels must wait on us by Your command (Ps. 34:7; 91:11).

The bride gets a new name from her bridegroom. O Lord Jesus, we receive a new name from You, so that we are no longer called children of wrath and hell's kindling, but rather God's children and dearest sons and daughters, and even God's saints.

A bridegroom gives his bride a ring as a token of his gracious love. O Lord Jesus, You give me the Holy Spirit as a token of Your constant fidelity. In the Holy Supper You give me Your body and blood as a token that You will be mine and I Yours.

A bridegroom accepts what his bride offers him and requites it according to his means. O Lord Jesus, You also accept from us and give us in return. You make an exchange with us and say, Dear heart, give up your sin, receive My righteousness; give up your poverty and misery, receive My riches and glory; give up the eternal damnation which you earned with your sins, receive heaven and eternal life which I won for you with My obedience on the cross.

The bridegroom listens carefully to the sighs and complaints of his bride, and looks for a way to help her. O Lord Jesus, Your ears are open to hear us, and You mark our tears [Ps. 56:8] and take pains to assuage our misery. This brings our heart joy, rest, and relief in every care that weighs upon us.

A bridegroom uses his wisdom to the honor of his bride. He uses his strength to protect his bride. O Lord Jesus, You also use Your wisdom to comfort and help us and to hinder our foes, and You use Your strength to defend and protect us and to crush our foes.

A bridegroom is not fickle in times of scarcity or when his bride is sick. O Lord Jesus, You also stick with us. You do not change Your mind when we are sick and ailing.

A bridegroom provides food and drink and necessary clothing for his bride by hard work. O Lord Jesus, You provided for my heart by Your holiest work of all, of which You say, "Yea, you have made work for Me with your sins, and you have made toil for Me with your iniquities" (Is. 43:24). You are my soul's heavenly bread, my heart's best food. You are my most pleasant drink of refreshment in every anguish. You clothe us inwardly in the greatest splendor, with golden garments of pure, sumptuous gold, and in such finery set us at Your right hand (Ps. 45:9). O Lord Jesus, You know what honor means. You spread Your cloak over us and cover our shame (Ezek. 1[6]:8). You give us of the cloth of Your righteousness for a robe. You clothe us with Your innocence. You have "put garments of salvation on me, and clothed me in the robe of righteousness" (Is. 61:10). You give us the new shoes of a steady willingness to amend our life. You gird us up with the girdle of Your grace. You give us a coin-purse, that is, a heart filled with beautiful, wholesome, heavenly comfort. You give us beautiful bracelets, that is, the joyful power to lift our hands in every need and call on Your Father in Your name. And You give us the certain promise that we will be heard.

A bridegroom is most delighted when his bride has an honest disposition and virtuous way of life. O Lord Jesus, You also are most delighted when we are faithful at heart and virtuous, and serve You according to the Ten Commandments. This is why You let Yourself be nailed to an X (which is how Germans usually write "ten"),[311] that You might cleanse us from our sins committed against the Ten Commandments, and set us upon a blameless way of life according to the holy Ten Commandments; which, though begun in this life, shall not be perfected until we are in heaven.

A bridegroom speaks soothingly to his beloved bride. O Lord Jesus, You speak soothingly to our heart so that we do not faint while bearing our cross.

A bridegroom, bringing his venture to completion, then celebrates his evening homecoming with great joy, beautiful music, and lovely company; for bride and groom belong to the same house. He receives the bride courteously, embraces her, surrounds her with joys, and gives her the keys to the whole house. O Lord Jesus, on the evening of the world You will likewise celebrate Your happy homecoming. There the angels will be trumpeting in the field. There in beautiful fellowship we will be conducted into the house where "there are many dwellings" [John 14:2]. For You, O Lord Jesus, and we will be members of the same household, as You Yourself say: "Father, I desire that they also, whom You have given Me, may be with Me where I am" (John 17:24). Oh, what joy, bliss, and blessedness will be there! If You do such great good to us in this life, what will be done in eternity?

O Lord Jesus, most dearly beloved Bridegroom of the soul, You are mine; this is my greatest honor. I am Yours; this is my most exquisite comfort. You love me as a faithful bridegroom; this is my highest blessedness. Oh, help me always to love and worship You in return. Grant me to rule myself by and be mindful of Your will, to learn to know Your ways and Your precepts; never to anger You in word, deed, or gesture. Enable me to look up, incline my ears, and forget my people and my father's house and

311 I.e., the Roman numeral.

all worldly things, that You may desire my beauty (Ps. 45:11). I know Your heart. I praise Your kindness. I extol Your gifts, and take comfort in Your benefits. I thank You for all the honor which You have bestowed on me. For this grace my heart will remain true to You. Without You, it is never well with my heart. If I have You, I do not care for all the treasures in the world [Ps. 73:25]. You will not leave my heart and mind day or night. Oh, continue in Your old kindness and I will be content! To Your glory I will behave chastely, that is, I will keep myself from sin, follow at Your beck and call, and as Your dearest bride aspire to all honor and decency. O Lord Jesus, I desire it; grant me also to carry it out [Rom. 7:18]. Amen.

XXI. JESUS,

The Oldest, First, Best, and Noblest Preacher of Evangelical Comfort, the Sweet Comforter of Our Heart (Gen. 3:15).

There are in the Bible three chapters in particular that everyone should pay close attention to: Genesis 3, John 3, and Romans 3. For these three chapters clearly display two things: first, where sin and all adversity come from; second, where one should look for the righteousness that avails before God, and for every blessing. Evil comes from the devil, good from Christ Jesus. Now Genesis 3 is the spring and source, and shines throughout the Bible like the sun in the sky. Thus the old Wittenbergers implored Luther to expound this chapter to them one more time, and he even promised to do so, but death prevented that beautiful work. Therefore we must take a little time to consider this beautiful chapter. But let us restrict ourselves here to considering how Jesus Christ comforted Adam and Eve after the fall and wasted no time showing them the long-lasting, steady, rock-solid comfort which alone can strengthen and sustain all troubled hearts in the midst of their anxieties.

With great artistry God created man, gracefully adorned him, and richly blessed him with dominion over the whole world. In return for such benefactions, God desired nothing at all but a thankful heart and a God-praising mouth, and He set apart one single, solitary tree in Paradise from which man was not to eat, that God might thus discern his obedience. The envious old devil would not begrudge man this great prosperity, nor would he suffer man to be dearer to God than he was himself. He therefore transformed himself into a serpent, or perhaps spoke through a possessed serpent, and deceived the Joy of Adam's heart first, and then, by way of her smooth words, Adam as well, and thus brought them both into trouble and misery.

First, the devil worked doubt in Eve's mind regarding God's Word, posing the first question in the world: "Indeed, has God said, 'You shall not eat of any tree in the garden?'" This is the root of all heresies, when doubt is cast on God's Word and it is not trusted purely and properly. Then the devil lied, "You will surely not die." This was the first lie in the world, and it was the devil who spoke it. Thus Christ rightly called him a murderer and a liar from the beginning (John 8:44). Next, the devil said that God knew that, after having taken of the fruit of the tree, they would be like God, and that God was envious and would not begrudge them this. Lies, devil, lies! Third, the devil deceived our first parents with villainous, treacherous phrases, saying, "Your eyes shall be opened." This they took for a good thing, but the devil meant it for ill.[312] What a prankster! He further promised them great benefit and good: "You shall be like God"; for just as he himself is a proud donkey, he likewise stokes pride in others. Finally, he made the tree of sin seem goodly to Eve, just as he still dresses up sin today, clothing it with beautiful masks so that men think it something pleasant. But once it has been committed, the devil pulls off the shapely disguise, reveals the sin in its proper misshapenness, and makes every effort to bring men to despair.

Thus Eve was deceived and Adam seduced at the same time; and thus Adam and Eve fell under God's righteous wrath and forfeited His grace, and all that had been beautiful in them before was darkened, disfigured, and destroyed, so that our knowledge after the fall is now in part, piece-meal, patchwork, scraps, fumbling, and beggary. And God was justly and rightly angered; for God was not concerned about an apple, like that fellow once said: "I would give God a sackful of apples if only He would forget that single one," or like Julius III,[313] who once had a peacock on his platter at breakfast. Its taste pleased him, so he said to his cook, "Put this dish away until evening and serve it to me cold in the garden, for I am going to have some fine people here." But when the cook found out that the servants ate up the peacock without his permission, he had to prepare something new. That evening, then, when the holy father did not see the dish from breakfast,

---

312   Cf. Gen. 50:20.
313   Pope Julius III (1487–1555).

he asked where it was. The cook told him that the servants had gobbled it up, whereupon he cried out, "Bring me my peacock, in despite of God!"[314] (How terrifying to hear!) Then the cardinal said, "Come, your Holiness, do not be so angry." Julius answered, "What? Should I who am God's vicar not be angry on account of a peacock, when God was so enraged on account of an apple eaten in Paradise? For surely a peacock is worth more than an apple."[315] Oh God, what foolishness! In God's eyes, it had nothing to do with an apple, but obedience. It had to do with the fact that God's narrow, strict will was scandalously cast to the wind to the delight of the devil. Consider yet how great Adam and Eve's sin was: God exalted them with great honor over all creation, yet they were not content with this; they would not be satisfied with their situation, but wished to seize the crown from God and be like Him. They despised God's clear commandment and heeded the devil's advice. They put the devil in God's place. They followed the devil; they abandoned God. God cannot deceive, yet they doubted His true words, and thus made God out to be a liar. They refused to trust in God alone any longer. They were impertinent, concerning themselves with unhatched eggs, and that which they were commanded they forgot. They became murderers of their souls and bodies, and of those of all their children and descendants. God had not failed to give them anything. They had the whole world and all Paradise full of gorgeous fruit, yet what shameless ingratitude they showed their Lord and Benefactor! After they committed their sin, they were still just as self-assured as if they had never rippled the waters. They did not even shed a tear. They sewed skirts of fig-leaves together, hoping to cover their shame—as if they could sell God a foxtail.[316] He was not supposed to see their shame. They thought that they could pull the wool over God's eyes and trick Him. When God summoned them to the judge's bench, and their own consciences terrified them, they shamelessly tried to excuse themselves. Adam blamed his wife, in fact, God Himself, for he said, "The woman whom You gave to be with me, she

---

314   "Al dispetto di Dio!"

315   Cf. Foxe's Book of Martyrs, book 11; and the Legend of Tyl Ulenspiegel, ch. 11;

316   I.e., attempt to sell something which may be gotten freely.

gave me of the tree." Eve blamed the serpent: "St. Nobody[317] did it." So if God had not created Adam, Eve, or the serpent, He would not have had any grievances against Adam or Eve. But how could God not be greatly angered by such shame, iniquity, arrogance, crudeness, impudence, and rebellion? Did they not owe God service and obedience on pain of death and forfeiture of all that they had?

Thus Adam, Eve, and all their descendants were lost. They had to flee from God forever, hide away, and never enter His presence with joy again. They had a restless conscience, and were forced to look with unveiled eyes upon their shame and uncleanness at every moment, saying, "I am afraid." This was the first lamentation in the world, and it came from their sinful condition. If man had not fallen into sin, he would never have had anything for which to be sorry, but everything would have proceeded according to his heart's desire and joy. Oh, how often we poor men must now say with Eve, "The serpent deceived me." So here you have the missing coin, the lost sheep, and the prodigal son that the Lord Jesus talked about (Luke 15:4[–32]).

The Lord Jesus, then, took up the cause of poor, prodigal man, pleading for his life before His Father and offering to suffer death Himself, which is why He is called "Counselor" (Is. 9:6), for He devised the counsel for our salvation. St. Bernard delights in this, saying,

> When man fell, two Virtues of God came before God's court: Righteousness and Mercy. Righteousness said, "O strict, zealous, angry, righteous God, You said, 'Touch not this fruit, lest you die; for in the day you eat of it, you shall die your death.' Your unchangeable will has now been trespassed; therefore let man die the death which Your righteousness demands. Since You, O Eternal God, have been spurned, the penalty must also be eternal. You are an unchangeable God, so it must always be according to Your solemn will. Pour out Your wrath upon this wicked, neglectful people." But Mercy sighed and lamented, and said, "Oh God, in the midst of Your wrath, remember Your boundless mercy. You are not only a righteous God, but also a gracious God, full of goodness and mercy. Have mercy, Lord, and do not let Your noble creation perish so miserably!" Then the Lord Jesus rendered the verdict: "A righteous one must die for the

---

317 Germ. *Sankt Niemand,* a fictional scapegoat; cf. "St. Nemo."

unrighteous people; then mercy will abound and righteousness not be a vain thing." Then the two Virtues went out and sought a righteous one who might bring this to fruition. They approached the holy angels: "Are you righteous?" They said, "Oh, no! We cannot stand before God's strict judgment." They went on: "O Sun and Moon, O dear Stars, are you righteous? O Trees and Flowers, are you righteous?" No one in the whole world could be found who was righteous. They returned in sorrow and said, "Dearest Lord Jesus, since You have given the counsel, may You also accomplish the deed,[318] for You alone are righteous." Then our Lord Jesus consented to help man through His own death.[319]

Thus the righteousness of God was appeased. For our Lord Jesus bore the rightful penalty. Nor was mercy withheld at all, for wretched man was delivered of his misery.

Here the Lord Jesus made a clear announcement of His gracious intent to poor Adam and sorrowful Eve, and thus became the first, best, and most lovely Preacher of evangelical comfort. The Lord Jesus Himself even spoke in this fashion in Isaiah 61:1–2: "The LORD has sent Me to preach to the poor, to bind up the brokenhearted, to proclaim liberty to the captives, and to those who are bound, that it may be opened to them; to proclaim a gracious year of the LORD, and a day the vengeance of our God; to comfort all who mourn," etc. In Luke 4:18, the Lord Jesus plainly connects these words to Himself in His first sermon, delivered in His fatherland of Nazareth where He was brought up.

And of this comforting work, Christ says, "The only-begotten Son who is in the bosom of the Father, He has made Him known to us" (John 1:18). Jesus also says that He is "He who spoke to you from the beginning" (John 8:25), that is, "I am He who spoke comfortingly to the patriarchs from the beginning of the world, and made pledges to them in their grief." Just as our Lord Jesus was the speaker in the work of creation as discussed earlier, as found in the First Article of the Creed, He is also the speaker in the work of redemption here, as found in the Second Article of the Creed. Thus the Chaldean Bible says, "They heard the voice of the Word of God

318 "Qui dedit consilium, ferat auxilium."

319 Bern. *In Annunc. sermo* I.

our LORD."[320] So the whole world should listen to and love this preacher of comfort, as Moses says in Deuteronomy 18:15, and as God the Father Himself says in Matthew 17:5.

Oh my Lord Jesus, You are the first and most pleasant preacher of comfort, and You will remain the most beautiful, noblest counselor to all godly hearts until the end of the world. I pray You, graciously also fulfill Your office in me in my every need.

> I trust, O Christ, in You alone;
>   No earthly hope avails me.
> You will not see me overthrown
>   When Satan's host assails me.
>   No human strength, no earthly pow'r
>   Can see me through the evil hour,
>   For You alone my strength renew.
>   I cry to You!
> I trust, O Lord, Your promise true,[321] etc.

The whole hymn is relevant here.

Therefore, when all manner of empty comforts and human trifles are foisted upon you, simply reply: Jesus Christ is the best comfort in every trouble. He is the oldest source of consolation. I will stay with Him. It is good to keep what is old. The old God and the old comfort are always best. Others have no lasting power. The heart cannot be at peace apart from Christ's comfort. New bread, new calendars, new things each year—I count them but trifles. The old God and the old comfort are always best.

A certain Dr. Creutzenach celebrated many masses, fasted often, even built a house for repentant sinners where they could be fed without resorting to sin and disgrace on account of their poverty. When he was about to die, he reflected on one good work after the other, hoping to be comforted thereby, but it was no use. At last he said, "Well, if nothing else will help, this will: Have mercy upon me, O Lord God, for the sake of Your dearest Son Jesus Christ!" Then his heart found peace.

---

320 "Audiverunt vocem Verbi Domini Dei"

321 From the hymn "Allein zu Dir, Herr Jesu Christ" (attr. J. Schneesing, 1542), st. 1; tr. *LSB* 972.

A monk once tried to console an important lady with the intercession and gray robes of Mary and with the mass for dead souls, etc. As he departed, a fine, young fellow approached—a pedagogue and teacher of children, who later became a well-known preacher—and told her of Jesus Christ's sufferings, blood, death, and merit. Then the godly lady said, "This gives me strength and comfort. That other stuff would not penetrate my heart."

In the same way, Emperor Maximilian II (d. 12 Oct. 1576)[322] refused to let the bishop of Naples, Dr. Lambert Gruter,[323] depart from him during the throes of death. The bishop promised him to speak of nothing else but Christ's merit, anguished sweating of blood, and bitter death. The bishop spoke aptly, graciously, and comfortingly of the benefits of the Lord Jesus, and finally asked him if his imperial majesty wished to die in such faith and consolation, to which the pious emperor replied, "I desire nothing else."[324] And thus he departed serenely for eternal life.

O most dearly beloved Lord Jesus, experience shows that You are the best giver of consolation. Your benefits are the surest, most enduring, most stalwart comfort of all, able to strengthen me in every need. Oh, do not forsake me! You visited and comforted father Adam and mother Eve in their misery. I beg for Your comforts from the bottom of my heart. How will You despise me? If You were able to speak so comfortingly here without being asked, what will You do for my tear-filled prayer? Like Adam and Eve, I too have sinned. I too deserve Your wrath. Oh, ancient, comforting preacher of the Gospel, come in mercy! Absolve me of my sins! Console me with the news of Your benefits, so that I do not despair. Support me in Your consolations so that I may pray with boldness, live a Christlike life, and in the comfort that You give to the soul be saved. Amen, Lord Jesus! Amen.

---

322 Maximilian II von Habsburg (1527–1576), king of Bohemia, king of Hungary, emperor of the Holy Roman Empire from 1564.

323 Lambertus Gruterus (fl. 16th c.), imperial court minister.

324 "Non aliter faciam"

XXII. JESUS,

The Woman's Seed, Shall Trample the Serpent's Head: The First Gospel, Which Vividly and Clearly Describes Jesus Christ's Person, Work, and Merit (Gen. 3[:15]).

God passed judgment on and condemned the devil who had disguised himself as a snake. Adam and Eve, however, He absolved upon the intercession of Christ the Serpent-Trampler. He released them from the everlasting punishment which they merited with their sins, and by grace exchanged it for a temporal and bearable punishment. Once again, the words spoken here are Jesus Christ's, so let us all listen devoutly and carefully consider what He reveals about His person, work, and merit.

Hitherto we have considered the Lord Jesus in many beautiful mysteries, images, and figures of speech. Now we find Him expressly named in clear, vivid terms known by everyone. Hence the Jerusalemite and Onkeli Targums also clearly understood these words to concern the Messiah.

Night has departed, day has come. Up till now, we only had starlight, which is, to be sure, lovely and comforting as well. But now the bright sun is shining, and now we find the Lord Jesus in the bright light of noon-day in His own words as He says to the serpent, "And I will put enmity between you and the woman, and between your seed and her seed; He shall trample your head, and you shall prick His heel."

Here Jesus gives bright and clear proof that He would have a constant conflict with the evil one and oppose him, and would engage him in a valiant battle, in a manly fight, mightily claim the victory, overthrow the devil and all his minions, and hold the field victorious. Yet it would cost Him much blood. Because of it, He would have to suffer death, but He would break free and restore all that had been ruined by sin nevertheless. Jesus did not say of Eve or of Mary that one of them would trample the serpent's head. Rather, He assigned this great work to the woman's Seed, the Messiah, as is clearly seen in the Hebrew as well as the German. In fact, the word *Hu* ("He") requires it to be a male person, not a female, to resolve any conflict. Thus our Lord Jesus also holds this name *Hu* among the honorific titles with which He styles Himself, as readily apparent in the Hebrew text of Isaiah 41:4, 42:8, and 43:10. The same is seen in Psalm 24:7–10:

> Open wide the gates, and lift up the doors of the world, that the King of glory may come in! Who is this (*Hu*) King of glory? It is the LORD, strong and mighty, the LORD, mighty in battle. Open wide the gates, and lift up the doors of the world, that the King of glory may come in! Who is this (*Hu*) King of glory? It is the LORD of Sabaoth; He is the King of glory.

This is clearly to be understood as Jesus Christ, the most mighty *Michael* ("He who is like God"), who fought valiantly against the dragon and got glory for Himself upon the foe of our salvation. O my most beloved Lord Jesus, indeed You are He who has delivered us from the power of the devil, death, and hell. For this may You alone be praised. May we give glory to no one else but You.

The Lord Jesus went on to describe His person, work, and merit in a pleasant, suitable, brief, and comforting manner, calling Himself the woman's Seed. For He would become a physical man, possessing every human attribute, yet pure and sinless. Unlike other men, He would be

> Begotten not of human seed,
> But by the Spirit's mystic deed[325]

That is, by Holy Spirit's power, working, and overshadowing of a Virgin, without any spot or uncleanness, for

> Such birth befits the God of all.[326]

Mary was a betrothed Virgin, and so was called a "wife,"[327] since betrothal is part of marriage in God's eyes.

---

325 "[non] ex virili semine, / sed mystico spiramine"; from Ambrose's hymn, "Veni Redemptor gentium," st. 2, lines 1–2.

326 "Talis decet partus Deum"; ibid., st. 1, line 4.

327 Germ. *Weib*.

Adam was created from virgin earth, that is, from soil that had not yet been tarnished by innocent blood. With outstretched hands upon the tree he took the exquisite fruit and committed sin. Likewise, the Messiah was a Virgin's Son. With outstretched hands upon the tree of the cross he tasted the bitter draught of vinegar and gall and atoned and paid for Adam's guilt, says St. Andrew the apostle.[328]

It was quite fitting for Him who would make atonement for sins to be born of a woman. For it was by a woman, seduced by the devil, that sin and every ill were first brought into the world. Moreover, St. Paul alludes to this when he writes to the Galatians: "But when the time was fulfilled, God sent his Son, born of a woman," etc. (Gal. 4:4).

Furthermore, this woman's Seed was to trample the serpent's head, that is, to take away all its power, dominion, and claim, for the serpent's life is located in its head. If that remain whole, no other misfortune can harm it. The Lord Jesus was not merely to subdue a piece of the devil's kingdom, but to crush it so wholly and completely that the devil could have no power over the hearts of those who believe in Christ. Thus John says, "For this reason the Son of God appeared, that He might destroy the works of the devil" (1 John 3:8). No mere man could have performed this great work. He had to be true God. He had to be stronger than the evil foe and all the gates of hell. He had to have divine omnipotence and a claim to heaven. Therefore the Lord Jesus is the true almighty God.

Finally, the Lord Jesus also clearly foretells His bloody suffering and death: the serpent would prick His heel. It would cost him His own blood to help us. Therefore our Lord Jesus presently told Eve, "Dear Eve, it will give you great pain to bear children, but My pains will be a thousand times greater when I give you and your children new birth unto heaven, that you may all become newborn infants of God"; and to Adam, "Dear Adam, you will experience much grief and heartache, but the grief for which I am bound in order to assuage your grief will be inexpressibly deeper and greater. You will be forced to sweat and labor, but as for Me, I will be made to sweat the bloody sweat of anguish; For 'you have made work for Me with your sins, and you have made toil for Me with your iniq-

---

328 From *The Golden Legend*; see Ryan I 17.

uities' [Is. 43:24]. The field shall bring forth thorns and thistles for you, but My heart shall have to bear the stinging thistles of God's wrath. My head shall have to bear the heavy crown of piercing thorns so that I may deliver you from the curse which has been put upon your body and soul, and win for all believers the crown of righteousness. I shall offer Myself up to death that I may take Your death away; yet I will not remain in the tomb, but I will survive, subdue, and subjugate all our enemies. And finally on the Last Day I will come and crush the serpent's head, cast all our foes into hell's abyss, take you from your tomb, and restore you to a perfect estate, and honor you even more highly than you were honored before the fall." By this Adam and Eve were consoled and uplifted.

Adam preached this Gospel until his death. All the writings of the Prophets are simply postils on this text, and the object of their contemplations is the power concealed in these words. That is why St. Peter says that to this Lord Jesus "all the prophets bear witness that everyone who believes in Him receives forgiveness of sins through His name" (Acts 10:43). How Adam must have preached! "Dear sons, dear daughters, we should have perished eternally for our sins when the serpent deceived us. But for the sake of the woman's Seed, the promised Messiah, we will be saved from all sin and adversity.[329] In Paradise I heard the pledge; in it I take comfort, and in such comfort I will live and die. This is my confession of the Messiah: He is true God and true man; He is mightier than the devil. By His bloody death He will restore everything that was corrupted by my sin and the devil's deceit. Let this be my last will and testament. I bequeath to you the true faith in Jesus Christ, the promised Serpent-Trampler, Sin-Atoner, and Redeemer, that by Him you may all be saved."

When he prayed, Adam said, "Oh heavenly Father, be gracious to me, forgive me my sins, receive my cry, and help me for the sake of the promised woman's Seed who will give up His blood for me and trample the serpent's head."

When Eve lay in the pains of childbirth, she said, "I deserve these pains because of my sins, but I will bear them patiently. O Lord, Heavenly Father, guard me from eternal torment for the sake of the promised

---

329 "Serpens decepit, sed Semen mulieris salvabit nos"

Serpent-Trampler. He will endure far greater pains for my sins than I experience in my childbirth."

Likewise, in the midst of his grief, toil, and the sweat of his face, Adam never once grew unmindful of the Lord Jesus, the Savior of the world, but said, "Oh what misery and sorrow come from sin! But courage! All will be well. By His grief, by His bitter toil, by the sweat of His anguish, the promised Messiah will take this all away and bring me with all my faithful children into the estate in which I lived before the fall."

This is the ancient, Christian, catholic faith which has been confessed by all God's blessed children since the beginning of the world. By this right knowledge and confession of the woman's Seed, Jesus Christ, they were all saved. Thus the apostles manifestly declared at the First Council, "We believe that we will be saved through the grace of the Lord Jesus Christ, just as they," our fathers in the Old Testament (Acts 15:11).

Thus in 1528, when Luther was commenting on these words, He said it very well: "Time has no bearing on the faith. The faith is one from the beginning of the world to the end." Oh Lord Jesus, thank You for conveying and bringing me also to the true, ancient, catholic, Christian faith. Help me to persevere steadfast in it, to sacrifice health and wealth for it, and through it to be saved forever.

This knowledge of Jesus Christ's person, work and merit is the only sure foundation on which the Church and the communion of God's children is built, for "there is salvation in no one else, for there is no other name given among men whereby we shall be saved" (Acts 4:12); and "No other foundation can any man lay than that which is laid, which is Jesus Christ" (1 Cor. 3:11).

Therefore, wherever Christ's person, work, and merit are not rightly taught, and wherever Jesus is not publicly confessed to be both God and man and our only Salvation, do not to look to find the Christian Church or the children of God.

O Lord Jesus Christ, I also thank You from the bottom of my heart for causing me to become a member of the true evangelical Church which is firmly and solidly rooted in the ancient and First Gospel[330] which You

---

330 See Iren. *Adv. Haeres.* 23.7.

Yourself preached in Paradise. I know that the gates of hell shall not prevail against us [Matt. 16:18], since we put our heart and trust in You.

O Lord Jesus Christ, I acknowledge and confess that You were made true man; in fact, I count this my greatest glory and advantage above all the angels and other created things. You are a Virgin's pure Son, conceived without sin by the Holy Spirit (for whoever is to cleanse others cannot himself be stained). You are far stronger than the evil one. You can and will trample the serpent's head and the seat of his power. You are almighty and invincible; for You are not merely man but also true God. This is my consolation, yea, my highest defense against all my foes. From the cross You extended Your unbroken legs down to the earth, even to hell, to announce that there on the cross is where You were exalted; that You, by Your bloody death, trampled the head of the serpent, blotted out the sins which I committed on earth, crushed the tyranny of hell, and regained for me the lost state of innocence, God's grace, and eternal salvation. You are the Man whom Adam and Eve were told of in Paradise. You have a man's bold and fearless heart against all Your foes. You let Your heel be pricked, that is, You gave up Your precious blood to save us. Oh, how frightful, huge, abhorrent, and unbearable the load of my sins must be, since there was no other way to atone for them! Dear Lord Jesus, I promise You in turn that for Your glory I will even shed my blood. I desire it; grant me also to carry it out [Rom. 7:18].

In Freiberg, a man was once subjected to a severe spiritual attack. The devil came to him in the form of a great, powerful prelate carrying a long scroll of paper, a pen, ink, and a writing-case, and said, "Just wait! I must make a record of your sins. How do you possibly think to stand before God?" The ailing, afflicted man was horrified, but he recollected himself and said, "All right, if it must be written, then write away! But at the top of it, write: THE WOMAN'S SEED SHALL CRUSH THE SERPENT'S HEAD."[331] When the devil heard this, he vanished, leaving behind an awful stench; for he was prevented from taking revenge.[332] May every pious, Christ-believing heart do like this man. If you should become fearful as you

331 "Semen mulieris conteret caput serpentis"

332 This story is also referred to in part 1, meditation 1.

examine your sins, then with bold faith take hold of this beautiful Gospel where Adam and Eve and all pious hearts are absolved of their sins and are pointed to the Serpent-Trampler and Sin-Atoner, Jesus Christ. Then all fear will vanish.

Oh God, Holy Spirit, it is Your particular office to glorify Jesus Christ in our heart. Oh, glorify in my heart the great Friend of my salvation, Jesus Christ, by the remembrance of this comforting Gospel, that I may never despair of sin, but like Adam and Eve rejoice in the merit of Jesus Christ, and in such blessed joy pray with confidence, bear my cross patiently, overcome every spiritual attack and death itself, and inherit the crown of glory prepared for all who by faith lay hold of the Serpent-Trampler. Amen!

In addition, dear heart, notice how the Lord Jesus prophesies concerning the prosperity and bloody estate of His Church. The serpent would prick His heel, that is, the devil would vex the Messiah's limbs—taunt, plague, and afflict pious Christians. This was soon experienced by the pious Abel. He too confessed the Lord Jesus; it immediately cost him life and limb. So shall it be until the end of the world.

> "On blood the Holy Church is founded,
> From blood its form did first ascend;
> With blood its path is all surrounded,
> Through blood it shall attain its end." [333]

Oh my Lord Jesus, how the evil one pricks and stings all about with his heresy and tyranny! There is no more afflicted creature in the world than a pious Christian who wants to serve You faithfully and uprightly! Oh, grant us the long-suffering and perseverance through bloodshed, distress, and death to remain true to You to the end, and not only to confess You with words but also, if need arise, with life and limb, with all our health and wealth, that You might also confess us before Your heavenly Father. Thus may we, like Your angels and hosts, overcome the ancient dragon by Your blood and by the word of our testimony; and love not

---

[333] "Sanguine fundata est ecclesia, sanguine crevit, / Sanguine succrevit, sanguine finis erit"; a saying of Erasmus (corr. "crevit" for "capit").

our lives even unto death, as it says in Revelation 12:11. Finally, grant that we may lift our heads with joy when You come on the Last Day to stamp out the devil's kingdom completely and with a final "crush"[334] destroy the serpent's head, that together with You we may all enter into joy everlasting. Amen!

334 "Conteret," lit., "he shall crush," from Gen. 3:15.

XXIII. JESUS
Restores Everything That Adam and Eve Ruined in the Fall
(Gen. 3:15; Luke 1:31–32).

Now let me briefly compare the account of how the angel Gabriel brought the message to Mary that she would be the mother of our Lord Jesus Christ (Luke 1:31–32) with the present account of the fall of Adam and Eve; for all the circumstances of that event clearly indicate, signify, and prove that everything that Adam and Eve lost here has been repaired and restored by Jesus Christ.

Here, Adam and Eve were immediately seduced by the evil one at the beginning of the first year[335] of the first world. And right at the sixth day of the first week, about eventide, the Lord Jesus came and promised them that He would save them from the power of the devil. Likewise, the conception of Jesus Christ, who was to bring salvation from Adam's fall, was announced on the twenty-fifth of March (as the ancient doctors of the Church believe), the very dawn of the spring-time of the New Testament, six months after John the Baptist was conceived. And thus it was about eventide on the same day on which Adam had fallen 3,969 years earlier that Mary heard the news that she would be the mother of the Messiah.[336] For everything that had been ruined in Paradise was to be restored by the Lord Jesus.

Before the fall, man was God's most beloved creature. The image of God shone and radiated within him. In other words, man's mind knew God, his heart loved God, and his will served God. In his mind there was bright light, in his heart joyful faith, and in his will beautiful obedience. His mind knew what it ought to know about God, his heart trusted God and burned with heartfelt love for God, and his will honored God. In his

335 As formerly reckoned, on March 25 (clarified below).
336 See Victorinus, fragm. *De fabrica mundi.*

mind there was wisdom, in his heart righteousness, and in his will a swift readiness to do every good. In such a state, moreover, man was meant to flourish and live forever. But when he sinned everything was turned upside down. God, for His part, was angry and hostile toward mankind and raged against him. Man, on the other hand, had lost all of his beauty. The image of God was obscured in him. Man's mind no longer knew God, nor did his heart believe anything, nor his will do anything that pleased God. His mind was filled with thick darkness, his heart with a fearful lack of faith, and his will with sin and disgrace. His mind did not know God, his heart did not trust Him, and his will did not honor and serve Him. Lastly, man was required to "die his death," that is, to feel the anguish of death forever but never be rid of it—to perish, yet never disappear. Accordingly, the Lord Jesus Christ made sure to announce His conception in the same season, on the same day, and even at the same hour when Adam and Eve had fallen so that all the world would know that He would correct everything.

O Lord Jesus Christ, thank You! Because of You, everything that had been ruined by Adam's fall is now rectified, restored, and made worthy again. When by grace You took up our cause, Your heavenly Father became affectionate, gracious, and kind to us again. The image of God in us was renewed and scrubbed clean. Now our mind knows the faithful, fatherly heart of God in heaven, our heart rejoices in Him, and our will urges our whole body to thank God for it. Our mind is filled with bright light, our heart is filled with beautiful faith, and our will is adorned with many good works. In short, we have been made brand new men by Your Holy Gospel and the cooperating power of the Holy Spirit. Just as the wind makes itself heard and felt, so the Holy Wind of Pentecost rushes and sweeps the Gospel into our ears and whispers of Your merit. At the same time, He uses His comforting breezes to make us feel and know that this is the very truth of heaven, and works mightily to make us grasp it with our mind, lock it in our heart, and gladly be content with such consolation. Thus we are renewed, changed, and reborn, and thus the image of God is reestablished in us, and in this new adornment we are blessed and live forever.

Here when Adam and Eve sinned a wicked angel came of his own audacity, desire, and wantonness, and tricked Eve. There, however, a holy angel came sent by God and delighted Mary. For everything that started wrong and went astray here was begun in a right and proper manner, proceeded successfully, and concluded masterfully in what Christ did. The angel Gabriel, who bears the name of God's might,[337] was designated to serve as legate in this errand because Mary was bringing into the world that Lord whom Isaiah calls "Mighty" (Is. 9:6). He redeems us mightily from the dominion of the evil one, and works mighty wonders for us in every need. An angel was designated to bring this announcement to Mary, for the angel with a "drawn and brandished sword" (Gen. 3:24) does not forbid our entry to Paradise any longer. Paradise—heaven, and the heart of God—stand open to us. Angels have become our good friends and glad companions once again—indeed, they have been appointed as our bodyguards, for Jesus Christ has brought us into His family. What an honor this is!

Here, the evil spirit came to the children of God in the midst of Paradise, where everything budded and bloomed, and where the tree of life stood, which was to intended to sustain man's health forever. There, by contrast, a good Spirit came to the land of the Jews, where the people of God dwelt, where Paradise had stood long before, in the vicinity of Nazareth, which means "green branch." For the true green tree of life that gives us everlasting health and life was planted in the midst of Paradise, that is, under the chaste heart of the virtuous Virgin Mary, as our dear forefathers used to say. The true heavenly Flower of Paradise from the withered root of Jesse began to flourish. Our High Priest Jesus was conceived, as indicated by the priestly rod of Aaron which budded and blossomed [Num. 17:8]. O Lord Jesus, I will plant You, the true Tree of Life, in the midst of my heart's garden, that You may blossom and live in me and I in You forever.

Here the name of Eve, the first sinner, is mentioned by Moses as proof that her name and the names of all her children were condemned to be written in the Book of the Dead, God's blacklist. There, on the other hand, the name of Mary, who would carry the Sin-Atoner under her heart, is mentioned as proof that our names are blotted out of the Book of the

---

337 Or, "bears the name 'God's Might.'"

Dead and written with Christ's blood by God's own hand in the Book of Life, yea, in the very heart of God in heaven.

Here the devil first deceived a woman. There, however, a woman was the first to be gladdened by the news of the Messiah. For everything that had been ruined by the first woman's sin was repaired by the Lord born of Mary. Womankind, moreover, which had been cast into dishonor by the devil, was conversely exalted to full honor in the person of Mary.

Eve, the first sinner, was still a virgin. She was hardly a few hours old, and was in the flower of her youth. Likewise, the Mother of the Lord Jesus also had to be a virgin. She was a tender maid of fourteen years, as Isaiah provides with the word *almah* [Is. 7:14]. For by the Lord Jesus, born pure of a Virgin, we receive pure, virgin hearts. This is how faithful Christians are described in Revelation 14:4: "They are virgins and follow the Lamb." Oh my Lord Jesus, give me a chaste, virtuous, virgin heart. Adorn me with Christian modesty. Grace me with moral virtue. Grant me to wear the virgin's wreath of my Christian name honorably, shunning the make-up of all hypocrisy in my divine service, that I may always take care of this name, since it is Yours. Help me to keep my mouth veiled and silent as I bear my cross, nor to grumble impatiently at You, but to look to You, my Bridegroom, in every need. Lastly, grant me to sing Your hymns in heaven with the soft, clear voice of a virgin.

Eve was a new bride, having been pledged to the world's first builder, for Adam was supposed to build up Paradise. Mary was a bride, too, having been betrothed to a skillful craftsman, Joseph, for she was to bring into the world the Craftsman of heaven and earth, of which we have already said a great deal. O Lord Jesus, You have built for us many mansions in heaven. Help us to have the joy of occupying them.

In Paradise the devil spoke first, but gave no greeting, for his heart was treacherous, cunning, stealthy, and wicked. With Mary, the angel, too, spoke first, but he greeted her amiably and kindly because his heart was good. For the sake of our Lord Jesus Christ, an angel's heart was good toward Mary, and is good toward all believers. But Jesus Christ's own heart is far better. "Greetings come from the court," [as they say].[338] O Lord

---

338 I.e., the commoner does not speak to the nobleman unless spoken to first.

Jesus, You go further and propose Your love to us. You treat us as kindly as if You were our equal. You will also greet us and address us like a friend in our every need. Mary was not meant to be the only one called "full of grace." Rather, every one of us who believes in You is full of Your grace, love, faithfulness, and favor, too.

Here the devil had God on his lips but gall in his heart. In God's name all calamity was born. But there the angel had God on his lips and in his heart. In God's name our eternal prosperity was born.

Here the devil made Eve doubt God's Word. But there the angel made Mary certain of God's opinion of her heart, saying, "The Lord is with you." For now that Jesus has become our Immanuel, God wants to be in us and with us, and us to dwell in Him and with Him forever. Thus we may boldly proclaim with Isaiah 8:9–10, "Be wicked, O nations, and take flight! Give ear, all you of far countries; arm yourselves and take flight. Take counsel together, and it will come to nothing; speak a word and it will not stand, for here is Immanuel."

Here Eve had no fear. She did not once reflect on how much danger she was in. But there Mary was dismayed and contemplated what it could all mean. For now that the Lord Jesus has become our Brother, we are brought to a blessed knowledge of ourselves and our salvation. We are dismayed by our sins and God's wrath, and yet do not lose hope in such anxiety, but rather look to the mercy of God secured by Christ.

Here Adam said, "I heard Your voice in the garden and was afraid." But there Mary heard a different voice: "Do not be afraid, Mary" [Luke 1:30].[339] For by the merit of our Lord Jesus all the fear of our wicked conscience is quelled. In short, we know and feel in our heart that we have found grace with God.

Here Eve stood in awe of false glory, for she thought she would be like God: "And she saw that the tree was good for eating, and pleasant to behold, and that it was a desirable tree." But there Mary stood in awe of God's grace: "'What manner of greeting is this?' This is too much for me." There was arrogance in Eve, but humility in Mary. For the Lord Jesus

---

339 The rest of the quotations from Luke will not be explicitly referenced here, but follow in order hereafter.

won so much for us that we ought to stand in awe forever, saying: Jesus was conceived for our comfort; what manner of treasure is this? He was born for our good; what manner of grace is this? He suffered in our stead; what manner of salvation is this? In this way we should go through all the benefits of Jesus Christ and stand in awe of them, here in time and there in eternity.

Here the devil spewed lies so thick that they could have been cut with a knife. He said, "You will surely not die your death." "O you knave, where is your 'surely not?' Behold, we all die,"[340] says St. Bernard. But there, the angel spoke nothing but truth: "You will conceive in Your womb"; this was so. "You will...bear a son"; this came true. "You shall call His name Jesus"; this was fulfilled. For by the Lord Jesus we have been freed from the thrall of that liar the devil and placed into eternal truth.

The devil did not approach Eve in his true form but dressed and disguised as a serpent, for he is a beguiler and deceiver in all his doings. The angel, however, came to Mary without duplicity in the form of a fair youth, not from a deceptive heart, but to the honor of mankind which had been so highly dignified in the person of Christ. Furthermore, the angel said that the Son of God would not reveal Himself in His divine light but take on our flesh and blood. Yet He would not merely disguise Himself in the form of man but *become* true man for our eternal honor and consolation, that we might fully know, perceive, and understand that He came not to deceive us but to deal honestly and openly with us.

The devil made Eve imagine that she would be like God and become wise, yet there was no substance to this claim. It was a villain's invention. The angel, however, depicted the great glory of the Lord Jesus Christ to Mary, saying, "He will be great"—in respect to His person, His work, His merit, and His gifts. Then he said that Jesus would "be called (and be) the Son of the Most High." The fact that we have such an invincible Protector and Lord is our greatest bastion. Finally he said that Jesus would be a king. Through the Gospel He would establish His kingdom in Jerusalem and reign forever, accomplishing the salvation of all believers. This is

---

340 "O Nequam, Nequam, ubi est tuum Nequaquam? Ecce omnes morimur"; Bern. *In nat. Dom. sermo* 2.3.

no waterless mirage; these are no vain or empty words but clear, certain, spotless, and rock-solid comfort. No pious heart should let himself be cast into doubt about this.

Eve's mind was filled with the deceptive thoughts of sin. Mary's mind was filled with the holy thoughts of God's works. She said, "How will this be?" In the same way, our joy is no longer found in sinning but in meditating on the treasures of God's grace.

Eve was shamefully deceived, but Mary was given the whole story. For the angel said, "'The Holy Spirit will come upon on you,' make you into God's temple, and set apart and consecrate a droplet of your blood within you. You will conceive a child by the overshadowing and power of God's Spirit. You will give birth to the fountain of all holiness, the eternal Son of God. Believe firmly, 'for with God nothing is impossible.' And let this be your sign: You will find your cousin Elizabeth already six months with child, in her old age, contrary to the laws of nature." Thus we have a clear account of our salvation from henceforth: first, by the clear, intelligible words of God's grace; and second, by the sure, unambiguous signs of His grace, so that our heart never need doubt God's mercy.

Eve agreed to sin and angered God. Mary, however, agreed to God's plan and served Him. With humble submissiveness she said, "Let it be to me according to Your word." For now that the Lord Jesus has come to our aid, we have received the Holy Spirit, who inclines our heart and works in us the desire to obey God's will with readiness and speed.

When Eve consented to sin, nothing but grief and calamity ensued: Adam was also led astray. God was angered. Adam and Eve were both summoned and interrogated. They fled from God. They were afraid. They hid themselves. They were cast out of the garden. Abel was murdered. Cain did no good. Everyone grew sick, withered, and died. Corpse followed corpse. The ground was cursed. Men found sorrow and misery wherever they turned. At last the world was drowned in the flood. By contrast, when Mary consented to God's plan, nothing but joy and bliss ensued: New tidings began to spread. Pious hearts were filled with joy. Elizabeth heard Mary's greeting and became a prophetess. John leapt for joy under his mother's heart. Mary sang. Zechariah chanted his Benedictus. Christ was born. The angels proclaimed and sang about it. The Wise

Men from the east came looking for Him. Simeon and Hannah spread the news abroad, etc. For by the Lord Jesus, conceived by the Holy Spirit and born of the Virgin Mary, all that was corrupted by Adam and Eve's sin was corrected. All the details of these accounts testify to this.

Thus it is true when the psalmist says, "Great are the works of the LORD: whoever studies them finds pure pleasure in them" [Ps. 111:2].

O Lord Jesus Christ, thank You for this good work. Oh, look at my heart, my mind, and my whole life; restore all that is corrupted by sin, and make it well pleasing to You. Amen.

XXIV. JESUS

Clothes Adam, Eve, and All Repentant Hearts with the Garments of His Righteousness and the Lambskins of His Innocence (Gen. 3:21).

At the close of chapter 3, Moses informs us of three things. First, Adam named His wife *Eve*, that is, "mother of life," the grandmother of all mankind. At the same time Adam here hoped in his spirit that the Captain of Life, Jesus Christ, who was to restore the life lost by sin, would be born to Eve or one of her daughters. You furthermore see here that Adam had in his heart the same words that St. Paul spoke: "Christ is my life, death is my gain" (Phil. 1[:21]). Oh Lord Jesus, You are the Fountain of life. You are the Way, the Truth, and the Life. You are the Resurrection and the Life. I will carry You in my heart as Adam did when he named his Eve the "mother of life." I will cling to You with true faith in my hour of death, that through You I may obtain eternal life.

Second, Moses tells us that God clothed Adam and Eve with skins of animals as a certain sign of His friendship and love. Earlier, God had filled the ears of these two grief-stricken souls with a comforting word of grace. Now He filled their eyes with a visible token of grace so that their hearts would overflow with comfort. What God had said before with clear words in the First Gospel He repeated here with a beautiful picture, as if to say, "A Virgin's Son will save you from sin and calamity by His blood. Do you want to know how this will come about? Behold, I will show you. Your Savior will be slaughtered just like this sheep, and you will be clothed with His merit. By His innocence your sins will be covered."

Therefore the garments and hides of lambskin were Adam and Eve's Sacrament, their visible word,[341] by which their hearts were assured of God's grace promised in Christ Jesus.

---

341 "verbum visibile"

Third, we learn that Adam and Eve were cast out of Paradise, proving that they merited expulsion and rejection with their sins. The Lord Jesus redeemed us from such hardship and misery by His flight into Egypt, His exile in the desert. He obtained for us the joyous entrance into eternal life by His being led out from Jerusalem, that we might have access to the tree of life and not be driven back from heaven's path by any sword. Indeed, "there is...nothing condemnable in those who believe in Christ Jesus" [Rom. 8:1].

Also notice a mystery of the most blessed Trinity, for the conversation of the persons in the council of the most blessed Trinity is reported in the words, "*Jehovah Elohim* said, 'Behold, Adam is become as one of Us.'" Adam did not become like God, as the serpent's lips had lisped. Rather, God spoke as a father to his son when his wrath has somewhat relented, "Alas, how close you were! You wanted to become as one of Us. Alas, how close you came! Now back to school with you, Ink-pot, and learn the answer that you sought!"

At this point, let us consider the clearest, brightest, and loveliest part of our Lord Jesus: how He and His benefits are fittingly and fully portrayed and propounded to us in Adam and Eve' animal-skin coats.

Our Lord Jesus was also involved in the clothing of Adam and Eve, for Moses says, "And the Lord God (*Jehovah Elohim*) fashioned coats for Adam and his wife"; that is, the God who is one in substance but revealed in three persons (namely, Father, Son, and Holy Spirit) skillfully covered and clothed the first parents with the skins of a lamb.

Oh my gracious Lord Jesus, here I see what a constant Friend to man You are; indeed, what faithful love and friendship You have for all repentant hearts. As soon as Adam and Eve, at Your prompting, confessed, regretted, and mourned their sin, as soon as their hearts repented and longed for Your grace and took comfort in Your Gospel, You received them into Your care again. Not only did their hearts find perfect consolation, but their bodies were also equipped for the many hardships which they would face after the fall, and in this needful gift of clothing given proper provision.

Dear Lord Jesus, deep in my heart I will plant this consolation, that You still have the same attitude today toward all humble and afflicted hearts that are sorry for their sins and take refuge in You.

Dear Lord Jesus, God honor the trade![342] You were the first butcher: You slew a lamb. You were the first tanner: You worked the skins with the skill of a master craftsman who has in his hands all that is needed to make a fine garment. When You clothed Adam and Eve, You did not regard showiness, pride, or frivolity, but respectability, suitability, richness, and usefulness. All God-fearing people today would do well to consider these. This clothing reminded Adam and Eve of their sins every day and acted as a salutary repentance-sermon for them. Every morning as they put on their clothes, they talked about their situation thus: "Oh God, what miserable souls we have become! Not only are we forced to walk in shame before all creatures but even before ourselves. Our own bodies are shameful to us. Before, every part of us was beautiful, graceful, and lovely. In those days there was no fear, no weakness in us. We were never ashamed. Oh, what miserable souls we have become since we first committed sin. Oh, forgive us our sins and take away our shame and disgrace, for the sake of the promised Virgin's Son!"

We should think such thoughts as these every morning: Dear God, my clothes are "visible signs"[343] that I am a sinner and cannot stand before God. Oh, help me not to boast in or show off my clothing, but let them remind me of my tragic estate. Help me to be constantly clothed in a concern for the salvation of my body and soul. Whoever worships clothing is like the thief who tried to boast of the noose around his neck which he had to wear as a reminder that his life had been given to him freely by grace. Thus St. Benedict says, "It is like a villain who struts about with his forehead branded because of his crimes."

Besides this, the skin garments that God fashioned for the first parents were a beautiful reminder of the means by which the injury of their souls would eventually be healed. The Messiah would let Himself be slaughtered and killed like a lamb, and by this bloody sacrifice on the cross the sins of mankind would be covered and forgiven. This is the jewelry and adornment of all faithful hearts.

---

342 The traditional greeting between members of a guild.

343 "signa reatûs"

Thus the Chaldean text calls these garments "clothes of glory and splendor."[344] Concerning these garments of Jesus Christ's imputed righteousness and innocence, Isaiah 61:10 plainly states, "I rejoice in the LORD, and my soul is joyful in my God; for He has put garments of salvation on me, and clothed me in the robe of righteousness, like a bridegroom decked with priestly ornaments, and like a bride that is adorned in her jewels." This is the true wedding garment which our Lord Jesus Himself requires of the heavenly wedding guests (Matt. 22:12). Whoever is not clothed with the lambskins of Jesus Christ's innocence will be gagged and bound hand and foot on the Last Day and thrown into the outer darkness, where there will be howling and gnashing of teeth. Of this, St. Paul says, "Put on the Lord Jesus Christ" (Rom. 13:14); and, "As many of you as were baptized have put on Christ" (Gal. 3:27). This is furthermore why our Lord Jesus let Himself be nailed to the cross naked and bare, stripped of His clothes, showing the whole world that He was the one who would take away our nakedness, disgrace, and shame and give us the clothes of His holiness, innocence, and merit so that we would not perish.

O my most beloved Lord Jesus, what good sermons You give me about Your benefits in my daily clothing! Clothing warms me. It blocks the harsh wind. It holds in the radiant warmth of the body and provides me with heat naturally, keeping me healthy. Oh dearest Lord Jesus, Your benefits are my best clothing. Your merit warms me so that no evil spirit can harm me. Your kindness gives me strength. You warm my ice-cold, fainting heart so that I do not despair.

A nice fur coat is useful for the winter's cold. O Lord Jesus, You are splendid, beneficial, and useful for the winter of my misery, the winter of all spiritual attack, the chilling winter of my death. You sustain me so that I do not fall into the eternal fever, trembling, and gnashing of hell.

When a man is nearly frozen and is then wrapped in a warm fur, his spirit rises again and he is revived. You do this for me, too, O Lord Jesus. When I am already half-dead in great anguish of heart, You come to me, wrapping me in Your benefits and clothing me with Your kindness, and immediately I am so revived and full of joy that I can scarcely express the

344 "vestimenta splendoris"

comfort in my heart. Hence Adam and Eve's clothing is also called "the clothes of quickening and revitalization"[345] in the Hebrew.

Clothes make the man; put some on if you can. Long ago there was a famous poet in Marburg who once walked through the market in the daily clothes of a commoner. No one gave him any respect. Then he went back, got his fine robe, and took the same path as before. Everyone instantly bowed their knees and paid him homage. Angered, the gentleman went home and trampled upon the fur, saying, "Are you the poet or am I?" It is true, a fine garment attracts the world's attention and gives its owner prestige. Whoever honors it in secret will be honored by it in public. Oh Lord Jesus, You give us the most beautiful adornments in Your gifts of grace. Whoever wants to enter Your Father's presence with success and be a welcome guest must come wearing Your imputed righteousness.

Clothing shelters the body from the rain, snow, and all kinds of bad weather. It also covers the unsightly parts of our body. O Lord Jesus, You are our shelter from the beating rain of God's wrath and the storms of hell, concealing everything in us that has become unsightly and misshapen by sin. Clothes of leather and hide are especially good; they hardly ever wear out. Blessed is the man who is joined to You in the bond of kinship and has acquired the garment of Your innocence. You have been used and worn since the beginning of the world, yet not worn out. We too will get by with You until the end of the world, indeed, we will rejoice in You for all eternity. Imagine, dear heart, how happy Adam and his Eve were made when God skillfully fitted them out and dressed them with the skin garments. How they must have hugged and kissed the blessed garments with joy. Just think of how the smallest gift is treated when it is received as an honor from a great nobleman; it is all treasured more highly than it is worth in itself.

Adam must have said, "Dear Eve, this clothing comes to us from a loving hand. Blessed be the hour when God provided us with these warm clothes! Blessed be God's grace that fills us with such profound joy! Oh warm, beautiful garment, what good you do for my numb body! Oh sweet grace of God smiling at me from within this garment: what good you

---

345 "vestes resuscitationis"

do for my heart! With these clothes I cover my nakedness and all that is unsightly in me. But with the merit of the promised woman's Seed, who will also be slaughtered like a lamb, my sin is covered and blotted out, and everything that was corrupted in me is hidden."

We should think such beautiful thoughts every morning while we are dressing. Blessed is he who can cover his body with a good fur. Yea, "blessed is he whose transgressions are forgiven, whose sin is covered; blessed is the man to whom the Lord does not impute iniquity" [Ps. 32:1–2]. Oh dear heavenly Father, cover my sin with the true lambskins of of Your most adorable Son Jesus Christ's innocence. Bishop Wulfstan[346] once said, "Others may wear what they like; marten and sable I may not have, for in church, only the Agnus Dei ('Lamb of God') is sung. My lambskins remind me of the lambskins of Adam and Eve, and the true raiment of God's children from the fabric[347] of Jesus Christ's merit."

When you get out of bed, think: What would happen to me if I passed through the town thus naked before the eyes of all? Likewise: What would happen to me if I came in my own shame and nakedness before the eyes of God the Father? I suppose that I would be shown the gates of hell. Thus, just as I cover my body, I will also wind and bind and wrap my soul in Jesus Christ's benefits. When I die I will wrap myself in Jesus Christ's wounds. In these will I live and die. A brave man in Frankfurt-an-der-Oder once said as much when he was near death: "Thus will I boldly and confidently enter the presence of God the Father, in the certain hope that I will be pleasing to Him."

If anyone is poor and has nothing on his back but patches and rags, let him reason: Since Adam and Eve, God's dearest children, did not wear satin and silk, either, but simple garments of hide without any lace or trim or lining, why, then God will not be any farther away from me because of my meager clothing. Did not St. Bartholomew (as they used to tell children) have little silver ornaments on his robes? And when he repented to Christ for his noble estate, Christ was supposed to have said, "Just wait! You had no desire to let go of your robe, so for that you will have to give up your

---

346 Wulfstan of Worcester (d. 1023), archbishop of York.

347 Or, "by the testimony" [*aus dem Zeuge*].

hide and skin."[348] A poor man in a threadbare tunic and coat may well be much more in God's eyes than a proud man who flaunts showy garments yet under his beautiful clothes conceals a filthy heart and immoral body. Indeed, Hebrews 11:37 also says of many holy martyrs, "they went about in pelts and skins of goats, with destitution, sadness, and affliction," and in the hope of eternal prosperity overcame temporal hardship.

Over 150 years ago[349] at his wedding in Brussels, Duke Philip of Burgundy[350] conceived of the Order of the Knights of the Golden Fleece.[351] Its membership boasts the greatest rulers in Christendom. Their clothing is white and red, and they wear a gold chain. The links of the chain are made to look like firesteels, the jewels like flints. Its pendant is shaped like a golden sheepskin with locks of fleecy wool. Each member is required come to the aid of the other. They must all strive for honor and virtue. We Christians are all brothers of one spiritual order of chivalry. We must fight boldly against the devil, sin, the world, and death. We wear the mark of Jesus Christ's red blood, and the renown of the snow-white innocence imputed to us by our Savior. We all carry on our heart the golden lambskin of the Son of God's benefits by which our wounds are bandaged. This is the consolation in which we strike and kindle our fire. In it we find our light and life, and share with one another a perpetual Brotherhood of the Lamb. With true fidelity each man comes to the aid of the other. The hearts of believers are all united and joined in Christ. Oh Lord Jesus, let me live chivalrously, fight valiantly, and die blessedly in this worthy noble order! St. Paul said, "We groan for our dwelling that is from heaven, and we long to be further clothed with it, if indeed we may be found clothed and not naked" (2 Cor. 5:2–3). Here he is clearly saying that all who by true faith have been clothed in the lambskins of Jesus Christ's innocence will be further clothed; but that whoever wishes to be naked and not believe in Jesus Christ, but meet his end with an

---

348 "non vis amittere pallium, amittes pellem." (According to legend St. Bartholomew was flayed alive.)

349 Precisely, in AD 1430.

350 Philip III (1396–1467), duke of Burgundy.

351 "Aurei Velleris"

unrepentant heart, will remain in his shame; he will have "clothed himself with cursing as his coat" (Ps. 109:18).

In Deuteronomy 22:11, God says, "You shall not put on a garment of wool and linen mixed together." With these words God not only wished to dissuade His people from hypocrisy (such as cheating in measurements and dealing with neighbors underhandedly and falsely) but also by the same token to instill in them the realization that man's works and human merits are not to be added to the clothes of righteousness won by Christ. The incense and sacrifice of Jesus Christ, the Lamb of God, is our best clothing and most beautiful adornment in the sight of God. The homespun linens of our own good works are not worth one stitch in respect to God's strict justice, even if they amount to as much toil as it takes to make linen.

Oh Lord Jesus Christ, preserve me from reckless thoughts that presume themselves sufficient to pass muster by the fanciful appearance of their own piety. This is no different from Adam and Eve's attempt to cover themselves in God's sight by sewing together garments of fig-leaves. For it is only by Your grace and merit that we are kept from the wrath of Your heavenly Father. O Lord Jesus Christ, let Your innocence be my Sunday clothes and my workday clothes. I cannot wear these out any more than the Israelites wore out their raiment in the desert.[352] Clothe me, cover me, warm me, adorn me, that by You all my sins may be covered, my body and soul concealed from all evil, and myself preserved by Your grace both now and forever. Amen.

Glory to God in the Highest!

---

352 See Deut. 8:41; 29:5; Neh. 9:1.

PART TWO: GENESIS 4–15

DEDICATION OF PART TWO (1602)

TO MY DEAREST HOMELAND,
THE ROYAL CITY OF FRAUSTADT,

Its honorable, reputable, most wise council, its renowned, honorable lords of the court, its right honorable lords, jurors, and elders, its respectable testamentaries, its whole Christian citizenry, and all my faithful professors and well-deserving friends there who share my own heart and blood:

Honorable, reputable, most learned, most wise, respectable patrons and friends! Next to Almighty God, I owe no more debt of gratitude to any one else in the world than to my most beloved Homeland that raised me, my dear professors who instructed me, my friends who nourished me, the honorable testamentaries who through the praiseworthy gift of the respectable, reverend, and blessed Doctor Lampertus served as benefactors to my studies; and especially to the honorable, reputable, most wise Council, which out of exceptional favor requisitioned me from the University of Leipzig and entrusted to me the youth of its school for an entirety of six years, finally transferring me from its school to its church, and for thirteen years has kindly and graciously listened to me in that post, and furthermore supported me honorably in my need, and granted and furnished all my fortune and prosperity.

Whereas, according to the Law and instruction of Solomon (Prov. 3[:9]), I have committed to the Lord God the First Part of the mysteries of Jesus Christ in Genesis, therefore it is my judicious desire to dedicate this work to my dear Homeland and to my beloved preceptors as a testimony of my requited love and a witness of my gratitutde, and in indebted humility to hold in reverence your honorable, reputable, very wise lords as the pillars and foundation-posts of my dear Fatherland. I pray your honorable and esteemed sirs will accept my thanks with goodwill and, as they have hitherto done, assist me in loving, honoring, extolling, praising, and worshiping our sweet Lord Jesus.

Oh my dearest Fraustadters, see what a great treasure God has given you! "Let the Word of Christ dwell among you richly in all wisdom" [Col. 3:16].

When St. Andrew was introduced to our Lord Jesus, these were his first words to his brother St. Peter: "We have found the Messiah" (John 1:41). May you Fraustadters speak these words of joy at all hours and every moment: "We Fraustadters have found Jesus the Messiah." As St. Paul wrote to his Galatians, "Christ was portrayed[353] before your eyes as if He had been crucified among you" [Gal. 3:1]. Oh, may you be benefited by this noble treasure!

Remember your crucified Lord and Savior whenever you see your town's coat of arms. In it are two crosses on top of each other. Between them are two rings or wreaths. You have something great to contemplate in this.

You plainly have *two* crosses. First, there is the cross of Jesus Christ by which the Gospel is highly exalted among you. Second, the courtly insignia of Jesus Christ is found in your daily house-cross [*Hauskreuz*].

Courage then, dear citizens of Fraustadt! Do not always keep both eyes focused on the lower cross. Do not always brood and focus upon your daily, private cross, but lift your eyes also up to the higher cross of Jesus Christ. Remember what your Lord Jesus won for you on that cross.

The cross of Jesus Christ can sweeten all your crosses, just as Moses' tree sweetened the bitter water (Ex. 15). The cross of Jesus Christ will lift your heavy, iron hearts upward to heaven, as Elisha's tree made the sunken axe-head float (2 Kings 6). The cross of our Lord Jesus is able to banish all your crosses. By the cross of Jesus Christ you will overcome all your foes,[354] dear Fraustadt, following the example of emperor Constantine.

---

353 The crest of Fraustadt (Wschowa) has a blue field with a white double-cross and two white rings between the arms. There is further description in the next paragraph.

354 "In hoc vince"

The cross of Jesus Christ is your soul's mithridate,[355] antidote, and remedy, in the same way as the copper serpent raised up on Moses' cross was the supreme cure for the Jews' stinging wounds.

From the holy cross, the dear sun shines upon our heart. Behold our Lord Jesus, the great Sun of righteousness, with the unaverted gaze of the eagle, and you will be blessed. Do not think that your courts are represented by the eagle for no reason.

Your heart should be the posthole in which the cross of Jesus Christ is planted by true faith.

The cross of Jesus Christ should be painted upon your hearts, as St. Elizabeth used to say to the sisters in her cloister, and as St. Clare's heart said long ago.

Under the cross of Jesus Christ you have shelter in every heat of anguish, as did the beasts of the field under the great tree (Dan. 4[:12]).

If you behold the cross of Jesus Christ with eyes of faith, then all the misfortune of your souls will subside, no matter now large it may be. Look at what happened on July 22, 365, when the ocean billows receded from the Epidaurians after St. Hilarion drew the sign of the cross three times on the seashore and prayed three times in the name of the crucified Lord Jesus.[356] The holy cross is the sign that preserves all believing Christians from every ill (Ezek. 9[:4]). Tertullian writes, "The cross of Jesus Christ is the precious Book of Life." Behold this beautiful Book of Life, dear Fraustadt:

The paper and the pages of this Book are our Lord Jesus Himself. Our Lord Jesus is bound between two endboards, or cross-beams. His iron nails are the gorgeous hinges and clasps with which the Book of Life is studded. Jesus' holy corpus [or body] is full of script and letters, that is, full of red wounds and violet scars. Isaiah was wonderfully skilled at reading this script: "By His wounds we are healed" (Is. 53[:5]). St. Peter recalls these letters when he says that "We have been healed by His wounds." (1 Peter 2:24). Dear Fraustadters, you too should learn to read the Book

355 Mithridate: an ancient antidote for poison.
356 See Hier. *Vit. S. Hilarion.* 40.

of Life. Repeat this as your consolation: Lord Jesus, by Your stripes we Christians are dressed for eternal life.

Oh, if you are friends and not enemies of the cross of Jesus Christ, as St. Paul writes, you will receive a crown of life (Rev. 2:10)—which, incidentally, the great seal of your city stamped on my call-document[357] seems to depict. Our Lord Jesus crowned Mary[358] with a golden crown. Mary is a pattern of all Christians who love to be under the cross of Jesus. They can all await "a beautiful crown from the Lord's hand" (Wisd. 5:16). Paul delights in this: "I have fought a good fight, I have finished the race, I have kept faith. Henceforth there is laid up for me the crown of righteousness, which the Lord, the righteous judge, will give me on that day; yet not me only, but also those who love His appearing" (2 Tim. 4:7–8). St. Paul is generous in his comforts; he even shares with us Fraustadters!

You are often called "Fronstadters."[359] Oh, my dear friends, may you be "Frommstadters."[360] Lift your hearts to Jesus Christ, for in this way you will have eternal good [*Frommen*]. For "to love Jesus surpasses all knowledge" (Eph. 3[:19]) and "I count everything as loss compared with the excellent knowledge of Jesus Christ" (Phil. 3:8). If you are "Frohstadters,"[361] be joyful [*froh*] for the grace of Jesus Christ. That is a blessed joy.

The grace of Jesus Christ be with you all. Amen.

Your honorable and reverend Servant,
Steward of the Mystery of God,
VALERIUS HERBERGER

---

357 "vocatio," issued by the consistory.

358 Mary is mentioned here hecause of the name of the city Fraustadt, meaning "City of our Lady," and the city church, St. Mary's.

359 This can mean "citizens of the Lord."

360 This can mean "citizens of the good or pious city".

361 This can mean "citizens of the joyful city."

Jesus...was made to us wisdom from God, and righteousness and
sanctification and redemption.
—1 Corinthians 1:30

In Christ are hidden all the treasures of wisdom and knowledge.
—Colossians 2:3

We have found the Messiah.
—John 1:41

I. JESUS,

The Richest Treasure of Our Heart, Hereditary Lord of All that Eve has in her Heart, Mind, and Mouth During the Birth of Cain (Gen. 4[:1]).

Adam dwelt with his beloved Eve in true love, constant favor, and marital bliss. Thus Eve, the mother of the living, looked forward to her first son with joy. But this firstborn of men was a wicked blemish and child of death from the beginning. Oh, what a terrible misfortune! The effects of sin are manifest in this misery. Had Adam and Eve not transgressed, no parents in the world would have to mourn that their children were wayward or selfish. But Eve was so fully convinced that it would be the promised Messiah that she did not even call him "son," but referred to him as Lord, exclaiming with joy, "'I have begotten the Man, the LORD.'[362] At last I have begotten that noble man and very mighty Lord who will rescue me from all the misery in which I have wept and groaned myself nigh to death. Simply by praying I have brought forth the Counselor from heaven. I have now beheld the blessed hour for which my heart was yearning: 'Blessed be the Messiah, who comes in the name of the Lord. Hosanna in the highest!'" Likewise, she also gave her first-born son a powerful title and noble name by calling him Cain, that is, "her heart's treasure, salvation, joy, comfort, jewel, and portion—her very mighty and richly endowed hereditary lord, possessor of heaven and the whole world."

Our dear grandmother Eve thought that it would be the Savior of the world who had been promised in Paradise, for to Him alone and no other would such a title be rightly given; but in this supposition she was sadly deceived. The possessor and heir of heaven whom she bore turned out to be the possessor and heir of hell and eternal damnation. Here we see another example of the great calamity which sin wrought upon man. Good,

---

362 "Acquisivi virum Dominum."

pious grandmother Eve had a darkened heart, dimmed understanding, and weakened memory. It had already slipped her mind that the Messiah was to be the seed of a woman, not begotten in the course of wedlock, but the son of a Virgin. Moses writes of Eve, "Adam knew his wife." But the mother of Christ would say, "I have known no man" [Luke 1:34]. Such misunderstanding about the most central matters of our faith is a result of sin. If we had not been corrupted by sin, we would know and comprehend everything with full clarity and free of doubt.

We also see the nature of a true, unaffected faith here. It is not buried, but breaks forth and gives light to everyone. Eve set and fixed her faithful heart and mind on the Messiah, the promised Savior. As soon as the first man was born, the faith that was hidden in her heart became visible and manifested itself. She immediately began to praise the Messiah. So if faith never demonstrates itself in beautiful virtues, it is no true faith but only a tale of the tongue, and a baseless boast—which point James 2[:17–26] emphasizes well.

Therefore, just as grandmother Eve eased the pains of her childbirth by thinking and talking about the Messiah, so even today all pious women who believe in God should learn to sweeten and lessen their anguish by remembering, discussing, and meditating on the benefits of Jesus Christ. Let them pray thus: Dear Lord Jesus, when mother Eve was in the throes of childbirth she remembered You and Your benefits, and was so cheered that she forgot all her pain. The oldest comfort is still the best, the most precious, and the most valuable, so let it be mine as well. Oh sweet Lord Jesus, as painful as it is for me to bring my child into the world, so painful was I to You, yea, and far more painful, when on the cross You gave me a new, heavenly birth! Oh Treasure of my soul, noble Heir, Lord Jesus, assist me! Sweeten, lessen, and ease my pains for me, and grant me to see a good, healthy, blessed child. Spare me from an angry, condemned Cain. Give me a child with the humble, pious, well-behaved little heart of Abel. So will I gladly and willingly bring him up to the glory of Your holy name.

We also see with what great yearning all the pious hearts in the Old Testament looked forward to Christ. Therefore we ought all the more to turn our heart to Christ now, since for us He has already come and everything needed for our salvation has been accomplished.

Now, although Eve was wrong in her identification of Jesus Christ, she was not wrong in her confession of Him, which she attributed to this child out of a good heart and a sincere desire, albeit mistakenly.

On this account let us carefully consider our grandmother Eve's ancient, catholic confession of faith in the Lord Jesus, strictly contemplating in this section how she called Jesus both the Treasure of her soul and her hereditary Lord.[363]

O dear Lord Jesus, I cannot call You Cain, for, although the name in itself is choice and good, it was first borne and dishonored by a wicked, merciless man. But You are sincerely good and faithful, yea, You are the fountain of all mercy, so You possess the power of this name nevertheless. You are my heart's treasure, inheritance, comfort, joy, possession, delight, and salvation. "If I have but You, (O Lord Jesus,) I ask nothing of heaven and earth. Though my body and soul should fail, yet You are forever the ease of my heart, and my portion" (Ps. 73:25–26). "I will love You, O Lord (Jesus), my strength; O Lord my rock, my fortress, my deliverer, my God, my refuge in whom I trust; my shield, and the horn of my salvation, and my treasure" (18:1–2). You are my noble treasure of gold, worth more than all the world's wealth, possessions, and riches [17:14]. You are my light and salvation; whom shall I fear? You are the strength of my life; of whom shall I be afraid? (27:1). Thus with St. Ignatius I will say of You, "My heart's delight died on the cross."[364] If anyone does not love You as his greatest treasure, "let him be accursed" (1 Cor. 16:22). From this we have an old riddle; see if you can get it: A pious man once asked a scoundrel for a gift, and the gift was larger than heaven and earth, and the scoundrel gave it to the man. In other words, Joseph of Arimathea asked that scoundrel Pilate for Christ's body and received it for burial. Truly, O Lord Jesus, You are the gift of my heart. I count You as my possession, and prize You more highly than heaven and earth. If I have but You, I need not doubt my salvation any more. If You are with us, for us, and beside us, who can be against us [Rom. 8:31]?

363 "Possessionem vel Possessorem"

364 "Amor meus crucifixus"; Ignat. *Rom.* 7.5.: ὁ ἐμὸς ἔρως ἐσταύρωται is perhaps better understood: "my passions have been crucified"; also see Ryan I 141, 143.

Besides this, You are also the true "Heir of all things,"[365] as Hebrews 1:2 says. You are my gracious hereditary Lord, my feudal Lord. I am Your bondservant. I am delighted to dwell in Your kingdom. I am Your possession (Ps. 2:8). The devil has no right to me or power over me. You are a rich Lord. Heaven and earth are Yours. If I am poor in worldly things, if I have neither money nor property, You are the richer. A brother cannot leave another in time of need. You are my Brother, neither will You leave me. You will save me from my poverty, and I will gladly make do with You. If You will not give me my food by the shovel-full, then give it to me by the spoonful. I will be content, and receive the smallest crust of bread from Your hand with a reverent bow and humble thanks. Yet because You are the hereditary Lord of heaven, You have the authority to take me to heaven. Indeed, You have a double right to heaven (I say with pious Bernard):[366] first, because You are God's natural Son, and second, because You won heaven with Your blood; keep the first right for Yourself, and give me the second, and my heart will be entirely assured of salvation and heaven by Your grace. Oh Treasure of my soul, Comfort of my heart, my most beautiful Possession, Lord Jesus, be my hereditary Lord and let me remain Your inheritance and possession!

365 "Possessor"

366 From Guillel. Abbas *Vita Bern.*; See Ryan II 102–3.

*The Noble Man Whom Eve Confidently Expects in Childbirth
(Gen. 4[:1]).*

Dear Lord Jesus, You are the true Man, the noble *Ish*, as Eve called You. Moses also used this term below in chapter 32, verse 24: "a man (*ish*) wrestled with [Jacob] until the dawn broke." This was You, Lord Jesus. Isaiah 53:3 also calls You the "man (*ish*) of sorrows and grief." And Zechariah 6:12 says, "Behold, it is a man (*ish*), whose name is Zemah;[367] for it shall grow under Him, and He will build the temple of the Lord" (Zech. 6:12). And Peter says in his sermon on Pentecost, "You have crucified and slain Jesus of Nazareth, the man attested to you by God with miracles and wonders and signs" (Acts 2:22–23). Therefore let me weigh the word *ish* ("man"), and contemplate in it Your goodness and beneficence.

To the Hebrews, *ish* normally meant "man," as can be seen in Psalm 1[:1]: "Blessed is the man who walks not in the counsel of the ungodly," etc. Oh my Lord Jesus, You took on the form of a servant and became like a common man, an *ish*, and were found in countenance as a man. Thus St. Paul says, "There is one God, and one mediator between God and men, namely, the man Christ Jesus" (1 Tim. 2:5). St. Paul does not mean that Jesus is a mere man, but simply means to show that He is the same *ish*, or man, that Eve expected in this passage.

Oh my Lord Jesus, You truly took on a human nature. This is mankind's honor, glory, and pride over the angels, beasts, and all creatures. Thank You for the great honor of courting and betrothing Yourself to us in our own nature. Through sin the devil put man to shame and mockery, but through Your incarnation You lifted us to eternal honor. The more the devil abased us, the more You blessed and honored us. After the devil

---

367 Heb. *zemah*, "branch."

deceived man, You restored man's nobility and splendor by Your incarnation. Through one man, sin, death, and every calamity entered the world [Rom. 5:12]. Therefore You willed to be true man so that through You as true man, innocence, eternal life, and all salvation and prosperity might be restored to the world.

Man was separated and wrested from God, so You took on a human nature, that man might thereby be reunited with God. For as certainly as God and man are united in Your person, so certainly have God and mankind been joined, reconciled, connected, bound, and united in eternal friendship through Your merit.

One man sinned and incurred guilt, so You became a true man in order that by one man our guilt might be atoned for, sin blotted out, and God's righteousness satisfied.

The Messiah was to die for the sins of the world, so You assumed a true human nature in order that You might be able to suffer death. For Your divine nature did not die, but rested, and empowered and strengthened Your human nature to endure its great agony, lest in the state of such great anguish it should fall apart. Oh Lord Jesus, how comforting it is that You are true man, our brother and kinsman by blood! Oh, how honored we shall be forever and ever because You have brought our flesh and blood into the secret council of Your Father and the Holy Spirit! We will see this in heaven and heartily rejoice at it. Oh, what tremendous, sweet comfort it gives us to hear that as true man You tasted, tried, and partook of our human misery! So Hebrews 2:17 says that You had to be made like Your brothers in all things so that You might become merciful, and a faithful high priest before God to make propitiation for the sins of the people; and, "we do not have a high priest who cannot sympathize with our weaknesses, but who in every respect was tempted as we are, yet without sin. So let us draw near with boldness to the throne of grace, that we may receive mercy, and find grace in the time when we will have need of help" (4:15–16). A man looks to his ruler for every good, even if he has known poverty and much misfortune in youth. How then should I not look to You, O Lord Jesus, for every good, since You have suffered all our adversity and are well acquainted with all man's grief and affliction?

Ish does not merely signify "a man of plain, lowly, and common origin," a son of the earth,[368] like *Adam,* or "a forsaken man of sorrows and grief" like *Enosh*—which are other words for "man" in Hebrew. For You, O Lord Jesus, are no mere common man, but the center of the whole human race, the glory and splendor of all men. Neither do You have a low estate in the world. You do not have a weak memory, but You keep the record of our names safe and secure in Your heart and never forget us. *Ish* means "a valiant, noble, noteworthy man." Thus You are a true nobleman on your father's side and your mother's side: begotten of the Father's heart from eternity, and born of the royal Virgin Mary in time. "You are the most handsome of the children of men" (Ps. 45:2). Eve saw well that the Messiah could not be a woman and so gave him this valiant, manly name. Therefore, O Lord Jesus, no one in the world can persuade me to ask the most blessed Virgin Mary for what can only be found in You.

Ish means "a man who has a manly heart and a lion's courage." This name is Yours by right, O Lord Jesus, for like Samson You have a true noble, manly heart against all the foes of my salvation. You alone have dared to fight them all, and attacked them directly. Thus You earned an honest battle-scar.[369] You were wounded on Your front side, not on your back, for You did not turn Your back to Your enemies, but courageously met them face to face. Oh my Lord Jesus, give me a true heroic, manly courage, too, that I may claim the victory and pass through temporal death to eternal life.

The word *ish* also means "a man of great power and authority," as does the Greek *iskhuô*[370] derived from it.[371] Dear Lord Jesus, You are a man "mighty in battle" (Ps. 24[:8]).[372] You are the *El-gibbor,* "the invincible" (Is.

---

368 "terrae filius"

369 "honestum vulnus"

370 "ἰσχύω" (from the verb meaning "to be strong").

371 The etymological connection drawn here is improbable.

372 Cf. part 1, meditation 22 for a discussion on the use of the Hebrew pronoun *hu* in Psalm 24:7–10

9:6). You are *Ish* [*milkhamah*], "the true man of war;[373] the Lord is Your name" (Ex. 15:3). Therefore I will always trust in Your invincible might.

> With might of ours can naught be done,
> Soon were our loss effected;
> But for us fights the valiant One,
> Whom God Himself elected:
> Ask ye, Who is this?
> Jesus Christ it is,
> Of Sabaoth Lord,
> And there's none other God,
> He holds the field forever.[374]

It is time for those who godlessly blaspheme against Christ to make themselves ready. This mighty Man of war can easily crush them, as He did Herod, Julian, etc.

Finally, *ish* also means "husband," as it says in Genesis 30:20: "Now my husband (*ish*) will dwell with me again." Dear Lord Jesus, You are the bridegroom of my soul. In Baptism, You and my heart were joined in spiritual wedlock, and death shall not part us. You are my husband. Here I recall St. Paul's words: "I betrothed you to one husband, that I may present you as a pure virgin to Christ" (2 Cor. 11:2). Oh sweet Lord Jesus, grant me to fix my heart on You, as a chaste bride on her noble, handsome, virtuous groom; for the love of You, O Lord Jesus, surpasses all knowledge (Eph. 3:19.)

Dear Lord Jesus, You are both God and man, for which great honor I cannot thank You enough. Yet You are a just, worthy man and a master more excellent than heaven and earth. You are a man of great courage; comfort me in my timidity. You are mighty; support me in my need. And You will do this, for You are the blessed Bridegroom of my soul. Blessed are You forever because of Your goodness! Amen.

---

373 "vir praelii"

374 From the hymn "Ein feste Burg ist unser Gott" (Luther, 1529), st. 2; tr. *LSB* 656:2.

III. JESUS,

The Lord, Jehovah, of Whom Eve Speaks in Childbirth, and By Whom She Overcomes Her Anguish (Gen. 4[:1]).

Eve not only called her Lord Jesus a man (*or* human), but also Lord, saying, "I have gotten the Man, the Lord." She did not say "a man of the Lord." She did not call her Lord Jesus a "man of God," as the prophets were called. Rather, she described Him as a man (*or* human) who was simultaneously a person of God, *Jehovah* ("the Lord"). And when the words are examined, they run thus: "I have gotten (*or* acquired) the man who is simultaneously Lord."[375] This is properly necessitated by the particle *eth*.[376] Here in this passage our Lord Jesus was first given the name *Jehovah*.

This honorific title, moreover, is also ascribed to Him in the Prophets and the New Testament. Jeremiah 23:6 says, "This is the name whereby He will be called: The Lord, our Righteousness." Thomas says, "My Lord and my God!" [John 20:28]. In all these verses you should read *Jehovah;* for Greek, not having the word *Jehovah,* employed the word *Kurios*[377] instead. Hence it has come about that wherever the Hebrew reads *Jehovah,* the Vulgate always has *Dominus,* and the German, "Lord"[378] (with capital letters, since our God *Jehovah* is the greatest Lord of all).

Abraham, too, ascribes this splendid title to our Lord Jesus: "Oh Lord, do not be angry" (Gen. 18:30); likewise Moses: "Lord is His name" (Ex. 15:3); and David: "The Lord is king" (Ps. 93:1). Our Lord Christ declares as much Himself: "You call me Master and Lord, and you speak

---

375 "Possedi, vel acquisivi hominem, qui pariter est Dominus."

376 A Hebrew particle commonly denoting the object of a verb or preposition.

377 "Κύριος"

378 Germ. *Herr*

rightly, for so I am" (John 13:13). St. Paul, too, came to learn this: "We proclaim...Jesus Christ as Lord" (2 Cor. 4:5); "We have...one Lord, Jesus Christ, through whom are all things, and we through Him" (1 Cor. 8:6). St. Peter says that "He is Lord of all" (Acts 10:36). St. Paul calls Him "the Lord of glory" (1 Cor. 2:8). He asserts, moreover, that this is the particular confession of God's children who are indwelt by His Spirit: "No one can call Jesus Lord except in the Holy Spirit" (1 Cor. 12:3). Thus the apostles took care to include this honorific title in the Creed, in which we say, "I believe...in Jesus Christ, His only Son, our Lord." In the high Mass, moreover, the Christian Church always sings:

> Thou only art holy; Thou only art the Lord.
> Thou only, O Christ, with the Holy Ghost
> art most high in the glory of God the Father.[379]

This agrees with St. Paul when he says, "We have...one Lord." You should not take this to mean that God the Father and the Holy Spirit are not the Lord; for "the Father is Lord, the Son is Lord, and the Holy Spirit is Lord, and yet there are not three Lords, but one Lord," sings Athanasius in his creed.[380] Orosius writes that, around the time of the birth of Christ, Caesar Augustus no longer wished to bear the title "Lord."[381] Augustus had his own reasons, but God wonderfully arranged it so that the emperor would unwittingly concede this title to the Lord Jesus. Tiberius did the same thing at the time of Christ's Baptism, and Trajan once again about a hundred years after Christ's birth. O my dearest Lord Jesus, I too will honor You with my body and heart, bowing my knee and confessing that You are "Lord, to the glory of God Your Father," as St. Paul says in Philippians 2:11. Emperor Domitian, too, tried to pass himself off as Lord, shamelessly including in his imperial edicts: "Your lord and god Domitian wants this to be observed by you."[382] Woe to such powerless lords!

---

379 "Tu solus sanctus, tu solus Dominus, tu solus altissimus, Jesu Christe, cum Sancto Spiritu, in gloria Patris"; from the Gloria of the Mass.

380 "symbolum"

381 I.e., "Dominus."

382 Suet. *Dom.* 13.2.

O Lord Jesus, You are Lord in name and deed. You are, with Your Father and the Holy Spirit, called Jehovah, for You are of the very same eternal, omnipotent divine essence. You do not belong to the common class but to that of the great LORD. You are the eternal Father's natural Son: true, essential, majestic God with Your Father and the Holy Spirit. You are the high, noble Lord, rich in wealth and benefice, upright, amiable, and gracious, not frivolous or haughty. You bear the name Jehovah with great justice and honor, for everything that this name comprises is powerfully evident in You. You are true Jehovah because You are Lord from eternity, and shall be so forever, and even at this moment live and reign. And all three of these tenses, past, future, and present, may be happily found in this Hebrew name. You are not simply "perpetual" (i.e., without end)[383] as the Samosatenes rave, but "eternal" (i.e., without beginning or end).[384] You are true Jehovah because You are not merely some invented God like the heathens' idols, which are nothing at all but the conceits of men. Rather, You have a true existence even without our conceiving it. You are true Jehovah, for You live and powerfully prove Yourself to be no dead thing. You are true Jehovah because You were not given Your life and existence, nor received it as a gift as did Your creatures, but are Yourself the very fountain of life. You give and sustain the life of all that moves. In You we live and move (Acts 17:28). You are true Jehovah, for Your being is unchanging and constant. You do not grow old and gray. You do not grow sick, weak, or frail. You do not die. Your omnipotence is not diminished. Your wealth is not spent. Your thoughts, will, and counsel are unshaken. You are not fickle-minded. Yea, all the promises of God are Yes in You, and Amen in You (2 Cor. 1:20). God be praised! They all have the force of an oath and cannot be broken.

Here, dear heart, consider why our Savior had to be the LORD God of such might and power. Anselm says, "Only God could accomplish

---

383 "perpetuus"

384 "aeternus"

the mighty work of mankind's redemption; only man could pay the debt that man had incurred."[385]

Oh Lord Jesus, we had to be saved from all our misery by Your omnipotence. You had to bear the wrath of God, which calls for strong legs and broad shoulders. Human strength would have been too little for this. Your own arm (Is. 63:5), Your divine strength, had to reveal itself in this work. You had tremendous foes; You crushed all the foes of our salvation. This would be impossible for mere man to manage. You fill a great office; You are at once King and High Priest. Neither did You delegate this task to servants, but You did everything Yourself. Mere man would not have lasted longer than butter in the sun.

You paid off a great debt; You cleared the debts of all men. No man's purse would have been big enough. You paid enough for every man. No one could do that but the LORD God. You are the rock of our salvation, and our salvation can stand on no one else but the true God. Here, moreover, we see what the devil is trying to do through those who oppose Your divinity. His purpose is to make us doubt the ground of our salvation and to undermine us with a scoundrel's trick. If the devil convinced us that You were not true Lord and God, we would immediately begin to doubt whether the ransom for our sins was high enough. But the value of this transaction is greatly enhanced by the fact that You, the One who redeemed us, are no typical man, but true, almighty God. You gave Your life, so You must be true God, for God alone is the fountain and giver of life. The everlasting, infinite God was angered, so You also, Lord Jesus, had to be the everlasting, infinite Lord, that we might be reconciled to the same everlasting, infinite God by the infinite value of Your merit.

Now, since we Germans translate the word *Jehovah* with the honorific "LORD," let me meditate a little better on this word in godly fear.

Yes, Lord Jesus, You are Lord, just as we joyfully sing, "Lord Christ, the Sole-Begotten,"[386] etc. You are not one of those lords without land or people, but the possessor of a great dominion. I am Your servant and attendant, Your poor bondservant, Your peasant and subject. Oh, what a

---

385 "Deus qui posset; homo qui deberet"

386 From the hymn "Herr Christ der einig Gotts Sohn" (E. Cruciger, 1524); see *LSB* 402.

noble, grand, important insight Eve had when she recognized You as her Lord! In the old days, titles were not as cheap as now. You didn't have to address every other scoundrel as "your lordship."[387] O Lord Jesus, Eve did not think of You as some simple country squire, but as sovereign ruler and lord of the land. This is what cheered and comforted her through her birth pains. I too have such a high conception of You, Lord Jesus. Whenever I call You my Lord, I recognize and confess that You are my Lord Protector, my Benefactor and Helper. I am comforted by the fact that You are my Lord and Bridegroom, just as Sarah called her husband Abraham "Lord." I am cheered by the fact that You are my gracious Captain, my Colonel, and our Governor and Custodian. You are my Lord and Supporter, and my Patron and Defender from every foe. You are my dear Lord and Heir (Heb. 1:2). You are my faithful "Lord of the household,"[388] as Simeon calls You in his swan-song.[389] I am the tenant of Your household. "As the eyes of servants look to the hands of their master, and as the eyes of maidservants look to the hands of their mistress," so our eyes look to You, O Lord Jesus, our God, till You have mercy upon us (Ps. 123:2). O Lord Jesus, I will find an empty seat at Your table. There is no need for me to cry myself to death in times of scarcity. Every day You deck my table and stock my kitchen, saying, "Children, have you nothing to eat?" (cf. John 21:5). Oh, how well off we are with You in years of scarcity—just as a true, charitable lord's poor servants are.

Come then, dear heart! Get to know this rich, charitable Lord of yours to whom you were sworn in Baptism. Do not even think of serving the devil, for he pays his slaves with a noose. Hire your services to the Lord Christ every morning and He will give you more than you can earn. Do not be a double-dealer; do not labor half the time for the devil and half the time for the Lord God, for "no man can serve two lords" [Matt. 6:24]. So the valiant warrior Valentinian refused to be stained by heathen holy water, and the noble Marcus Arethusius would not pay one penny to an idol's temple. They both preferred to serve their Lord Jesus faithfully

387 "Dominatio vestra"

388 "δεσπότης"

389 I.e., the Nunc Dimittis, spec. Luke 2:29.

without alloy. How worthy this is of praise and honor! Whoever serves this Lord faithfully can pray boldly, saying like Daniel, "Hear us...for the Lord's sake" (Dan. 9:17). And those who thus call on Jesus Christ in their prayers are promised salvation by both Joel and St. Paul: "Whoever calls on the name of the LORD will be saved" (Joel 2[:32]; Rom. 10:13). Whenever cross and misery appear, we can happily say, "We have a...Lord of lords who rescues from death" (Ps. 68:21). I will not cry myself to death, nor run to a devil or soothsayer, as did Ahaziah (2 Kings 1:2), nor to a medium, as did the ungodly Saul (1 Sam. 28:7). After all, I have a Lord who is able to save me. "Did any ever trust in the Lord and was confounded? Or did any abide in the fear of God and was forsaken? Or which of those who called upon Him did He ever despise? For the Lord is gracious and merciful, and forgives sins, and saves in time of affliction" (Sir. 2:10–11). Oh Jesus Christ, demonstrate Your lordly power, that I may praise You with joy.

If the devil ever tries to attack you, if he ever troubles you with your sins, defy him in the name of the Lord Jesus: Begone, evil spirit! You have no power or authority over me. You are not my Lord. I have another Lord, whose own I am. He will not let go of me. "Ask ye, Who is this? Jesus Christ it is!"[390] "If He is for me (and on my side), who can stand against me?" [Rom. 8:31]. When you are going to die, say with Stephen, "Lord Jesus, receive my spirit" [Acts 7:59]. Consider the words of St. Paul: "Whether we live or die, we are the Lord's" (Rom. 14:8). Luther once wrote these beautiful words as a reminder on the wall of an innkeeper who would not let him pay for his meal, and said, "We are the Lord's and the lords."[391] In other words, we are His dominion, and by His grace we ourselves have dominion over sin, death, devil, hell, and eternal damnation. This is sublime, for it really is true.

When Ambrose was on his deathbed, many gallant persons of the nobility visited him, exhorting him to pray that God would extend his life, that his presence might benefit them yet a while, to which Ambrose replied, "I have lived in such a way that I need not be ashamed to live longer.

---

390 Cf. note 000/375; st. 2, lines 5–6.

391 "Domini sumus, in nominativo et genitivo"

Yet neither am I afraid to die, for we have a good Lord[392] and I shall go to Him." St. Augustine always used to praise these words highly, as may be seen in *The Golden Legend*.[393]

Hilarion, too, recognized Jesus Christ as his Lord and served Him faithfully. So when he was about to die, he said, "O dear soul, leave my ailing body. Why do you tarry so long? For you have a gracious Redeemer and Lord. You have served Christ your Lord for over seventy-five years, and will you now turn timid before Him and not depart with longing to be with your Lord?"[394]

The Jews say that they would not so much as speak the name Jehovah for all the world, giving as their frail and feeble support the book of Exodus (as I myself have heard them do). Yet, O Lord Jesus, I will confidently speak Your lordly name and Your honorific title *Jehovah* in life and death, in trouble and trial. For in it I find life, strength, and comfort. Yet I will never call on Your name irreverently. I pray You, preserve me by Your grace from ever thoughtlessly taking it in vain. Amen, O great and mighty and yet most gracious, humble, and kind Lord and *Jehovah*, Jesus Christ! Amen.

---

392 "quia bonum Dominum habemus"

393 "H. Lombardica mihi fol. 117"; Ryan II 125; cf. I 233.

394 This citation in Latin and with an alternate paraphrase is found in this part, meditation 16.

IV. JESUS,
The Lamb of God, depicted in Abel's sacrificial lamb (Gen. 4[:4]).

Moses continues by saying that God blessed mother Eve again with another son. This is noted by the Holy Spirit to the honor of holy matrimony and of all godly, honest matrons and midwives. For raising children and helping to fill heaven with blessed little sprouts is a holy and God-pleasing work.

Now Eve called her second son *Abel*, that is, "vanity, transience, impermanence, hardship, and toil"—the same word that the preacher Solomon uses five times in a row (Eccl. 1:2). This was because Eve was bitter from her birth pains. Here again we see what misery sin had wreaked. Had Adam and Eve not sinned, all mothers would have carried the fruit of their womb and brought it into the world with pleasure and free of pain. Oh, how exceedingly beautiful it is that though Eve possessed the realm of an emperor, she had no desire to train her children up in laziness, sloth, and loafing about, but in labor; for by the sweat of our face we shall eat our bread [Gen. 3:19]. All parents should note well this way of raising a child. Eve furthermore trained her children up in prayer and the fear of God, for "pray and work,"[395] as the saying goes. Without prayer, nothing will turn out well.

Cain, the rich wheat-farmer, brought a splendid offering of the delicious fruits of the field. This is the first sacrifice of which we read in Scripture. In this sacrifice, Cain was supposed to remember the Messiah and take comfort in Him with a faithful, penitent heart. While sowing his seed, he was to ponder how his Lord Jesus would also be sowed in the earth, that is, suffer, die, be buried, and rise again, and be "the firstborn from the dead" (Col. 1:18), "the firstfruits" of God's acre (1 Cor. 15:20), the

---

395 "ora et labora"; the motto of St. Benedict.

"breaker...before them" (Micah 2:13), who would prepare for us the way to life through the tomb and through death. Indeed, Cain should have considered how Jesus would be "the true bread from heaven" (John 6:32) that feeds our soul to eternal life. But he had no such goodly thoughts, no good heart, no humility, no repentance, no faith. He offered his sacrifice merely out of habit, for it was his parents custom, and he was of no mind to change it. He was a quarrelsome type, a restless troublemaker who prayed with an unrepentant heart, begrudged God's favor on his brother, and was as mad as a prodded goat when he saw it. If his heart would have burst into flame with one word, he would not have held back. He was an arrant hypocrite and the grandfather of all Pharisees. He despised his silly, simple, and meek brother: "What? Doesn't God owe me more for my choice fruits of the field than He does you for your miserable old sheep and goats?"

It was because of such arrogance that God was displeased with Cain's sacrifice. The fault lay nowhere but in his own wickedness. Thus God said, "Is it not so that if you do well, you will be accepted, and if you do not do well, sin is crouching at the door?" Here you see that God pays no attention to the outward finery of worship but looks at the heart and inspects its fundamental condition. Abel, who "brought of the firstborn of his flock and of their fat portions," honored the Lord his God. Here you see what a good, faithful heart is like. It refuses to give God the worst part, for God always gives us the best. Scholars claim that he said, "I'll make a sacrifice rather of fat than of lean things"[396] Here Cain inverts the heroic meter[397] and turns it into elegiac pentameter:[398] "Rather than of fat, lean will my sacrifice be"[399] This is a sublime piece of scholarly wit.

Now, in his slaughtering and offering of lambs, Abel was reminded of the true Lamb of God, Jesus Christ, as Hebrews 11:4 testifies: "By faith Abel offered to God a greater sacrifice than Cain." Of course, faith only looks to Jesus Christ, the Lamb of God. Abel learned this from his father

---

396 "Sacrum pingue dabo, nec macrum sacrificabo."

397 I.e., dactylic hexameter.

398 I.e., dactylic (elegiac) pentameter.

399 "Sacrificabo macrum, nec dabo pingue sacrum."

Adam and mother Eve when they explained the meaning of their lambskin garments. Thus, when he made his offering, Abel's thoughts and words would have gone something like this: "Dearest Father, Creator of heaven and earth, Friend of my parents' souls and of my own, I confess that I am a gross sinner by the debts of my father and mother, and that I have earned Your wrath also with my own countless sins and trespasses. But I appeal to Your mercy promised to my parents in Eden for the sake of the Messiah and, bearing in my arms this lamb, O Knower of hearts, I pray You to look within my heart upon the Blessed Lamb borne in my arms of faith, who will give His blood and be slain for my sins; for whose sake I pray You, do not refuse this my insignificant lamb which in true humility I now sacrifice to You as an offering of thanks." This humble, faithful heart pleased God, and He looked graciously upon Abel and his sacrifice—sending down fire from heaven and consuming it, as the ancient doctors of the Church say. Here you see that humility gets under everything[400] and finds favor before God and the world.

Now, O Lord Jesus, let me also regard You in Abel's lamb, following Isaiah who says, "When he was punished and afflicted, he opened not his mouth, like a lamb that is led to the slaughtering-bench," etc. (Is. 53:7); and following John the Baptist when he says, "Behold, this is the Lamb of God that bears the sin of the world" (John 1:29); and St. Peter, "You know that it was not with perishable silver or gold that you were redeemed from your futile way of life according to the tradition of your fathers, but with the precious blood of Christ, as of an innocent, spotless lamb" (1 Peter 1:18–19).

Oh dearest Lord Jesus, You are the Lamb that was slain from the beginning of the world. Throughout time every sacrificial lamb has been a portrait pointing to You. Since the beginning all pious hearts have taken comfort in Your sacrifice. Oh gentle Lamb, You are my treasure, comfort, joy, and salvation.

A lamb is a poor, needy, defenseless animal, without horns to thrust or claws to scratch. Sweet Lord Jesus, You laid aside Your divine omnipotence, came to us on earth in great humility, took on the humble form of a servant, and let yourself be abused and slaughtered, and did not defend

400 From the legend of St. Anthony; see Ryan I 94.

Yourself against those who afflicted You. For by Your humility You atoned and paid for my pride. You were born in deep poverty, You lived in deep poverty, and You died in deep poverty—naked and bare. You had nowhere to lay Your head [Matt. 8:20; Luke 9:58], that we might be rich and blessed in spirit.

How woefully a little lamb can cry and bleat when it is afraid. Alas, how miserably You cried in Gethsemane when Your soul was "grieved to the point of death" [Mark 14:34]. How pitifully You groaned on the cross to free us from eternal howling and gnashing of teeth.

A lamb is an innocent animal. It harms no one. O Lord Jesus, You are without blemish. Your innocence cannot but help me. You are like the innocent lamb that muddled the wolf's water.[401] In Your Passion You spoke as You pleased, so You had to go out and die.

A lamb is eventually slaughtered, for that is why it is bred. O Lord Jesus, You were slaughtered on the slaughtering-bench of the cross so that we would not have to fill hell forever with the smoke of our bodies.

A lamb can suffer and endure a very tremendous amount of pain with great patience, which fact both Isaiah (Is. 53:7) and Peter (1 Peter 2:23) regard with awe. Likewise, O Lord Jesus, with Your innocence You blotted out all my guilt, and there is nothing left to see in the final judgment.

Nevertheless, a lamb has such a strong head that it can take a blow and keep going. O Lord Jesus, You have such strong divine omnipotence that You were able keep going for a valiant distance. At last You broke through danger and death and, attaining the victory, lifted Your head on high.

A lamb is more beneficial than any other animal. Alive, it yields milk for food, wool for clothing, and dung for farming; dead, it yields meat for food, skin for clothing, and guts for stringed instruments. Yet, Lord Jesus Christ, You are far more beneficial. You benefit us with every one of Your words, works, and wonders. We can use You with very great benefit in physical, spiritual, and mortal distress.

Abel's lamb was of the firstborn. O Lord Jesus, You are "the firstborn of all creation" (Col. 1:15). As firstborn, You possess the right to both throne

---

401 See Aesop's fable , "The Wolf and the Lamb."

and priesthood. You are our brother, caregiver, and provider. Yours is by right a double portion [Deut. 21:17]: to You the one Christian Church shall be gathered together from both Jews and heathens. You have a double right to heaven: first, as natural heir; second, as valiant warrior and conqueror. For through Your bloody victory You won the promised land of heaven. The first right You keep for Yourself, and You give me the second.[402] Thus I too have a right to heaven and can look forward to salvation. You were the firstborn from the dead, that in all things You might have the preeminence [Col. 1:18]. Your resurrection also obtains for me a confident hope in the resurrection of my body to eternal life.

Whoever, therefore, would render sacrifice to God and pray successfully and know that he is well pleasing to God, let him approach God bearing pious Abel's Lamb, that is, in the knowledge and confession of Jesus Christ. Then he will be a welcome and warmly received guest in God's presence.

Themistocles wanted protection and mercy from king Admetus, so he took the king's youngest son in his arms, fell down before the king, and begged for mercy for the sake of his little boy. Then, because of the customs of the land, the king was unable to deny him. Likewise, O Lord Jesus, whoever seizes You in his arms of faith will obtain true favor and mercy every time, for Your Father loves You so much that, for Your sake, He cannot deny us anything ever.

> O Lamb of God, Lord Jesus Christ,
> Whose death for us hath all sufficed,
> Take all our sins and guilt away,
> And near us in all troubles stay. Amen![403]

---

402 From Bern.; cf. Guillel. Abbas *Vita Bern.* 1.12; see Ryan II 102–3.

403 From the hymn "Seht heut an wie der Messias" (M. Weiße, 1531), st. 16.

V. JESUS CHRIST'S
Heaven-Crying Blood Speaks Far Better than Abel's
(Gen. 4:10; Heb. 12:24).

Abel and Cain both had worthy forms of worship, but they conducted them with different hearts. Thus God kindled Abel's sacrifice with fire from heaven but would not look upon Cain's. This fire from heaven was Abel's sacrament, his visible sign of grace from which he could deduce with certainty that God was heartily favorable to him. Abel would have said, "Thank You, dear heavenly Father, for allowing my humble and pitiful heart to please You. Let Your old love and kindness be new for me every day; through the Messiah my Lord. Amen!" It was over this sacrament that the first quarrel in the world arose, so it is no wonder that there is still much strife over the Sacraments, and no doubt such sacramental strivings will persist until the end the of world. May God bring at last the blessed Last Day and make an end of all strife!

There is nothing in the world that infuriates human hearts more than religious debates. This is also seen here. Cain was so incensed at his brother that he turned murderer over the affair and right under the open sky killed the innocent Abel who once lay under the same heart as he. But God used this deed to demonstrate that the death of His saints is precious in His sight [Ps. 116:15]. Thus He lifted Abel up with His right hand, sent out the cry of bloody murder over the slayer Cain, and appointed Himself the world's first jury-bench. Cain, however, fell from sin to sin, ran blind-eyed into his own calamity, and did not shed one tear for his past sins. When God examined him, he shamelessly lied to His face. At last, he ended up in the biggest sin of all: he doubted. He complained that his sin was greater than could be forgiven him. "You lie, Cain," says Augustine, "for the mercy of God is greater than all the iniquity in the world."[404] Oh my Lord Jesus Christ, I have committed many sins against You! Oh, help me not to commit the most grievous sin against You! Let me not like Cain regard my sin as greater than Your merit. Strengthen me by Your Holy Spirit, that I may not doubt. For one single drop of the blood that You shed far outweighs all the sin in the world.

At this point it is well to mark the words that God spoke: "The voice of your brother's blood is crying to Me from the ground." To the world it seemed as though Abel had been completely forgotten. But in God's eyes he was alive. His blood cried out to heaven, and God had to exact punishment on the offender Cain.

In this heaven-crying blood of Abel's, the Holy Spirit Himself shows us the blood of Jesus Christ that cries to heaven: "[But you have come] to Jesus, the mediator of the new covenant, and to the blood of sprinkling that speaks better than Abel's" (Heb. 12:24). Let us humbly obey and receive this guidance of the Holy Spirit.

O my Lord Jesus, how sweetly You are depicted to me in the pious deeds of Abel! *Abel* means "a perishable, sick, ailing man."[405] He seems to have suffered from an ailment and been so sickly looking during his nursing that his mother Eve was almost always sure that he would not grow up. This is why he was so pious and meek, for cross and hardship teach piety well. "By the cross one's faith is sharpened as by a whetstone,"[406] said the pious Jerome. Here I contemplate Your thirst, O Lord Jesus. You were oppressed with misery from the time of Your youth. You were spared no misfortune. This affords me vast comfort in my sadness, for since You tasted our human thirst, You will be sympathetic with us and believe us all the more when we bring our needs before You as our High Priest.

Abel was not esteemed by mother Eve as much as her first son, the rich wheat-farmer Cain. O Lord Jesus, You are the best in heaven and earth, yet You were esteemed lower than the murderer Barabbas. You were not even valued by Judas and the rest of Your own faithless people

---

404 Cf. Bern. *Serm.* 16 *in Cantic.*
405 "homo bulla"
406 "Crux fidei coticula"

as highly as any other man, but were betrayed and sold away for a paltry thirty pieces of silver. Dearest Lord Jesus, You let Yourself be counted worthless in the world, that all who believe in You might be esteemed and highly valued in heaven.

Abel was an innocent child. O Lord Jesus, Your innocence is my precious treasure in which I take deep comfort.

Abel was obedient to his parents. You also were obedient to Your Father to the point of death, even the shameful death of the cross, and by Your obedience atoned for the disobedience of mankind.

Abel worked with sheep. You work with us men, and care for us as Your beloved sheep, and all Your work is spent on freeing us from sins and assuring us of eternal salvation. Indeed, I have made work for You with my sins, and I have made toil for You with my iniquities (Is. 43:24). O Lord Jesus, may Your holy labor be blessed and praised by pious hearts forever!

Abel was a shepherd and keeper of sheep. O Lord Jesus, You are the Good Shepherd. You wore the skin of your little sheep, that is, You put on our flesh and blood. Your clothes were pierced and slashed with many wounds and stripes. Your shepherd's club was the holy cross. You chased after us straying sheep, crawling through the thorn-bushes of our temporal affliction and feeling the thorns of our heart, our fears and afflictions. A branch of thorns was tangled around Your most sacred head. Oh, how Your head was pierced with the crown of thorns! How You were cut in every place! But You found us to bring us to eternal life. Therefore, in order to take us, Your sheep, upon your shoulders and carry us into heaven, You inclined Your head on the cross (Luke 15:5; John 10:9). Dearest Lord Jesus, You love our souls as a shepherd loves his own sheep. You lay down Your life for Your sheep. You are a physician. You know where we are broken. You often pour the salt of Your dear cross into the little troughs of our lives, for You know that it will make virtues prosper in us. After the salt, the sheeps' wool springs up abundantly. After Your dear crosses, our heart learns to spring up abundantly and trust God alone. We are often beaten to puddles by the hard rain of adversity. How often and mercilessly storms of every kind of abomination beat down upon us poor sheep! But then You faithfully pick us up and carry us in the arms of Your patient long-suffering and tender care. You are strong and able to protect us from all the wolves of hell. You stand watch for us day and night. You neither slumber nor sleep (Ps. 121:4). You call to us with the sweet-sounding flute of Your Gospel (Matt. 11:28). You always go before us, saying, "Follow Me" (John 21:19). You keep strong, watchful sheepdogs—rulers, preachers, and housefathers—who are all made to tend Your flock. Whenever we stray or doze off in respect to our Christian faith, You cry to us with goodly warnings. You cast clumps of dirt at us with Your spade; You allow us to suffer a little sickness so that we remember that we are dust and ashes. You hook us with your crook; You put hardships on our neck, yet in such measure that we are not hurt but eternally helped. You give us the blessed oats of Your consolation. You dress our scabs with a poultice; You give us Your Holy Sacraments along with Your Word. You quench us with Your merit, the well of salvation (Is. 12:3). You keep us from poisonous pastures, from every kind of heresy. May Your faithful, shepherd-like favor be blessed forever! Oh Lord Jesus, let me be Your dearest little lamb. When I am sick, heal me. When I stray, seek me. When I am defenseless, protect me. When I am weak, strengthen me. When I bleat with my trembling voice, hear me. When for Your sake I am slaughtered like a lamb [Ps. 44:22], quicken me again on the Last Day, and take me to the sheep-stall of eternal salvation. I pledge to remain a good little lamb and not turn into a big ram. I will be patient under my cross and a servant of all, like a good little lamb that yields great benefits in life and death. I will hear Your voice and follow and obey it. I will never be better off than with You.

> The Lord (Jesus Christ) is my shepherd; I shall not want. He makes me graze in green pastures, and leads me beside fresh waters. He restores my soul. He leads me in straight paths for His name's sake. And though I walk through the valley of darkness, I will fear no evil; for You are with me; Your rod and staff comfort me... [Ps. 23:1–4].

You shed Your blood for me. What greater love is there than this? "You ransom them dearly, You pasture them splendidly, You lead them carefully,

You keep them safely,"[407] I must say with Bernard. Oh good Shepherd, carry my soul to the joy of heaven!

Abel was also a priest, and conducted the divine service himself. O Lord Jesus, You are my High Priest, and You alone conduct the divine service that saves me. You teach us the Father's attitude toward our heart. You prayed for us on the cross, and You pray for us now at the right hand of Your Father. You hallowed and offered Yourself for us, and ascended into heaven with words of blessing, proving that You will speak blessing after blessing upon Your praying Christians.

Abel's sacrifice was very pleasing to God. The fire from heaven proves this. O Lord Jesus, Your sacrifice, Your "It is finished"[408] [John 19:30], was so pleasing to Your Father that, because of it, we too will please Him forever. Heaven and earth bore witness to this with great and unprecedented wonders during Your Passion.

Cain spoke politely to Abel out of a false heart. Your countrymen and kinsmen in Judea also spoke politely to You out of false, wicked, faithless hearts.

Abel was slain in the world's first murder. You were slain in the world's most notorious murder; they "crucified the Lord of glory" [1 Cor. 2:8]. The club of Cain that slew You was the tree of the cross.

Abel the shepherd was slain, and the sheep were scattered. You said this about Yourself (from Zech. 13:7) when You went across the brook Kedron to sweat the blood of anguish in Gethsemane and appease God's wrath [John 18:1; Luke 22:44].

Abel's blood cried to heaven. Your blood, O Lord Jesus, also cried to heaven; but it spoke far better than Abel's. For as Brother Grusch[409] says, "'The voice of Abel's blood cried out for vengeance; the voice of Christ's blood cried out for mercy':[410] Oh, mercy, mercy, mercy! O Heavenly Father, let Your mercy be on all who called for My blood and My death!"

---

407 "Redimis pretiosè, pascis lautè, ducis sollicitè, collocas securè."

408 "Consummatum est."

409 Perhaps Johannes Grusch, 13th c. religious painter.

410 "Vox sanguinis Abel est petitio vindictae; vox sanguinis Christi est petitio misericordiae."

Our blood-soaked Lord Jesus Christ's first words on the cross prove this when He says, "Father, forgive them, for they know not what they do" [Luke 23:34]. O Lord Jesus, if Your blood had cried for vengeance, we would have all perished. But thanks and praise be to God, it called for mercy and brought us eternal salvation. "My Lord Jesus is the best advocate for this reason," says Hugh [of Strasbourg] (in his *Compendium of Theology* 4.24), "that He speaks the Word to us with so many tongues, for He received many wounds and bloody scars on our behalf."[411] All Your wounds, all Your scars, every drop of Your blood—they all cry and plead for me, a poor sinner. Dear Lord Jesus, if Abel's blood could cry to heaven and be heard, how then will Your blood not be able to speak, pierce the clouds of heaven, and be heard? Surely You are greater than Abel. You are Abel's Lord and Savior. When because of the great anguish of my heart I cannot speak a word and my mouth is stopped, let Your heaven-crying blood avail for me. Let the blessed cry of Your most sacred blood attain comfort, help, and blessing for me. When the evil one afflicts me, saying, "You have sinned. The multitude of your sins cries to heaven"—for so our predecessors used to say that there were four sins that cried to heaven:

> To heaven crieth the voice of blood, and of sodomy's rages,
> Of the poor oppressed, and of workmen defrauded of wages.[412]

—if the evil one, I say, should try to frighten me with my heaven-crying sins, I will say, True, I cannot excuse my sins before God, but the blood of Jesus Christ also cries to heaven. If my heaven-crying sins are great, the power of Jesus Christ's heaven-crying blood far excels and outweighs them, for the blood of Jesus Christ cleanses me from all sins and obtains for me certain forgiveness of all my iniquity.

O Lord Jesus, when I start to pray, let Your heaven-crying blood go before and blaze a path to the heart of Your Father, that I may be heard.

---

411   "Christus ergo optimus advocatus qui tot habet linguas pro nobis loquentes, quot pro nobis vulnera accepit"; Hugh of Strasb. *Compend. theol. ver.* 4.24; form. attr. Albertus Magnus.

412   "Clamitat in caelum vox sanguinis, vox sodomorum, / Vox oppressorum, mercesque retenta laborum;" a traditional medieval distich.

When I am near death, let Your heaven-crying blood avail for my salvation. Let that be my comfort, wealth, joy, delight, and glory.

Dear Lord Jesus, here I see a great distinction between You and the saints. While Abel's blood could cry to heaven and obtain vengeance from You, no one can appease You with the blood of Abel or of the saints. Therefore, though I esteem the saints as Your beloved servants, nevertheless in my every need I will call on You as my only Mediator, Intercessor, Lord, and Savior.

God marked the murderer Cain with a constant trembling of heart, head, and hand, and with a gruesome appearance, that he might both be ashamed to live and afraid to die. O Lord Jesus, those murderers in Jerusalem who killed You were also marked with an awful doom. Heads began to tremble: all authority was shattered. Hearts quaked: the temple sacrifice and the priesthood were dissolved. Hands ceased their labors: chaos overtook the populace, and every beautiful thing in Jerusalem was horribly devastated. Also, just as the place where Abel's blood was poured out was called *Damascus*,[413] or "sack of blood," so Jerusalem became a true sack of blood, a scandalous pit of murderers, and of "all the righteous blood shed on earth, from the blood of righteous Abel to the blood of Zechariah the son of Barachiah" (Matt. 23:35).

O Lord Jesus Christ, let Your heaven-crying blood be on us and on our children [27:25]—not, as on the unrepentant Jews, for ill, but as on Your elect brothers and sisters for eternal life! Amen.

---

413   The capital of Syria. Its name was popularly related to Heb. *dam-*, "blood."

VI. JESUS,
The True Seth, or Immovable, Firmly Established Rock of our Salvation (Gen. 4[:25]).

At the end of chapter 4, Moses sets forth two genealogies: one of the children of this world from Cain, and one of the children of God from Seth. It seems strange that Moses should list the godless rabble of Cain first. This was not because he esteemed the vast swarm of Cain's ungodly offspring so highly, but because he wanted to show how fiercely these weeds had spread through the world, how violently they had burst forth, seized all authority for their own, and claimed the highest seat in the world. This was so that we would not despair nowadays when we see how the wickedest villains still have the best luck and the dirtiest pigs still gobble up the biggest beets, and how the godless rabble thrive and prosper while the godly fry up their troubles, melt down their cares, and are left with nothing. Yet in Luke 16:19–20, the rich man with his fat belly sits on high, and poor Lazarus down low; for butter always floats. Weeds don't wither, villains don't vanish. But on the Last Day, everything will be reversed [Matt. 19:30, par.]. Then the godly will be set on top of heaven's mountains,[414] and the ungodly cast down to the flames of hell, as demonstrated by the respective deaths of the rich man and the poor man, and the order in which they are told (Luke 16:22–23). Therefore, "fret not yourself because of evildoers; be not envious of wrongdoers. For they will soon be cut down like the grass" (Ps. 37:1). God sets them "in slippery places" (Ps. 73:18) and finally casts them down to the pit.

Cain built a city and named it after his first son. This was the first city in the world. Cain set his heart only on the temporal things of the world,

---

414 Cf. Is. 2:2; Micah 4:1.

thinking that as long as he had his pantry filled, heaven didn't matter. The heavenly city where he should have lived forever was completely forgotten. Oh, let us not for the love of temporal things forget the eternal, for we must leave behind that which is of the world. That which is to come will last forever. Help me, Lord Jesus, not to fix my heart on wealth, possessions, houses, land, and other idle pleasures, but to turn my thoughts to the heavenly city which You won for me with Your blood.

Lamech was the first who would not be content with one woman. By this wicked example many other saints have been led astray. Yet one should not follow wicked examples. Life is not to be lived according to [just any] example, but according to rules and good examples.

Lamech's children all turned out to be clever and happy fellows. Jabal was a rich wheat-farmer, country squire, and fieldworker. Jubal was an instrument-maker, leaper, hopper, and dancer who knew how to step his galliards and passamezzos.[415] Every stinge has his spendthrift. Tubalcain, the heathen Vulcan, was a skillful bell-founder, pewterer, and copper-smith. Naamah was a skilled needleworker and pearl-stringer, adept at backstitch and tatting, a beautiful damsel who never dipped a finger in cold water.[416] Her mother Zillah was a nurse of the belly, an able artisan of pancakes, marzipan, and doughnuts. In a word, it was as Christ said: "The children of this world are shrewder in their generation than the children of light" [Luke 16:8]. Oh Lord Jesus, help me to be a thousand times shrewder and better equipped for good than the offspring of the world, with all their trinkets and pomp, are for evil.

Moses ends with Lamech, and it seems that it is all for the sake of this one man that he has outlined this genealogy. Lamech was a cruel, insolent fellow who bragged about stealing the hearts of two women, and laughed down all God's threats to punish him. Indeed, he defied anyone to stop him. All his talk was mockery and sport. Rabbis think that Lamech shot his grandfather Cain while out hunting, having mistaken him for a wild beast, and that, in this wrath, he then slew his own son who had deceived him and misguided him. If this is so, then Cain was repaid with his own

---

415 Common dances of the period.

416 I.e., she was so skilled that she never stuck her finger on a pin.

currency. For "by whatever things a man sins, by the same also shall he be punished" [Wisd. 11:16]. Cain shed blood, and in return his children became his murderers, and his blood had to be shed. Some believe that it was a couple of pious followers of Adam and Eve in alliance with Seth and Enosh who slew Lamech. From this it would be clear that the apple doesn't fall far from the branch. Oh, dear parents, do not blaze a trail of sin for your children. For what the father and mother dare to do, the child soon thinks well done.

From this point on Moses restricts his chronicles to the children of God, making a precise record of the lineage of Seth's pious fathers to the glory of Christ. Tying up all the ungodly men in a bundle, he casts them out like exposed babes and people unworthy of the Book of Life; for "the generation of the upright will be blessed" (Ps. 112:2). On the Last Day, too, all the ungodly will be cast out, and the upright swiftly swept up into heaven.

For a long time Adam and Eve mourned the death of the pious Abel, and the wickedness of Cain, their wayward child. Then God gave them cause for new joy. He brightened their eyes with a good son. Such is the vacillation of gladness and woe which all the godly encounter. So do not boast when everything is going to your heart's desire, nor despair when crosses come raining and snowing. God will gladden you again with joyful sunlight in the midst of your long and weary private cross.

Eve was overjoyed, and gave her young boy a fine name, saying, "You shall be called Seth" (i.e., one who is firmly established). "I thought Cain would be the Messiah. Oh, how shamefully I was deceived! I thought Abel would be the forefather of the Messiah. Alas, how mistaken were my hopes! Now God has established you in Abel's place. You will be established among the forefathers of the Messiah. You will stand firm against Cain and all his horde. You will not be slain. No, rather you will establish a shelter for the flock of the upright. You will be firmly established in Your offspring until the time of the flood. While all the sons of Cain will drown, Noah, born of your line, will survive. You will be firmly established in your bloodline until the Messiah, my Lord and Savior, reveals Himself to the world. From Seth's blood the world's Savior will be born. You will be firmly established among the elect children of God. You will not desert God as Cain did, but remain stable and steadfast in the faith"—as St. Paul says in Colossians 1:23 when he compares the Colossians to the mighty and awe-inspiring pillars (*kolossoi*)[417] that gave their city its name. Oh, how the Holy Spirit displayed Himself in the pious heart of Eve to speak of the future with such clarity and simplicity! O Lord Jesus, send Your Holy Spirit into my heart also, that I may understand all that is necessary for my salvation.

Here again, O Lord Jesus, I see You in the fitting name *Seth*. You are the true, unshaken Seth; You are firmly established against all the gates of hell [Matt. 16:18]. You were "set for the fall and rising of many in Israel, and for a sign that is opposed" [Luke 2:34]. Help me not to sin against You. You were established by Your heavenly Father as the rock of my salvation, the cornerstone of Your church (Is. 28:16). "No other foundation can any man lay" and establish than You (1 Cor. 3:11). You were set forth as my mercy-seat by faith in Your blood (Rom. 3:25). You have set Yourself at the right hand of God's majesty [Heb. 1:3], so You will hear my cry and give me a good judgment. You have set Yourself by the heart of Your Father. You will speak a good word for me. Your royal scepter is sent forth from Jerusalem [Psalm 110:2]. You, our King, are set on the holy hill of Zion (Ps. 2:6). "Your throne has stood firm" (Ps. 93:2). No devil will depose You, and You will be my unfaltering helper and protector forever. Oh, send Your Spirit into my heart that, having been firmly established, anchored, fortified, and defended, I may trust in You and never be put to shame; for whoever believes will stand firm and not flee (Is. 28:16).

---

417   The basis of the city's name, from κολοσσός "gigantic statue, colossus."

VII. JESUS,

The True Enosh, or, Man of Sorrows, and the Lord Whose Name Men Began to Preach in the Days of Enosh (Gen. 4:26).

Seth had a son who was named *Enosh,* which means "an afflicted, aggrieved, miserable man of sorrows." *"Then men began to preach the name of the LORD."* The Church increased dramatically. Behold, when times were so grievous that men gave each other grievous names, the Church was at its most beautiful. From this we learn that tribulation and adversity do not suppress the Christian Church, but only sharpen it, improve it, purify it. "Heretics only serve to hone the wisdom of the Christian Church, and tyrants to hone its patience,"[418] said the ancients. The Christian Church never looked as beautiful as when it was distressed and afflicted.

Here, Lord Jesus, I find You twice: first, in the name of Enosh; second, in the beautiful title of Lord to which Enosh testified. O Lord Jesus, You are the true Enosh, the precious "man of sorrows, and full of grief" (Is. 53:3). You "bore our grief and carried our sorrows," that we might be freed from the eternal sorrows of hell and assured of heavenly joy.

Enosh also means "a man of forgetting," for forgetfulness is man's greatest affliction. Clearly we have in God's Word a sure comfort for every sorrow. Our frequent bouts of sadness can only blamed on our own forgetfulness. O Lord Jesus, You also are true man, yet not forgetful like man. You keep us fresh in Your memory. In the midst of Your suffering You were able to forget Your own divine glory and personal sorrows, but You could not forget ours. With Your very first words on the cross You prayed for us, forgetting Yourself, that we might not be forgotten any more.

"In the days of Enosh, men began to preach *the name of the LORD."* Here in the Hebrew is a word that means four things: (1) to call upon, (2) to

---

418 "Haeretici exercent sapientiam, tyranni exercent patientiam Ecclesiae;" paraphrased from August. *De civ. Dei* 18.51.

thank, (3) to preach and proclaim, and (4) to confess. So in these times men resumed the practice of going to church, called on the name of the true God, thanked Him, spoke and preached about His nature and will, refuted Cain's rabble, and confessed the truth with all their means and ability. There were bold, steadfast martyrs. Lamech was an expert in heresies.[419]

Now who is the Lord mentioned here? "The Father is Lord, the Son is Lord, and the Holy Spirit is Lord; and yet there are not three Lords, but one Lord," says Athanasius in his creed. Here you see the essence of the old, catholic, Christian faith in which we are still standing firmly today. Enosh recited his creed and confessed his faith as follows:

"I believe in God the Father, my Lord Almighty, Maker of heaven and earth, and of my parents, and of my own body; who also sustains me and kindly cares for me.

"I believe in the Messiah, the Son of the Virgin, who was promised to my grandmother Eve in Paradise; my dearest Lord and Savior, who by His blood shall redeem me from sin, distress, and death.

"I believe in the Holy Spirit, my gracious Lord, who hovered over the face of the waters during the creation of heaven and earth, and who shall always hover over my heart, bearing witness with me that through the Messiah I have the forgiveness of sins, the resurrection of the body, and the life everlasting. Amen!"

O Lord Jesus Christ, this is my creed, too. Oh, thank You for bringing me to the confession of this ancient faith. Strengthen me therein, that I may persevere until the end and receive the crown of glory.

Enosh learned all this from his mother Eve. She too had called the Messiah "the Man, the Lord." Eve taught her children, and prayed that God would preserve them from the wickedness of Cain, and her prayer was answered. Dear parents, teach your children what they need to know, and pray that God would bless them. When Monica was deeply worried that her son Augustine held false beliefs, Ambrose told her, "It cannot be that the son of such tears as yours should perish."[420] And so it was. Augustine examined himself and accepted all that he had previously neglected.

419 Or, "inquisitor of heretics" [*Ketzermeister*]

420 "Impossibile est ut tantarum lachrymarum filius pereat;" August. *Conf.* 3.12.21.

Here, then, for the second time I have heard it confessed that You are our Lord and Savior, and that Your holy name brings me temporal and eternal welfare. Help me always to contemplate this in my whole life, and to honor you and call upon You as Lord in my prayer. For "whoever calls on the name of the LORD will be saved," say Joel, Peter, and St. Paul (Joel 2:32; Acts 2:21; Rom. 10:13). Grant that in every cross I may rely on You as on my Lord, that in spiritual attack I may stand firm in You as in my hereditary Lord, that in life I may fear You as my sovereign Lord, and that in death I may confide in Your strong name of Lord, and in such blessed confession be saved with the pious patriarchs Seth and Enosh. Amen.

VIII. JESUS
And His Triumphant Ascension, Depicted for Our Comfort in
the Ascension of the Pious Patriarch Enoch (Gen. 5[:24]; Heb. 11[:5]).

Moses recounts the patriarchs from Adam to Noah with utmost care for the sake of the Lord Jesus Christ, who would be born from their bloodline. There were men of far greater riches and power living at that time in the world, but they have been forgotten. By contrast, our holy fathers have received an eternal, honorable remembrance because of Christ. Dear Lord Jesus, give me a steadfast faith, that finding sure comfort in Your precious name, I may remain steadfast in You and never be forgotten in heaven. For "the righteous man (the one who takes comfort in Your righteousness) will never be forgotten" (Ps. 112[:6]).

In this genealogy, Moses plainly states, "God created man in the likeness of God," and; "Adam begot a son after his own image." Here Moses clearly points out what a perfect creature man was before the fall, how the image of God shone in him, and into what grief and misery he then fell through sin, obscuring the image of God, so that what is born of flesh is flesh, as the Lord Christ explains in John 3:6. Accordingly, if we are to be restored, we must be born again of water and Spirit. Adam's guilt is passed down to us by carnal, physical birth; Jesus Christ's righteousness is imputed to us by spiritual rebirth. Dear Lord Jesus, by my physical birth I am thoroughly corrupt and deserve everlasting death. But by the washing of rebirth and renewal of the Holy Spirit let all that is within me be sanctified and set right, and "I will behold Your face in righteousness; I will be satisfied when I awake after Your likeness" (Ps. 17:15).

In addition, there are attached to each of the patriarchs two phrases which ought to be considered: (1) "and he lived"; (2) "and he died." This is a synopsis of all history, a microcosm of the world, and a brief report on the condition of our human indigence. Nothing is constant. The lives of men are like the leaves of a tree: one unfolds, another falls. We bring one to the font, another to the grave. This tragedy all arises from sin. "Your anger causes us to be thus consumed" (Ps. 90:7). In eternal life such vacillation will wholly and completely cease. There, freed from suffering, we will live forever without ceasing. Oh Lord Jesus, help me in all the inconstancy of this present life to take comfort in the certain constancy of the glory to come.

The patriarchs lived to a ripe old age, for their air was good, their food healthy and nourishing, the dry land not yet ruined by the flood, and people's lives moderate, sober, and restrained. In our world I do not count on living many years, for the climate is different, and so is our lifestyle. Food must be gotten wherever it can in these hard times, and grief and hunger strike us poor little earthworms and seize our hearts before their time. In short, aspiring to a ripe old age in these iron-hard times is futile, and even to some extent undesirable. "Our life lasts seventy years; and if it excels, eighty; and if it has been sweet, yet has it been labor and sorrow" [Ps. 90:10]. "Short and evil is the time of our pilgrimage, and does not attain to the time of my fathers in their pilgrimage" [Gen. 47:9].

Now let us turn to the account of the great and renowned patriarch Enoch. "There is none created on earth who is like Enoch," says Sirach 49:14, "for he was taken up from the earth." In the first world only Enoch had the privilege of not tasting death (just as after the flood Elijah did also), and thus Enoch became the first type of our Lord Christ, who triumphed and ascended into heaven.

Enoch lead a godly life, or as Jerome renders it, "he walked with God," or as Dr. Förster puts it, he was a great prophet, a mighty preacher, a devout priest, and an forthright preacher, and carried God in his heart, mouth, and whole life. In Hebrew it says, "He walked in respect to God,"[421] which is to say in effect, "He lived or conducted himself like God."[422] Had God desired to delegate His duties to someone else, Enoch would have

---

421 "Ambulavit Deum."

422 "Ambulavit quasi Deus."

been God's governor. The subjects of Duke Eberhard of Württemberg[423] are supposed to have said, "If there were no God, our duke would have to be God." Likewise, it is as if Moses said, "If there were no God, Enoch would have to be God, for God shone out of his eyes." If his heart could have been cut open, nothing but God would have been found inside. When he opened his mouth, God was his first word, and all his deeds were done only to further God's glory. He commended himself to God when he woke up and went he went to bed. In short, he believed in God with his whole heart, as Hebrews shows from Genesis: "By faith Enoch was taken up so that he should not see death, and he was not found, because God had taken him up; for before his being taken up he had the testimony of having pleased God. But without faith it is impossible to please God, for whoever would come to God must believe that He exists, and that He will be a rewarder of those who seek Him" (Heb. 11:5–6). Now Enoch did not believe in God all alone, but admonished others to do so, and diligently refuted Cain's faithless hordes. He not only put before their eyes the ungodly example of Cain, whom God had marked as a warning for all wicked scoundrels, but also faithfully alerted them to the coming judgment, when a precise account would be taken of how God's Word was received. So concerning the patriarch Enoch's teaching, Jude records in his epistle that he said, "Behold, the Lord comes with many thousands of saints, to exercise judgment upon all, and to punish all the ungodly among them for all their ungodly behavior, with which they have been ungodly, and for all the hard speech which ungodly sinners have spoken against Him" [Jude 14–15]. Enoch said, "Dear children, be godly, and fearers of God. Learn from others' mistakes. See how God punished Cain. This same God lives yet. If He should watch you for a length of time, I pray you, do not abuse His long-suffering! He will lay everything out in the open and demand an account of every single little word spoken in vain."

In addition, Enoch crowned his holy duties with a holy, blameless life and persisted steadfastly in whatever pious thing he began. He permit-

---

423   Eberhard I (1445–1496), Duke of Württemberg, beloved ruler renowned for his wisdom.

ted neither the threats nor the smooth words of the Cainish hordes to distract him. Even when cruel Lamech was about to kill him, the pious old gentleman had no intention of departing from the truth which he knew and confessed. Like Deus Terminus he said,[424] "I yield to no man";[425] and like the godly confessor Basil, "Tomorrow I will still be the same old Basil."[426] And lest anyone incite him to anything evil, he entered into holy matrimony at the age of sixty-five, earlier than all the patriarchs of the first world. (For praying earnestly, rising early, and marrying young should be regretted by none.) In short, "he walked with God." In all his deeds he consulted God, not the devil, nor the execrable example of the wicked world, nor his own flesh and blood. God enlightened his eyes, and his every word and action attested to his love for God.

Here you see the form, nature, and essence of the true faith, and how it demonstrates itself in so many powerful, beautiful virtues toward God and neighbor.

Therefore God set His heart on Enoch, for he pleased Him. When he prayed, God heard him. When he fell into trouble, God powerfully came to his aid, comforted, defended, delivered, and preserved him. Finally, God took him away. God would not let the thankless world vex him any longer. Enoch's earthly life was short compared to that of the other patriarchs, so Moses says, "And this was the day of Enoch"[427] whereas before, he always said, "And these were the days."[428] Enoch's heavenly life is eternal and unending. We have this consolation, too. Everything that is taken from us on earth will be richly repaid to us in heaven.

Our dear forefathers are of the opinion that Enoch was taken up into heaven in a time of devotion, no doubt while offering a sacrifice, and thus many witnessed it. This reminds me of Eusebius' description of the pious bishop Cheremon and his godly housemother who were visibly taken up

---

424 A Roman god believed to be the protector of boundary markers.

425 "Cedo nullis"

426 "Cras idem ero"

427 "Et fuit dies Henoch"

428 "et fuerunt dies"

to heaven while fleeing from Egypt to Arabia in great anguish. (Because of her age, she was not as quick on her feet as the younger people who were going into exile beside them.)[429]

The beautiful account [of Enoch's assumption] is proof that there truly is another life to hope for after this one. Thus the ancient doctors of the Church say, "Abel confessed another life after death, for his blood cried out and was heard. Cain acknowledged another life before death, for he was afraid to die. He thought that his temporal adversity would not last. Enoch confessed another life without death, for, out of temporal woe, he went straight to eternal life without the pangs of death."

Now ponder two beautiful mysteries here. First, Enoch lived in the world for 365 years. Then he was taken up to heaven. Our year has 365 days. When we have exhausted the 365 days of our years, and have dwelt in this world as long as God has ordained for us, He will call us also to the same abode where Enoch dwells.

Second, the first six patriarchs all died: (1) Adam, (2) Seth, (3) Enosh, (4) Cainan, (5) Mahalaleel, and (6) Jared. The seventh, Enoch, had the joy of ascending to heaven. Likewise, death and all calamity will only rule over the six ages of man living during the six millennia ordained for the world. But when the seventh millennium arrives, all those who lived godly lives like Enoch will have the joy of ascending also. After Enoch came Methuselah, who lived longer than any one else in the world. Likewise, after the blessed ascension of the elect, death will not be known any longer, but "the righteous shall live forever, and the Lord shall be their reward, and the Most High shall care for them" (Wisd. 5:15).

Here, O Jesus, I find You and Your triumphant ascension in the beautiful account of the most blessed patriarch Enoch.

The names of his grandfathers depict and portray You in terms of great beauty and admiration. As *Cainan* means "hereditary lord," so You, Jesus, are the "Heir of all things" (Heb. 1:2). *Mahalaleel* means "man who praises God." O Jesus, You praise Your heavenly Father in all Your deeds and bring us into the estate in which we shall honor and praise God forever. *Jared* means "sovereign lord and prince." O Jesus, You have

---

429 Euseb. *Hist. Eccl.* 4.41.

dominion from sea to sea (Ps. 72:8)—yea, from heaven to earth to hell. Yours is by right a threefold crown.

All this is admirable and comforting, but the image of Enoch outdoes all others. *Enoch* means "a man taught and instructed by God, into whose mouth God Himself puts the words." O Lord Jesus, You say of Yourself, "My teaching is not Mine, but His who sent Me" (John [7:16]).[430] Oh, how my heart is comforted to know that Your Father is of one mind with You. When You absolve me of sin, Your Father will never gainsay it, but will let it stand forever according to Your words.

Enoch further means "a man consecrated by God Himself." O Lord Jesus, at the Jordan and on Mount Tabor Your heavenly Father Himself consecrated You and appointed You to Your office. Woe to those who will not hear You nor acknowledge You as their Savior. What is more, Enoch also means "a man completely devoted to God, seeking nothing but God's glory." O Lord Jesus, here I am reminded of Your words of humility, when You said to John, "I do not seek My own glory" (John 8:50). Dear Lord Jesus, You devoted Yourself wholly to Your Father, even to the point of a contemptible death, that I, who on account of my sins was devoted to eternal death, might be devoted to the Father as His own and pulled from the jaws of eternal death. In return, therefore, I will devote myself, body and soul, to Your glory. O Lord Jesus, I want to be Yours only forever and ever.

Enoch was the seventh from Adam. O Lord Jesus, Your genealogy can also be divided into perfect sevens. From Adam to Abraham there are three times seven generations; from Abraham to David, two times seven; from David to the Babylonian captivity, two times seven; and again, from then to You, O Lord Christ, two times seven (Matt. 1; Luke 3).

Enoch walked with God. O Lord Jesus, You also walk with God, yet not only in the manner of Enoch, as Nestorius[431] long ago supposed, but in You "the whole fullness of deity dwells bodily" (Col. 2:9). You are true God and true man in one person.

---

430 Corr. for "John 5:24."

431 Nestorius (ca. 386–ca. 451), briefly Archbishop of Constantinople, taught that Christ had two separate persons.

Because of his godliness Enoch was a veritable man of wonders in the first world. O Lord Jesus, because of Your godliness You are a man of wonders forever. You could easily be called "the wonder of the world,"[432] as Emperor Otto was called long ago. You are a wonderful champion[433] (Is. 9:6). You alone have the glory of boasting, "Which of You can convict Me of a sin?" (John 8:46).

Enoch was a true preacher, priest, and prophet. O Lord Christ, this is Your office, too. Help me to heed Your warning. Enoch was taken up into heaven. You were also taken up by a cloud on the day of Your ascension, yet Your cloud was only obeying You, its sovereign, hereditary Lord. You ascended into heaven by Your own divine power and led captivity captive [Ps. 68:18; Eph. 4:8]. Enoch's ascension afforded the first world great comfort and good, for they saw unmistakably that God would come to their aid and give all the godly a better life after their present troubles. Oh dear Lord Jesus, Your heavenly ascension affords the whole world benefit and good. It was to our advantage, as You Yourself said, that You went away (John 16:7). Enoch's ascension may be comforting, yet it gains us nothing. Your ascension, however, has afforded, earned, and obtained for us indescribable riches. Therefore I cannot put You on par with saints. With You everything overflows. Whatever I lack, I can get. The saints cannot share their holiness with others, as the wise virgins were obliged to confess (Matt. 25:9). What is more, Lord Jesus, Your ascension has secured a joyous ascension for my prayers. By Your ascension the path to Your Father's heart was cleared for me, so that all my sighs pierce the clouds and are counted before God. In order to gain access to another's inheritance, one must obtain permission from a steward, court, or jury, and be officially introduced. O Lord Jesus, all authority in heaven and earth has been given to You [Matt. 28:18]. Thus on the day of Your ascension You fulfilled in Your own person the spiritual process of law, and gave us an official introduction so that we could keep and maintain our access to heaven without any suspicion.

432 "mirabilia mundi"

433 For the Heb. *gibbor*, "mighty (hero)."

Many times the evil one has told my weary heart, "Don't you know that your sins have earned you a sad descent into hell?" But now I know my firm consolation against such fearsome words: instead of a descent into hell, O Lord Jesus, You have won me a certain ascent into heaven. As surely as I deserve the penalty of hell for my sins, so certainly and truly have You cleared the road to heaven for me with Your merit. You took the prince of the air, the evil one, captive and defeated him. I can confidently say with Tertullian, "Rest easy, dear flesh and blood! In the heavenly ascension of Christ your forerunner, you already possess clear proof that you too shall ascend into heaven"[434] He is the "breaker before us" (Micah 2:13). We will all follow Him hence. Has He not clearly said that He would prepare a place for us and escort us there (John 14:3)? Therefore my heart is now assured that when I die by virtue of Jesus Christ's triumphant ascension, I too will ascend in my soul unhindered to heaven, for the Lord Jesus has cleared from my path all the enemies of my soul. On the Last Day, moreover, my body will be retrieved and in great gladness reunited with my soul, and there I will truly walk in the way that Enoch and my Lord Jesus trod. For Christ is my Head, and where the head goes, all the limbs go, too. When the Lord Jesus says, "No man ascends into heaven except he who descended from heaven, namely, the Son of Man who is in heaven" [John 3:13], I quickly reply with the pious emperor Maximilian, "Yea, those who believe in Him shall also ascend to heaven." Thus I will cling to my Lord Jesus by true faith, and be allied with Him in all humility, that He might take me along also, and draw me to Himself. After all, He did say, "And I, when I am lifted up (on the cross as well as to the right hand of God's majesty), will draw them all to Myself" (John 12:32). So although my Lord Jesus has truly ascended into heaven and been glorified with the glory which He had before the world was founded [John 17:5, 24], nevertheless He has not become haughty or proud in his heavenly glory and exaltation, but is mindful of me and blesses me (Ps. 115:12). He has made His dwelling so high that He can gaze far around. Indeed, "He beholds the humble things in the heavens and the earth" (Ps. 113:6).

---

434 "Securae estote, caro et sanguis, usurpastis in Christo et caelum et regnum" (Tertul. *De resurrect.* 51).

He has seated Himself next to the heart of His Father to make intercession for us, and as our faithful High Priest reconcile us to Him [Rom. 8:34; Heb. 7:25].

Blessed be Your comforting ascension into heaven, O Lord Jesus Christ! Give me a heaven-ascending heart at every passing moment, that all my thoughts may be turned toward You, that my heart may be where my treasure is (Matt. 6:21), and my mind set on things above (Col. 3:2), and my way of life in heaven (Phil. 3:20); yea, that with St. Paul I may say, "I have a desire to depart and be with Christ" (1:23).

Dearest Lord Jesus, send me Your Spirit, that, following Enoch's example, I may live in a godly manner, be well pleasing to You, and finally, out of affliction, be taken in body and soul to blessedness by that blessed ascension depicted for me in the ascension of Enoch and obtained by Your own. Grant me this, O Heaven-ascending Captain of Life, Lord Jesus Christ! Amen.

IX. JESUS,

*The True Methuselah, the Mighty Conqueror of Death and
Captain of Life (Gen. 5[:27]).*

Methuselah was the son of the pious, remarkable, and renowned patriarch Enoch, and was the grandfather of the great and notable prophet Noah. He was also the longest-lived man in the whole world, for he lived to be 969 years old. He lived for the last 243 years of Adam's life. Therefore Adam and Methuselah together lived through the first world,[435] for Adam lived 930 years, Methusaleh 969. Their lives overlapped 243 years. Subtracting this from the sum of the ages of Adam and Methuselah (1,899), that leaves 1,656. This is the year of the flood. Those people had healthy air and food and lived healthy lives, nor did they have as many cares and anxieties and we have now. Furthermore, the Lord God sustained their lives with a special grace to ensure that through their vast experience art and knowledge would be passed on to the next generation.

These days we must learn ancient history by carefully reading old books. But men in those days were able to recall everything from personal experience. Methuselah knew the entire history of the first world because he had the opportunity to talk about it and discuss it with Adam for two hundred years and with great understanding. Additionally, Noah, his son's son, prophesied about the flood 120 years before Methuselah died. Thus Methuselah was like a living library and beautiful bookshelf, or a "Library of Christ"[436] as Jerome called the astute Nepotian.[437] Methusaleh honored his elderly father Enoch, and so it went well with him and his days were long upon the earth [Ex. 20:12; Deut. 5:16]. All children should

---

435 I.e., the Antediluvian Era.

436 "Bibliotheca Christi"

437 St. Nepotian (d. 395), bishop of Altino and nephew of St. Heliodorus.

bear this in mind so that they do not sin against their parents. Also, just as God quickened Methuselah's heart and kept him strong, so is He able to preserve our lives today in all kinds of grief so that our youth is renewed like the eagle's (Ps. 103:5). He can lengthen our life as He did Hezekiah's (Is. 38:5) so that we live longer than we can imagine, and say with Paul, "Not I, but Christ lives in me" (Gal. 2:20). Yet we cannot aspire to the lofty peak of Methuselah's age. After the flood, everything went downhill. That great man Moses managed 120 years, but now things reflect more the lament of Psalm 90:10: "Our life lasts seventy years; and if it excels, eighty." Yea, if a man should manage fifty years, he should ready himself for his pilgrimage out of this world at any moment. What is this compared to 969? In our era[438] Johann de Temporibus,[439] who was Charlemagne's squire, attained 361 years, though he is noted by ancient historians as an exceptional wonder in this regard. But the more briefly we believers live in this world, the longer we have to live in heaven. Whatever is cut short for us here will be repaid there. Methusaleh died the same year as the flood. Yet contemplate this marvelous fact: when Adam died, his descendant of the eighth generation was still living in the world. But when this eighth descendant died, everyone else born of Adam died, too, save those eight who were preserved in the ark.

The Jews say that Methuselah died a mere seven days before the flood. Here we learn that altogether enormous changes follow upon the departure of great and important persons. The old, pious bishop Leontius,[440] once pulled on his hoary mane and said, "While I am alive, there shall be no great trouble. But when this snow melts, there shall be much mud." And so it was. Likewise, while Methuselah lived, there was no trouble in the first world, for he was able pray sincerely and stave off God's wrath. But as soon as Methuselah's hoar-frost melted and his gray hair was laid in the grave, the world turned to mud. The rain fell, a flood arose, and all the world was drowned.

---

438 I.e., the Post-diluvian Era.

439 John de Temporibus, *alias* John du Temps (d. 1014 or 1128), legendary long-lived squire of Charles the Great.

440 Leontius (348–357), bishop of Antioch.

When a storm is gathering, a linen-bleacher quickly gathers up her linens and puts them away. So, too, when adversity is coming, God always puts his elect away, through blessed death bringing them to their rest so that they neither see nor know of touble. No matter how careful a linen-bleacher may be with her linens, she never cared for them as much as God cares for His pious servants.

Ancient astronomers say that, three days before Methuselah's death, a comet in the shape of a fiery scourge appeared in the heavens. Heavenly signs are signs indeed. Whoever disbelieves this will be forced to find it out. What did this comet's tail entail? Trouble and distress. Methuselah, the oldest and godliest man, died three days later, and seven days after that the whole world perished. Oh God, help me not despise the signs that You set in the heavens! Alas, what can be the meaning of those fiery signs which were first seen marching at midnight[441] in the year 1560, and now at morning and noon?[442]

Some call it the anglers' parade [*Heringzug*]. Yea, it is the *angels'* parade [*Heerzug*] sent from our angry God as a preview of those armies by which He will punish the ungodly world. It is the vanguard of the final fire with which God shall burn the city (Matt. 22:7), yea, of the eternal fire which shall consume the wicked (Ps. 11:6). A certain farmer recently remarked about a large comet, "The snow is blooming."[443] Yea, calamity is blooming. The Last Day is blooming even now. Thus Christ our Lord Himself says that the whole world sprouts and shoots forth its blossoms of signs (Luke 21:30). So rejoice, dear heart! The summer of eternal salvation is coming. Our "redemption is drawing near" [v. 28]. Tremble, O congregation of the ungodly, for the day of wrath and vengeance is at hand!

Now the name *Methuselah* means "conqueror of death; sword against death; one who comes out of death and steals its power, and puts it to shame and mockery." Here I find another heartening image of the majestic power of my Lord Jesus Christ which I must investigate.

---

441 Or, to the north.

442 Or, to the east and south.

443 I.e., A snowy season is coming.

Dear Lord Jesus, You are the true Methuselah. You stood before Joshua with Your sword drawn, and You do the same to our adversaries, too (Joshua 5:13). You wield the sharp two-edged sword of Your mouth (Rev. 1:16). You alone can say in all honesty, "I will redeem them from hell and rescue them from death. O death, I will be your poison; O hell, I will be your pestilence" [Hos. 13:14]. "O death, where is your sting; O hell, where is your victory?" (1 Cor. 15:55). That I might believe it all the more firmly, You proved it, not only with word but with deeds as well. When the widow's son at Nain was carried to the tomb, You boldly faced death and, using the sword of Your mouth, cut the young man loose from death's grasp with a single word [Luke 7:14]. When the young daughter of Jairus, the pious ruler of the synagogue, died, You snatched her from the jaws of death [Mark 5:41; Luke 8:54]. When Lazarus died, and had already lain in the grave four days, decomposing, You released him from the bonds of death [John 11:43]. And just as Ezekiel walked among the skeletons and spoke words, and the bones came to life (Ezek. 37:1–10), so on Good Friday, dripping with blood, You carried Your cross to the Place of the Skull in the midst of all those bones and spoke seven powerful words, and a noise was heard, tombs broke open, and the dead came forth, all testifying to Your conquest of death. On Easter, by Your own might, You burst from death's prison, broke through the forces of hell, and returned as the glorious victor. On the Last Day You shall stand again upon the earth, as Job foretold (Job 19:25). And like Ezekiel (for You called Yourself the "Son of Man," just as Ezekiel did), You will walk among our dead bones, speak Your words, and make Your voice heard (John 5:28). Then a rustling will sound, all the tombs will break open, and "we shall be encompassed by this our skin, and in our flesh shall see God" (Job. 19:26).

Let this be my consolation in my final voyage hence. Dear Lord Jesus, I know that I must die a temporal death. All that I ask is that You defend me from eternal death, for You are the prince of life and conqueror of death. I will take hold of You, for You are the true, gleaming sword against all danger and death. With You, I can speak as that godly soul once spoke before he died, "How can I fear death? In my heart I have Him who consumed death." Though I am weak, Lord Jesus, You are strong.

Though I am small, You are great. I will trust in You in distress and death. With You I will pierce them both, pass into eternal life, and receive the crown of glory.

Methuselah had the longest life in the world. His years nearly numbered a thousand, which is the highest number of this world (for we have no word to count higher).[444] O Jesus Christ, Captain of life, You rose from the dead and die no more (Rom. 6:9). You will have the highest number of years in the next world, that is to say, You will live forever. Besides this, You have upheld the defense of Your Church against the Turk (the bane of Christians) for a thousand years, proving that You live and reign, as we see in Revelation 20:6. You will also grant us to rule and rejoice for a thousand years: You will graciously award us with the true golden age[445] of eternity. It is vain for us to dream of hills of gold in this world. We look forward to the world to come, which, O Lord Jesus, You shall give us.

Methuselah lived a long time, but he still had to die. O Lord Jesus, You will live a long time and never die. You are from everlasting to everlasting. Your years shall not fail. Heaven and earth shall pass away, but You shall endure (Heb. 1:8, 12; Ps. 102:12). And You will give me life, for You are "the Resurrection and the Life." Whoever believes in You shall live, even though he die, and whoever lives and believes in You shall never die (John 11:25–26). You are "the Way, the Truth, and the Life"—the true Way to eternal life (John 14:6). You can give us the rich gift of immortality which Alexander the Great could not give his wise counselors on his day of glory. You won eternal life for us by Your death. What is more, You have the power to destroy death single-handedly and give life to whomever You choose. Thus I will boldly proclaim, "Christ is my life, death is my gain. I have a desire to depart and to be with Christ" (Phil. [1:21, 23]).

Dear Lord Jesus Christ, You are the bane and death of death, You are the sword against death and all calamity, and You are my life. You preserve my temporal life, and assure me of the eternal. Oh, be my gracious patron, protector, and fortress. Strengthen me with Your power, that I too

444 I.e., all numbers higher were based on multiples of a thousand.

445 "aureum saeculum"

may conquer death and every distress, and inherit eternal life. Then I will serve You not only for 969 years (as Methuselah did in this world), nor even for a mere thousand, but will worship, praise, and adore You forever and ever. Amen!

X. JESUS,

The Comforting Noah, Who Brings Us Relief from Our Work and Toil upon the Ground Which the Lord Cursed (Gen. 5:29; Matt. 11:28).

The pious Lamech did not follow the bad example of his wicked, licentious cousin from Cain's branch, whose name was also Lamech, but followed in the footsteps of his sincerely pious father Methuselah, from whom he learned about Christ, the Savior of the world, often contemplating in his own name how the Messiah would suffer in the world (for *Lamech* means "man oppressed by poverty").[446] O dear Lord Jesus, surely You were oppressed and afflicted. You were born in deep poverty, laid to sleep in another's manger. You lived in deep poverty, having nowhere to lay Your head. You died in deep poverty, naked and bare. Though You were rich, yet for my sake You became poor, that through Your poverty I might become rich (2 Cor. 8:9). "Christ's poverty is my patrimony,"[447] I say with Ambrose. St. Eugenia[448] said, "He is rich enough who is poor with Christ,"[449] that is, who in the midst of his own poverty takes comfort in Christ's, patiently enduring his own poverty to the glory of Christ's.

No sooner, then, was a little boy born to the pious Lamech, than his faith in Jesus Christ was demonstrated. Thinking that this son would be the Messiah, he named him *Noah*, saying, "He shall comfort us in our work and toil upon the ground which the Lord has cursed." It is as if he said, "For my part, your name must be Noah ("Rest"),[450] for you will be

---

446 "oppressus paupertate"

447 "Paupertas Christi meum patrimonium"; see Ambr. *In Luc.* 2.

448 St. Eugenia of Rome (d. 25. Dec. 258), early Christian martyr.

449 "Assatim dives, qui cum Christo pauper est"; Hier. *Epist.* 14 *ad Heliod.* c. 1.

450 "quies"

a real *Noham* ("Consolation").[451] You must be called "Man of Rest," for you will be a counselor, and by your consolation give rest to our restless conscience. You will revive our troubled hearts, remove from us the toil of sin, and bring blessing and eternal salvation instead of the curse which the Lord put on the ground." O Lord Jesus, grant me also such a faithful heart, always to remember and ponder You. How ardently the blessed patriarchs longed at every passing moment for Your advent! Oh, help me to have the same ardor and devotion to thank You for Your blessed incarnation and to glorify Your grace.

Lamech mistook the person of the Messiah, no less than did his pious mother Eve. Here we see how hard it is for our mind to grasp that article of our faith which states that Jesus is a Virgin's Son. But since God covered over this and similar faults and errors of the patriarchs simply because they took comfort in the Messiah with true faith, we too have the certain consolation that this ancient and faithful God will also patiently bear with our infirmities.

Here, however, let us contemplate the beautiful confession of our Lord Jesus, for He Himself points us to this passage: "Come to Me, all who labor[452] and are heavy laden; I will refresh (*anapausô*)[453] you," (Matt. 11:28). I will enlarge your suffocating hearts so that you can catch your breath and take a break. "Take My yoke upon you, and learn from Me, for I am gentle and humble of heart, and you will find rest for your souls" [Matt. 11:29]. Behold, our Lord Jesus confirms that He is Himself our Noah and *Noham,* our "man of rest and comfort." Therefore St. Paul says, "We are richly comforted by Christ" (2 Cor. [1:5]). So, too, Epiphanius (bk. 1, vol. 2) plainly connected these words in Genesis to Christ. Consider, then, and ponder, dear heart, with what remarkable beauty our Lord Jesus is depicted for you in godly Noah.

Noah was his father's comfort and deepest joy. You, O Lord Jesus, are my heart's comfort and joy. "If I have but You, I ask for nothing in heaven and earth" [Ps. 73:25]. Titus Vespasian was called the "darling and delight

---

451   "consolatio"

452   "qui laboratis" (from the Latin; but LB: "who are weary...").

453   "ἀναπαύσω"

of all mankind."454 Oh Lord Jesus, You are the delight of every believing Christian's heart. I too say with Ignatius (whose heart was inscribed with Jesus' name in golden letters), "My heart's delight died on the cross."455

Noah was the grandfather of the second world. He was the real two-headed Janus,456 who saw the world before and after the flood. Everyone living in the present second world is descended from Noah. If we are faithful like Noah, he will rejoice over us on the Last Day as a father does over his own children. Theodoret calls him the Second Adam, for just as Adam filled the first world, so Noah populated the second one. Oh Lord Jesus, You are the Second Adam and Second Grandfather Noah. The next world is populated by You. Everyone who will be saved and live in it must be born again by Your grace. You are the Father of the next world,457 "The Everlasting Father"458 [or Father of Eternity], as Isaiah 9:6 calls You.

Noah was "a preacher of righteousness" (2 Peter 2:5), because he condemned all who believed that they would be justified and saved by their own works. He exhorted all who repented to take comfort in the righteousness of the Lord Jesus, and taught that unrighteousness should be earnestly avoided in daily life. Likewise, O Lord Jesus, You are also a preacher of righteousness. Condemning all who presume the ability to justify themselves by their good works, You say that "when we have done all things…we are still unprofitable servants." (Luke 17:10). Our own righteousness is all in vain. You point us to the source of righteousness in Yourself (Jer. 23:6). You plainly state that our righteousness is found in Your merit and in Your going to the Father, and that the greatest sin is to disbelieve in You, and to refuse to take comfort in Your righteousness (John 16:9–10). Yea, You also want us to lead our lives in the fear of God and adorned with righteousness, not in outward appearance but in utter truth, and You testify that, if we intend to be saved, our righteousness

---

454 "amor et deliciae generis humani"

455 "Amor meus crucifixus"; see note ooo in part 2, meditation 1.

456 Janus: the Roman god of doorways and passages, namesake of the month January; pictured as having one head facing forward and another facing backward.

457 "pater venturi saeculi"

458 "pater aeternitas"

must exceed and excel that of the scribes and Pharisees [Matt. 5:20] not only in belief but also in action. Noah "inherited the righteousness that comes by faith" (Heb. 11:7), but You, Lord Jesus, earned the righteousness that comes by faith. I cannot earn anything but must simply inherit by grace the salvation and righteousness obtained for me by Your merit.

Noah means "man of rest" or "man of comfort," for Lamech thought that his son would bring rest from hardship, toil, and God's curse. Oh Lord Jesus, this honorific name is only really fitting for You. You are my Man of rest, my Man of comfort. I was heavy laden, and You helped me. You redeemed me from the toil of my sin. You took away my curse and brought Your blessing. You are the very Son of comfort, a Master of counsel and consolation. You give my heart rest and peace in great affliction. You give me rest and peace from the devil, death, hell, sin, and eternal damnation. On Good Friday You laid to rest the great unrest between God Your Father and mankind. Your cleft side is the resting place of my soul. By Your rest in the tomb, You procured my everlasting rest. You are my sweetest Counselor in every trouble. Speak but a word and my heart will be consoled, my body made whole, and my soul healed.

Oh, my Lord Jesus, how much unrest, toil, trouble, and care fills my life! If I complained to the world, it would only add mockery to this. Therefore I will turn to You. With You I will find rest for my soul. You will comfort me in my toil and trouble on earth. You will not betray me. "Blessed are all who trust in You"; when they run to You, "their face is not ashamed" [Ps. 2:12; 34:5]. Wealth and the world no peace impart; blessed is he who has You in his heart,[459] O Lord Jesus, blessed Man of rest and comfort! Hence forever, faithless world! Jesus is my rest and comfort. Get behind me, Satan! You only cause unrest, trouble, and toil for my heart. You can tell me much of the curse attached to my sin, but you cannot pluck my Lord Jesus from my heart. He is my Noah and *Noham*, my rest and my comfort. He has the power to remove the curse. Though my sins are heavy and vast, His comfort and blessing far outweigh them by many thousand times. When I must die: Welcome, dear death, you are not fearsome to me, for in my heart I have the Lord Jesus who vanquished you. I have toiled away

---

459 Germ. *Welt ist Welt, wer sich drauf läßt, der fällt.*

long enough in the world. Now Jesus—my Man of rest and comfort, the Father of the world to come, the Comfort and Joy of my heart, the Fountain of my righteousness—is going to take me away, bring me to everlasting rest, and comfort me there forever. I will rest from all toil and trouble and sin—yea, from all the woes and penalties of sin. On the Last Day, He will rouse me again. Then I will hear those comforting words: "'Come, you blessed of My Father, inherit the kingdom prepared for you from the beginning of the world' (Matt. 25:34). 'Well done, good and faithful servant! You have been faithful over a few things; I will set you over many things. Enter into the (rest and) joy of your Lord' (v. 21). Now take your ease at Lazarus' side" (Luke 16:25). Amen, Lord Jesus! Amen!

XI. JESUS
*Places Shem Above His Brothers, and Honors Us Christians
Above All Unbelievers (Gen. 5[:32]).*

Noah, a young fellow at an old age, duly waited to grow out of his baby shoes before stepping into marriage. He was five hundred years old by the time he started courting. (Nothing like this can be found in any story in the whole world.) There's a young groom for you! These days, it would be as if a man of seventy were to marry a maid of fourteen. It might well be wished that young persons would let the yolk drip from their beak and gain some basic experience before embarking on marriage, for rascally birds and roguish wives have seen their best days. By this time, Noah had already preached of the flood for twenty years. Here he reminds me of Jeremiah, who prophesied that Jerusalem, already under siege, would succumb to the power of the Chaldeans. Then, buying himself a field, he became a rightful landowner to comfort careworn hearts with the knowledge that, even though Jerusalem would suffer great misery, yet God would look graciously upon the land and rebuild it after seventy years [Jer. 32:1–15]. Likewise, Noah saw in marriage a means to comfort all repentant hearts with the knowledge that God would certainly sustain them despite such a great disaster. God blessed Noah with three sons. Shem was the middle and best, Ham the youngest and worst (Gen. 9:22), and Japheth the oldest (Gen. 10:21). It is no doubt remarkable here that Moses did not list Noah's sons in order of birth. Yet he acted very intentionally by the guidance of the Holy Spirit. He put Shem, the most upright, first to the glory of the Lord Jesus Christ, who would be born from his line; for Shem, too, is among Jesus Christ's ancestors (Luke 3:36). For the same reason, Abraham, too, though younger than his brothers, is mentioned before them, as we will discover below in Genesis 11:27.

Here again I find my Lord Jesus, for whose sake Shem, Abraham, and all other believing hearts are honored. For now, I will restrict myself to contemplating my Lord Jesus in the figure of Shem.

Shem means "name." Oh dear Lord Jesus, I am now reminded of Your most holy name. Your name is the name above all names. "There is no other name…whereby we shall be saved" than Your most blessed name (Acts 4:12). You have been given a name above every name, that in Your name every knee that is in heaven and on the earth and under the earth should bow" (Phil. 2:9–11). Devils can do nothing but tremble when they hear a faithful Christian so much as pronounce Your name. You have become as much better than the angels as You have inherited a higher name than they (Heb. 1:4). All the prophets bear witness that everyone who believes in You receives forgiveness of sins through Your name (Acts 10:43). Whoever calls on Your name will be saved (Joel 2:32; Acts 2:21). Whatever we ask for in Your name will be given to us (John 16:23). "Ah, sweet name of Jesus! Ah, sweet name of Jesus!" Ignatius cried in his agony, and in this name, as he said, he felt such new comfort and strength at every moment that he could not forget it, for it was written on his heart with golden letters. Ah, sweet name of Jesus! Be my comfort and joy, too, whenever my heart is distraught.

Shem also means "renowned and illustrious, one who has a great name before God and the world, a most respectable, esteemed lord."[460] Hence Sirach 49:16 adds, "Shem and Seth had great honor among men," that is, they were members of the nobility. O Lord Jesus Christ, You are renowned and illustrious, respectable, and the noblest of all. You are noble by Father and mother both. In respect to Your deity, You are the Son of Your eternal Father. In respect to Your humanity, You are the Son of Mary, the royal Virgin. Just as a noble lord passes his title on to his children, so You pass Your noble rank on to us, Your children, who have been born again "by the washing of regeneration and renewal of the Holy Spirit" [Titus 3:5]. You bestow on our heart Your noble blood, and share with us Your noble name, so that (after Your name) we are called Christians, and children of God. You give us for our noble coat-of-arms a red cross

---

460 "illustris"

within a white heart. We are the true lords of the cross, duty-bound to make war upon the barbarians, that is, upon sin, the devil, the world, and death. You Yourself are the Grand Master of the Christian Order of the Cross. Your evangelical preachers are the commanders or heralds of Your cross.[461] As soon as we are baptized, we are marked with the noble sign of Your cross as a testimony that we will not be ashamed of it but take comfort in it, patiently bear all our crosses to Your glory, and, as much as in us lies, commit ourselves to a snow-white way of life. You assure us of our spiritual nobility with a beautiful certificate of rank: You cause Your Gospel to be preached and written, and blazon the divine city of the Christian Church with Your two great insignias, Baptism and the Lord's Supper. The Gospel declares and the Sacraments show that we are God's noble heirs. You give us powerful privileges and freedom from the control of the devil, death, and hell, and make us eternal barons [or free lords] in heaven (John 8:36). How can we ever repay You for this honor? Oh, grant Your grace, that I may execute my feudal service,[462] my vocation, as a true nobleman, and be ready at every passing moment to serve You, to do or do not according to Your will. Help me not to be too deeply involved in my secular affairs (for in olden days, those among the nobility who practiced common trades were refused admittance to tournaments). Neither do You desire among Your Christians such hearts as too eagerly pursue temporal things. So help me to turn my heart toward You in heaven, and to be wholly devoted to You.

Shem also means "he who is established or set down,"[463] (cf. Heb. *sham,* "placed, put"),[464] for he would be established among the ranks of the ancestors of Jesus Christ, and safely preserved through the flood. O Lord Jesus, You are established as my mercy-seat. For my consolation You have established and seated Yourself at the right hand of the Father. Who can cast You off Your throne? You are established and set down as the rock of my salvation. And if I trust in You, I too will, like the Colossians,

461 "commendatores crucis"

462 I.e., the military service owed a lord by his vassal.

463 "positus"

464 "posuit"

be established, grounded, firmly fixed, and safely preserved from all woe, yea, from the gates of hell, as I sufficiently learned above in Seth's name.

Shem was set above his brothers. O Lord Jesus, You are set above all Your brothers (Rom. 8:17). You were anointed with the oil of gladness more than Your fellows (Ps. 45:7; Heb. 1:9). You are "the firstborn of all creation" (Col. 1:15). Shem was set above his brothers, first, because he was related to the Lord Jesus by blood; second, because he was meek and humbled himself, not trusting in his good works but believing that he would be saved only by the grace of our Lord Jesus. For "whoever humbles himself (falling at the feet of God, like the tax collector or the indebted servant in the Gospels [Luke 18:13–14; Matt. 18:26]) shall be exalted." Third, to Christ's glory Shem bore the world's hatred patiently. Yet whatever the world throws away God lifts up. God regards the rejected. What the world despises God honors. What is afflicted in the world God fills with comfort and joy. Likewise, if anyone wants to have good standing with God, and be chosen as a child of the next world, and be set in the highest place of heaven, and not be cast down to condemnation, he must like Shem lay claim to and take comfort in his blood-kinship with Jesus Christ, and count as his greatest honor Jesus' having become our blood-kinsman. Then, abasing himself, he must humbly seek salvation only in Jesus' merit. Finally, he must all the while patiently endure the world's scorn, mockery, and contempt. Then he will have eternal honor and favor above all unbelievers. For whoever honors Jesus, Jesus will honor him in return; but he who despises Him shall be despised in return [1 Sam. 2:30]. Oh dear Lord Jesus, I too take comfort in Your having become my blood-kinsman. I humbly seek my salvation in You alone. I suffer the contempt of the world. Oh, do not spurn me, I beseech You, but grant me a little place of honor in heaven in the company of all the elect. On the Last Day, the ungodly will awake "to everlasting shame and contempt" (Dan. 12:2), but I to everlasting honor and glory. O Lord Jesus, You Yourself said that You would set Your beloved Christian sheep on Your right hand on high (Matt. 25:33). We will be set above all others; the stinking goats on Your left hand will be below us. You will also honor us pious hearts by speaking to us first. Our glory will be the first, best, and greatest. Then Your bride shall stand "at Your right hand in pure and sumptuous gold" (Ps. 45:9), in new wisdom, righteousness, and godliness. The wicked will be cast into the pit of hell, while I and every believer with me will be taken up to highest heaven and filled with everlasting glory and joy. "Such glory will all His saints possess. Alleluia!" I say with Psalm 149:9. Let us long for that glory while we are here. The idle glory of this world is passing away and profits nothing. God, save us! Just look at how many men exult when they reach the top of the world. They sneer with indignation, yet are never satisfied, beautified, or enriched by it! It lasts no longer than a dance at high mass. Should we then not rather seek after the true, blessed, and impeccable glory, and greatly rejoice in it? For by it we are satisfied, enriched, and blessed. The glory that Jesus won for us by His inglory on Good Friday should inwardly fill our heart with pleasure and outwardly make us boast with words. It should be sung out and extolled. Oh, what a great price many pay just to sit on top of the world! O dearest Lord Jesus, You gave life and limb to buy me the glory of heaven! Grant me in turn that I may be able to give life and limb, wealth and health, and not forfeit the highest place in heaven and the fellowship of all believers.

In the world, the pious and poor are always made to come last and bring up the rear, especially with regard to great noblemen. But with God there is no such notion. Whoever loves and belongs to Jesus comes first, even if he is the poorest beggar. When the rich man and Lazarus were both living (Luke 16:19), the rich man, with all his butter, floated on top and came first in the story. But when they died, the tables were turned. This time, Lazarus came first and was set in the highest place, Abraham's bosom. The rich man came last and had the lowest place, the fires of hell. So be of good cheer, dear heart! Though you may be despised in the world, you will be pulled from the gutter on the Last Day as long as you remain faithful to Christ. When in great tribulations the evil one says, "You have sinned too long, too grossly, too much! Down to hell with you!" I will reply, No, the unrepentant belong down there. I have mourned my sins. I have paid for them with Jesus Christ's merit. I belong to Jesus Christ, the Sin-Atoner and Serpent-Trampler, so I have an advantage over all unbelievers. My place is above, where God's children dwell in heaven, just as Shem was set above his brothers.

Why, then, should I be afraid of death? I will only be exalted thereby to the place that my Lord Jesus secured. Then I will sit on high; then I will mock all my foes and every calamity.

So begone, O worldly pomp and passing splendor! What benefit have I in being honored by the world, as Saul longed to be, saying, "Honor me before the eldest of my people,"[465] (1 Sam. 15:30)? Everlasting honor, everlasting possessions are the things that lift up the spirit. I will gladly come last and be ashamed in this world, yea, confess my own shame and disclose my sin, as did David (Ps. 51:4–5), Matthew (Matt. 9:9), and St. Paul (1 Tim. 1:15)—I will duly repent, if I might but have a share in everlasting glory.

Thank You, Lord Jesus, for setting me and all believers in the highest place of heavenly honor. Keep me from the lowest place of the damned in hell. In turn, I will to Your glory surrender the throne of my life. May You occupy the highest place in my heart and speech. May You be the subject of all my thoughts, the start of my every sentence, the companion of my whole existence, and the recipient of my worship and praise forever. Amen.

465 "Honora me coram populo"

XII. JESUS

Takes Counsel Concerning the Flood, and As Soon As It is Settled Upon,
He Kindly and Faithfully Warns the Pious Noah of the Coming Disaster;
and Noah Finds Grace Because of Jesus Christ (Gen. 6[:8, 13]).

God the heavenly Father discussed with Himself, His Son, and the Holy
Ghost how He should deal with the wicked villains of the first world. Here,
the solemn council of the Holy Trinity unanimously decided that, to address the flood of sin by which the world had been covered, there should
be a flood of seas, an outpouring of water, such as never was known
before. And no sooner was this decided than God the Father, through
His Word, that is, His Son, warned Noah of the coming disaster, advising
him to make ready a great ship and gather all the necessary provisions.
Noah had the great honor of having "found grace in eyes of the LORD"
[Gen. 6:8] and "inherited the righteousness that is by faith" (Heb. 11:7).
Like Mary (Luke 1:30), he believed in the Messiah and found grace for
His sake. Noah was upright and showed his faith with many good works.
He was unyielding and did not allow himself to be blinded, seduced, or
browbeaten by the vast throngs of the world. He reasoned: Better to be
alone than in bad company. He "led a godly life," and was a forthright
preacher (as was also said of Enoch). He carried God in his heart, mouth,
and mind, and as he lived God illuminated his sight. He did everything
that God commanded him. He preached with hand and mouth, with
word and hatchet, and filled both ears and eyes of his listeners. Oh my
Lord and my God, grant me such magnificent virtues also, that following
Noah, and in like measure, I too may be wholly devoted to You in heart,
speech, and life!

Here once again I find my Lord Jesus, for Moses says, "Then the LORD
said, 'Men will no longer let themselves be governed[466] by My Spirit.'"

---

466 LB: *straffen*, "chastised."

Behold, first we find the LORD God, the heavenly Father, then Jesus Christ, His Spokesman, and lastly, God's Spirit, with whom the children of the world strove. Moses further says, "And God said to Noah..."[467] God the Father kindly sent warning to Noah by His Word, that is, His dear Son. Third, Moses says, "Noah found grace in the eyes of the LORD." Here remember the rule of the ancient doctors: Wherever the words "grace" and "mercy" appear, Jesus Christ is present, too, for there is no grace apart from Christ. When the repentant tax collector said, "God be merciful to me, a (poor) sinner!" [Luke 18:13], in his heart he said, "for the sake of Jesus Christ." Thus Noah, too, believed in Jesus Christ and found grace for His sake. Peter alludes to this when he confesses his belief that he would "be saved through the grace of the Lord Jesus Christ, just as they," his fathers in the Old Testament (Acts 15:11). Here you see the essence of the ancient, apostolic, catholic faith, to wit: "By grace you have been saved through faith, and that not of yourselves: it is the gift of God, not of works, so that no man may boast," as St. Paul says in Ephesians 2:8–9. Fourth, God says in this passage, "I will establish a covenant with you." What kind of covenant was Noah and no one else in his generation set apart for? Nothing other than this: Noah would be the ancestor of the Messiah. God would spare and preserve Noah through the flood so that the Messiah would be born from his line. Here is our Lord Jesus once again. Therefore, dear heart, devoutly contemplate your Savior Jesus Christ in these events in truth and for your consolation.

Dear Lord Jesus, I have learned that You are that most judicious Counselor with whom Your Father took counsel concerning the flood. Isaiah, Your cousin (Is. 5:1), was not without cause to call You "Counselor" (9:6).

Oh Lord Jesus, be my Counselor also in every perplexing situation! When no one can help me, advise me of the best way to get rid of my grief. You are a just Lord, for You affirmed that the sin and disgrace of the first world had to be punished. "You are not a God who is pleased by ungodliness; whoever is evil will not stand in Your presence" (Ps. 5:4). Though You may be silent for a time, You keep Your eye on the wicked, noting everything carefully, and at last hold it up before their eyes: "Mark this,

467 Perhaps meaning Gen. 6:7 "And the LORD said..." rather than v. 13.

then, you who forget God" (Ps. 50:22). Oh, help me to fear Your righteous anger and stern judgment!

You are never unjust to anyone. In order that the whole world might know that You justly rewarded the people before the flood according to their merit, You had the warrant and deposition of the committed crimes recorded in Genesis, the book of evidence, as an eternal reminder: Fornication was perpetrated at home. Men knowingly lived in incestuous relationships. They went to and fro like dogs in heat. The children of God were seduced and came to blow the same horn as the children of the world. They ate, drank, sang, and danced in the streets (Matt. 24:38). They caroused over apple-cider and goodly cinnamon-water—which they made better than any Malvasian (beer and wine not yet being in use). Cain's spawn devoured meat without God's permission (for Noah was not permitted until after the flood), and God's children licked it up right alongside them. Thus it was like that proverb: those who cling together, swing together—who dine together, pine together; who drink together, sink together; who nibble together, quibble together.

God's Word was despised in church. The children of God turned apostate and forsook the old faith. Factions, sects, and heresies arose. Men no longer submitted to the chastisements of God's Spirit. So God lamented, saying that He would not suffer His Spirit and Word to strive with that wicked people any more: "My Spirit will not strive with man."[468] The Holy Spirit indwelling the hearts of the godly preachers was no longer to be grieved (Eph. 4:30). Instead of His Word God would send beatings. Instead of the Spirit working with the Word He would send utter calamity. He would proclaim nothing but woe. That faithless people would find their faith too late. The government was full of conceited, proud, puffed-up bullies and tyrants who perpetrated injustice without remorse, nor would they suffer any one to shed a tear over it. They were like that Tryzus described by Aelianus[469] who at first forbade his citizens to speak (for he was despised as much as Pilate). Next, he forbade their winking, which they had learned to make use of when prevented from speaking. Finally, he even forbade

---

468 "Non contendet Spiritus meus cum homine."

469 Aelian. *Var. Hist.* 14.22.

them to weep, the only thing left for expressing their sorrow. Such were the shameful fellows that filled the government in those days. Briefly put, "The wickedness of men was great on earth, and every intention and thought of their heart was only evil" [Gen. 6:5]. O Lord Jesus, You had this written down to show that You are never unjust to anyone. I can only say with Daniel, "O Lord, You are righteous, but we must be ashamed" [Dan. 9:7]. "O Lord, You are righteous, and all Your judgments are just" (Ps. 119:137), I must confess with the repentant emperor Maurice.[470]

Dear Lord Jesus, You are a gracious and long-suffering Lord. You had no desire to rush in upon the wicked scoundrels. You gave them 120 years to think and repent. Oh, how great is Your grace! Now I see that You speak truly when You say, "As truly as I live, I take no pleasure in the death of the ungodly, but that the ungodly should turn and live" (Ezek. 33:11). Oh, guard me from being secure in my sins. Help me not to sin willfully against grace, and do not snatch me away instantly when I do sin, that Your forbearance and long-suffering may lead me to repentance (Rom. 2:4) and make me turn before it is too late.

O Lord Jesus, in these events I see how careful You are in Your work. No sooner had the Most Blessed Trinity in His private council decided that there would be a flood than You went to Noah and revealed the whole secret to him. It is Your proper work to declare the secret counsels and thoughts of Your Father. "No man has ever seen God; the only-begotten Son who is in the bosom of the Father, He has made Him known to us" (John 1:18).

And in this, O Lord Jesus, I see Your friendly heart. A good friend warns another. You cannot leave us unwarned. Thus You warned Jerusalem with words and bitter tears. Thus You also warned us of the final judgment. You gave the first world a definite length of time to exist and specified the number of its years. But You have not revealed a definite length of time to us, for in our case, no specificity of time would help. You opted for another method, preferring to see whether we might be persuaded if the time remained unspecified. "One day is hidden from us,

---

470 St. Maurice (d. AD 287), leader of the Theban legion.

that we might take heed every day."[471] You said that You did not know the time of the world's end: You did not wish to make a revelation because it would not have been good for us to know.[472] Oh, be our faithful friend forever! Be our faithful Eckhart,[473] and warn us of every danger. Every day You warn us with clear words, with celestial signs, with diverse chastisements, with the words of close friends, and with fortuitous thoughts and ideas. Oh, help us to receive Your warning with thanks! Mordecai warned Ahasuerus of his courtier's treachery [Esther 2:22]. Jonathan warned his dear friend David [1 Sam. 19:2]. Those were good and faithful friends.

Oh dear Lord Jesus, You are, to put it simply, the best, most dependable, most enduring, most faithful friend, and we are Your beloved friends. You have made us Your confidants. You say so Yourself: "No longer do I say that you are servants, for a servant does not know what his master does; but I have said to you that you are friends, for all that I have heard from My Father I have made known to you" (John 15:15).

Dear Lord Jesus, You know Your own (2 Peter 2:7[–9]). The whole world was full of wicked men. Only Noah—one single housefather—was godly. You knew about him. You were concerned for him. You love those who love You, and You have a wondrous way of leading them (Ps. 4:3) and protecting them. You can feed them and sustain them—just like those six thousand Christians whom Simeon led over the Jordan to the town of Pella when Jerusalem was besieged by the Romans.[474] To You all things are known. You see the wickedness of the world (Sir. 23:19). You saw Noah's uprightness. Your wisdom, Your all-knowing majesty is my comfort in every need. Though nothing in creation may know me, You do, and in Your grace You are mindful of me and bless me (Ps. 115:12).

As gracious as You are to godly hearts, so wrathful can You be to all who abuse Your grace. With the holy You are holy, with the faithful,

471 "Latet dies unus, ut observentur omnes"; see Hilar. *De Trin.* 9.67.

472 "Noluisti dicere, quia nobis non expedit scire."

473 From Germanic folklore; usually imagined as an old, bearded man, supposed to warn travelers of danger.

474 See Euseb. *Hist. Eccl.* 3.5.3.

faithful, and with the vengeful, vengeful. "You are prepared to love and to hate,"[475] as Ennius said.

1,536 years before, You said, "Let Us make man" [Gen. 1:26]. Now You say, "I am sorry that I have made them." Your Father was of the same opinion as You; You relayed His words. And yet later at the Jordan, when in Your body You began to cleanse and wash away our sins, He said, "'This is My beloved Son, with whom I am well pleased' [Matt. 17:5, par.]—indeed, for whose sake I am well pleased in all men who believe." As we sing in that beautiful sequence:

Forgotten are God's former words, "It repents Me that I made man"[476]

So when I feel Your grace in my heart, I will not grow secure in my sins. Your anger would be rekindled. When I merit Your wrath, I will not despair. "He who ceases to sin renders the anger of God such that it must vanish," says Lactantius.[477] I will earnestly seek pardon for my sins. I know that Your wrath will subside and Your heart will regard me graciously again.

To conclude, O Lord Jesus, I see that, even if You delay the penalty a long time, You do not forget a thing. "The delay of Your vengeance is made up for by the severity of the punishment," says Valerius Maximus.[478] When men neglected the hour of repentance, You were roused to anger at last, and to such ferocity that not only did men suffer destruction but their dwellings, too. Oh Lord Jesus, help me not to sin against grace, lest I be repaid with eternal disgrace. Help me not to abuse Your patience by multiplying my sins. Help me not to tie around my neck the twofold noose of divine wrath and earthly disaster, but in Christian humility to acknowledge, glorify, praise, and extol the kindness of Your heart which You have shown me.

Lastly, just as Noah believed in You and found grace with Your heavenly Father, so let me always find and receive grace in Your name whenever I have need of it, in life and in death. Amen, Lord Jesus! Amen.

---

475 "Amicitiam et inimicitiam in fronte promptam geris"; Ennius 3.41.

476 "Veteris oblita sermonis: pœnitet me fecisse hominem"; from Notker's sequence for Epiphany, "Festa Christi omnis."

477 Lact. *De ira Dei* 22.

478 Val. Max. 1.1.3.

XIII. JESUS

Commands Noah to Enter the Newly Built Ark Eight Days Before the Flood; and When Noah Is Inside, the Lord Jesus Shuts the Door Behind Him (Gen. 7[:1, 16]).

There is a limit to how long a pitcher can be taken to the well before its handle breaks. There is a limit to how long an ungodly man can work his wickedness before he is stamped out. No evildoer has yet gone on sinning for a thousand years, for God always arises and rewards each and every one according to his labor. The people in the flood found this out, too. For 120 years the news was spread about that God would bring His retribution. There is a limit to how long a thing is talked about before it comes true. All of a sudden, the ungodly found their faith in their hands[479] and water in their throats, for when the 120 years had passed, disaster struck. God waited seven days, exactly as He had told Noah. The forty days and forty nights went just as the Lord said. Here you see that all God's words have the force of an oath, and are just as true and certain as if they were sworn a thousand times. Oh dear God, grant that I may tremble at Your threats and not cast Your warning to the wind, lest like a fool I be made wise at my own expense! Help me also to rejoice heartily in Your consolation, and never to cast doubt on Your words, for it is impossible for You to lie [Heb. 6:18]. You are not a deceiver of men. "Heaven and earth will pass away" [Matt. 24:35, par.], but Your words will stand forever.

The flood came in 2314 BC when the world was 1,657 years old; and it wrought its havoc in the month of May, the fairest time of the year, when the youth of all nature is renewed. Likewise, the Son of God said that the fire of judgment would come "at an hour that you do not expect" (Luke 12:40). Oh my Lord Jesus, help me to be ready for Your coming at every passing moment!

---

479 I.e., were forced to believe when it was too late

Moses also tells us where so much water could come from so as to rise ten cubits above all the mountains. First, God opened all the fountains, not with diggers of ditches, miners, or makers of wells, but with His mighty Word. Then, all the dams of the sea were made to burst open and overrun the limits which God had prescribed for them at creation [Job 38:10–11]. If lakes can sweep away a few villages, as they often do, what can the ocean's mighty currents accomplish? Third, God removed the pillars with which He had propped up the clouds so that their torrents came down in great abundance. Here you see that, when God is angry, any created thing can act as His army. Grass, foliage, earth, and water stand ready to serve Him. He "will take His zeal as His suit of armor, and arm creation for vengeance upon His enemies" (Wisd. 5:17). Oh God, what a powerful Lord You are! With You as my ally, all creation must fight for me and turn its powers on those who persecute me.

If God is slow in bringing His grace and assistance, yet He does so with all the more splendor and magnificence. Observe in Mark 5[:22–42], Matthew 9[:18–26], and Luke 8[:41–55] how Jesus did not hasten to the daughter of the ruler of the synagogue in Capernaum, but was delayed on the way by the woman with the issue of blood. All the same, He took care of every last detail and missed nothing. Had He come earlier, He would have only healed a sick body; because He came late, He raised a dead one. This was far more glorious and splendid. In the same way, when God delays His wrath and punishment, He will be all the more stern and severe and take care of all that He seemed to have neglected before. This should be noted carefully in relation to our present passage. Through His Word, that is, through His dearest Son, the eternal Father commanded Noah to get into the ship that he had built. Jesus then urged Noah on so that he would not be late. Finally, after Noah was inside, Jesus Himself closed the door behind him, as Moses says, "The Lord shut him in." This is the same Lord Jesus in whom Eve took comfort during the pain of her childbirth above, and whom we extol as Lord in our Creed. These are the most beautiful words in this account: "The Lord (Jesus) shut him in." And that Jesus Christ was fully at work here is proved by John 1:3: "All things were made by Him." In other words, Jesus has always acted as Creator, not only during the creation of heaven and earth, but in every noble work by which God has revealed Himself to mankind.

Carefully contemplate here the kind, faithful, and benevolent heart of Jesus Christ. He remembered Noah. When disaster was nigh, He warned him abundantly. The world was full of men, but out of them all Jesus set His heart only on Noah, for Noah's heart was set on Him also. Jesus proved that He was telling the truth when He said, "I love those who love Me" (Prov. 8:17). He urged Noah on so that he would not miss the opportunity. And when Noah had gone inside and found no way to secure the door against the waters, Jesus shut it Himself. He pitched, plugged, and plastered every little crack so carefully that not one drop of water could get through, and no wave, no gale, and no jagged rock could harm the ark. Truly, God was Noah's very own captain, watching him and keeping him safe from every woe. Oh, how loving, tender, and full of blessings You are, Jesus Christ! With what living consolation You warm my heart as I read these events! O my Lord Jesus, I often fall into such distress that, like Noah in the ark, I can only think, What will I do now? I have built the house, and done this and that to the best of my ability. What do I still have to do? How can I secure the door? It can't be done from within, nor can I do it from without. Things have never been as bad as now. How will I make it through? All effort and toil is in vain. But this is my comfort: what Noah could not do, You did. What Noah could not reach, You reached for him. Like Noah I, too, will do as I am commanded to the best of my ability, and leave the rest to You. When I cannot find a way to do something, You will. You have the power to secure me in the cabin of my calling. On You I will rely, and my building will stand high. Blessed are all who trust in You [Ps. 2:12]. He who believes will see it come to pass [Mark 11:23].

O Lord Jesus, Lot was another one who fell into great distress. But when the rulers of the city of Sodom tried to hurt him, You gave Your angels charge to shut the door behind him, and prevented those ruffians from finding him all night. How often You kept the pious Athanasius safe in the very midst of his adversaries! How faithfully You cared for Moses, and kept the stubborn Israelites from trampling him to death! When a certain pious Christian[480] was chased by persecutors and hid himself in a cave, a spider quickly spun a web over the cave's mouth, and his enemies passed by, assuming that no man could be hidden there. Here again You closed up the hole and kept Your loved one safe. When Christ is there, a spider-web can be a wall of steel. When Christ is absent, a wall of steel is as a spider-web, and nothing can help [Job 8:14].

Dear Lord Jesus, make Your old favor new for me every day, for I am a poor sinner. Do not forsake me. Take me into Your care when the world casts me off. Stand by me when the world attacks me. Urge me on by Your Spirit, that I may escape all disaster, and do not let me miss or sleep through my opportune hour as I live in this body. Help me to serve You faithfully and do what is pleasing to You, to rest and to dwell at peace in the vessel of my vocation, not to cry myself to death in difficult times, nor to shorten my life by my own doing, nor to worry my heart away, but to take comfort in the fact that You will shut the door behind me, enclose me in Your grace, secure me from all adversity, and preserve me from all harm of body and soul, goods and honor.

O Lord Jesus, shut the door of my house behind me also whenever I go to the ark of the church, and turn away all wicked men in the meantime, that no one may do my household harm. Shut the door behind me also when I go to sleep. Deliver me from fire and sudden death. Take my soul to heaven when I must die, and enclose me in Your kingdom, that no trouble may plague me. Finally, take me on the Last Day to Yourself in heaven. Conduct me to the heavenly wedding that You have prepared with Your blood for Your wise virgins, Your repentant Christians. Then the door will be shut (Matt. 25:10), that is, no one will ever harm or plague us again, and we will dwell there in everlasting rest and peace. Amen, Lord Jesus! Amen.

---

480 St. Felix of Nola (d. 14 Jan. 255), martyr; see Ryan I 91.

XIV. JESUS,
Noah's Vessel of Grace, the Mighty Fortress and Ark in Which We Escape the Flood of God's Wrath (Gen. 7[:7]).

Moses records two great and wondrous works. First, he describes how God wiped out all mankind. The waters rose fifteen cubits above every mountain, rushed over the world with great force, knocked down houses, uprooted trees, and removed mountains. Evidence found in underground mines prove how devastating the flood was. Oh God, how mightily You rage! To have a wrathful God far outweighs every kind of misery. Oh God, grant grace that I may fear Your wrath, keep myself from sin, and put away all immorality, lest I invite upon my poor soul the ravaging fire of Your wrath. For You are still as enraged by sin today as You always have been. You are still just as angered by shamefulness and immorality as ever before. What benefit to the ungodly was their great society which they had built up in their sins, now at the very moment of their demise? It would have been best if they had amended their ways and heeded Noah's good advice. Indeed, it would have been markedly better if they had imitated lonely old Noah and been preserved with him rather than run with the great throngs of the world and join them in condemnation. At the same time, Moses is careful to say, "And all flesh died." He does not say "all souls...." For some of them, having climbed up into a tower or tree, and seeing their fellows drown before their very eyes, beat their breast, praying to God for the forgiveness of their sins. In such cases God spared their soul, though because of their sins their body still had to die. It is a powerful comfort to know that God will have mercy on the vilest sinners, and that, even though He must put their body to death, He will still be gracious to their soul if they sincerely repent and turn to Him.

Second, Moses speaks of a great miracle whereby Noah, the emperor, and his seven electors[481] were kept alive in their great ship. God will never be so angry as to neglect the faithful in the midst of His wrath. Although pious hearts must suffer great agony when God permits plagues to strike the wicked (for he who stands under the eaves in a heavy rain still gets splashed), yet the faithful will fare better. God will turn a gracious eye upon them: "Surely the righteous will enjoy His fruit" [Ps. 58:11]. Thus we find yet another image of our Lord Jesus Christ in this great ark or ship of Noah's. Augustine saw this, for he says, "Just as Noah was kept alive in wood and water, so all believing hearts are saved by the merit of Christ on the cross and the water of Baptism."[482]

Dear Lord Jesus Christ, You let Yourself be nailed to the tree of the cross, and became a curse in our stead, that You might win for us the blessing of God's grace. You have included this merit of Yours in Holy Baptism and instituted for us "a washing of regeneration and renewal of the Holy Spirit" [Titus 3:5], "not as a removal of dirt from the body," 1 Peter 3[:21] states, but rather as the gracious cleansing of our sins, that we may escape God's wrath. This is the healing flood—not a flood of wrath but of grace—in which we are cleansed from all the wickedness that we inherited from Adam, as well as that which we ourselves have done. As sinners were drowned in the flood, so our sins are drowned and submerged in Baptism. Just as when Noah was about to embark upon the waters God told him, "With you I will establish a covenant," God likewise tells all baptized Christians, "With you I will forge an eternal alliance." Thus Peter calls Baptism "the covenant of a good conscience with God." We promise to serve God alone. He promises to show us everlasting kindness. Therefore, dear heart, take comfort in your Baptism whenever you are in distress, just as Blandina did during her agony, saying, "I am a Christian."[483]

481 I.e., Noah and his sons and their wives, compared with the rulers of the Holy Roman Empire.

482 "Noa per aquam et lignum liberatur: Ecclesia per aquam Baptismi et lignum crucis"; August. *Contr. Faust. Manich.* 12.14.

483 "Christiana sum" (the German gloss adds the word "baptized" here for clarity); Euseb. *Hist. Eccl.* 5.1.19.

And when Wandregisel[484] was tempted by the evil one and unable to find solace in his cloister, the words "I am a baptized Christian"[485] were his blessed breastplate. And when Friedrich Barbarossa fell off his horse into the water, and was pulled out again, and was about to die from the ordeal, he said, "My God, what a washing I've had! Now I take comfort in the washing of regeneration of the Baptism to which I was brought as a child. Oh God, let that old comfort which You promised me in the waters of Baptism when I was a child be renewed for me, a wretched man, who have fallen into waters of great peril, and take me to Yourself in eternal life as You have promised."

In addition to this, the ark is itself a type of Jesus Christ, the friend of our soul.

Noah's ark was enormous: three hundred cubits long, fifty wide, and thirty high—as wide as our city church in Fraustadt, but five times its length and six cubits higher than its roof. The ark had three decks or balconies. The livestock was on the bottom, grain, straw, hay, and food were kept in the middle, and Noah and the birds lived on the top. This was a great load to bear, O Lord Jesus, yet You are also great. Your person is great (You are true God and true man), Your office is great, Your benefits are great, Your power and glory are great. Oh, let my love for You also be great forever.

The ark's measurements and proportions agree with the measurements of the human body, for as Augustine and Philo say, when man is lying on the ground, his body is ten times as long as it is deep, and six times as long as it is wide. O Lord Jesus, You are an incomprehensible, immeasurable God, and yet to our honor You took upon Yourself a human nature with finite lengths, bounds, and measures. Oh, thanks be to You forever and ever because of this!

In the measurements of the ark, the numbers thirty and fifty are both present. So in Your Baptism, Lord Jesus, thirty and fifty are also both present. You were thirty years old according to Your frail humanity, and it was thirtieth year of Moses' jubilee. At the same time, it was also a year

---

484 St. Wandregisel (ca. 600–668), Benedictine abbot.

485 "Christi lavacro tinctus sum."

of fifty, that is, the eightieth jubilee since the creation of the world (80 x 50 = 4,000).[486]

The ark was tough and durable. Water could not soak through it, wind could not tip it, whales could not upset it. Nothing touched it for a whole year. Dear Lord Jesus, You are strong, firm, and enduring. You can take a beating. Death cannot hold You [Acts 2:24]. The gates of hell cannot prevail against You [Matt. 16:18]. Before You all the proud waves of cruel tyrants must be stayed [Job 38:11]. No one can slake or break Your power. You put the devil, death, grave, and hell to shame and mockery. Your almighty power is my shield and refuge. In You I put my trust. Who trusts in You builds well and true.[487] A mighty fortress is our God, a trusty shield and weapon.[488] O Lord Jesus, You are my impregnable castle. With You as my armor I can simply defy all my foes.

Forty days after the great waters (which stayed for 150 days) a raven flew out of the ark, just as forty days after Your Baptism in the Jordan and Your fast, the black raven of hell, the devil, came out into the wilderness and tried to sway You from Your task. Not long after [the raven left the ark], a dove brought a green balsam-leaf[489] to Noah, just as at Your Baptism a beautiful dove also appeared when the Holy Spirit descended upon You in a bodily shape like a dove, showing that Your Father's comforting words referred to You. Thus He declared that You are the One in whom we find the true balm that can heal the wounds of our conscience.

Noah's ark carried the whole new world, the whole of mankind, all the people that would be left after the flood. It sustained man and beast and preserved their temporal lives. O Lord Jesus, You carry and sustain the entire race of man before and after the flood. No one can live without You. Indeed, You give all believers life everlasting.

---

486 Herberger places Christ's Baptism 4,000 years after creation; for more on this chronology, see note ooo/xxx in part 1, meditation 2.

487 See the hymn "Wer Gott vertraut hat wohl gebaut" (J. Mühlmann, 1598); *LSB* 714.

488 From the hymn "ein feste Burg ist unser Gott" (M. Luther, 1529) st. 1, lines 1–2; see *LSB* 656:1.

489 Imagined here is the leaf of a tree from which curative balm (< "balsam") is produced.

Noah's ark had a skylight (which the Jews think was made of crystal)[490] and by this he was able to see what the weather was like. Dear Lord Jesus, Your every word is a skylight to heaven, yea, to the heart of the heavenly Father. When I hear You speak, I see the weather of heaven, Your Father's disposition toward me. Through Your Holy Spirit remind me of Your comforting words in all my troubles, that I may know the gracious will of Your Father in heaven and behold it in a clear light.

Outside of the ark there was nothing but danger: no salvation, no life. Outside of You, O Lord Jesus, there is no salvation. Outside of You there is no life, but utter calamity and destruction. Happy were all who were in the ark with Noah. They stayed warm and dry as it rained and snowed outside. Happy are all who are in Christ Jesus. They are protected from every stormy blast and evil spirit, and the gates of hell shall not prevail against them. Even if the whole world were filled with calamity, the faithful would not be lost.

The ark was Noah's comfort through his lengthy sorrow. The year was long, the days many, the hours much more, and the thoughts innumerable. But whenever he had great feelings of anxiety, Noah reasoned, "In spite of all this, dear God, You must love me, for this ark is proof of it. You commanded me to build it and go inside, and You shut the door behind me. Your love is my source of comfort. Your love will bring be back to land." When like Noah in the ark I suffer from long-lasting misery, when thought after thought comes beating like waves of the sea, when everything around, below, and above me is frightening, when I am inches from death, when there is no one in the world to comfort me—O Lord Jesus, then I turn my thoughts to You. Then like Noah contemplating the ark, my heart is consoled and I shout with joy, "In spite of all this, dear God, You must love me, for I see it in Your Son. Here You declared Your love by sharing Your heart with me, and giving me Your Son, the most beautiful piece of heaven. May Your love be my comfort and joy. May Your love be with me and help me. May Your love save me forever. Amen!

---

490 *Ber. Rab.* 31.11; *Sanh.* 108b. Rashi 8.22: "Some say it was a window. Others say that it was a precious stone which shone, giving them light."

XV. JESUS

*Is the Noble Balsam Shrub; His Benefits Are the Healing Leaves of
Ointment Which God's Spirit, the Holy Dove of Pentecost, Ushers into
Noah's Spiritual Ark, That Is, into Noah's Heart and Ours (Gen. 8[:11]).*

For a whole year Noah was stuck inside the ark, [locked up] much like
Daniel in the lion's den (Dan. 6), during which time he concluded that
God had forgotten him—as is our habit whenever God's presence cannot
be instantly seen with our eyes or touched with our hands. Yet Moses says,
"And God remembered Noah." Our Lord Jesus is not fickle or forgetful.
His heart remains steadfast in its kindness toward us. "The Lord is mindful of us and blesses us," says Psalm 115:12. And so in Isaiah, the Lord Jesus,
the Redeemer of Israel and His saints, says, "Can a woman forget her
child? ...Behold, I have engraved You on My hands," etc. (Is. 49:15–16). O
dear Lord Jesus, grant that Your constant faithfulness and kindness may
be upon me and my house forever. If all the world should forget me, be
mindful of me and comfort me.

Further consider how every created thing stands at the beck and call
of the Lord Jesus. The wind was made to lick up the waters with its huge
mouth. The stormy clouds were defied to fall any longer; the sky was made
to hold them up. The rain was stopped, the springs were dried up, the vast
sea was pushed back to its former bounds. O Lord Jesus, how can I not
rely on You? Are not heaven and earth and all that is in them required to
obey You?

Lord Jesus, You were not only able to dispel the physical flood that
swept over the world, but also the emotional one that smothered Noah's
anxious heart. Oh Lord, when the brooks of Belial pass over me [2 Sam.
22:5; Ps. 18:4], and my heart is crushed by a flood of tears and sadness so
that it faints, let Your Spirit, Your Holy Wind of Pentecost, breathe and
blow into it. Command all my foes to turn back and retreat from me, that
my afflicted heart may be filled up, relieved, and revived.

Something else worthy of consideration is that the flood topped all the mountains in forty days. It was done quickly. So it goes today. When adversity comes, it comes by the ton; when it leaves, it leaves by the ounce, or less. In a flash we are sick, poor, miserable, and weak, yet how long it takes to get back on our feet! Do not let it fret you, dear heart. Our Lord Jesus is not always the "Lord of Hasting"; He is often a "Lord of Waiting" or "Lord of Whiles."[491] He may take His time, but He doesn't forget a thing. Rather, He makes up for His delay with blessings all the richer.

When it stopped raining, Noah released a raven which, according to Jerome's interpretation, fattened itself on the carcasses that floated here and there, and did not return. This is exactly how masquerading church-boys and pseudo-Christians behave. Though they join the communion of believers for a while, they are fickle, and as soon as they figure out how to get goods and profits in the world, and how to fill their bellies, they become rebellious apostates and heretics and persecute Christians far worse than those who never heard the truth, until finally they receive their reward with the black ravens of hell. Such a ravenous nature is possessed by all the enemies of the Gospel. In 1534, Duke John Frederick, elector of Saxony,[492] visited a beautiful church in Annenberg and heard one such fellow squawking blasphemies against the Gospel, whereupon he said, "The cage is pretty, but the bird can't sing any good songs." This was another one of those black ravens.

Noah then released a dove, which, because it could find nowhere to land, returned to him. Those of the dove's species remain in the community of God's children.

After seven days, Noah sent out another dove, and this one came back at evening carrying a green oily leaf from a balsam bush. Then Noah rejoiced inside the ark, reasoning, "The waters must have greatly receded if the humble little balsam bush is already visible!" Now in this passage I prefer this reading of "balsam shrub," which is what *zaith* in

---

491 I.e., the Lord does not always act quickly; Herberger playfully couches the appropriate adjectives in phrases that sound like noble titles.

492 Johann Friedrich I (1503–1554), elector of Saxony.

Exodus 30:34 plainly refers to. And in Psalm 133:2 it is called "ointment."[493] So Luther rendered it "balsam" there, for "balsam" is a new word and is not found in the Hebrew Bible, only either *zaith,* in our passage here in Exodus 30:34, or else *shamen,*[494] as in Psalm 133:2.

Here take thought, dear heart, and notice a great mystery. You have heard mention of a flood, an ark or vessel, a dove, a leaf of ointment, and evening-tide. Let the reader understand: the first 2,000 years of the world's existence are its morning, the second 2,000 years its noon, and the last 2,000 years its evening. We have nearly reached evening, if the prophecy from the house of Elias is true. What occurred in the New Testament at evening? Counting 4,000 years from the creation of the world, when the final 2,000 years began, Jesus Christ was baptized in water. As God drowned sins before, so Jesus Christ drowned all our sins in the Jordan and consecrated Holy Baptism for us as a gracious flood and washing away of our sins. Immediately, the Holy Spirit appeared like a dove, and descended upon our Ark of grace, Jesus Christ, testifying that He is the noble Branch that grew out of the roots of Jesse [Is. 11:1], that He bears the precious leaf of ointment that heals our wounds, and that the comforting voice of God the Father referred to none other than the baptized Lord Jesus. Nazianzen took great delight in expounding this mystery: Just as Noah's dove flew from the ark's chamber, so the Holy Spirit, who testifies of Christ, flies from the treasure-chamber of Jesus Christ's good heart and is poured into the little chamber of our heart, as St. Peter proves in his sermon on Pentecost (Acts. 2:14–36).

O Lord Jesus Christ, just as Noah surely must have regarded You in the blessed balsam shrub and leaf of ointment, let me now contemplate You in it also.

The noble balsam shrub grew only in the land of the Jews and some parts of Egypt. Modern balsam is exported from Spain, but it is not the good, old balsam. I have personally observed that this balsam is left out

---

493 Germ. *Öle,* as dinstinct from LB: *Balsam.*

494 The word "balsam" is supposed to be derived from Heb. *baal,* "lord" and this word, Heb. *shamen,* "oil."

of theriacs[495] and replaced with a different, distilled, artificial ointment for the simple fact that true balsam cannot be found on earth any longer. O dear Lord Jesus Christ, You also lived and showed yourself only in the land of the Jews, as well as in Egypt when You were a child. Nowadays, You do not even allow Yourself to be viewed with the eyes or grasped with the hands, as You did after Your resurrection, but You visit the world in veiled form. When we hear Your Word, use Your Sacraments, and call on You, You are in the midst of us, powerfully and palpably demonstrating Your gracious presence with comfort and blessing. On the Last Day, however, we will see You with our very own eyes, just as You were seen in the land of the Jews. For You will come in the same way as You went into heaven, as the angels said [Acts 1:11]. "I will behold Your face in righteousness, I will be satisfied when I awake according to Your likeness" (Ps. 17:15).

The balsam shrub is low to the ground, as tall as a man at most, and has small leaves like rue. O Lord Jesus, You also made Yourself lowly, came down from heaven to us in this world, and did not despise our lowliness. You humbled Yourself to the point of death, even the shameful death of the cross [Phil. 2:7–8], that we might but be pulled from the depths of our sins and established on high in heaven.

The balsam shrub was drowned by the great waters of the flood, but it held on until it peered out over the waters again, and flourished all year round. O Lord Jesus, You too were drowned by the flood of God's wrath during Your Passion: All His waves and billows went over You, as You lamented in Psalm 42:8. You drank a bitter draught from the brook by the way, from the murky river of death; You lifted up Your head (Ps. 110:7): You conquered, rose again from the dead, and flourished. You live and reign all year round, and die no more [Rom. 6:9]. Indeed, You shall be our joyous Comforter forever.

After three years, the balsam bush bore its fruit and produced its remarkable gum. O Lord Jesus, for three whole years You preached and performed miracles in the land of the Jews. In the fourth year, You sang Your joyous "It is finished"[496] on the cross [John 19:30], and everything

495 Medicinal tonics or antidotes for poison.

496 "Consummatum est."

that was required for man's salvation was finished. This is the blessed balm that can heal our wounded conscience.

When a balsam bush is sliced with a stone knife or cut with a fine bone, it exudes its precious balm. In Your circumcision You were sliced with a knife of slate. In Gethsemane You were squeezed in the press of Your Father's wrath. In the Praetorium You were cut with the reeds and the crown of thorns. On the cross You were pierced with cruel nails and the spear of Longinus. Then You exuded the precious balm of Your blood that cleanses us from our sins, a sweet-smelling balm far better than the precious oil of Aaron's priestly garments (Ps. 133:2). Thus the Gospel, which is a testimony of Your blood, is also called a sweet savor. Yea, You pour out the Holy Spirit, the true oil of gladness and most precious comfort that we have in life and death.

When a serpent is put under a balsam bush it loses all its venom. O dear Lord Jesus, You put the serpent, the devil, under Your feet, crushed his head, and took away all his power so that he could no longer harm any believing heart.

Balsam oil completely heals the most serious wounds from all pain within three days. It was out of a particular grace that God gave this precious ointment to His people, knowing that they would constantly have to fight difficult battles. O Lord Jesus, You were wounded on the cross, but by the third day You had healed Yourself completely. On the third day You were alive. After two days You will revive us; on the third day You will raise us up, and we will live before You, as Hosea 6:2 promises us. First comes our day of death, second, our day of rest in the tomb, and third, the Last Day, when we will all be made alive by virtue of our Balm, Jesus Christ. Then all our wounds will be healed also, as that pious mother once said about her invalid infant.[497]

Balsam oil greatly eases every pain. The Samaritan understood this quite well (Luke 10:34), for he poured ointment on the wounds which he had first sterilized with wine. O Lord Jesus, You ease all my pains whenever I think about You and find Your consolation in my heart.

---

497 Perhaps a reference to Herberger's second child, a pious son that died at a young age.

Balsam oil was used to consecrate kings and priests for their office. O dear Lord Jesus, You loved us, and cleansed us from sin with Your blood, and made us "kings and priests," as it says in Revelation 1:6 and 5:10. We are "the royal priesthood," as 1 Peter 2:9 says. Through prayer we can now enter into the most holy heart of God in the hope that He will graciously receive us.

Balsam branches were used as tokens of peace. When balsam could not be found, some other kind of resinous branches was used. In peacetime, moreover, Greek children used to celebrate a festival of games with olive or laurel branches on October 8, calling it *ōskhophoria* or *eiresiōnē*,[498] (the "branch-festival"). O Lord Jesus, You are my token of peace, my Prince of Peace. You have won me peace with God and my conscience, and peace in eternal life.

Balsam was very valuable. The Jews defended their balsam gardens as their own life and limb, and would not suffer the Romans to use their precious produce. O Lord Jesus, You are my richest and most valuable Treasure. I will fight for You as for my own life and limb. If I have You, heaven is mine as well.

The branches of the valuable true balsam each had ten leaves. Oh Lord Jesus, here I am reminded of the blessed ten phrases of the Second Article of the Creed, wherein Your benefits are summarized and contained. These are beautiful, green leaves of consolation in which all sad hearts can take pleasure. For my consolation You (1) were conceived, (2) were born, (3) suffered, (4) were crucified, (5) died, (6) were buried, (7) descended into hell, (8) rose again, and (9) ascended into heaven; and for my joy You (10) sit at the right hand of God's majesty. Thanks be to You forever because of this.

Noah's dove plucked a leaf from a balsam bush and carried it to Noah inside the ark. O Lord Jesus, the Holy Spirit, who caused Himself to be seen like a dove at the Jordan, is He who takes Your benefits and carries them into my weary heart, filling me with joy. Thus You say, "He will bear witness of Me," "He will glorify Me...He will take of Mine" [John 15:26; 16:14–15]. It is the proper work of the Holy Spirit to remind me of Your

---

498 "ὠσχοφόρια *oder* εἰρεσιώνη"

bountiful merit and to assure my heart that I have been reconciled to God through You.

Noah's dove picked up a resinous leaf in its beak. The Holy Spirit proclaims the Lord Jesus through His little mouthpieces and messengers, that is, through faithful preachers of the Gospel. Thus the office of preaching is also called the office of the Spirit. So wherever a faithful preacher teaches about Jesus Christ, there God's Spirit is active and busy, bringing the Word to life in the hearts of the hearers so that, thus consoled, they begin praising and worshiping God. O God, Holy Spirit, grant that the precious balsam branch of Jesus Christ's merit may be profitably conveyed by all preachers of the Gospel into the arks of their Christian hearers' hearts. So whenever a pious child of the Church hears a sermon about our Lord Jesus, let him say: This preacher, too, is a mouth of the Dove of Pentecost; He carries Jesus Christ on his lips. O Holy Spirit, let this beautiful comfort be preserved and kept safe in the treasure-chest of my heart.

When Noah saw this branch or leaf of ointment, his heart was elated, and he thought, "Praised be the hour! Now God has turned to me again. Now God's wrath will relent. Now everything will be better." Such also are the thoughts of my heart whenever I hear, read, or speak of our Lord Christ: Praised be the hour! for now I have heard of the precious balm of Jesus Christ's benefits which smile at me in the blessed balsam bush of Christ. Since Christ is preached, presented, and given to me, there is nothing to worry about. Every flood of wrath has been stopped. All my sins have been taken away. God's love and kindness will rest upon me forever.

O God, Holy Spirit, blessed Dove of Pentecost, display Your proper work in me in my every need. When I am about to pray, show me the precious leaf of the ointment of Jesus Christ's merit, that I may have fresh courage in prayer. When I suffer hardship, point me to the sweet-smelling balm of Jesus Christ's benefits, that I may not despair. In my tribulations, show me the balm of Jesus Christ gracious working, that I may not die. As long as I live, frame in my heart the blessed Fountain of anointing, Jesus Christ, that I may lead a Christlike life to His glory. When I must die, be like Noah's dove and fill me with joy. Remind me of the precious ointment that was poured out from the balsam shrub of Jesus Christ in the garden, in the Praetorium, and on the cross, that I may be assured that no flood of wrath will go over me, but that I will live and dwell forever in God's grace, Amen. O God the Holy Spirit, Amen, in Jesus Christ's name! Amen.

XVI. JESUS

Speaks to Noah, Saying, "Go Out from the Ark." Noah's Joy, As of One Risen from the Dead and Come Out of the Tomb, Foreshadows the Paschal Joy That Our Heart Will Have on the Last Day (Gen. 8[:16]).

The waters dried up and receded. Noah's sadness was turned to joy. Oh how comforting this is! "Merciful and gracious is the LORD, patient and of great goodness. He will not always chide, nor keep His anger forever" [Ps. 103:8–9]. Noah took off the roof so that, like those who have spent a year in prison, he and his children might adjust gradually to the fresh air and not be physically hurt by the sudden change; for God wants every man to take care of his health and to attend to it as well as he can. Then Jesus Christ, the ancient Spokesman of the heavenly Father appears—the One who earlier brought Noah warning, urged him into the ark, shut him in, and called him out again. O dear Lord Jesus, You are ever the same old Jesus, the same old Comforter and Friend, in fair weather or foul. You still remembered Noah on that day as You had for 120 years before. Your steadfast, unchangeable faithfulness is my source of comfort forever and ever.

O dear heart, pay attention to the words of Jesus Christ in this text. He is a man of honor, and He knows what honor means. When He spoke, He put master Noah first as the head of His household, his wife beside him, the children next, after them the children-in-law, and the senseless beasts last. Oh Lord Jesus, help me also to learn propriety and good manners from You, and to show honor to those to whom honor is due [Rom. 13:7]. Help me also to demonstrate my love according to such proper order, putting You first before all else, and thinking of my fellows in the faith and my family next, and then my servants, and my material possessions last of all.

Noah hearkened to the voice of Jesus Christ. For when opportunity comes, one should not be caught sleeping. When someone offers you a pig, get your sack. Oh Lord Jesus, nothing can turn out well for those who ignore You. So give me Noah's obedient heart, that I may constantly live according to Your will.

Here we find the Spokesman of the heavenly Father, Christ Jesus, in His proper and comforting work, for He is the same Lord who spoke to the godly men of the Old Testament from the beginning (John 8:25).

The Lord Jesus is present in this passage as the Lord High Chancellor, speaking to Noah on God the Father's behalf. O dear Lord Jesus, if You can relay Your Father's words to us men, then You can also relay my words back to Your Father. Since Your Father entrusted His words for me to Your care, I too will entrust my words for Your Father to Your care. I know that You will speak them effectively. You can speak far better than I. Every little scar and wound that You received on Your holy body for my sake is a tongue to plead my cause. Oh, how powerfully Your holy nail-prints cry and plead for me, a poor sinner! And so, dear Lord Jesus, since the world is unreliable, I will commit my business with Your Father strictly to Your care. I would gladly have Him as an ally. Oh, grant me a good word! You will not say anything for Yourself personally, for You have no need. You and the Father are one. You will plead my cause justly and fairly. Oh, do so, Lord Jesus, for the glory of Your name! Amen.

In this passage the Son of God says to Noah, "Go out." This is an old, gracious word of comfort from which we learn that He is a "Master to help" [Is. 63:1], and that there is no trouble so great that He cannot and will not help.

Noah prayed himself nearly to death during this long, weary year. But now it was made clear to all the world that he had not groaned and sighed in vain. Oh Lord Jesus, do not let me cry so long. Hear my prayer also, even as You answered Noah's cry. Say to me also, "Go out from your wearisome misery, and be saved in body and soul." Noah had a wearisome year of hardship that gave him anguish beyond measure, yet one day it came to an end, and he received comfort and found help.

O Lord Jesus, comfort me in my wearisome misery, that I may not despair, but await with Christian forbearance the joy of that final hour when You shall say to me, "Go out from of your long-suffered cross." Oh Lord Jesus, speak this gracious message today to every oppressed and worried heart! If the condition of Noah's heart during that year could only be seen, God help us, what great and heavy tribulations would be found there! It was no daily Martinmas and hourly carnival in Noah's heart. Distressing thoughts raced through his mind, one after another. But then the Lord Jesus said, "Go out," and every bit of sadness and melancholy disappeared. Oh Lord Jesus Christ, look also upon my woeful, afflicted, and oppressed heart! With love and kindness say, "Go out from Your tribulation," that my heart may be glad.

When Noah was about to die, he thought about this day, saying, "A long time I sat in the ark; finally, my Redeemer said to me: 'Go out.' Oh, how glad I was then! Now, too, I have dwelt long enough in the world, and my Redeemer is calling me out of it just as He once called me out of the ark. Blessed be His gracious will! Oh, how happy I shall be when I take my first step in heaven." O Lord Jesus, when I have lived long enough in this world, You will say to me likewise, "Go out, faithful servant, from the ark of your cross and 'enter into the joy of your Lord'" [Matt. 25:21–22]. I will gladly and willingly follow You, and tell my soul (like the pious abbot Hilarion), "Go out, my soul! Why do you doubt? For you have a gracious Redeemer and Giver of reward. For nigh seventy years you have served Christ, and do you now fear death?"[499]

"And Noah went out," says Moses. This was Noah's Last Day and Easter feast. He had entered the ark on a Sunday the previous year, right around the same time of the month, as both Cedrenus[500] and the *Encyclopedia of History*[501] place it. We likewise will have our Last Day and Easter feast, and go out from our graves and coffins (which are made in exactly the same proportion as the measurements of Noah's ark), and there will be only the joy of the eternal Sunday, as pointed out earlier on the subject of the Sabbath.[502] Our Lord Jesus will make His voice heard,

---

499 "Egredere, anima mea; quid dubitas? Habes enim misericordem Redemptorem et Remuneratorem. Septuaginta prope annis servisti Christo, et mortem times?" Hier. *Vit. S. Hilarion.* 45; "Habes…Remuneratorem" added from an unknown source.

500 Georgios Kedrenos (11ᵗʰ c.), Byzantine historian.

501 "Fasciculus temporum"; first published by Werner Rolewinck in 1474.

502 See part 1, meditation 13.

and say once more to all who lie in their graves, "Go out from your chambers of sleep, mankind!" All who lie in the earth will obey this call. Remember the power displayed in Jesus Christ's words when He says, "Young man, I say to you, arise," "Young woman, I say to you, arise." and "Lazarus, come out." Oh Lord Jesus, do not tarry long in bringing that joyous day!

Now imagine, dear heart, if you can, what the condition of Noah's heart was at this time! What joy must have filled it! Surely Noah must have said something like this: "Praised be the blessed hour! Oh, how deeply I have yearned for this day. This is the day that You have made, O Lord. Let us rejoice, dear children. Who would have imagined that I could be preserved for such a long time among so many wild beasts? Who would have thought that I could survive such an awful stench? Who would have believed that this great edifice, so often knocked and beaten about, would endure through such great tempests and stormy blasts? Praised be the almighty power of God that kept me safe! Oh, where shall I find words to express my joy? Rejoice, dear children! Praise God with hearts united! Let us always persevere in such praises. Dear God, where shall I find a sacrifice to give You? I will offer You a sacrifice according to the custom of my grandfathers, yet I will sacrifice myself up to You. Oh, let this my sacrifice be pleasing to You. Praise to You, O Lord and Savior, my Redeemer, who shut the door behind me and preserved me till this very hour! Alleluia! Shall my heart not rejoice? God has turned back to me, His love has been shown me, my prayer has been answered, my misery is past, and misfortune has vanished. God Himself has brought me comfort. He knows me and calls me by name, and pledges me His favor and grace. I will never be able to thank Him enough for this. I was not worthy of this wonderful grace, but I was in need of it. Therefore blessed be the mercies of God forever. Amen."

Our hearts will similarly rejoice on the Last Day when Christ calls us out of our graves. Thus says Bernard:

> In whatsoever place I be,
> I long for Jesus constantly.
> What joy of joys when Him I meet!
> What rapture when His face I greet!

His kind embrace, His kiss divine,
Are sweeter far than honey-wine,—
O Christ, what blessing to be Thine![503]

Just as Noah leapt for joy, so we too will rejoice and say, "Blessed is He who comes in the name of the Lord!" Blessed be the long-awaited hour! Oh, how eagerly we longed for this day. "This is the day that the Lord has made." This is the day of our redemption. "Let us rejoice and be glad in it" [Ps. 118:24.]. To our reason it seemed unlikely that we would be kept safe in our coffins for such a long time, and that our bones would be preserved in the ark of the earth. Now we have witnessed the almighty power of our God. Be praised, O Lord Christ, for preserving our ashes, and regarding our bones, and giving us back all the good friends that death had taken. The sorrow of our heart was great in that life. Now sorrow is gone, and that joy is come which no man shall take from us [John 16:22]. The joy of our heart is greater than any grief ever was. Though all the stars were scribes, and all the waters ink, and all the trees their feather-pens, and heaven and earth their paper, yet they could not commit our joy and blessedness to writing. Though every blade of grass were a tongue, yet our glory could not be expressed. Blessed be God the Father who has given us this glory. Blessed be Jesus Christ who purchased this treasure for us with His blood. Blessed be the Holy Spirit who made this joy known to us in the Gospel, and strengthened our hearts in the faith. O beloved angels of God, assist us in praising our God, that our Alleluia may be sung with power. O elect and blessed children of God, let your glorified voices resound to the glory of God our Savior. As for ourselves, let us offer up every vessel, thought, utterance, and deed to God forevermore. Let us sing praises to God who has granted us a blessed departure from the former world, strengthened us in death, and preserved us unto eternal life. Now we step into a new world, yet not as Noah into the world after the flood, but into that far more beautiful world of blessed eternity. Our misery is gone, our grief is ended,

---

503 "Quoconque loco fuero, / Semper [corr. for "Mecum"] Jesum desidero, / Quam laetus, cum invenero, Quam felix, cum tenuero, / Tunc amplexus, tunc oscula, / Quae vincunt mellis pocula. / Quam felix Christi copula!" From the hymn *Jesu dulcis memoria*, attr. Bernard.

the wrath of God has been drowned. Now we see God face to face, now we hear God Himself speak. He calls us and knows us by name. How can we ever repay Him for this? Oh, how is it that we poor clods of earth should come into such glory? Blessed be God's mercy! We did not merit this from God. It is a free and gracious gift from His unspeakable love. May His love rest upon us forever. May His love flow out over our bodies and souls. May His love be requited with everlasting and unceasing praise. Amen.

Note one more thing, dear heart: all the wild animals behaved tamely for Noah. They came to him two by two, as orderly as young ladies and young men at a ball. So will it be in the new world, too, when all strife and discord will cease, and pairs, partners, and matches will be made with beauty and tenderness. For heaven and earth will not be annihilated in the last fire, but renewed, purged, and scoured clean. In a fire, gold remains gold and silver silver. Its essence is not lost, only its form and shape. Yet it is greatly refined and freed from impurity. Likewise, the new heaven and new earth will be much more beautiful. Neither will we be locked up in heaven as in a prison, but will be swift, agile, and fleet of foot like the angels of God. We will be able to race back and forth between heaven and earth in the blink of an eye, beholding all of God's creatures properly, and so praise His almighty power, wisdom, and goodness because of them. All creation will be man's amusement, to come and go according to his will. No trace of hostility or hatred will be known any more. Oh, if only we were there!

O Lord Jesus Christ, come and keep the blessed Easter feast of Your Church. Let Your tender voice exclaim, "Go out, O pious hearts, from the ark of your grave!" and lead us into the joy, exultation, and blessedness of eternal life which words cannot describe. Oh, come, Lord Jesus! Equip Your poor flock that it may do Your will, and in Your rest hereafter eternally praise Your name. Amen.

XVII. JESUS,

The Altar of Christendom, Depicted in the First and Oldest Altar, and in Noah's Burnt Offering (Gen. 8[:20]).

Noah, the emperor of the second world, was not ashamed of worship, but took diligent care to restore and provide for it. Oh Lord Jesus, grant that no one in the world may think himself too lofty for prayer and the divine service, but that everyone, including those of high station, would lower themselves in Christian humility to serve You.

The first thing that Noah did after the flood was to build an altar, and this is the first altar recorded in the Bible. Behold, Noah followed the verse, "Seek first the kingdom of God and His righteousness, and everything else will be added to you" [Matt. 6:33]. To be sure, God also deserved this of Noah and his children since He had wonderfully preserved him and their families for a whole year. Oh dear God, help me to be grateful to You also, and never to forget Your benefits. For whoever thanks You for a past benefit will get another one from You.

By no means, however, did Noah preside over this altar and its sacrifices in silence, but clearly preached the Messiah to whom all sacrifices pointed. In this you see that even in the Old Testament the death of the Lord Jesus was proclaimed prior to His coming in the flesh. How much more should it be so now? Here in Noah's altar our Savior is portrayed to us again.

Noah began the first year of the new world with an altar which was a depiction of Jesus Christ. We too should begin every new year, yea, every single thing we do, with Jesus Christ (Col. 3:23). Then it will be free to prosper, for Jesus is "the Alpha and the Omega, the beginning and the end" (Rev. 1:8[; 21:5–6]).

Of course, in Hebrews 13:10 our Lord Jesus is plainly called our altar: "We have an altar from which those who serve the tabernacle have no right to eat." So just as Noah laid his sacrifice on the altar, so may you lay and establish the sacrifice of your prayer on Jesus Christ. Whatever you ask of the heavenly Father in the name of Jesus Christ, He will give it to you [John 16:23]. Psalm 51:19 prophesied that this would happen in the New Testament: "Then You will be pleased with the sacrifices of righteousness, with burnt offerings and whole burnt offerings; then bullocks will be offered on Your altar." Oh Lord Jesus, build the altar of my heart with grace and purity, and grant that in the fire of ardent love I may offer sacrifices to You of Christian humility and thankfulness (as Augustine says in *The City of God,* ch. 4). Also, when I pray in times of distress, be Yourself my consecrated altar. I will lay my groans and Our Fathers upon You and Your merit so that the sacrifice of my lips may be well pleasing to Your heavenly Father.

Noah's sacrifices likewise depict Jesus Christ, for "He made His soul an offering for guilt," as Isaiah 53:10 says; and Jesus "gave Himself for us as an offering" (Titus 2:14[; 1 Tim. 2:6]). Noah's sacrifices were of clean animals. O Lord Jesus, You are completely clean and spotless, purer than the angels, free of sin or blemish. You also cleanse us with Your blood so that we are made "as white as snow" (Is. 1:18). Noah's sacrifices were slaughtered. O Lord Jesus, You also were slaughtered (Is. 53:7) to redeem us from the slaughterhouse of hell in which we should have been torn apart by death. Noah's sacrifices were devoured by fire. Oh Lord Jesus, You burned with ardent love for us and were liquefied in the hot fire of Your Father's wrath to deliver us from the flames of hell. O Lord Jesus, You are the true sacrifice for our souls, and our priest as well. You offered the true thank offering of Your hymn on the evening of Maundy Thursday. You offered the true prayer offering on the cross with a great cry of supplication. You offered the true sin offering in Your own blood. You offered the true guilt offering when You suffered in body and soul. You offered the true burnt offering in the fire of Your Father's stern wrath, obtaining for us the eternal blessing.

There are three kinds of altars that we find in Scripture: first, of earth (Ex. 20:24), second, of stone (Ex. 20:25; Deut. 27:5), and third, of wood overlaid with gold (Ex. 30:1[-3]). O Lord Jesus, You likewise had three kinds of altars. First, You sacrificed Yourself upon the earth of the Garden of Gethsemane, obtaining comfort for our souls by Your sweat of anguish. Next, You sacrificed Yourself on the stone pillar, and on the stone pavement of Gabbatha, obtaining eternal rest and glory for us by Your suffering and ridicule. After that, You made satisfaction on the altar of the wooden cross, which You overlaid with the gold of Your crimson blood, obtaining eternal life for us by Your death. Finally, You let Yourself be locked and sealed in a tomb of stone so that all our sins would be buried, hidden, and sealed up forever. Because of this, Lord Jesus Christ, may You be worshiped and glorified forever and ever. Amen.

XVIII. JESUS,

The Heavenly Father's Heart, with Whom the Heavenly Father Decides That A Flood Shall No More Go Over the Earth (Gen. 8[:21]).

Noah offered a sacrifice of clean animals and birds, for of the unclean Noah had only taken one pair of every sort (Gen. 6:19), but of the clean, three pairs, plus one for a sacrifice. This is what the text of Genesis 7:2–3 means with the two "sevens." There was no doubt about whether Noah would be so thankful to God that he would offer Him a sacrifice as soon as he came to land. Moreover, he kept his promise just as soon as he stepped out of the ark. So you also should "perform your vows to the LORD" [Ps. 50:14]. When you are in trouble, do not promise more than you can or wish to keep—as did that seaman who promised St. Nicholas a candle as big as his ship's mast.[504]

Noah then attests that God took heartfelt pleasure in this sacrifice and smelled its sweet savor. (Moses speaks of God in these terms for the sake of our comprehension.) Here we see that thanksgiving is the highest form of worship.

Thereupon God decided never again to destroy every living thing; in the midst of His wrath He would remember His mercy. He also lamented that man was thoroughly and entirely corrupt, and so we rightly sing:

> Our works are fruitless and in vain,
> And merit but endless pain. Kyrieleis! [505]

O Lord, let Your mercy avail for our good. "O LORD, You are righteous; we must be ashamed," for "when we have done all things…we are unprofitable

---

504 In this legend, the seaman is saved, but then offers St. Nicholas a penny candle instead; the second time he is in danger, the man shipwrecks and drowns.

505 From the hymn "Dies sind die heilgen zehn Gebot" (Luther, 1524), st. 12, lines 3–4; see *LSB* 581:12.

servants" [Dan. 9:7; Luke 17:10].

How powerful Moses' words are when he says, "God said in His heart" [Gen. 8:21]! In His wisdom and foresight God made a decision and never changed His mind. The Hebrew reads, "God said *to* His heart";[506] and the Chaldean Bible says, "God said to His *Word*."[507] Luther also pointed this out in his exposition of Genesis when he was quite old; for more and more can be found in God's Word each day, nor can Scripture be fully fathomed in a single study (Sir. 24:28). Mathesius[508] also reads it thus. The expression is the same as Psalm 110:1: "The LORD said to my Lord," or as the Chaldean text allows: "The LORD said to His Word." Of course this Word is none other than Jesus Christ, as John 1:1 proves. Here once again I find my Lord Jesus.

O dearest Lord Jesus, You are the heart of Your Father. Here, You and Your Father with one accord decided in favor of grace. You are His beloved Son, dearest to His heart; You have calmed and appeased the heart of Your Father. You are "of the Father's heart begotten,"[509] as Prudentius confesses, and as the Church sings with the wife of Dr. Cruciger. The heart of Your Father is familiar to You. You know all His secret plans. You have made known to us what Your Father thinks of us (John 1:18). Thus You are right when You say, "Whoever sees Me sees the Father" [John 14:9], that is to say, "Whoever knows Me knows the heart of the Father." Dear Lord Jesus, Your Father must love me a great deal since He has shared His heart with me—since He has given me You, His dearest heart, to be my own! Oh Lord Jesus, You are my heart. I will not say, "The Mass is my heart; you may not take it from me," as our pious Emperor did,[510] but rather, "Jesus is my heart; no devil or trial shall take Him from me."[511]

---

506 "Dixit Dominus ad cor suum."

507 "Dixit Dominus ad verbum suum."

508 Johann Mathesius (1504–1565), Lutheran minister and biographer.

509 "Corde natus ex parentis" (the hymn by Prudentius, here with its German paraphrase, "Herr Christ, der einig Gotts Sohn"; see *LSB* 384, 402).

510 "Missa cor meum, hanc mihi non debes eripere"; said by the Emperor, prob. Charles V, to Count Wilhelm von Nassau.

511 "Jesus cor meum, hunc mihi nemo eripiet."

O Lord Jesus, when I pray in Your name I reach Your Father's heart, for You are His heart. If I would steal the heart of Your heavenly Father, Lord Jesus, all I have to do is take hold of You. If in times of bearing my cross I want certain knowledge of Your heavenly Father's heart, I will simply cling to You. If when I die I join Stephen and commend myself to You, then I will be commended to the heart of Your heavenly Father, and it will be impossible for me to perish. O Lord Jesus Christ, most beloved Heart of hearts, my heart will cherish You, keep You, and honor You forever. Amen.

XIX. JESUS,

The Blessed Man For Whose Sake God the Father Will Never Again Curse the Ground (Gen. 8:21).

God goes on to say in our text that He will "never again curse the ground for the sake of *the man*." Thus Jerome reads the text, as does Dr. Forstemius,[512] the pious Mathesius, and Adam Reusner[513] as well. Also, the Hebrew is in the singular. Here is yet another mystery. God the Father was willing to lift the curse for the sake of His dear Son who in the fullness of time would become man. So in this passage, "the man" is Christ Jesus, as St. Paul says (1 Tim. 2:5). To our honor, moreover, the Lord Christ refers to Himself in this way (Matt. 13:24) because He is man's faithful friend, and His "delight is in the children of men." [Prov. 8:31]. It was for the sake of this blessed Man that God the Father promised to have mercy.

Just as for the sake of one man's sin death reigned, so also through one man, Jesus Christ, the fullness of grace and of the gift for righteousness would be restored. "Just as by the disobedience of one the many were made sinners, so by the obedience of one many are made righteous," says St. Paul (Rom. 5:19). In veiled terms God reiterated the First Gospel from Genesis 3:15: For the sake of one man God had unleashed all His wrath; for the sake of the Lord of men (as Eve says in Gen. 4:1) He would be gracious. Isaiah builds on this when he says, "'With everlasting kindness I will have mercy on you,' says the LORD, your Redeemer. 'This is like the days of Noah to Me: as I swore that the waters of Noah should no more go over the earth, so I have sworn that I will not be angry with you or rebuke you'" (Is. 54:8–9). Before, in chapter 3, God promised that He would forgive sins for the sake of Jesus Christ. Here for Christ's sake He consented to dry up the flood.

---

512 Johann Vorstheimer (1496–1558), Lutheran scholar and expert in Hebrew.

513 Adam Reusner (1496–ca. 1575), scholar and hymn-writer.

So behold, dear heart: for Christ's sake God will do good to us in body and soul, in time and eternity. And just as for Christ's sake no flood of water will go over the earth, so for Christ's sake no flood of wrath will go over the earth of our hearts. For "there is…nothing condemnable in those who believe in Christ Jesus" [Rom. 8:1; cf. John 5:24]. Pious hearts have known this well. Thus Daniel prayed, "Hear us…for the Lord's sake" (Dan. 9:17), and the Church ends every prayer and collect with these words: "for the sake of Jesus Christ our Lord (let our prayer be efficacious)."[514] Also, St. Paul says that all the promises of God are Yes and Amen in Christ [2 Cor. 1:20].

Dear heavenly Father, You have promised to be gracious for the sake of Your Son, our kinsman by blood. Your dear Son also says, "Truly, truly… whatever you ask of the Father in My name, He will give it to you"[John 16:23]. Relying on this promise, then, I will lay my troubles and misery before You today and every day, beseeching You to fulfill Your trustworthy word in me and let me reap the benefits of my dear Brother, Jesus Christ, the dearest Son of Your heart. For His sake lift the curse of Your wrath and let me be saved in the benediction and consolation of Your grace. Amen.

514 "Per Dominum nostrum Jesum Christum."

XX. JESUS

Pronounces His Blessing Upon Noah and His Children, Reminding Them in a Veiled Way That Life Is Found in His Blood (Gen. 9[:1–4]).

God is a lover of order. Therefore, in order that everything might proceed in an orderly fashion, He ordained three holy estates: teaching, labor, and defense.

First, He graciously took pleasure in Noah's sermons, sacrifices, and prayers, and in this way church was provided for. Second, God blessed the marriages and households of Noah and His sons. Third, God bequeathed the regular authority of the sword with these words: "Whoever sheds man's blood, by man shall his blood be shed." Accordingly, just as God Himself ordained these three holy estates, so, too, He preserves them from the devil and all his horde until the end of the world. A pious preacher should thus be comforted in difficult situations by the fact that his office, his estate, has been sanctioned by God, for which reason he can occupy it in good conscience. A pious homeowner and laborer, in the bitter sweat of his brow, has the assurance and comfort that his estate pleases God also. In it he can pray with a happy heart, knowing that God will renew His old blessing for him. So, too, an honest ruler can in good conscience support the death-penalty, hold a public trial, and sentence the murderer according to his conviction, nor need he make satisfaction for it by living out the rest of his days in a Fransiscan's cap. For God Himself commands the victim to be defended and capital punishment imposed. Indeed, God Himself brought the slain man Abel to justice and sent out the cry about Cain.

We further see that God is mankind's friend. He not only took pains to provide Noah with honorable employment (as the ancients used to say of the three sons: "Shem, you be the pastor, Japheth the mayor, and Ham the laborer"),[515] but He also provided for Noah's kitchen and pantry, mak-

---

515 "Tu supplex ora: Tu protege: Tuque labora."

ing sure that he would always have something to eat by granting Noah and his children the right to eat meat. For just as Adam lived on exquisite fruits in Paradise, so he and his children had to get by on roots and vegetables outside of Paradise, and become gentlemen farmers. It is as if God said, "Noah, dear Noah, I see that your strength has diminished in your year-long imprisonment. Nature, too, has been sorely impoverished by the flood. You would get by very poorly on roots and vegetables, so I must provide you with stronger food. Flesh produces flesh. You may prepare for yourselves dishes of wild game, young hens, and old pike. You may have your vegetables as a side dish, and add meat as your main course. This I gladly grant you." In this way Noah became the first butcher and fisherman, and God Himself built Noah's butcher shop and fish market, and thus the teaching that forbids the eating of meat is not of God but of demons (1 Tim. 4:1).

Next behold how great God's concern for Noah's health was, for He forbade him to eat meat that had blood in it and was still alive. "Dear Noah, make sure you don't do yourself harm by eating meat. You are not used to the new food, so proceed carefully. Do not devour lambs as a wolf does, nor chickens as an eagle does: raw and with the blood dripping from your chin. Do not eat of the flesh that still pulses with blood; do not eat meat that is still warm from living, but let it cool off and it will be tastier. Let the blood drain completely first and it will be healthier for you." See, dear heart, what great care God had for Noah's health, for blood is quite unhealthy for men and quite hard to digest, and whatever has not been kept cool before it is cooked often causes great harm as well. But since God Himself cares for our health, by no means should anyone willfully hurt himself. Food should be kept impeccably clean. Medicine is worst when it is mixed in with food; but it is best when the food is healthy, and very medicine itself, say experienced doctors. Those in authority should certify that no sick livestock or rotten fish or herring are sold. A decent hostess should make every attempt to be a good, clean cook, and not waste food through coarseness or laziness. All this pleases God, as can be seen in this passage.

In addition, God wanted to engrain in Noah and his children a wariness of blood, lest by small degrees they should get used to great evil, learning to esteem the blood of man lightly by esteeming the blood of animals lightly. Just look at how executioners use young pups to get used to shedding blood, and how a dog learns to eat meat by first chewing on leather.

It took the flood to cleanse the first world from Abel's innocent blood. Therefore God issued a warning against staining the new world with innocent blood also.

Under the new covenant, however, we Christians are no longer bound to this law against eating blood. We may eat both blood and food made with blood. Yet the apostles forbade the new Christians who came from heathendom (Acts 15:29) to do so because they did not want the formerly heathen Christians to offend the weak Jews. Thus Paul says that he would forgo the eating of meat if his brother should be offended by it (1 Cor. 8:13). A Christian should, moreover, always have this verse of St. Paul in sight: "I have a right to all things, but not all things are helpful; I have a right to all things, but not all things are edifying" (1 Cor. 10:23). Scholars furthermore think that it was to the glory of Jesus Christ, in whose blood our salvation and life reside, that God forbade Noah to eat blood.

Pause here, dear heart, and contemplate firstly who the Lord is that pronounced a blessing upon Noah. It is our dear Lord and *Elohim*, Jesus Christ, present here in His office of Bishop and High Priest. O Lord Jesus, You are the blessed Seed through whom all the nations of the earth are blessed [Gen. 22:18]. Blessing, prosperity, consolation, and life are to be sought and found in You. You are mindful of us and bless us (Ps. 115:12). You blessed Noah and his children when they entered marriage. You bless all pious spouses. You gave Your blessing to the wedding at Cana in Galilee. Let Your blessing also rest upon me and all my family.

When You were about to ascend into heaven, You raised Your hand in Your parting work and blessed Your disciples, and with this blessing proceeded to seat Yourself at the right hand of Your Father's majesty as an everlasting testimony that You would do nothing else but bless, comfort, and help us; and You still do so today. Accordingly, whoever wants happiness and blessing must take refuge in You alone. Raise Your hand, O Lord Jesus, and pronounce a blessing upon Your Church. Grant that Your Gospel may dwell among us richly. Pronounce a blessing upon our city hall, that all things may work together for Your glory and the increase of the common good. Pronounce a blessing upon all just citizens and laborers, that all things may prosper in every way. Let us sit, stand, live, and linger in Your blessing, that we may be consoled while bearing our cross, defended in times of trial, and blessed forever, and on the Last Day hear those words of honor and gladness: "Come, you blessed of My Father, inherit the kingdom prepared for you from the beginning of the world" (Matt. 25:34).

Next, contemplate the veiled words that the Son of God uses: "The blood is alive," or, "Life is in the blood." Concerning this passage our dear forefathers said that here the blood of Jesus Christ is presented for us to contemplate in the mystery of Noah. For life is in Christ's blood, and in this blood the Jews were hideously drowned "by man," that is, by the Roman soldiers. For the statement "His blood be on us, and on our children" [Matt. 27:25] cast the Jews up to their necks in great misery, and still oppresses and weighs heavily on them today. Just as a threat is here placed upon every animal that sheds the blood of man, so Psalm 22:13 threatens those great beasts that shed Christ's blood. However, let our passage be glossed thus: "In Christ Jesus is all our comfort and blessing. In Christ's blood is our life." "In Him was life," says John 1:4. And Jesus Himself says, "I am the resurrection and the life; he who believes in Me shall live, even though he die. And whoever lives and believes in Me shall never die" [11:25].

But how did the Lord Jesus bring us life? Through His blood: He paid with His precious blood, and thus bought us life everlasting.

O Lord Jesus Christ, You are the true Pelican. You wept over our injuries and sprinkled us, Your young, in the Garden of Gethsemane, in the Praetorium, and on Golgotha with Your blood, giving us poor sinners the life that we had lost through the serpent's deceit.

Now let me contemplate why You had Yourself nailed to the cross in the Place of the Skull, a place filled with the bones of the dead. Ezekiel walked among the dead men's bones and prophesied as he was commanded, and immediately the dead bones came to life [Ezek. 37:1–10]. You too, O Lord Jesus, stepped through the dead bones to the holy cross, and one by one spoke Your seven words of power, sprinkling them with Your blood. What happened? The graves were opened. The power of

Your blood was displayed: "Truly, truly, life is in Your blood." By tradition, painters paint a skull at the foot of Your cross, showing thereby that Your blood has the power to blot out our death and take it away. This then shall be my armor against danger and death.

Mary had herself buried on the Mount of Olives[516] not far from the place where Christ sweat blood, for she knew very well that life is in Christ's blood. Mary's faith is my faith, too. I seek my blessing and life in You, Lord Jesus, for I know that Your blood brings me life everlasting. Therefore I thank You, Lord Jesus, for giving me life through Your blood. O Lord Jesus, let me dwell in the power of Your blessing and live forever in the strength of Your blood. Amen.

516 The Church of Mary's Tomb is located at the base of the Mount of Olives near Gethsemane.

XXI. JESUS,

The Beautiful Rainbow, the True Witness of God's Grace (Gen. 9[:8–17]).

A burnt man fears the sight of fire. So it was with Noah. He was once caused much grief by water, so whenever dark clouds started to fill the sky, he trembled at the thought of a flood. God had plainly pledged never to wreak such harsh punishment with water again, but Noah's face remained firmly buried in his hands. When he saw black billows roll across the sky, he fell into an terrible anxiety and grief and forgot all about his consolation. So it is with me too, for whenever I suffer great distress and lengthy misery, my heart does no different. God has revealed His will to me plainly and sufficiently, to be sure, but when such lengthy misery weighs me down, I forget all about my consolation, as if God had died, as if there were no longer any comfort or deliverance in the world. Oh dear God, help me by the aid of Your Spirit to resist such stupidity and senseless fear. God knew of Noah's worries, so He thought of a way to help his listless, fearful heart. Oh, how sweet and delightful God's mercy is! "He will not quench the smoking flax; the bruised reed He will not break" [Is. 42:3].

In order to make Noah's heart overflow with living comfort, God first filled his ears with a word of grace so oft-repeated that, in spite of his sorrow, he would not miss it at all but grasp it firmly and hold onto it, and then filled Noah's eyes with a splendid token of grace visible enough to sense and see that God would be gracious to the new world: "Listen, My dear Noah! You need not fear another flood. I will never allow the world to be drowned again in such misery. This is My covenant which I pledge to you with the force of an oath and testament. I shall not change My mind. It is as certain as if it were sworn with a thousand oaths. I tell you twice for two thousand times, so shall it stay. The rainbow in the heavens bears witness. Just as hitherto you were distressed whenever you saw black clouds, so henceforth I will comfort you with them. The rainbow is My sign. I tell you this thrice, lest you anymore doubt My grace."

Behold, dear heart, such is God's gracious way from of old. When He wishes to convey His grace to our heart, He gives us a bright, clear word to which he attaches His assuring token of grace. Adam had a clear Gospel, and with it, in lieu of a sacrament, the skins of a lamb. Abel also knew of the Gospel concerning the promised Seed of the woman, and with it the fire from heaven. Noah likewise received a clear word of grace, and with it the sacrament of the rainbow. In our day, I have the shining Gospel of Jesus Christ, and with it the two worthy sacraments of Baptism and the Lord's Supper. Just as Noah had a guarantee that no flood would come, so I, too, have a guarantee that no flood of God's wrath shall destroy me. Blessed be our God who by His faithfulness and providence so deeply assures us of His grace!

God skillfully fashioned the rainbow to serve firstly as a preacher of repentance to the whole world, and secondly as a comforter for all mankind. This is what the rainbow tells us whenever it shines in the heavens: "Repent, dear people! God can use water to drown willful sinners. Though I am proof that God shall never wreak destruction by such means again, He has a thousand other ways and means by which to punish the ungodly. Look at both of my colors: I not only show you the color of water, by which judgment was poured out upon the first world, but also the color red, that you might keep the fires of the Last Day in mind. Consider how God will reward the impenitent with hellfire, and sincerely repent and return while there is still time. Think of the carter's rule: Do not take on more than your cart can carry. Do not overload your conscience; it may well prove too heavy for you. Dear men, at every moment you merit both God's wrath and a terrible flood with your sins.

"Yet do not despair in your sins, for 'the grace of God far outweighs all your sin and iniquity.'[517] No matter how great and heavy your sins may be, God will never again wipe out the world with a flood. In the midst of His wrath He will remember His mercy. Howbeit do not wantonly, knowingly

---

517 "Exuberat gratia supra peccatum." (Rom. 5:20.)

sin against grace, for he who does such wickedness shall receive the terrible reward of eternal disgrace." For this reason the ancients also used to call the rainbow the "bow of mercy."[518]

The rainbow is above all a beautiful witness and pleasant portrait of our friend Jesus Christ. God Himself suggests this in Psalm 89:34–37 when He says, "I will not violate My covenant or alter what has gone out of My lips. I swore once by My holiness: I will not lie to David. His seed shall be forever, and his throne as the sun before Me. As the moon it shall be established forever, and like the witness in the clouds be certain. Selah." In other words: "Look up, dear heart, and remember: Just as the rainbow bears witness to My grace for you, so shall My Son Jesus Christ bear witness to My mercies for all the world." In the same manner Isaiah 54:8 connects our Messiah to the word of grace that God spoke to Noah as discussed above. Based on this text, moreover, our forefathers used to depict Jesus, the coming Judge, on a rainbow, saying that this sign of Noah would appear among the clouds, as Christ says in Matthew 24:30, just as there is a rainbow around Christ's throne in Revelation 4:3. The Antichrist, who pretends to be Christ's vicar, also has a rainbow upon his head (Rev. 10:1). Accordingly, just as Sirach says, "Look at the rainbow, and praise Him who made it; for it has beautiful colors" (Sir. 43: 11–12), so I will say, Dear heart, look at Jesus Christ, and praise the heavenly Father who gave Him to us; for He has beautiful words, works, and benefits.

The rainbow is an undeniable witness of God's grace. Dear Lord Jesus, You are a certain witness of Your Father's grace. You bear witness of Your Father's affectionate heart with clear words, saying, "Truly, truly... whatever you ask of the Father...He will give it to you" [John 16:23]. "For God (My Father) so loved the world that He gave His only begotten Son, that whoever believes in Him should not perish but have eternal life" [John 3:16]. You bear witness to Your Father's gracious heart with all Your miracles, yea, with every drop of Your blood. As many drops of blood as fell in Gethsemane and on the cross, so many thousands of witnesses do we have that we will not perish. So when the evil one attacks me, when my wavering heart is in anguish over my sins, I will simply appeal to You

518 "arcum clementiae"

as my credible witness, rely on Your testimony, and join St. Paul in saying, "Who will condemn? Christ is here, who has died" [Rom. 8:34]. O Lord Jesus, no evil spirit will make me doubt Your testimony. Therein will I be saved. To Your glory I will also become a witness, testifying to You and Your benefits with all my possessions and strength until my final day.

The rainbow heralded new blessings to men. O Lord Jesus, You bring us a far greater blessing, for You are the Seed of Abraham through which we have all been blessed. You promise and grant us Your blessings in time and eternity. You bring us the forgiveness of sins, heaven, and life everlasting.

After the rainbow brightened the sky, no great floods came any more. O Lord Jesus, after You came to our aid, no believing heart in the world will perish any more. The flood of the wrath of Your Father shall not overwhelm us repentant sinners. With Your song of victory, "It is finished" [John 19:30] You obtained eternally bright and fair weather for us in body and soul.

The rainbow always appears just before the sun, for it is a reflection of the sun. O Lord Jesus, You are always our advocate and intercessor before the heavenly Father, for You are also "the radiance of His glory and the exact image of His being" (Heb. 1:3; Col. 1:15), of equal majesty, worship, and honor. You speak well of us to Your Father and reconcile us to Him (1 John 2:1; Rom. 8:34). By Your intercession we must be saved.

Whoever would see the rainbow must look up at the sky. O Lord Jesus, whoever would view and know You rightly must lift up his heart from temporal, transient things and set his affection "on what is above, not on what is on earth" (Col. 3:2). Whoever acts like a pig with its acorns and only gazes at what is on earth will never know You rightly. Oh Lord Jesus, direct me by Your Spirit, that where my treasure is, there my heart may be also [Matt. 6:21, par.].

The rainbow is never without clouds, and is usually followed by rain. For three days at least it threatens rain, for which reason villagers call it the "storm-flower." O dear Lord Jesus, no sooner does one come to love, praise, and confess You than the dark clouds of adversity and cross appear, and with them the numerous beating rains of misery. Your Gospel is always followed by the storms of the blessed cross. Oh grant grace that it may not part us from Your love, that we may not be embittered by the grief in which all Christians must live, but take comfort in the fact that You will scatter every cloud in time, and give us eternal brightness instead. Julian was a black cloud that hung over Christians; but of him Athanasius said, "This little cloud will soon pass,"[519] and so it was.

Dear heart, consider the beautiful colors of the rainbow. The ancient doctors of the Church discern two colors: the first, that of water or the flesh, and the second, red. In these they contemplate the two natures of Christ: true man, born of the Virgin Mary, and true God, begotten of God the Father. On the other hand, some scholars count three colors, such as Aristotle,[520] the great Philosopher; and in our day, my gracious lord and friend Dr. Wolfgang Meurer,[521] and Chytraeus[522] as well.

First, [the rainbow] is red. O Lord Jesus, this signified that You would deal in red blood, for without blood there is no atonement (Heb. 9:22). At Your circumcision You shed Your first drop of blood. In Gethsemane You stood in a sweat of blood. In the Praetorium You appeared red with blood. On the cross You hung in Your blood. For You wished to appease the heart of the heavenly Father with Your blood, that our blood-guiltiness might be washed away, and our blood-red sins made "as white as snow" (Is. 1:18; 4:4). In this way You are our High Priest.

Second, the rainbow is yellow, for as our mighty King, You rightfully possess the crown of yellow gold. By right You wear a threefold crown, for heaven is Yours to command, earth to rule, and hell to scour as You please. All creatures stand at Your beck and call. In this way You are our King.

Third, the rainbow is green. O Lord Jesus, You are the true green hue, our heart's green pasture. You strengthen the eyes of our faith just as the color green soothes our eyes. Our heart is best off with You. You are the green wood, the true green Tree of Life from which we draw our sap and strength. Aaron's green, budding rod was but an image and shadow of

---

519 "Nubecula citò transitura."

520 *Meteorologica* 3.2, 4.

521 *Alias* Meurerus (1513–1585), doctor and philosopher in Leipzig.

522 David Kochhafe (1530–1600), German theologian, co-author of the Formula of Concord.

Your ever-greening merit which always avails to save us. [In this way You are our Prophet.]

The rainbow spreads its arms down from the sky as if it to embrace the earth and draw it up. O Lord Jesus, You embrace heaven and earth. You are true God and true man: God of heaven, man of earth. Heaven is Your throne, the earth is Your footstool [Is. 66:1; Acts 7:49]. You climbed up into the sky on Your cross and spread out our Your arms as far as You could. You reached for our souls, for the soil of our hearts. For You said, "I, when I am lifted up, will draw them all to Myself" (John 12:32). You would draw men up into heaven and bring them to Your Father. You still spread Your arms out wide today in the Holy Gospel, calling to us as a hen does to her chicks to gather them under her wing. If anyone follows You, obeys Your voice, and comes to You, You draw him up to eternal life [John 10:27–28].

The rainbow frightens and comforts, for it reminds us equally of God's wrath and God's grace. O Lord Jesus, Isaiah 35:4 says the same of You: "Behold, your God who is coming for vengeance; God, who repays, is coming and will save you." You wreak vengeance on the devil, death, hell, tyrants, and heretics, but to all pious hearts You give grace and salvation.

In the rainbow the eyes and heart of both God and Noah met. For God said, "Behold," and again, "The bow is seen." Noah was to look at the bow and know in his heart that God was his ally. Then God added, "Therefore My bow will be in the clouds, that I may look at it and remember the everlasting covenant." In this way the rainbow is a sort of median or center[523] at which the eyes and hearts of God and man meet. Oh Lord Jesus, how beautifully You are depicted to me here. You are the Median, the Mediator.[524] Your Father's eyes and heart are focused on You, and it is for Your sake that He will be gracious. So I too must and will set my eyes and heart on You. When I look to You, I have peace with Your Father, for on and in You dwells all the fullness of Your dear Father. You are like a precious memory-ring in Your Father's sight. You are also the golden memory-ring of my heart. Oh, help my eyes and heart never to stray from

523 "centrum"
524 Germ. *Mittler*, "median; mediator."

You. Where Your Father has turned His eyes and heart I too will turn. There I am helped forever.

Whenever great storms appeared and darkened the day with their black clouds, Noah searched for the rainbow in great earnest. Likewise, O Lord Jesus, whenever great distress, misery, and need strike me, I will swiftly and speedily search for You. Let the solution for Noah's worries be mine also in every affliction, and my anxious heart will be healed. Oh, how Noah's heart must have smiled whenever he saw the rainbow! He would have said, "Blessed be God's grace and truth! Blessed be God's love of old now shining on me from heaven again." Likewise, O Lord Jesus, when I remember You, my heart feels as though I were sitting in heaven with the holy angels. I start worshiping, extolling, and praising God with more joy in my heart than words can express.

Just as Noah, then, was no doubt overjoyed to talk about his rainbow and its meaning, so, O Lord Jesus, I too will be heartily glad to talk about You for as long as I live. Your praise shall continually be in my mouth [Ps. 34:1].

O Jesus Christ, most beloved Witness of my salvation, one thing I ask of You, that would I gladly have [Ps. 27:4]: that You, O beautiful Bow of grace, would shine on my soul in every trouble and gladden me with Your beautiful colors. Remind me that You are my intercessor, protector, and comforter. When my eyes are darkened in death, let Your light and life shower down on my failing heart. Spread Your arms, O mighty Rainbow, reach for the soil of my listless heart and comfort me. Embrace my soul and press me to Your loving heart. Draw me up to You and Your heavenly Father, to eternal life, and I will rejoice a thousand times more than Noah when he contemplated the rainbow. Let the words of Bernard be my words, too:

> When I must to death betake me,
> Do not, Savior, then forsake me,
> At the very brink of dying,
> Tarry not to heed my sighing,
> O Jesus, come, defend my cause!
>
> When from hence I must be going
> Jesus dear, Your face be showing,

Friend, oh, let me then behold You
Where Your healing streams enfold You
Upon redemption's bloody cross.[525]

Let my heart behold You spreading Your arms like the beautiful rainbow, reaching down, and lifting my soul to heaven, and I will be satisfied. For this I will worship You forever. Amen.

---

525 "Dum me mori est necesse, Noli mihi tunc deesse, / In tremenda mortis hora / Veni, Jesu, absque mora, / Tuere me et libera // Cum me jubes emigrare, / Jesu care, tunc appare, / O amator amplectende, / Temet ipsum tunc ostende / In Cruce salutifera" (from the hymn "Membra Jesu nostri," section "ad faciem," st. 5).

The Noblest Vine in Noah's Vineyard and in the Garden of Every Pious
Christian's Heart (Gen. 9[:20]).

Moses says that Noah became a worker of the field and lived off his bitter labors. Blush for shame, idle sloth! Noah had the holdings of an emperor but did not go loafing about the streets. You scarcely have bread to eat yet will not lift a finger for it. "Go to the ant, O sluggard" (Prov. 6:6), as we said in part one.[526] "Noah planted a vineyard." This is the first vineyard that we read about in the Bible. God blessed old Noah in his sorrows with a sweet drink of gladness, and furthermore caused the healing, pure, invigorating, warmth-giving grape to grow for him to help him digest the meat that God had allowed him to eat. Here once again you see how concerned God is for man's health and welfare. Since, then, He has given us wine for our health, the noble juice of the grape should not (while drinking to another's health, as is the world's unfortunate custom) be used to the detriment of our health. If God has granted it, a draught of wine may be taken with a good conscience. The poor have a poor cross. As the saying goes, Consult the purse, not the bottle. St. Paul writes, "No longer drink water, but a little wine also for the sake of your stomach, and because you are often sick" (1 Tim. 5:23). These days, so many people fruitlessly squander this precious drink that God refuses to give us any more excellent vintages.

Here let us collect these thoughts somewhat, looking at Noah's vineyard with our spiritual eyes. The Christian Church is often compared to a vineyard. When he wished to describe how our Lord Jesus would manifest Himself in God's people, Jacob said, "He will bind His foal to the vine" (Gen. 49:11), that is, He will wash His garments in red wine, shed His blood, and die in God's vineyard, in Jerusalem of Judea. Isaiah

---

526 Part 1, meditation 11.

5:1 does the same: the prophet sings a song of a vineyard in honor of Christ Jesus, his cousin, born from his own branch. This is the very same image that the Lord Jesus Himself uses in Matthew 21 (and ch. 20 as well). Thus Cyprian fittingly says, "The Church is a garden of heavenly plants, day by day sprouting forth vines and branches out of the Vintner's blood."[527] Yet the Christian Church is compared to a vineyard chiefly because it is in her that Jesus Christ, the noble Vine from whom we derive our sap, strength, comfort, and life, is loved, honored, and confessed. And surely Noah, too, had this Vine in his vineyard. He loved Him in the garden of his heart and spoke of Him and His sweetness in the precious vine of his vineyard. Therefore let us also reflect on this mystery somewhat.

O dearest Lord Jesus, You are the true Vine, as You Yourself declare: "I am the true vine, and My Father is the vinedresser" [John 15:1]; and again: "I am the vine; you are the branches" [v. 5]. Oh, how skillfully You depict Yourself to my heart! Vinewood is ugly, gnarled, thorny, dirty, and pale. Oh Lord Jesus, "You are the most handsome of the children of men" [Ps. 45:2], and for my sake became ugly. You turned pale in Your death on the cross, and had "no beauty that we should be pleased" (Is. 53:2), that I might become beautiful and well pleasing to Your Father.

Vine-wood is cut with a vinedresser's knife. O Lord Jesus, You were quickly circumcised on the eighth day after Your birth, that blood and forgiveness of sins might flow from You. This first droplet of Your blood already outweighed all my sins. Then, in Gethsemane, You were cut with the knife of Your Father's wrath and Your whole body dripped with blood. Oh, how the wrath of Your Father pierced Your holy heart and filled it with anguish for my sake! And again, when You said on the cross, "My God, my God, how You have forsaken Me!" you spoke those words in my stead, that I might never have to lament in such agony. Your heavenly Father pruned away my sins in Your holy body, for You took my sins upon Yourself. For this be praised forever!

---

527 "Ecclesia est seminarium divinarum plantarum, ex sanguine Vinitoris quotidie protrudens vites et palmites"; see *Apost. Const.* 1, prologue.

Wood weeps[528] when it is cut. Alas, how You wept, O Lord Jesus! You "offered up loud cries and tears on the cross" (Heb. 5:7), that I might rejoice forever.

The vinedresser attacks the roots with his hoe as if to rip out the vinestock completely, and then pours stinking manure all around, one cartload after another. O dear Lord Jesus, You too were deprived of life and limb, You were "cut off" (Dan. 9:26). You had to die, but Your death procured my life. You were put to death and shame on the cross, You were made to stink like manure, but Your shame won my eternal glory.

A vine has its leaves stripped off and is bound to a stake. O Lord Jesus, You were stripped naked and bound, and at last even nailed to the stake of the cross with iron nails. But You laid aside Your clothing, that we might be covered with the robe of Your innocence and righteousness. You were bound so that we would be set free from the bondage of our sins and from the power of the devil and eternal death.

A vine can get "eyes."[529] O Lord Jesus, You got lesions and scars. Your whole body was covered with eyes that all wept nothing but blood. What are red eyes (Gen. 49:12) if not these? In my grief, when my eyes gush water and my heart weeps blood, this gives me utter comfort.

A vine puts forth blossoms. O Lord Jesus, You have gracious, sweet-smelling blossoms. Your seven powerful words on the cross are pure and beautiful flowers that revive our fainting heart in distress and death.

A vine shoots up so fast that the vintner must prune it frequently or it will get too big for itself. Likewise, O Lord Jesus, You did not remain in Your state of humiliation. Death and the grave could not hold You. You shot up from the earth and broke out of the prison of Your tomb. You came out like a captain of war, and at last ascended and seated Yourself at the right hand of God's majesty. Your invincible, wonderful power is my comfort in all misery.

A vine bears many grapes. It produces the most delightful juice and drink on earth. O Lord Jesus, You produce beautiful grapes; Your merits strengthen us in prayer, cross, temptation, life, and death. Your grace gives

528 Germ. *weint*, a play on Germ. *Wein*, "wine."

529 I.e., knots, or scars left by the pruning of branches.

us the best consolation in the whole world. Just as a bottle, flagon, or flask is filled with the juice of the grape, I will fill my pint, the chamber of my heart, full to the brim with Your comfort; from Your fullness I will receive (John 1:16).

Some vines produce red wine, some white wine. O Lord Jesus, You produced both red and white wine at the same time: both blood and water issued from Your opened side. With Your red blood, as with a costly Malvasian, You wished to strengthen us and keep us from despair. With Your clear water, as with a white Rhinish wine, You wished to cleanse and wash us, and make us as white as snow and holy.

When a vintner knows of a good varietal, he does not rest until he has planted it in his vineyard. Likewise, O Lord Jesus, my heart cannot be content without You. O Lord Jesus Christ, my heart shall be Your plantation. The deep furrow is already prepared. In true humility I confess my unworthiness, and so I fall at Your feet. Oh, do not despise me in my misery. I will seize You with both hands of my faith and plant You deep, deep down in the furrows of my humble heart, that in You I may have strength and life. Take root, O Lord Jesus, in the vineyard of my heart. I will plant You well, honor You in newness of life, serve You, and worship You. You will find good, fresh, sandy soil in my heart: I will live in unswerving fear of God and remember that I am but dust and ashes. I will pitch my heart toward the east [Gen. 12:8; Num. 2:3] I will seek the kingdom of God and His righteousness at all times [Matt. 6:33]. Let the sun of Your love fill me with warmth, the wholesome air of Your Spirit breathe on me, and the cooling rain of Your grace quench me. Root and tear out of my heart the cankers and weeds of all worldly sorrows, and give increase, that I may be blessed. I will make a hedge around You with prayer and love for God's Word. I will speak of You gladly and learn of You often. Make this hedge around my heart firm, O Lord Jesus, that I may not lose You in any spiritual attack.

Here let me also meditate on the words of the Lord Jesus when He says, "You are the branches. Every branch in Me that does not bear fruit (My Father) will take away; and every one that bears fruit He will prune, that it may bear more fruit"; and again, "As the branch cannot bear fruit by its itself, unless it abide in the vine, neither can you, unless you abide in Me. I am the vine; you are the branches. Whoever abides in Me and I in him, he bears much fruit; for apart from Me you can do nothing. Whoever does not abide in Me, he is thrown away like a branch and withers; and they are gathered and thrown into the fire, and must burn" [John 15:4–6]. Oh Lord Jesus, grant grace that I may not be a fruitless rhizome, a worthless Christian of the tongue only, who steals comfort from others' tongues, boasts highly of his own Christian faith, and has nothing to show for it in deed. For such will be pruned away and of no use but as fuel for the fire of hell (Ezek. 15:4). Rather, let me be a good, straight, fruitful branch, grafted and planted in You. Give me understanding to perceive Your love when You prune me with the shears of cross and woe, when You strip me and uproot me with all kinds of sorrow. For it is only for my good and benefit. Since, moreover, I find in You all my strength and energy, life and salvation, grant grace that I may bring forth grapes profitable to my neighbor also, and do to him as You have done to my soul. Teach me to cling to the stake of Your holy Ten Commandments and not willfully to turn awry in sin and disgrace, but to grow straight and tall in every Christian virtue. Let me yield to and be guided by the soft twine of Your good words in the Gospel, that, contemplating Your great benefits, Your Father's love, and Your Spirit's goodwill, I may begin to serve You without constraint. Strip me of the broad, useless leaves of my pride. Defend me in the summer of prosperity from the pests and devilish vermin of sin, and cover me with Your Spirit, lest, being frozen in the winter of adversity, I fall away from You; and I will extol You and praise You forever.

O Lord Jesus Christ, precious Vine of my salvation, from You I derive all my sap, strength, power, comfort, life, and gladness. "If I have but You (in the vineyard of my heart), I ask nothing of heaven and earth. Though my flesh and heart should fail, You are forever the ease of my heart, and my portion" [Ps. 73:25–26]. Therefore my heart will honor, love, extol, worship, and praise You forever. Amen.

XXIII. JESUS,

Shem's Most Blessed Lord and God, in Whom Japheth's Children, the Vast Mass of Heathendom, Will Also Have a Share (Gen. 9[:27]).

Our pious farmer Noah had exceptional success in growing grapes. Thus the heathen named him *Janus* (for *yain* means "wine" in Hebrew), portraying him with two faces because he saw the world before the flood and the world after the flood. Noah, then, having labored all through the summer, celebrated Martin's Eve[530] with great festivities (for there is no village too small to throw a Carnival at least once). He refreshed himself with the noble juice of the vine, and was astonished at the delicious result: "My God, how can I ever repay you for this blessing? How can I praise You enough for this marvel? You have turned water into wine. The vine soaked up the rainwater while beneath the vine's ugly wood Your almighty power miraculously transformed it into a delectable wine." With this, Noah took another sip and thanked God for granting success to his labors. So as pious Noah sat amusing himself sip by sip, imbibing the noble juice of the vine with increasing generosity, he fell, quite by accident, into the state of drunkenness; for he did not yet know that this noble drink could do harm when taken to excess. He presently lost his balance, fell over in his tent, remained lying as naked and bare as a rock, and forgot all good domestic propriety and decency.

Here you see that no kitchen is free of broken pots. Only Christ is without sin, so no saint is ever without fault. It may furthermore be seen that old seasoned officials and careworn souls who, for the frailty of their head, unexpectedly fall into a stupor after a single drink, should not be hastily handed over to the devil. Here I'm sure some "carnival brother" will say, "Now that's a verse for me! After all, if Noah drank himself silly

---

530 Martinmas, celebrated on November 11, traditionally marked the end of harvest.

and flouted all decency, I can, too. If I happen to do some unseemly things, it doesn't matter. It's been done before." Peace, brother! Noah's affair has nothing to do with your filth. All his life long, Noah only crossed the line once. How often have you gone overboard? Perhaps more than 360 times a year, or perhaps even three times a day? Enough, you speak to your own shame! Noah did not do this on purpose and knowingly, but, as a man full of sorrow, fell into it quite unsuspectingly. You, on the other hand, fully aware, wantonly seek to fill yourself like a wash-basin. This is all wrong. From Noah you are not to learn to get drunk but to be wary of strong drink, lest like him you fall in the muck and make someone stumble. If you wish to be merry, by all means be merry. God would happily grant you a good drink and nourishing things to eat. But "when you eat, drink, or draw a breath,[531] forget not God and your own death"—nor the death of Jesus Christ. To this end, men long ago used to have a picture of Jesus' cross put in the bottom of their tankards. "Go to the table as to the altar,"[532] says Bernard. "The time for eating is right and pleasant when people remember that Christ is present,"[533] they used to say long ago.

Everyone in the world ought to have sympathized with Noah, since he became drunk by accident. But wonder of wonders, that old blundering centenarian Ham, Noah's youngest son, when he learned of his drunken father's nakedness, burst out laughing and made great sport of it. He noised it abroad to everyone, disparaged his natural father before his good brothers, and sought to convince them with his barefaced babbling and gossip and turn them against their father. Therefore he was justly accursed along with his wicked brood. Ham had many comrades in the world who could do nothing but root through the muck and stench with their snouts like filthy pigs and were never happy until they had hauled their neighbor over a carding-comb. Older people often do this, too, though they should know better. Age does not always improve wisdom. Yet let every pious child

---

531 A traditional saying; the words "or draw a breath" are added by the translator to preserve the rhyme.

532 "Ad mensam [quasi] ad aram."

533 "Tum bene prandetur, cum Christus adesse videtur."

be wary, lest he invite on himself the curse of his parents; for the father's curse sticks well, as both experience and the present example bear out.

Now the two good sons, Shem, ancestor of the Jews, and Japheth, of the heathens, remained dead silent. They wanted to keep the whole thing hushed and hidden from the whole world. They went in backward and covered their dear old father. Ah, blessed piety, goodness, honor, and decency—how worthy you are of great praise! "He is wise and erudite who puts whatever's wrong aright." Thus these two received the blessing while Ham and all his shameless swine were cursed.

Noah was 950 years old. Here you have a 950-year-old cross-bearer, so when you suffer cross do not fear. Since Noah's had an end, yours cannot last forever, either.

Here once again we find our Lord Jesus Christ, first in a veiled manner as Cyprian found Him. Noah planted a vineyard: Jesus built the spiritual vineyard of the land of the Jews. Noah became drunk and fell asleep naked: the Lord Jesus died and hung on the cross naked. Noah was scoffed at by Ham: likewise, our Lord Jesus was mocked by many wicked men. Noah was honored by Shem and Japheth: likewise, the Lord Jesus was honored by Joseph, Simon, Nicodemus, John, etc. Noah's scoffer was cursed: those who despise our Lord Jesus will perish forever. By contrast, those who honored Noah received his blessing: likewise, those who in true faith honor Jesus Christ receive eternal life. O dearest Lord Jesus Christ, help me not to resent Your nakedness and humble appearance on the cross, nor to join the unbelieving Jews and heathens in slandering You, but, approaching Your cross with blindfolded reason, to seek my highest pleasure in You, and so receive the eternal blessing. Amen.

Second, we also find our Lord Jesus here in the clear words, "Blessed be God the Lord of Shem." This is Jesus Christ, who was to be born from Shem's lineage and family. Therefore it promptly adds, "May God enlarge Japheth," or as it says in the Hebrew text, "May God speak kindly to the heart of Japheth"—may He dandle and soothe him with the gentle, sweet speech of the Holy Gospel, fill his hearing with such lovely words that his heart may be enlarged with joy, and let him become very powerful people and dwell with all his descendants in the tents of Shem, that is, join the community of God's people, and in the true confession of Shem's God and Lord be saved.

Behold, dear heart, how beautifully this passage declares that Jesus is not only the Savior of the Jews who come from Shem, but also of the heathen who originate from Japheth. O sweet Lord Jesus, You are the Blessed God and Lord of Shem. You are my *Baruch Jehovah Elohim* ("blessed Lord and God") also. With the apostle Thomas I say, "My Lord and my God" [John 20:28]. You are the true God, and eternal life. You are my sovereign Lord. Your manners are noble, honorable, gentle, and gallant toward me in my every need. (What was said about *Elohim* in Genesis 1, and LORD in Genesis 4 is again relevant here.)[534] You are the Blessed and Most Blessed forever [Ps. 21:6]. In You I find all my blessing, comfort, and salvation. You are the source of my eternal happiness and of all welfare of body and soul.

Oh sweet Lord Jesus, let me dwell in the tents of Shem, let me be a true member of Your holy, catholic Christian Church which honors and confesses You, that I may dwell forever in Your heavenly tents which You purchased with Your own blood. Oh, thanks be to You forever for giving us such a great honor and promising us poor heathens (descended from Japheth) that we would have a share in You. Therefore, just as surely as the Jews boast that they are the people of God, inasmuch as they are able to find proof for this in Genesis, so surely will I also boast that we poor heathens have by true faith been adopted by You and are members of Your people, since we can find no less solid proof for this in Genesis. Japheth was to dwell in the tents of Shem; the heathen born of Japheth were also to come to faith in You through the Gospel, and by their faith be joined to the company of all the pious hearts in the Old Testament who through You would be saved in the tents of Shem, among the Jewish people. Thus St. Peter said rightly, "We believe that we will be saved through the grace of the Lord Jesus Christ, just as they," our fathers in the Old Testament (Acts 15:11). This will also be confirmed by oath a little later in Genesis 22:16 and 18: "By Myself I have sworn…through your seed shall all the nations on earth be blessed"; and in Genesis 49:10, Jacob says, "To Him shall the heathen cling." In Isaiah 49:6, God the Father says, "It is too light a thing that You should be My servant to raise up the tribes of Jacob and to bring back the preserved of Israel; rather, I have also made You as

---

534 See part 1, meditation 4; part 2, meditations 1–3.

the light of the heathen, that You may be My salvation to the ends of the earth"; and in Psalm 2:8, "Ask of Me, and I will give You the heathen for a heritage, and the ends of the earth for a possession." Therefore godly Simeon called the infant Jesus "a Light to lighten the heathen" (Luke 2:32); and St. Paul put it aptly: "Jesus was a servant to the Jews for the sake of God's truthfulness..." (for God plainly said that the Messiah would be a Jew by birth) "...that the heathen might glorify God for His mercy" (Rom. 15:8–9). Therefore, "Praise the LORD, all heathendom! Extol Him, all nations! For His grace and truth abound to us forever. Alleluia" (Ps. 117). O Jesus Christ, You are full of grace and truth. May Your kingdom abound to us forever. Amen.

Indeed, Lord Jesus, do not the heathen love You far more than Your own people who are related to You by blood? Who was first concerned about Your birth in Jerusalem? In truth, it was the heathen from the east. That was but the vanguard. Yet when Your disciples proclaimed You throughout heathendom, the rest came in droves, as seen in St. Paul's epistles. Not only were simple bricklayers friendly and receptive to Your Gospel, but so were mighty rulers. Philip was the first Christian emperor. After that, Constantine the Great. Jovinian accepted the Christian faith, and by his princely example led a powerful army to the knowledge of Jesus Christ. How widely the Church is spread throughout the world in our own time! The pious emperor Maximilian, in the throes of death, would hear nothing but the precious merit of Jesus Christ. Elector Augustus, as a lord who believed in Christ, hoped merely to be a blister on His foot in eternal life. His mother, the lady Katharina, wanted to cling to her Lord Jesus like a burr to a frock. Many other such famous examples could be mentioned. Oh Lord Jesus Christ, single Treasure of my soul, I am a poor Japhethite, and my grandfathers were heathens, too. Yet I know that in You I shall be blessed. You have called me by the Gospel into the tents of Shem, the fellowship of Your true Christian Church. I have confessed You: You are "my Lord and my God" [John 20:28]. You are the Most Blessed Forever. Oh, let me be faithful here and blest forever! In this world let me dwell in the tents of Your Church with a true faith and good conscience, and hereafter abide continually in the eternal tents not made by human hands! Amen, Lord Jesus, Savior of all, Redeemer of both Jew and heathen! Amen.

XXIV. JESUS

And His Sibling Christians Hold the Highest Place in the Eyes of God the Heavenly Father, But Are Always Counted Last in the Eyes of the World (Gen. 10).

Through the flood God had destroyed all but eight persons. Now the new world was to be repopulated by Noah's three sons. I will restrict myself to discussing our own ancestors and those of our neighbors, and leave other nations to address their own provenance.

From Magog came the Turks and Tatars.[535] *Magog* means "a man who lives only by plunder, not dwelling in cities or houses, but always staying in the country," which is precisely how these peoples are. From Meshech came the Muscovites.[536] *Meshech* means "a good shot," and so these people are fierce warriors even today. From Ashkenaz came the Germans. *Ashkenaz* means "a priest of the holy fire; a man who can call down fire from heaven." From Elisha came the Silesians. *Elisha* means "God's salvation; a man who knows and confesses the Savior of the world, Jesus Christ." These last two men, Ashkenaz and Elisha, learned about the Lord Jesus in Shem's church, and, as it were in the midst of wolves, bore witness to the heavenly truth. By this we see that God often finds pious hearts even in the enemy's camp. From Riphath came our Poles. *Riphath* means "a huge giant," which is borne out by the fact that big, tall, strong men can still be found among this people.

No other author in the world could have given us such an account, from which it is evident that Moses was the oldest, noblest, best, and most trustworthy historian. From this passage, then, it is clear that Japheth

---

535 A fanciful, though not uncommon, explanation at the time; so also the others without exception. This section may draw on one of many ancient or medieval conjectures; cf. Josep. *Antiq.* 1.6; Isid. *Etym.* 9.26–33, 89; Johannes Magnus *Hist. de omn. Goth.* 1.4–5, et al.

536 I.e., the people of Moscow; see previous note.

was the ancestor of all of us who inhabit these lands. We are all Japheth's children, and Noah's prophecy (Gen. 9:27) that we, Japheth's children, would dwell in the tents of Shem, has come true, for through the Gospel we have all been brought to the knowledge of the same Jesus Christ glorified in Shem's church. Eternal thanks and praise be to God for this! From Ham, Noah's youngest son, there came nothing but wicked scoundrels and enemies of God's people: Babylonians, Philistines, etc. Like breeds like. The apple does not fall far from its branch. As the old sing, so do the young. Bad hair and bad hide always make a bad pelt. Hawks don't hatch eagles.

Nimrod was a mighty tyrant "before the LORD," that is, by God's allowance and permission, for without God's permission and will no tyrant could lift a foot, nor could Pilate have had any authority [John 19:11]. Nimrod was the first king of Babel, a mighty warrior feared by all men like a hunter by hares. He was, as his name implies, a bitter, savage ruler,[537] who forced his people to labor and wait on him like bondservants. He might as well have been called "Take-bread," [*Nimm Brod*], for he took the bread from the mouths of his poor subjects so that they never had any bread [*nim Brod*], and he never so much as blushed [*nimmer roth*] about it. He was not ashamed of any villainous trick. He had the shamelessness[538] of Caligula, who thought that his most commendable characteristic was that he did and said what he pleased and had no shame before anyone. But "He is lost who is lost in shame."[539] Behold, I pray you, the worst scoundrels steal away the most power and glory in the world. The fattest pigs always gobble up the biggest beets. The worst rogues always have the best luck. While these enjoy the fat of the land, the most godly bear their cross and chew the tablecloth of hunger.

From Shem came the children of Eber, the *Hebrews*. In German this means "pilgrims, wayfarers, and strangers in the world." Such are God's people; they are constantly made to move and wander the world, enduring many afflictions as members of one household. They also know that

---

537 "amarus dominator"

538 "ἀδιατρέψιαν"; Gk. "shamelessness, inflexible rigor"; see Suet. *Caligula* 29.

539 "periit cui pudor periit"; Plautus *Bacch.* 3.3.80.

they have no lasting city here. Therefore, like strangers and pilgrims, they set their hearts on the eternal fatherland in which they will abide forever. For so our Lord Jesus carefully calls the heavenly dwellings "mansions,"[540] or "permanent abodes" [John 14:2].

Here again we find our Lord Jesus in a beautiful mystery. Before God our Lord Jesus does indeed take first place and receive the greatest glory, as do His kinsmen. But in the world's eyes He always comes last and is left with nothing. Mark how beautifully clear this is in Genesis. When Moses lists Noah's sons at the beginning of chapter 10 (v. 1), he puts Shem first even though he is not the oldest but the second-oldest. This Moses did to the glory of the Lord Jesus Christ who would be born from Shem's bloodline. Thus, as demonstrated above, Shem has the first place for the sake of the Lord Jesus. Japtheth is put last because the circle would be joined in him: in matters of faith Japheth's children would take after the children of Shem. When masters receive their diploma,[541] the last place is the place of grace.[542] Thus Japheth is here put in the place of grace,[543] since the children of Japheth would "glorify God for His mercy," as St. Paul says (Rom. 15:9).

Ham, the wicked villain, comes between them, since as the true tare among the wheat he would afflict and harrass the children of God, even as has assuredly come to pass. This is one reason. Shem has the first place in the beginning of this chapter to the glory of the Lord Jesus. But when his children according to the flesh are counted, and their names recorded as they stood in the sight of the world, Shem is pushed to the back and put last. The first place is given to the largely wicked clan of Japheth and the entirely corrupt seed of Ham. So it goes with the world. The worst scoundrels always get the greatest glory. It often cuts the pious to the heart to see it with their own eyes. Psalms 37 and 73 are heavily plagued and afflicted with such grief: "Thus my heart was grieved, and I was pricked in my kidneys," says Psalm 73:21. Cain, too, was the big man around town, and

540 "mansiones"

541 "In promotionibus magistrorum"

542 "locus gratiae"

543 "in loco gratiae"

built himself the first city while Abel was left in the dust. Herodias and her lewd dancing daughter got the rose-garden and malthouse, and John got the kiln. In Pilate's question and in the Jews' hearts, that bad bird Barrabas came first; Christ came dead last. Likewise in our text, Magog, Meshech, Nimrod, and the Philistines come first while Shem's children are forced to eat their dust and breathe their stench. The former were a land-full, the latter barely a handful. The former had big castles, the latter were poor pilgrims, etc. So do not let it grieve you when, in this world, you and your Gospel are swept aside:

> Fret not yourself because of evildoers; be not envious against the work-ers of iniquity. For they will soon be cut down like the grass and wither like the green herb…fret not yourself over him who prospers in his way…For the evildoers shall be cut off…In just a little while, the un-godly will be no more; and if you seek for his place, he will be gone. (Ps. 37:1–2, 7, 9–10)

Where are the haughty braggarts of Ham's lineage today? Neither hide nor hair can be found of them anywhere in the world.

But devout Christians are seen quite differently in God's eyes than in the world's. The kinsmen of Shem, those committed to Christ, come first in God's sight, as can be seen at the outset of this chapter and as is once again brought to our attention at the chapter's end. For Moses says that Shem was "the father of all the children of Eber." Here he passes over ten names, making Eber the fourth after Shem in Christ's genealogy (Luke 3[:35]). Again, he does this on purpose to the glory of the Lord Jesus. For from Eber came the Hebrews, the Jews, from whom Jesus Christ was born. Moses therefore focuses on him more closely, counting the oth-ers as rejects, as though they were nobodies compared to this ancestor of Jesus Christ. Here observe that, even though devout Christians are despised in the world, they are nevertheless greatly esteemed by God for the sake of the Lord Jesus Christ, to whose family they are joined.

Dear Lord Jesus, You said, "You will weep and wail, but the world will rejoice" (John 16:20). You knew that we evangelicals would always be the most miserable and forsaken people in the world. Oh, help us not to shrink from such humiliation, but letting the world discount, despise, deride, and belittle us, to suffer all for the sake of Your glory. Grant us patience when the world takes us for rejects and rubbish, and let us recall Your humiliation when for the sake of our salvation You let Yourself be esteemed little and reckoned far less than a murderer and evildoer. Help us to take comfort in the fact that, because of You, we have all the more respect in the eyes of Your heavenly Father, that He does not despise or reject us, but treats us lovingly, exalts us, and honors us, and that on the Last Day we will have the first place at Your right hand, occupy the first and highest place of heaven, and with Your first and foremost words be honored and addressed, as You Yourself attest. Meanwhile, all our foes and those who mocked Your Gospel will be passed over as rejects unworthy of Your kingdom, and cast down beneath Your left hand—down to hell. Though we are last in this world, we will be first in the next. Though we have no lasting city here, we will dwell forever in the heavenly Jerusalem. Though we may not be granted a powerful family here, yet we have a greater family to look forward to in heaven. O Lord Jesus, let my heart consider this, that no dishonor or humiliation in this world may separate me from You! Amen.

XXV. JESUS,

The Only Heavenly Tower in Which We Are Safe from All Calamity,
Contemplated in the Tower of Babel (Gen. 11[:1–9]).

The story of the wondrous and splendid tower of Babel is especially noteworthy inasmuch as it tells us how there came to be so many languages,
which is something that no other history is able to account for. Herodo-
tus describes how Psammetichus, the king of Egypt, had two boys raised
among sheep to find out what language they would speak naturally. When
at last he called for them, they were supposed to have said, "*Bekos, bekos,*"
which means "bread" in Phrygian—not unlike the German "baker" and
"baking" [*Bäcker und Backen*]. But this is all nonsense. The goats and rams
simply taught these lads how to bawk and bleat. Moses shows that the Hebrew language was the oldest, and that the other languages did not appear
until the tower of Babel was built. Petrus Galatinus[544] believed that we will
all speak Hebrew in heaven. After all, the heavenly hosts sing "Alleluia!"
(Rev. 19:1). By the grace of Jesus may we find out the truth.

About 131 years after the flood (as estimated by Berossus),[545] a large,
magnificent tower was erected in Babel. The builders of this tower were
like bad students: they didn't worry themselves over a shilling. The master
builder Nimrod, being the egotistical man that he was, lived by the rhyme:

> Now build your buildings, make them large,
> Since you're the prince and man in charge.

He had a vast retinue of men who were nothing but wicked scoundrels,
for like and like are glad company.

Many hands made light work: one cut the bricks, another mixed the

---

544 Pietro Colonna Galatino (1460–1530), Italian friar and scholar of Hebrew.
545 I.e., Pseudo-Berossus = Annius of Viterbo.

mortar. This was a special kind of pitch which, according to Pliny, became like steel or iron when dried. Those clever people wanted to make their building able to withstand any kind of rain. It is disturbing that the children of the world can be so clever, but the good thing is that God holds all their cleverness in the palm of His hand and can put it to shame with His own wisdom.

Babel swarmed, teemed, and bustled like an anthill. Wheelbarrows creaked, huge windmills turned, timber went up, scaffolds were fixed in place, levels and right-angles were on hand, and everything proceeded with speed.

They put the tower in the country of Shinar, the fat of the land. Behold, they chafed of their fur lining. Their bulging purses were ready to burst. The good life spoiled them.

The city had a circumference of twelve miles. The tower must have reached a great height; for the great and mighty king Alexander, intending to rebuild the edifice, made ten thousand strong men carry away the fallen rubble for a whole eight weeks. When he died in the process, however, no one was able or willing to incur further expenses. Long ago it was said in the cloisters that the tower had been nine miles high: three miles were eroded by weather, three collapsed to the earth, and three were left standing. From the top, moreover, the angels could be heard singing. They had no wish to put an end to a fairy tale. On the other hand, Strabo[546] writes that in his time it was still standing 416 cubits high, laid out in a square, and 416 cubits long on each side. What an edifice! It must have seemed rather like a small city.

The tower's builders themselves admit why this splendid construction was begun: "Let us make a name for ourselves, lest we be scattered abroad into every land." Philo says that the masters of the project cut their names in the bricks so as not to be forgotten. They wanted to establish a powerful border-palace and build a strong bunker in which they might surmount and escape God's wrath in the event that He ever punished them with water again, as Nicholas of Lyra and several other doctors of the Church believe.

---

546 Strabo (ca. 63 BC–ca. AD 24), Greek historian.

These people were despisers of the divine Word and the Holy Sacraments. For God had promised them with clear words that He would never again destroy the world with water, and added to this, in lieu of a sacrament, the rainbow in the clouds of heaven. But they esteemed one no more than the other. When, therefore, they attacked these as cleverly as possible, God simply took another path, canceled their calculations, and thwarted their plans. They were like the monk with the honey-pot.[547] God confused their tongues. No one could understand anyone else. They looked at each other like lazy cats, and instead of the glory which they thought to acquire for themselves, they had shame and disgrace. God put a curse on their arrogance. The building was left unfinished, and even to this day God's curse haunts the place, for it is so infested with poisonous insects and vermin that no one can come within a half-mile of it except in the harshest, coldest winter when the pests are still underground. Here take note: God is not asleep in heaven, but watching and examining every word and deed, and He has a thousand ways to punish those who despise Him. So be faithful, and whatever you do, begin with God and prayer, and you will begin, continue, and end well. When you neglect God, you are sure to be adding insult to injury. To be insulted by the world is simply salt in the pickling.[548]

Now attend, dear heart: The height of this tall tower of wonders could never have reached heaven; it could not and would not have done so. For this would have been an offense to the glory of our Lord Jesus Christ. He alone is the tower of wonder by which we ascend to heaven. He is "the way and the truth and the life" [John 14:6], the true way to eternal life. He is the blessed ladder and portal of heaven. The apostle Matthew likewise proclaims this of Christ, His Gospel, and His Church (in *The Golden Legend*):[549] Just as the languages were confused when the tower of Babel was being built, so the knowledge of many languages was given to

---

547 A traditional fable about a monk who happens upon some honey, and putting it into a pot, dreams of how, by a series of increasingly fortuitous transactions, he will transform it into a great fortune, but ends by accidentally breaking the pot and losing all the honey.

548 I.e., "it comes with the territory."

549 "Lomb. Hist."; Ryan II 184.

the apostles in the New Testament when the Christian Church, in which Jesus Christ is confessed as the true tower to heaven, was to be built. Just as here by the confusion of languages many schisms and idolatries were brought into the world, so by the gift of tongues the one Christian faith was spread and idolatry routed.

The Lord Jesus was active in this work, too, for Moses says, "The Lord said, 'Let Us go down,'" etc. Here God the Father took counsel with our Lord Jesus and God the Holy Spirit. However, let us restrict ourselves to contemplating the image of the Lord Jesus in this tower of Babel.

O Lord Jesus, You are the mighty Tower to heaven, the Tower of wonder. These people trusted in their tower of pride; I trust in You alone. You are my heart's Palace and Bunker. "A mighty fortress is our God, a goodly shield and weapon." You are our God, our Immanuel, and our Kinsman by blood. You are our Fortress, as we sing of You, "Ask ye, Who is this? Jesus Christ it is."[550] Your name, O Lord Jesus, is "a strong tower; the righteous man runs to it and is sheltered" (Prov. 18:10). Through You Your heavenly Father has magnified His name in all the world, for all the world marvels at this great grace, namely, that Your Father has shared His heart with us. Of this the angels sang on Christmas Eve, "Glory to God in the highest, and on earth peace, and goodwill to men" [Luke 2:14].

You are laid out with four corners: You are very fittingly presented and revealed to us in the writings of the four holy evangelists.

Whoever dwells in You in true faith surmounts and escapes the wrath of God and the flood of all calamity and has an everlasting remembrance in heaven (Ps. 112:6). In You the singing of the angels is heard just as it was on Christmas Eve, for they are employed in all Your works. In fact, whoever trusts in You has the holy angels to watch over him also. Our names are engraved on Your hand, on Your heart, and we will never be forgotten (Luke 10:20; Is. 49:16).

Your benefits are Your most blessed steps, spiral staircase, and rising ramp. Whoever takes comfort in them will at last ascend to eternal life.

---

550 From the hymn "Ein feste Burg ist unser Gott" (Luther, 1529), st. 2, lines 5–6; see *LSB* 656:2.

From the top of a tower I can see far, both above and below me. Likewise, since I believe in You, I have the comfort of seeing the gracious heart of Your Father in heaven above, and also of knowing which way to go in my Christian life below, that I may serve and please You.

A high tower can be seen from very far away. O Lord Jesus, You are seen from the world's remotest climes, for by the Gospel You have been exalted and made known in all the world.

A high tower with a bright light is very helpful to sailors when they make for port, enabling them to find the right course. Oh Lord Jesus, how helpful You are to the vessel of my heart on the dark sea of this world, guiding me to heaven's port by the bright light of Your Gospel! For if I sail straight for You, I am taking the sure course to the promised land of eternal joy.

A high tower gives prestige to the whole city. O Lord Jesus Christ, You give prestige to the city of God, the whole Christian Church, in the sight Your heavenly Father so that He exhibits gracious kindness toward us. My heart, too, is a little city and palace for God to dwell in. Oh Lord Jesus, be my heart's beautiful Tower of wonder, be my Glory and Jewel, and give the palace of my heart an everlasting prestige in the sight of Your Father, that thereby I may pray and be heard, find comfort when bearing my cross, have protection in spiritual attacks, and enjoy You continually. And when I must die, stand in the city of my heart as my own wondrous heavenly Tower, that my soul, surmounting every calamity of this world in You, may ascend into heaven and reach eternal joy. Amen, dearest Lord Jesus, Glory and Jewel of my heart! Amen.

XXVI. JESUS

Makes an Eternal and Noble Name for Shem, Arpachshad, Salah, Eber, Peleg, Reu, Serug, Nahor, Terah, Abraham, and All His Family (Gen. 11[:10–26]).

Moses continues Shem's genealogy up to Abraham, showing that he was of Shem's lineage and bloodline in the tenth generation. Here you see that all these saints, Shem, Arpachshad, Salah, Eber, Peleg, Reu, Serug, Nahor, Terah, and Abraham lived married lives. From this it should be learned that marriage is a holy and God-pleasing estate in which one can live and serve God with a good conscience.

It can also be seen that man's lifespan quickly decreased after the flood, for the fruits of the field were greatly diminished by it, man found it somewhat harder to nourish himself, and strong drink became more common. Consequently, man's lifespan grew shorter and was cut off before its time.

It can also be seen that everyone was free to move from one land to another. Everyone could seek to improve his situation. Terah, Abraham's father and Lot's grandfather, moved around in search of a better life for himself and his children.

Note here, dear heart, what an exceptional thing it is that Moses lists so many names in a row and says absolutely nothing about them save only that each one left a particular son behind. Surely he must have had a good reason for this? Indeed he did. For Moses, it was all about the Lord Jesus. He wanted to display the ancient noble pedigree of Jesus Christ (according to His human nature), and to show that He was not only a son of Abraham but also of Shem. For all these men that Moses lists in this passage are in the lineage and genealogy of Jesus Christ, and every last one of them is an ancestor of His, as Luke, following Moses, clearly recounts in chapter 3 of his Gospel.

O Lord Jesus, here again I see Your long, laudable, and gallant pedigree. You are the most venerable nobleman in the whole world. No person of nobility can count so many of his ancestors so far back. You are noble by Father and Mother both. We share Your nobility when we do the will of Your Father. This is the will of Him who sent You, that everyone who looks on You and believes in You should have eternal life [John 6:40]. You clearly say, "Whoever does the will of My Father in heaven, the same is My brother, sister, and mother" (Matt. 12:50). Therefore, if I hold You dear in my heart, confess You with joyful lips, and live a Christlike life to Your glory, I am a part of Your noble family and am perfectly noble in the sight of Your heavenly Father, even if I am low-born in the world.

Oh, what an honor this is! Lord Jesus, send Your Spirit into my heart that, contemplating this noble honor, I may be comforted by it in all the dishonesty of this world and not subject my noble Christian status to any dishonor. Let me act nobly and not serve the evil one or the world, which would be a stain upon my noble honor. But rather, as one of noble blood, let me remain true to You, honor You, extol You, and praise You forever and ever.

Just as the highest honor of the people mentioned above is that they were blood-kinsmen in Your family, so I too count it my highest honor to be called a Christian after Your name, saying with the apostle Matthias, "Christian is not a name of shame, but the most glorious title that a man can be given."[551] And when I suffer for being a Christian, I need not be ashamed, but may regard it as my eminent glory and give God the glory in the process, in accordance with 1 Peter 3:14.

Now this is lovely beyond all measure to contemplate: For Christ's sake, these two esteemed men [Shem and Abraham] were given an everlasting name and a glorious, lasting, and noble remembrance, so that they will be spoken of as long as the world stands. Likewise, O Lord Jesus, all who believe in You receive an eternal remembrance. Hence it says in Psalm 112:6, "The righteous man will never be forgotten,"[552] and they are

---

551 "Christianum esse, non est criminis, sed gloriae"; from *The Golden Legend*; see Ryan I 170.

552 "In memoria aeterna erit justus."

righteous who take comfort in Your righteousness, oppose willful unrighteousness, and serve You in new holiness and righteousness. My name is written in heaven, and I rejoice because of this, as You Yourself say (Luke 10:20). My name is engraved on Your hand, as You clearly inform me (Is. 49:16). Therefore I can never be forgotten. The world may forget about me, but You are mindful of me and bless me (Ps. 115:12).

The builders of the tower of Babel wanted to make a great name for themselves with their proud edifice. I want to make a great and everlasting name for myself in heaven with true, unfeigned faith. They received an infamous reputation with their arrogance. I want to build an honorable reputation with Christlike humility. Herostratus forged a powerful remembrance and lasting reputation for himself by means of a daring prank when he burned down the great temple of Ephesus,[553] which it had taken all of Asia 120[554] years to build, and which had 127 enormous columns, each contributed by a different king, and then confessed his crime himself, saying that he had dared to do it so that all the world would know of him. Skeptical that he could earn great fame with valiant deeds, he tried to bring it about with this act of villainy, the result being that the name Herostratus was forbidden to be spoken in all Asia upon pain of death. Oh, how many there are of this sort, making a name for themselves with blatant robbery, immorality, tyranny, and other evils, just to be remembered for a long time. But, just like Pilate in the Creed, it is an accursed remembrance that they get. Oh Lord Jesus, keep me from such evil-doing. Strengthen me in the faith by Your Spirit, for then I will have an eternal, good, and honorable name.

Perillus made a name for himself with a fake bull made out of brass in which he had people locked up and tortured for his pleasure. Though Phalaris did not do much else good, he did act justly when he made this inventor scream inside his own invention. These people all became famous in the world, but it would have been better if they had never been born. So, Lord Jesus, I will remain in Your family. I will love You sincerely, confess You boldly, and honor You as long as I live. Thus I will be part of

---

553 I.e., the Temple of Artemis.

554 Corr. for "220 years"; cf. Plin. *NH* 36.21.95.

Your family and receive from You a glorious remembrance in the world before my honorable fellow Christians. Yet much more than this, I will receive an eternal and honorable name in heaven before Your heavenly Father. Blessed be Your honorable name, O Lord Jesus, which has made my name so renowned and noble in heaven! In return I will never forget Your glorious name, but worship and bless it forever. Amen.

XXVII. JESUS,
The Seed of Abraham in Which All the Families on Earth
Shall Be Blessed (Gen. 12).

Up to this point our Lord Jesus was always proclaimed to the world as follows: "A Virgin's Son shall crush the serpent's head." But now that the world was greatly multiplied and the lands inhabited by many nations, God was no longer content to leave it at this, but wished to add to it, and to make known and declare plainly in which land and nation this Virgin's Son would be born. Thus God set apart Abraham for Himself and commanded him to move with all his household, establish a particular kingdom, and take possession of a particular land. Oh Lord Jesus, how much must depend on You, since Your heavenly Father took such great pains not only to make Your birth known but Your ancestors and homeland, too! Much depends on You indeed. All our salvation and blessedness depends on You, for "in You all the families on earth shall be blessed."

Abraham did not depart until God gave him explicit directions, for no one should rush off without a certain call. Oh Lord Jesus, govern me by Your Spirit that I may remain in my calling, turning neither to the right hand nor to the left, doing only what is pleasing to You. For Your angels keep us in all our ways (Ps. 91[:11]), and when we walk in Your will, we go with safe conduct, no matter how the devil may try to break it, or every tyrant try to hurt us, or all the gates of hell try to prevail against us. When we do what You and our conscience demand, then all goes as it should. Oh, help me not to leave Your escort.

At the same time, Abraham was a pilgrim. He had already moved to Haran; now he had to move again to Canaan. Here we have a picture of our earthly life; there is no constancy in it. We must ever wander on. We are "guests and strangers on the earth" [Heb. 11:13]. "Here we have no lasting city, but we seek the one to come" [13:14]. Oh Lord Jesus, help me not to set my heart on temporal things, which are all fleeting and impermanent, but grant me grace to turn my thoughts and attention to what is eternal. That will last. There I will no longer have to keep walking and wandering on like this, but will live and dwell with You forever.

Abraham did not quarrel with God. He did not contest God's will. He did not say, "What, am I supposed to let go of what is certain to trust in what is uncertain? A bird in the hand is better than ten on the fence. I know what I have here, but who knows what I might encounter elsewhere?" He thrust all such thoughts from his heart and, trusting solely in God and paying heed only to His will, he went forth, and knew himself not whither. He left that to God, reasoning (as the students used to say in Wittenberg, "Wherever Philipp is, Wittenberg is, too."),[555] "Wherever God is, my homeland and fatherland is, too. God is everywhere, and good bread can be had in any country. So since He commanded me to go, let Him be my guide. He'll manage well. Let Him cook, I'll fetch the water." This is a champion's faith. Thus Hebrews 11:8 praises him: "By faith Abraham was obedient when he was called to go out into the land that he was to inherit; and went out, and knew not whither he went." Oh Lord Jesus Christ, grant me such a noble faith. Help me to be so quick to obey You. For whoever loves father or mother (or something temporal) more than You is not worthy of You (Matt. 10:37). Help me, with Abraham and Peter, to leave everything, follow You, and please You forever.

Abraham, having been an idolater (Joshua 24:2), was not as highly praised at the beginning of his story as were Noah, Job, and others. Nevertheless, God preferred him to all others, and set him apart from mankind like a precious kernel from the pods. Here God's inexpressible goodness, graciousness, and mercy shine before our eyes. Abraham could not boast before God that he had earned this of Him. God was good to him out of sheer unmerited grace and love. Nothing avails before God but grace and favor. O Lord Jesus, it is my most beautiful comfort also that my happiness and bliss, my salvation and blessedness, do not depend on my good

555 "Ubi Philippus, ibi Wittenberga."

works but simply on Your grace and goodness. Let Your goodness, grace, favor, and mercy dwell upon me and avail me for eternal life.

Out of sheer love, then, God promised Abraham seven great gifts of grace. First: *he would become "a great nation."* Here the Jews, born of Abraham, are themselves called *goy,* so it is gross blindness when they slander us with this word. Second: *God said, "I will bless you."* In other words, you will have an invincible kingdom, and your descendants will never be wiped out until the Messiah comes. Third: *"I will make your name great"*—you will be acclaimed throughout the world, and all men will speak of the Jews and the wonders that took place among them. Fourth: *"You will be a blessing"*— through your children, many will be brought to the knowledge of God and their salvation. Fifth: *"I will bless those who bless you"*—whoever gives your children a cup of cold water to drink will not do so in vain [Matt. 10:42]. Sixth: *"I will curse those who curse you"*—whoever denies you anything will only be kicking against the pricks, just as Pharaoh learned to his disgrace. Seventh: *"In you all the families on earth shall be blessed"*—Jesus Christ, the Savior of the world, will be born from your descendants. This is where Abraham saw in the Spirit the day of Jesus Christ and rejoiced (John 8:56). Moreover, everything was fulfilled and took place in exactly this way.

Now pause here, dear heart, and contemplate your Savior Jesus Christ in His person, office, and benefits. O Lord Jesus, You were to be born from the seed of Abraham, so You had to be true man. Thank You for this great honor with which You have adorned us wretched pieces of earth. At the same time, You were to bless all the families on earth, so You had to be true God, for that is a purely divine work. It is my greatest comfort that in You I have such a mighty, powerful Lord and Protector. You were to bring blessing. Your calling was to to take away the curse that resulted from sin, to restore and fix everything that was corrupted by sin. Your benefits are unsearchable, for every family on earth without exception (even I, a poor sinner) was to benefit from and be blessed by You.

Oh, Lord Jesus, be my blessing! I know that I will be blessed by You. When I bear a cross, I will draw comfort from You. When I pray, I will be heard because of You. When I am attacked by the world and the evil one, I will find protection in You. When I die, I will be blessed by You. On the Last Day, I will not hear an evil verdict but those comforting words, "Come, you blessed of My Father" [Matt. 25:34], and finally receive eternal life from You.

Blessing is the most beautiful word that I hear from You in the Old Testament. *Eternal life* is the most beautiful phrase that I have from You in the New Testament. Oh Lord Jesus, Source of all blessing, let the power of Your blessing fall on me and I will be freed from my sins, and assured of Your Father's grace, and know that the evil one cannot catch me, nor death hold me. Yea, then I will have all that I need for eternal life. Through You I have these three articles in the Creed: the forgiveness of sins, the hope of the resurrection of my body, and the life everlasting—yea, truly, and amen! You are the true Blessed One of the Lord.[556] O Lord Jesus, my Blessing, grant me Your blessing.[557] Now if Moses could say, "Behold, I set before you today the blessing and the curse: the blessing, if you obey the commandments of the LORD...the curse, if you will not obey," etc. [Deut. 11:26–27], I can say all the more, "Behold, dear heart, I set before you the blessing and the curse: the blessing, if you believe in Jesus Christ; the curse, if you reject Him." You have before you life and death; take which you will. Follow the rule of St. Paul: "Approve what is excellent" (Phil. 1:10). Take blessing and life, and you will be blessed forever. O Lord Jesus, surely I will take the blessing, and this I find in You. I will remain faithful and true to You, for then I know that I will have comfort to the full, and in the end, eternal life. Amen. O Lord Jesus, grant that in this I may remain steadfast. Amen.

556 "Benedictus"
557 "Benedictus benedicat"

XXVIII. JESUS,
The Lord Whom Abraham Preached (Gen. 12[:8]).

Abraham went as the Lord directed him. He did what God commanded, and refrained from what God forbade. For "obedience is better than sacrifice," says 1 Samuel 15:22. Oh Lord Jesus, grant Your grace that I may submit my whole life to Your will, and so walk as You have directed me in Your Word.

Yet God could not leave pious Abraham unconsoled. Therefore, immediately perceiving that Abraham was obedient to Him, God prodded the heart of his nephew Lot, who then consented to go with him. "Dear uncle Abraham," Lot might have said, "I do not want to part from you. I have to see what wonderful things that God will do for you. What you suffer, I too will suffer. Where you stay, I too will stay. I will walk with you even unto death, and risk life and limb at your side." Oh, how the heart of Abraham must have leapt for joy when God gave him such a trusty fellow traveler to whom he would be able to open his heart along the way, and make the long miles short with many pleasant discussions. Lot was Abraham's caravan. All who serve God have this comfort, that though they must encounter much opposition as they fear God, their friends will always be greater than their foes.

Sarah followed her dear master without question. All good wives should keep this in mind, that they may learn to yield and submit their will to that of their head and master. At the same time, like Abraham, husbands should not ask anything of their wives contrary to God, honor, and conscience. In this way God will dwell with them, and in this way their household will thrive and prosper, and through unity their little possession will be enlarged.

Up to this point, Abraham had followed God, forsaking what he knew and departing at God's command into the unknown (for God had not yet revealed to him the Promised Land by name). So as soon as he entered Canaan, God said, "To your seed I will give this land," thereby ridding Abraham of his unspoken concerns. Here we see that God does not leave His own to wallow in worry continually. Thus Psalm 55:22 says, "Cast your cares on the LORD who will sustain you, and will not leave the righteous man in disquietness forever." Abraham, receiving this comforting promise with a grateful heart, immediately built an altar and publicly thanked God for His grace; for everyone who prays devoutly should also give thanks sincerely. Whoever thanks God for an old benefit will receive a new one from Him.

So when Abraham found out that Canaan was the land that God would give him, he established himself on mount Ephraim between Bethel and Ai, only two miles from Jerusalem, so that He would have the honorable Melchizedek near him for a neighbor and be able to discuss with him the essential questions of religion and faith. A good neighbor is a precious jewel. Thus when Themistocles[558] had his free holdings put up for sale, he added that he had a good neighbor, thinking that this would fetch him a higher price. Jews curse their bad neighbors. Florian Sarus, who got his belly sliced open in the battle against the Knights of the Cross in Prussia, remarked to the king of Poland that he had been made to suffer far worse pains from his bad neighbor. So whoever is able to get good neighbors, let him take heed and keep his relationship with them in good shape.

Abraham, then, having decided to stay in that place, built another altar and went to church. All those in authority should thus take the greatest care that churches and schools may be rightly and well provided for, since "the fear of the LORD is the beginning of wisdom," and of all welfare [Ps. 111:10; Prov. 9:10].

Though Abraham was godly, even he was not able to avoid bearing his cross. Famine pressed upon him until he had no hope of finding a means to live. At great cost he had to move again, and soon came to fear

---

558 Themistocles (ca. 524–459 BC), Athenian politician who was forced into exile.

losing life and limb for the sake of his darling, the beautiful Sarah. Here you see that it is true when Sirach 2:1 says, "My child, if you will be a servant of God, prepare yourself for tribulation."

God, however, did not forsake Abraham, for "who ever trusted in the Lord and was put to shame? Or who ever persevered in the fear of God and was forsaken? Or who ever called upon Him and was neglected by Him?" (Sir. 2:10). Abraham did not starve to death, no one hurt him on the way, and this difficult situation worked out for his good (Rom. 8:28). For by it he became known at the king's court, his name was more widely spread about, and he grew wealthier than he had been before, all because of the king's good favor. He was given safe conduct. Oh God, how great is Your goodness! You lead your saints in a wondrous way [Ps. 4:3], but in the greatest need You demonstrate the greatest help. Therefore, "you who fear the Lord, trust in Him, for it will not fail you. You who fear the Lord, hope for the best from Him, and you will ever find grace and comfort" (Sir. 2:8–9).

It is comforting beyond measure that God graciously prevented the anxious Abraham and kept him from perishing in his foolish plan, and on the contrary made Abraham's wicked deeds work together for good. Abraham instructed his wife to lie; this was wrong. By his silence, he put Sarah's honor and fidelity at risk; this is not to be commended. Nevertheless, God did not let him come to ruin. He saw that Abraham was not acting out of a wicked, mischievous heart, but out of poor judgment, human frailty, fearfulness, and the love of this temporal life. For once in his life, Abraham did not consider what a dangerous thing he was doing. For a moment he lost sight of all his comfort and reasons why he should not fear. He had trusted God with a champion's faith before, but now he forgot that God was still as able to protect him as ever. Others, too, who truly love God have experienced such grief. So take note of this sweet consolation that you have here, dear heart. Serve God out of a true heart and be assured that He will not leave you. When out of human frailty you likewise ignorantly put yourself in danger, God will by grace stop you on your perilous path of error, give you His hand, and help set you right again.

If Pharaoh would refuse to dishonor himself by taking another man's wife, how much more ought Christians to shun adultery and immorality?

Here again we find the Lord Jesus. Abraham built two altars and on these offered his sacrifice to the LORD God. Our altar is Jesus Christ (Heb. 13[:10–12]),[559] as demonstrated above with Noah's altar. Just as Abraham laid his sacrifice upon the altar and thus, calling upon God, was heard by Him, so we lay our trouble upon our Lord Jesus Christ and thus, kindling our sacrifice of prayer with ardent devotion, are heard. For the Lord Jesus plainly says, "Truly, truly…whatever you ask of the Father in My name, He will give it to you" [John 16:23].

Next it says that Abraham "preached the name of the LORD." Here again we find the Lord Jesus, for "the Father is Lord, the Son is Lord, and the Holy Spirit is Lord, and yet there are not three Lords, but one Lord."[560] Thus Abraham plainly preached the most blessed Trinity, and above all the Messiah, the Lord Jesus, of whom Eve said, "I have gotten the Man, the LORD" [Gen. 4:1], whom Jeremiah 23:6 calls "the LORD, our Righteousness," and about whom the apostles say, "I believe in Jesus Christ, His only Son, our Lord."[561] Now this is expressed in the Hebrew in such a way that it manifestly must be understood that Abraham *plainly preached and taught about the Lord*. He said, "As I have experienced the grace of the Lord as an example for you, so may you also trust this dear God. He too will be your Lord and Provider, and you too will find proof of His grace." Second, Abraham *called on the name of the Lord*, for Joel 2:32 uses the same expression, saying, "Whoever calls on the name of the LORD will be saved." When Abraham was done preaching, he would collect his sermon into a fine prayer, praying sincerely, "Oh dear Lord, be my Protector. 'Your grace is sufficient for me.'[562] O Lord, renew Your old favor to me, and I will be saved in body and soul." Third, he publicly *thanked the Lord* for the favor that He had shown him. Fourth, *he confessed the Lord and the true faith* over against all fanatical heresies, and refuted the false opinions of idolaters by sound argument. But this has been sufficiently discussed

559 Corr. for "Heb. 11."

560 From the Athanasian Creed.

561 From the Apostles' Creed.

562 "Sufficit mihi gratia tua" (2 Cor. 12:9).

above concerning chapter 4,[563] where Moses told us how in the days of Enosh men began to preach the name of the Lord.

Oh Lord Jesus, Protector of Abraham, my Lord and my God! Be my Protector also. I am Your servant. Provide for me and be my Lord, and I in turn, as is fitting, will extol and praise You as Lord forever. Amen.

563 See part 2, meditation 7.

XXIX. JESUS

Is Never Let Out of Abraham's Heart (Gen. 13).

Because of a famine, Abraham was an exile and had to dwell in Egypt for some time. Then the sun began to shine on him again and he was able to move back to the land of Canaan. So "cast your cares on the LORD who will sustain you, and will not leave the righteous man in disquietness forever" (Ps. 55:22).

Now it is quite remarkable that Abraham and Lot grew rich despite all these travels, for it usually goes, "An oft-rolled stone is not overgrown." Here we plainly see that "the blessing of the LORD enriches without effort" (Prov. 10:22). "God gives to His friends while they sleep" (Ps. 127:2). "By orderly housekeeping the rooms are filled" (Prov. 24:4). "Seek (and regard) first the kingdom of God and His righteousness, and everything else will be added to you" (Matt. 6:33). The ancients tell how, once upon a time, a holy father prayed often to God that he might learn how to manage his affairs prosperously. God therefore made three angels appear before his eyes: one prayed, another dug up roots from the earth, a third gathered the dug-up roots and carried them into a house. All this shows that when prosperity is sought in one's living, one must first pray. "I lift up my eyes to the hills, from whence help comes to me. My help comes from the Lord, who made heaven and earth" [Ps. 121:1–2]. Second, one must work until one stinks and the sweat drips in one's face, for a blister on the hand is better than a rope on the neck. Third, one must save and keep track of all that has been earned by bitter toil. And finally, all the household must dwell together with the harmony of angels. Where this happens, everything thrives. Our present passage testifies to this by the example of the two godly homeowners, Abraham and Lot.

Moses also informs us that a disagreement and dispute arose between Abraham and Lot over some grumpy herdsmen. Here we see that even saintly men may often err, and a spark may often flare up between two godly neighbors. As the saying goes, If every road were smooth, who wouldn't want to drive a cart? But Abraham, being the oldest, was the wisest, and he thought to himself, "I ought to patch things up with this young duckling." He relinquished his advantage and bought peace for himself at the costly price of patience, for these are three good Ps, as Philipp says, "Peace must be purchased with Christlike patience."[564] Therefore, "let your gentleness be known to all men" (Phil 4:5). "Blessed are the meek, for they shall inherit the earth" (Matt. 5:5). This is clearly shown here, for no sooner had Abraham done this than the Promised Land was pledged to him a second time. Here comes the cut that made the hole. He incurred no harm when to the glory of God and for the sake of peace he went to live in the lesser plot and the dry patch of land. Lot grabbed the butter-barrel and the honey-jar, but it did him as much good as grass does a dog, for right away in the next chapter he becomes involved with ungodly neighbors and is forced to relinquish all his worldly possessions to the flames of Sodom. So it goes for all who try to take care of themselves and not look to God's hands. Besides this, Moses laments the fact that there was good, rich land around Sodom but it was inhabited by wicked people. This happened frequently, even in Bethlehem; for you need strong legs to make it through the good days. But a great grace is often followed by a great disgrace, as will be discussed below.

In this chapter our Lord Jesus is remembered twice. First, when Abraham arrived between Bethel and Ai, he "preached the name of the LORD"; then at the end of the chapter, when Abraham dwelt in Hain Mamre, which is at Hebron, "he built an altar to the LORD." These words have all been clearly and thoroughly explained above and connected to our Lord Jesus. Note here this one detail: Abraham carried the Lord with him everywhere. In every land, city, village, and hamlet, day and night, he never let his Lord Jesus out of his heart, and in this found comfort and blessing.

---

564 "Pax patientiâ paratur."

Oh my Lord Jesus, give me Abraham's heart. Help me to keep You with me day and night, and like a precious jewel never to let You go, but to love You with my heart, extol and confess You with my mouth, glorify You with my whole life, and say with the holy apostle Paul, "Far be it from me to boast except in the cross of our Lord Jesus Christ" (Gal. 6:14); and with dear Ignatius, "Oh sweet name of Jesus! Oh sweet name of Jesus!"; and with devout Bernard, "In whatsoever place I be, I long for Jesus constantly."[565] Help me to rise, move, and go out in You; to begin the day, continue it, conclude it, and fall asleep in You. Grant me never to forget You for one moment. Be my companion and escort on the way,[566] and I will be content. For whoever carries You with him, You will in turn carry him like a beloved lamb to everlasting life. O Lord Jesus, I carry You in my heart; You know this. I carry You in my mouth as I confess You. I carry You constantly in my thoughts as I ponder You. I will carry You in my prayer, cross, tribulation, and death. Oh, carry me also in Your heart, and treat me with true faithfulness. Yea, carry me, Your sheep which once was lost but now is found, into the everlasting joy of heaven. Amen.

---

565 "Quocunque loco fuero, / Semper Jesum desidero"; see note 000, part 2, meditation 16.

566 "Vade-mecum"

XXX. JESUS,
The King of Righteousness, the Priest after the Order of Melchizedek,
Instituter of the Holy Supper (Gen. 14).

In good, rich meadows, calves grow lusty. This is apparent in the lands of Sodom and Gomorrah: there was good soil there but wicked people. They chafed of their fur lining. They sat among the reeds, cutting whistles where they wished. Then when life was good they began to go bad, and cursed each other in their drunkenness. Finally, having become too close for comfort, they declared a frivolous war. When the donkey feels good, it dances on the ice and breaks its leg. Oh God, help us when life is good not to forget You, but always to reason thus: Dear God, if You can give us so much in this life when we continually sin and anger You, what will You give us after this life when we will serve You in eternal innocence and holiness?

But God used this war as a hint to the inhabitants of the land that they should guard themselves from severe punishment. For God's way is ever to sprinkle and threaten with lesser adversity before severe punishment. He is like a pious father who first lays his switch out in the light before grabbing it in anger, turning around, and striking in earnest. Oh dear God, help us to amend our ways during lesser adversities, to be converted while there is still time, and to escape the greater afflictions.

The five kings fought against the four as rebels, for they had been subjects of Chedor-laomer for twelve years. Nevertheless, they were beaten, for treachery always strikes its own master. Oh God, help us not to oppose our regular authorities, lest we thereby fall under Your righteous anger. Earlier, Lot set his sights on the butter-barrel and sent his old uncle Abraham off to the less valuable piece of land. But now he was the worse for it, whereas Abraham had peace and quiet. Therefore do not get yourself too mixed up with the ungodly. Whoever mingles with the slop is fed to the hogs. Jehoshaphat, too, caught one on the snout when he allied himself with Ahab. As they say, those who cling together swing together.

Moses also informs us that Abraham entered into a brotherhood and confederacy with the men Aner, Eshcol, and Mamre. Abraham's heart, however, did not depend on the help and assistance of men but only on God's help and protection, for "cursed is the man who trusts in men" [Jer. 17:5]. So while there is therefore nothing wrong with making a pact and alliance with one's neighbor in the world, one's heart should only rely on God, not any man. Oh Lord my God, give me also a heart that clings only to You!

Abraham came to the aid of his captured nephew. He made no mention of disagreements from time past, as the world does which says, "A loan is no gift. Old debts gather no rust." It is still becoming of families today to spring to each other's aid in times of danger and put old disputes aside.

Abraham fought in the war personally. Who then can condemn honorable soldiers who have just cause to fight and are compelled to do so out of need? An honorable soldier pleases God just as much as did Abraham, David, and Judas Maccabaeus.

A handful fought a land-full. What are 318 unprepared, unexperienced servants compared with the forces of four mighty kings? Yet they won, for victory can only be found in the hand of God, and He holds it out to whichever party He will.

Nevertheless, it is evident that Abraham managed his affairs with great caution. He divided his host so that one group would be able to relieve the other, and he came upon the enemy by night when they would surely have been carousing. For advantage is the most important thing in warfare, and whoever has justice on his side may with a good conscience make use of his advantage.

How exquisite it is that, although Lot had to suffer a short time among his wicked neighbors, he was eventually rescued, and so were many wicked men because of him. Thus many an ungodly soul often benefits from a single godly man. The way in which hardship affects the wicked differs greatly from the way in which it affects the pious. It makes an end of the wicked, but brings the pious much good. For God knows His own, and He is able to deliver them from trouble. Adversity is nothing but a school for the pious in which they learn their *mores,* so that they recognize their own transient, human frailties, and pray to God for forgiveness. Yet "the desire of the righteous man must turn out well" (Prov. 11:23). "The righteous man must suffer many things, but the LORD delivers him out of them all" (Ps. 34:19). Accordingly, as Abraham was returning from battle, the king of Sodom came out splendidly to meet him, for "when the pot is full, the flies come swarming."[567]

> When there's fat in the pail and good mugs of ale,
> Your friends all say "Good cheer!":
> But when the fat has gone shy, and the mugs are all dry,
> False friends all like flies disappear.

Abraham's good old friend, the venerable priest Melchizedek, also exhibited princely manners by thanking the victor for restoring his fatherland to peace and quiet, and by being a magnanimous host toward these strangers who could find no room at the inn. This is praiseworthy in him, as it is in all those who make sure to show grace and kindness to worthy guests.

Abraham gave him a tenth part of the spoils,[568] for everyone is obligated, according to his means, to support churches, schools, hospitals, and poor tenants from out of his own wealth. Even though the king of Sodom offered all his possessions to Abraham if he would only let him have his worthy knights (probably to use them as his own imperial guardsmen), Abraham refused, lest he should be promoted and advanced prematurely. For it is best not to be mixed up with those who do not share our faith. Abraham was very gracious and generous here, yet he would not deprive his allies—the men Aner, Eshcol, and Mamre— of their portion, for one ought not to trim others' property like a felt hat. A shoemaker gets no reward from God for stealing leather and then giving the shoes away in God's name. If you want to be generous, do so with your own things.

---

567 "Fervente olla fervet amicitia"; here translated from the paraphrase provided in the text, lit., "When the pot is boiling, friendship is warm."

568 "decem"

Now as bright as the sun in the sky we see the worthy deed of the venerable old priest Melchizedek, who blessed the victorious Abraham and strengthened him and his weary army with a square meal of bread and wine. For this is a type of our Lord Jesus Christ, who likewise deals in blessing, strengthening, and nourishment.

Psalm 110:4 teaches us to regard this account in this way: "The LORD has sworn and will not change His mind, You are a priest forever after the order of Melchizedek." Here it is not only asserted with clear words but also confirmed with a priceless oath that Melchizedek is an image of Jesus Christ. This should be noted very clearly. The Holy Spirit also regards this account in the same way in Hebrews 7, all of which is pertinent here. Likewise, among the Jews, Rabbi Pinhas Ben Yair pointed to the Messiah in this passage. This is the basis for the beautiful things that Luther says in [Luther's Works,] vol. 7, fol. 332.

Melchizedek means "king of righteousness," for in his realm he defended the Gospel, which avails as righteousness before God, and pointed to the merit of Jesus Christ, the Savior of the world. Moreover, since he was also a priest, he himself clearly conveyed this righteousness of ours.

O Lord Jesus, You are the true Melchizedek. You are my King, as Your title on the cross, I.N.R.I. ("Jesus of Nazareth, King of the Jews"), displays. The beautiful Psalm 93 supports this:

> The Lord is King, and adorned in splendor; the Lord is adorned, and has founded a kingdom as wide as the world, and prepared it, that it should remain. From that time forth Your throne has stood firm; You are everlasting, O Lord. The floods lift up, the floods lift up their rumbling, the floods lift up their waves on high. The waves of the sea are great, and rumble terribly; but the Lord on high is mightier still. Your word is a true teaching; holiness is the adornment of Your house forever.

O Lord Jesus, when my troubles weigh and press upon me, I will seek audience with Your faithful, royal heart. Support my cause, as a true king does that of his oppressed subjects. Defend me. Have You not given up Your blood for me? (This reminds me of how King Alfonso used the image of the pelican to represent his motto "For the Law and the Flock.")[569]

You are the King of righteousness. You are the royal Fountain full of righteousness. In summer and winter You overflow with the righteousness that avails before God. From Your fullness I receive all that I lack. You are "the LORD, our Righteousness" (Jer. 23:6). You were made to us righteousness from God (1 Cor. 1:30). You are the righteous Servant who by His knowledge makes many to be accounted righteous (Is. 53:11). You are our "Advocate...who is righteous" (1 John 2:1). "As by the disobedience of one the many were made sinners, so by the obedience of one (You) many are made righteous," [Rom. 5:19]. You are none other than that "Righteous One"[570] whom Righteousness and Mercy look for (in St. Bernard).[571] You died for us poor sinners so that there could be satisfaction between God's righteousness and mercy. O Lord Jesus, I am unrighteous, for which I am ashamed. But You are righteous, for which I rejoice. You are my righteousness, for what is Yours is mine. Let Your righteousness blot out and cover my unrighteousness. Let Your righteousness be mine, and then my righteousness will exceed that of the scribes and Pharisees [Matt. 5:20], for Yours exceeds that of the holy angels and all creation. Thus do I recognize my unrighteousness and my righteousness: My unrighteousness springs from my own sins, but my righteousness springs from Your precious merit. O Lord Jesus, my unrighteousness grieves and accuses me, but my righteousness, which is founded on Your righteousness and merit, gladdens and absolves me. If my unrighteousness is great, my righteousness is far greater, for my righteousness is Jesus Christ.[572] O Lord Jesus, though my unrighteousness points me to God's wrath and eternal damnation, my righteousness in You brings me God's grace and eternal life. Since, moreover, this righteousness imputed to me exceeds that of the scribes and Pharisees, I know for certain that I will enter into the kingdom of heaven. Oh Lord Jesus, help me to Your glory to hate and oppose all unrighteousness, to pursue Christlike righteousness, and to

569 "Pro lege et grege."

570 "Justus"

571 I.e., Bernard's allegory, from *In Annunc. sermo* 1.

572 "Abundat injustitia mea in me ipso, abundat quoque justitia mea in Jesu Christo."

serve You without fear all the days of my life, in holiness and righteousness pleasing to You. Help me to be devoted to You in my heart, actions, words, and deeds, and yet to hope not in my self-righteousness which flows from my good works but in my righteousness which You obtained for me with Your good works on the cross. In other words, help me to trust in that righteousness which You have given me, and be saved.

Once upon a time, an old pilgrim tested his young monks, asking them one by one which works they had been practicing. The first boasted that he had never eaten meat, the second, that he had never slept in a bed, etc. At last, the old master said, "My work is the best, and I will tell you what it is. For it is fitting for the young to learn from the old. When the sun rises, I face the dawn and fall on my knees and say, 'Oh God, be gracious to me, a poor sinner. As the sun rises in the heavens, dear heavenly Father, let Your mercy rise in my heart, that I, an unrighteous man, may be saved.' When the sun stands at high noon, I face the noon[*or* south] and say, 'Lord Jesus, You are the Sun of righteousness, You are my Righteousness. Let Your righteousness help my unrighteousness, that I may be saved.' When the sun is setting, I face the evening and say, 'O Holy Spirit, as the sun of heaven sets, let not the Sun of my righteousness, Jesus Christ, set in my heart, but glorify Him so that at every moment I may be mindful that through Him I have the forgiveness of sins, the hope of the resurrection of the body, and the life everlasting, Amen, verily, and truly. Govern my heart also, that I may conclude my life in holiness and righteousness pleasing to You.' When it has grown dark, I face the midnight [*or* north] and say, 'Dear God, as it is dark, so my eyes also will darken. Oh, help me, God, when the dark night of my death comes, that I not despair. Forgive me my sins, as I also gladly pardon those who have done me ill; and help me to depart this world blessedly and inherit eternal life. Amen.'" This old, pious pilgrim counted his own righteousness as nothing, and confessed to the contrary that he was full of unrighteousness. He sincerely longed for the imputed righteousness of Jesus Christ's merit, and was furthermore resolved, as far as he might, to lead his life in holiness and righteousness. This is a blessed work. Grant me this, too, O Lord Jesus, my great King of righteousness, my most blessed Melchizedek. Amen.

It is also worthy to note here that Moses makes no mention of Melchizedek's father or mother. For the Holy Spirit carefully guided his pen so that a type of the Messiah might again be discerned, just as Hebrews [ch. 7] demands. O Lord Jesus, You have no mother according to Your divine nature, and no father according to Your human nature, for You are God from eternity, begotten from the heart of Your Father, and true man, conceived and born to a pure, spotless Virgin by the overshadowing of the Holy Spirit.

Of this Lactantius writes very beautifully in book 4, *On True Knowledge*, chapter 13:

> When the most holy God and Father of all wished to convey His religion, He sent a teacher of righteousness from heaven so that in and by the Same He might give His new servants a new law; not by a man as He had already done some time before. Rather, He caused Him to be born a man such that in all respects He would be like the heavenly Father. For God the Father Himself, as the origin and beginning of all things, having no parents, was most accurately called by Trismegistus *apatōr* and *amētōr* (i.e., "fatherless" and "motherless"), since He was made by no one. Therefore, His Son, too, had to be born twice so that He would be fatherless and motherless. For in His first and spiritual birth He was without mother, since He was begotten by God the Father alone without the participation of a mother. In His second birth, however, when He came in the flesh, He was without father, since He was conceived in the womb of the Virgin without the participation of a father.[573]

Melchizedek was lord of Salem, which was later called Jerusalem. O Lord Jesus, You are Lord of the heavenly Jerusalem where I shall dwell forever. Oh, how I long to enter there, that I might dwell with You forever!

---

573 "Summus igitur Deus ac parens omnium, cùm religionem suam transferre voluisset, doctorem justitiae misit è caelo, ut novis cultoribus novam legem in eo vel per eum daret: non sicut ante fecerat per hominem, sed tamen nasci eum voluit tanquam hominem, ut per omnia summo Patri similis existeret. Ipse enim pater Deus et origo, et principium rerum, quoniam parentibus caret, ἀπάτωρ atque ἀμήτωρ à Trismegisto verissimè nominatur, quod ex nullo sit procreatus. Idcirco etiam filium bis nasci oportuit, ut ipse fieret ἀπάτωρ atque ἀμήτωρ. In prima enim nativitate spirituali ἀμήτωρ fuit, quia sine officio matris à solo Deo Patre progeneratus est. In secunda vero carnali ἀπάτωρ fuit, quoniam sine patris officio virginali utero procreatus est." .

Salem means "peace." So when I say "Melchizedek was lord of Salem," it can be translated as follows: "Melchizedek was lord of a peaceful land." O Lord Jesus, Isaiah alluded to this when he called You "Prince of Peace" [Is. 9:6]. Indeed, Lord Jesus, You are the true Prince of Peace. With You as my ally, I have peace, rest, and comfort in my conscience, and peace from Your heavenly Father's wrath, and the devil and all the world must leave me in peace, and with joy I can look forward to the everlasting peace of eternal life.

Melchizedek was a priest of the Most High. O Lord Jesus, You are our Priest and Advocate before the Most High. I am Your parishioner. You teach me how to be justified and saved. You intercede for me (Rom. 8:34). I commend myself to the piety of Your prayer. Put in a good word for me with the faithful heart of Your Father, and I will be preserved.

Moses does not say a word about when Melchizedek entered his office or when he died. This brings to mind Your blessed immortality. O Lord Jesus, You are from everlasting to everlasting. "Your throne stands firm. You are everlasting" (Ps. 93:2). Thus I can take comfort in You forever. "You are able to save forevermore those who come to God through You, and You live forevermore, and make intercession for them" (Heb. 7:25).

Melchizedek made a splendid meal of bread and wine, and thus strengthened Abraham and his weary soldiers. O Lord Jesus, You prepare the great Supper of the Holy Gospel and serve us to the full in the great hall of Your Christian Church. "You prepare a table before me in the presence of my enemies, You anoint my head with oil, and fill my cup full. Goodness and mercy shall follow me all the days of my life, and I shall dwell in the house of the LORD forever" (Ps. 23:5–6). This great Supper is also described by You Yourself in Luke 14:16[–24]. When we become Christians and sit at table, the pitcher of the holy water of Baptism is before us. At last You feed us the Holy Supper, not with mere bread and wine, like Melchizedek, but with Your own body and blood, for You are superior to Melchizedek and therefore act with far greater honor and nobility. You strengthen and nourish our weary hearts with Your own body and blood, and You give us Yourself in the Holy Supper as our very own, just as You offered Yourself up for our sins on the tree of the holy cross, so that we are now Your possession and can never be parted from You. Accordingly, Your heavenly Father can no more disdain and oppose us than He can disdain and hate You. He can no more cast me out of heaven than He can You, O Lord Jesus, for You and I have been united in the pledge of the Holy Supper. You are my Head, I am Your limb. Where You are, there I must be also. You are in me and I in You. Temporal death cannot part us. Yea, because of this guarantee and sworn pledge, I cannot remain in the grave, but shall live again and be with You forever. Wherefore we justly sing:

> O sacred banquet, in which Christ is received, the memory of His Passion renewed, and a pledge of future glory given to us.[574]

This, even this, gives me more strength than Abraham and his servants got from Melchizedek's bread. This gives me greater joy than Abraham and his people got from Melchizedek's wine.

O Lord Jesus, You purposefully used bread and wine in the Holy Supper so that You might be more easily found in the story of Melchizedek. Yet You were not content to leave it plain bread and wine, but with them You give Your true body and blood—not merely a sign, not a mere comforting picture, not only Your benefits, but Yourself and all Your riches. You are the Master of the feast, and the Feast Yourself, for we have far greater enemies than Abraham had, and need far greater strength and armor. As Abraham was afflicted by four kings, so we are in constant battle, and must defend ourselves from (1) the evil one; (2) the offensive example of this perverted world; (3) our own flesh and blood, which are ever inclined to wickedness; and (4) eternal death and the gates of hell, that we not fall into doubt. These are four mighty foes. Oh, help us, Lord Jesus, that we may "wage the good warfare, holding faith and a good conscience" (1 Tim. 1:18–19), and as the warriors of Christ (Eph. 6:11) gain the victory.

---

574 "O sacrum convivium, in quo Christus sumitur, recolitur memoria passionis ejus, et futurae gloriae nobis pignus datur"; the antiphon for the feast of Corpus Christi; perhaps significantly, the words "mens impletur gratia," lit., "the mind is filled with grace," are lacking.

Melchizedek dealt in words of blessing. He said to Abraham, "Blessed be you, O Abraham, to the Most High God, who possesses heaven and earth." O Lord Jesus, You also deal in words of blessing. Even Your last work as You ascended into heaven was to give a blessing. Oh, speak a powerful blessing on my body and my soul. Forgive me of my sins, announce to me Your Father's grace, and grant me heaven and eternal life.

Since therefore Abraham received the blessing from Melchizedek, Abraham and all who come from him, including Aaron and the children of Levi, must be inferior to Melchizedek; as is required by Hebrews 7:5. Indeed, O Lord Jesus, You are without doubt superior to Abraham, Aaron, and all the levitical priests. What they could not accomplish, You can. In them there is only shadow; in You there is nothing but truth. Indeed, You are superior to Melchizedek himself, for even Melchizedek needed to be saved by You and Your righteousness. Thus I too believe that I shall receive the crown of righteousness through no one else but You.

Melchizedek accepted a tenth part from Abraham. O Lord Jesus, You also want a tenth part (or tithe)[575] from me. The tithe that You desire is a broken and contrite heart that is sorry for its sins of breaking the holy Ten Commandments, and has wept through the Ten Commandments, one by one, yet with a joyful faith takes comfort in Your ten benefits wherein You (1) were conceived and (2) were born for my consolation; (3) suffered for my good; and (4) were crucified, (5) died, (6) were buried, (7) descended into hell, (8) rose again, (9) ascended into heaven, and (10) seated at the right hand of the heavenly Father for my consolation, just as we recite in the Second Article of the Creed, and as was discussed above on the subject of Paradise.[576]

After this, You require new obedience of me. I am to serve God by the instruction of the holy Ten Commandments according to the means that God provides. Oh Lord Jesus, govern me by Your Holy Spirit, that I may gladly and willingly give You Your tithe, confessing my sins against the holy Ten Commandments, rejoicing in Your comforting ten benefits, and starting afresh to serve You according to the Ten Commandments,

---

575 "decimae"

576 See part 2, meditation 25, regarding the balsam leaves.

nor to be ashamed of the holy cross, which is painted in the form of the numeral ten,[577] but to serve You as I ought in righteousness and godliness. Amen.

577 "in forma decussata", i.e., the Roman numeral X.

XXXI. JESUS

Says to the Greatly Troubled, Melancholy Abraham, "Fear Not, Abraham, I Am Your Shield and Your Very Great Reward" (Gen. 15:1).

Moses tells us that the Lord Jesus comforted Abraham with extraordinary words, but says nothing of Abraham's worries, what was bothering him, what he was lacking, or what oppressed his heart. By this Moses seems to imply that Abraham had fallen into such deep melancholy, anxiety, and despair that he was rendered utterly speechless by it. He could not even find the words to express his sadness. All words were insufficient. His inner turmoil was far too heavy and profound. He sat down, bowed his head, and buried his face in his hands. He meant to cry himself to death. His heart melted away inside him. He fretted himself with secret thoughts and would not reveal them to anyone. He was ashamed to speak his thoughts or complain to anyone. An indescribable, insufferable grief swept over him and he did not know if he was dead or alive. He mourned as though God had died, as though there were no more help in the world. He forgot every consolation, every wonder that God had shown him in the past, and wanted to die because of the affliction in his heart. Thus not even Moses himself understood enough to describe Abraham's melancholy and profound tribulation. Oh Lord Jesus, how often pious hearts still fall into such griefs which they are unable to express, and which others cannot even understand or describe! May You and Your sweet consolation not forsake these troubled hearts!

Shortly before, Abraham had the towering, noble courage of a champion. He dared to take on four kings. But now his heart hung down to his knees. It was like a sudden April shower in Abraham's heart. Indeed, such sudden showers often appear in our heart, too. One day we are as happy and confident as if we were in heaven with the holy angels; the next, we are as sad as if we had fallen a thousand miles under the earth. One day we see our comfort in bright light; the next, we have forgotten everything (for forgetfulness is our worst ailment). Then our disposition is overshadowed with a dark, black cloud. We go back and forth between pondering and weeping, thinking only of our misery, and finally fall into an abyss, a deep valley, where we have no idea what will happen to us. "The holy children of God always have the Spirit, but this Spirit shows itself stronger at one hour than another."[578] The Lord Jesus referred to such sudden affliction in John 16:19 when He said, "A little while and you will not see Me, and a little while longer and you will see Me." For a short time, every comfort vanishes from our heart, every sweet verse that we have heard in church melts away, and no word of encouragement will stick. A little while later, and suddenly Jesus Christ, the Sun of righteousness, sends His beams into our darkened hearts and fills us with joy. Then we see God's grace again, and our heart is well. David too must have experienced this April shower, this sudden vacillation between sadness and joy in the heart, for in Psalm 30:6–7 he says, "And I said in my prosperity, 'I shall never be cast down; for by Your favor, O LORD, You have made my mountain strong'; but when You hid Your face, I was troubled." So, too, when the king of Sodom congratulated Abraham, and the king of Jerusalem gave him a victor's feast, he said, "'I shall never be cast down.' God be praised, I have found out that God is my ally. A handful defeated a land-full. I defy the next man who would dare attack me." But soon an insufferable grief came and passed over Abraham's heart like an April shower. Then all joy was gone. Then Abraham could do nothing but weep, sigh, groan, and lament. O Lord Jesus, You treat us as a mother does her child. One day she hugs, kisses, and smiles at her little one; the next, she hides behind a coat or huddles in secret to see if the child will call for her. Then, when the child begins to groan and whine, she jumps out again and comforts him. In the same way, Lord Jesus, one moment You make our heart overflow with Your comfort; the next, You hide away and let us experience for a while what our flesh and blood can do without Your grace so that we may learn to ascribe our joy not to our own powers but to Your grace. Yet when our troubles have reached their height, You leap out again and shine the love of Your boundless grace and mercy upon us.

578 "Sancti habent eundem Spiritum, sed non semper idem robur Spiritus."

Now since our Lord Jesus is a master of speech and always uses the words best suited to the hearts of His hearers, the kind of agony that Abraham must have had in his heart can surely be inferred from this beautiful little verse of encouragement: *"Fear not."* Abraham was very afraid; his heart raced and trembled. *"Abraham."* Abraham must have doubted in his heart whether God, in His grace, still remembered his name as before. *"I am Your shield."* Abraham must have been terrified at the might of his great enemies. *"[I am] Your very great Reward."* Abraham must have pitied himself because of the world's treachery and ingratitude. Here we see how sick at heart Abraham must have been. Bodily distress is painful, to be sure, but spiritual distress surpasses all.

Thus it is evident that, with men who have suffered such spiritual attacks and been so afflicted, no comfort will stick or help for a long time. Abraham wondered and wept and knew no end of his misery. Every rustling leaf seemed to him an armored soldier. Thoughts came on and on like waves of the sea: "Oh, what have I done? I beat and routed four kings, and now I am stuck in a veritable hornet's-nest. The people are angry. They are not on my side, for they are not of my faith. They have a large following. Soon they will strengthen themselves, make every neighbor side with them, pound me into the dust, and neither hide nor hair will be left of me and my people. Who am I, and who are my people? We are nothing but a fly compared to this huge elephant. True, God is omnipotent, but when does He ever use His omnipotence? Many a good, honorable man with a just cause has had to experience great hardship at God's disposal. Who knows if God will be as kind to me as last time? Long ago He promised me a son, and swore that I would become the grandfather of many nations. Where is this divine promise now? My Sarah is still as barren as she has been for many years. I must have forgotten something. I must have angered God somehow. He will choose someone else to be the Messiah's ancestor. It is all over for me. If my enemies ever attack me again, how long will I last? No longer than butter in the sun. My nephew Lot should have kept that oath that he swore to me. How true it is! 'Cursed is the man who trusts in men' [Jer. 17:5]! Ingratitude is the world's best reward. When you save a man from the gallows, he helps you up to the noose. There's little money to be made in that market. When a man deserves the most thanks, he gets the least. The king of Sodom may have offered me his great friendship, but the favor of noblemen rides on hares.[579] Whoever hopes in them will be sorely disappointed when need arises. The venerable Melchizedek is my best friend, but he is now old and frail. He can't fight any more. When he dies, all my plans will be ruined. Where can I go? How can I stay? I would be better off dead. Oh, if only I were buried in the earth! Oh, if only I had died long ago! Poor forsaken man that I am, I must now weep myself to death," and so on. Now that is an afflicted man.

So, dear heart, when this happens to you, do not be alarmed. It does not mean that you are any farther from God. Abraham was a saintly man, but encountered hardship nevertheless. Our Lord Jesus Himself fell into such painful anguish in the Garden of Gethsemane when He said, "My soul is grieved to the point of death" [Matt. 26:38; Mark 14:34]; and on the cross, "My God, My God, how You have forsaken Me!" [Matt. 27:46; Mark 15:34]. In His heart He felt the anguish that we should have felt who, because of our sins, ought to have been forsaken by God forever, and thus He spoke as one forsaken.[580] Speaking in our stead, He lamented Himself as forsaken, that we might never need to speak such words of sorrow. David was a godly man, and yet he, too, was cast into this furnace and squeezed through this sieve of anguish. Thus he says, "I said in my haste, I am cut off from Your sight" (Ps. 31:22); "My spirit is distressed within me, my heart is consumed within my body" (143:4). Isaiah recalls this great misery also: "Zion says, 'The LORD has forgotten me, the LORD has forsaken me'" (49:14). St. Anthony found strength in such a distress. Therefore, when he recovered, he said, "Oh Lord Jesus, where were You then?"[581] Immediately he heard a reply: "I was here. Had I not been with you then, you would not have made it through. I saw your struggle and helped you to conquer and overcome."[582] Therefore, dear heart, when such adversity befalls you, do not think it something new. Do not consume your heart

---

579 I.e., it is transient and subject to sudden changes, like the way a hare runs when chased.

580 "Sentit dolores derelicti, ideo loquitur verba derelicti."

581 "Domine Jesu, ubi eras?"

582 "Hic eram; eventum pugnae tuae praestolabar."; see Ryan I 93–94.

with ceaseless introspection, as that certain margrave of Brandenburg[583] did when he simmered away his heart so that it was found shriveled up like a baked pear. Instead, remember that such things have befallen even the greatest of saints. The more a saint is recognized by God, the bigger a cross he has to bear. The most pious of all have had to bear with such sadness. The dearer to God, the closer to the rod.[584]

Even St. Paul, that great apostle who studied his Gospel in the third heaven, laments such secret suffering by means of a veiled expression: "Lest I should be exalted above measure because of the profound revelations, a stake was given me in the flesh, namely, a messenger of Satan to harass me, lest I should be exalted above measure" (2 Cor. 12:7). Twice St. Paul says "lest I should be exalted above measure." Likewise, lest Abraham should be exalted above measure by his great, miraculous victory and the great friendships of the kings of Sodom and Salem, God sent him this great cross. For God always bestows great crosses with great gifts, or else the gifts would be abused. St. Paul, however, speaks curiously of his affliction of heart, with veiled, even obscure, expressions. He barely touches on it. Thus one might infer that he suffered great inner turmoil because of his persecutor, despiser, and slanderer (1 Tim. 1:13); for his conscience would often bleed, reasoning, "Is it even possible that God could forgive and forget such horrible sin, blood-guiltiness," etc.? Likewise, the fact that He always suffered from a diseased body, daily headaches, and a constant ailment of the bowels, and was also forced to endure many treacherous tricks by false brothers, and experienced much hardship during his faithful service—in view of these things, scholars believe that there is in this passage a secret which St. Paul carried with him to his grave. He was too ashamed to speak of it clearly. Nor is it wise to reveal everything, for the children of the world are too uncivil. "He who has not been tried knows nothing about it,"[585] and thinks that it is just a fairy-tale.

Therefore, dear heart, if you also suffer such things and cannot ease the pain of your heart, if you are too ashamed to reveal it, if you often say

---

583 Perhaps Joachim II Hector (1505–1571), Elector of Brandenburg.

584 "Deo carissimi, flagellis proximi."

585 "Non tentatus, qualia scit?" Sir. 34:11 (Vulgate).

that things are well and hide the truth, if you are afraid that you will be mocked or that your worries will be doubled, and that you will have to keep it inside you and take it with you to the grave: take comfort! See how both Abraham and St. Paul suffered in the same way. Reveal your heart to God who is faithful and who will not mock you. He will not rebuke or betray you, but comfort you truly.

Now St. Paul called this thing a "stake in the flesh," meaning that he would rather have been impaled alive, like the 20,000 men impaled by Vlad Dracula in the Moldau. Birds came to nest in their bellies, and even the Turkish sultan was horrified. This kind of anguish cannot be expressed with words. Whoever does not believe it need only speak with those who have suffered such tribulations. To be sick at heart is the greatest woe on earth. Many may not have one sick soul in their house, but in their breast there is a sickbed where an ailing heart lies, groaning loudly. That will take the smile off your face. Hence it is that St. Paul calls it "Satan's messenger," for melancholy is the devil's bath.[586] The devil is a sadistic soul, and pushes down the drowning and drenches the soaked. He turns a little infraction into a great, terrifying sin unto death. He embellishes everything to the extreme. Out of a speck of dust floating in a sunbeam he makes a huge mountain. He sharpens all thoughts into daggers and stakes for the heart, and makes men despair of ever finding a silver lining.

Dr. Pommer and Dr. Justus Jonas have written remarkable things about that exceptionally gifted man Luther ([in *Luther's* Works] *Jena* [Edition,] vol. 3, German, *fol.* 458, etc.): In the year 1527, on the Saturday before the Visitation of Mary, he too fell into one such sweat-bath. Luther himself told Dr. Jonas the next day about it: "'I must tell you about yesterday. I was up at the school then, and I was in a feverish sweat-bath.' The Lord took him to hell and back [1 Sam. 2:6]. He went on to say that the spiritual attack was far greater and more grievous than the bodily one." In his great anguish his prayer went thus: "My dearest God, You are a God of sinners and wretches who feel their anguish, trouble, and woe, and sincerely desire Your grace, comfort, and assistance, as You say, 'Come to Me, all you who are weary and heavy laden; I will refresh you.' I am in great

---

586 "Melancholia balneum diaboli."

anguish and trouble. Help me on account of Your grace and faithfulness. Amen." And once again: "O my dear Lord Jesus Christ, who said, 'Pray, and it shall be given to you; seek, and you shall find; knock, and it shall be opened to you'; by virtue of this Your promise, O Lord, let it be given to me, for I pray not for gold or silver but for a strong and steadfast faith. Let me find, for I seek not pleasure or worldly joy but comfort and new life through Your blessed, comforting, saving Word. Let it be opened to me, for I knock. Nothing do I desire that the world counts great and high, for by such things I am not made a hair's breadth better in Your sight. Rather, send me Your Holy Spirit to enlighten my heart, to strengthen and comfort me in my anguish and distress, and to preserve me in the true faith, that I may trust in Your grace until I die. Amen."

Such distress he often had to suffer, just as he himself said, "Many suppose that, because I sometimes act happy in my outward behavior, I walk in a world of roses. But God knows how it really is with me," etc. And in the same year, for that matter, on the eve of Simon and Jude, he wrote to a good friend, "Pray devoutly for me, a poor, rejected worm, who am so harshly afflicted with melancholy and sadness of spirit according to the good, gracious will of the merciful Father in heaven, to whom be glory, honor, and praise, even in my great anguish and distress." Mathesius also writes about this (*Luther's Life, fol.* 56, 172, etc.). From all this we see how comfortingly Luther was able to address such people (ibid.; *Jena,* vol. 8, *fol.* 413). This essentially consists of six parts: (1) People under such temptation should not be left alone, but have the Scripture spoken to them, for it is the pharmacy of the Holy Spirit. Then they should be shown: (2) that their thoughts are only the attack of the devil; (3) that they should strike such thoughts from their heart and bluntly turn him away, for arguing with him will not help; (4) that they should receive the comforting sayings of Holy Scripture as though the God of heaven were speaking to them Himself; (5) that they should pray earnestly and not forsake the prayers of the gathered Church; and (6) that they should boldly seize the victory and not let the devil weary them. Oh, what beautiful things he said to Elsa, that spiritually afflicted woman whose story I shared in part one![587]

587   See part 1, meditation 4.

Scholars, being forced to read through all the learning and correspondence of the world, often suffer from this sort of private cross the most. Master Anton Musa,[588] Pastor of Rochlitz, once came to Luther complaining that he often did not himself believe what he preached to others. Luther said, "Well, thanks and praise be to God that for once I have heard another man of my disposition." Musa was never able to forget that comfort his whole life. Mathesius also fell into this kind of anxiety. Once, having been directed to his own books and comforting writings, he said, "I know all that stuff very well, but it doesn't penetrate my heart." Then those standing around him said, "Well then, let it penetrate the heart of Jesus Christ," and he immediately recovered.

Philipp said that a student at Wittenberg was once stuck in this kind of anxiety for three whole days. At last, regaining his senses, the student said, "Thanks and praise be to God who helped me overcome this. Whoever believes in Jesus Christ shall have everlasting life. I believe, therefore I shall have everlasting life."[589]

In 1490, Wessel Gansfort,[590] a highly learned scholar from Frisia, also fell into this kind of anxiety and began to doubt the truth of Christianity. His good friend, hearing this, left him in great sorrow. After a few hours, Wessel asked him to come back, saying that the storm in his heart was past and he was again certain of his consolation. Also, Dr. Weller[591] passed through such a sieve and with great nobility suffered being raked over the coals of his cross. Hence it was that, at the suggestion of many fine persons, he came to write his beneficial book on the account of Job as a comfort for the spiritually afflicted. In January, 1597, in Breslau, a well-born lady said to me, "Please, dearest sir, etc., pray, pray that God would not take my joyfulness from me," and cried so bitterly that a stone would have been filled with pity. As I began to reply with words of comfort, she said,

---

588 Anton Musa (1485–1547), *alias* Wesch, West; reformer, theologian, and composer.

589 "Deo gratia, qui dedit nobis victoriam. Qui credit in Filium, habebit vitam aeternam. Ego Nicolaus credo, ergo habebo vitam aeternam."

590 Wessel Harmensz Gansfort (1419–1489), pre-Lutheran reformer from the Netherlands.

591 Hieronymus Weller (1499–1572), the "Prophet of Freiberg," theologian and friend of the Luther household.

"Just let me weep a little. I will get better." I have met with many more such examples, about which I would now be wise to keep silent.

A pious woman once came to Luther and lamented pitifully that she was unable to believe. He said, "Do you know the Apostles' Creed?" "Yes," said the woman, and prayed it. Then Luther said, "Do you hold this to be true and to be your own?" She said, "Yes." Then the blessed man said, "Forsooth, dear woman, if you hold it to be true and believe in it as the utter truth, then you believe more strongly than I! For I must pray every day for more faith." At this, the woman thanked God and went home with joy. It is well to note this, lest a heart oppressed by such a cross should imagine that no pious man in the world ever met with such suffering before.

Now contemplate further, dear heart, the gracious, old love and kindness of our Lord Jesus for all afflicted souls. He answered Abraham when Abraham had not even sought Him out. He consoled Abraham when Abraham had not even asked Him for it. He allayed Abraham's worries precisely to a tee when Abraham had not even revealed one word to Him. This is a mighty consolation for all afflicted hearts. If only we would be earnest to pray morning and evening and sigh to God whenever we are in our right mind, we would also be preserved from evil and calamity in times when out of the weakness of our flesh and the sheer weight of our grief we forget to pray. O Lord Jesus, You will run to us without being asked, and lift us up with Your comfort. Oh, had You not come unsolicited to our aid so many times, we would have perished long ago! Display Your old love to us. And if in some accursed moment we forget our dearest treasure, the precious gift of prayer, yet do not forget us, for You know our weakness. We do not do this out of hatred, but our many crosses cast dark clouds over our mind and we do not always think and reason as we should. Oh, answer us before we pray. You know our worries far better than we can describe them to You. You proved this when You comforted Abraham and when You answered Moses on the Red Sea. Prove it also to me, poor sinner that I am, that I may not perish.

Also contemplate our Lord Jesus' word of comfort: "Fear not." Do not grieve, dear heart, dear friend, the old God is still alive. He is still as strong as He was a thousand years ago. He is all-powerful; who can have dominion over Him? If God is with you, by you, before you, behind you, and around you, who can be against you? "The angel of the LORD encamps round about those who fear Him" [Ps. 34:7]. Remember His wonders of old [77:11], and in view of them, "wait on the LORD, be confident and despair not, and wait on the LORD" [27:14].

"Abraham, you heard well. You wondered if I were still as gracious as many years ago. Listen, Abraham, I know you, not only by face but by name as well. You—yes, you—will be the forefather of the Messiah. My original grace and truth will not change. 'I am your Shield.' Let the four kings rage. I will defend you. One little word and they will be knocked over. Rely on Me. Cast your burdens on Me, for I have a broad back. I can easily bear them. You can hand them over to Me. 'Who trusts in God, a strong abode [in heaven and earth possesses].'[592] I will be your guardian and your reward. You have done well to aid your nephew and your neighbors. What they do not repay you, I will. Should one whose friendship you deserve fall away, I will give you a hundred instead, or if they are not enough, a thousand. I will be your constant friend. I will profit you better than the world can. I am your very great reward. Indeed, I assure you, whatever you lack in temporal things shall be richly repaid in eternal, incorruptible goods. Therefore, 'let My grace be sufficient for you' [2 Cor. 12:9]."[593] Oh Lord Jesus, as You comforted Abraham, as You encouraged St. Paul, so refresh my weary heart. Say also to me, "Fear not, (dear heart), I know you by name, and you have found grace in My sight" [Ex. 33:12]; "I am your shield and your very great reward"; "Let My grace be sufficient for you." O Lord Jesus, indeed, Your grace shall be sufficient for me. Let Your grace and truth be great toward me forever, and I will thank You like Abraham and dear St. Paul. As soon as You rescued pious David from his anguish, he said first, "I extol You, O LORD, for You have lifted me up," and last, "O LORD my God, I will give thanks to You forever" [Ps. 30:1, 12]. In the very same way, O Lord Jesus, I too will extol Your comfort, praise Your wondrous works, and glorify Your name forever and ever. Amen.

---

592   From the hymn, "Wer Gott vertraut hat wohl gebaut" (J. Magdeburg, 1572); see *LSB* 714.

593   "sufficit tibi gratia mea."

XXXII. JESUS
Counts to Abraham as Righteousness Abraham's Faith in Him
(Gen. 15[:6]).

The Lord Jesus gave the deeply afflicted Abraham living consolation, saying, "Fear not, Abraham, I am your shield and your very great reward." In addition, He also assured him that he would have a son, and that a great nation would come from him, that, in fact, the Messiah would be born from his bloodline. For the Lord Jesus Christ repeated to Abraham His previous promise from chapter 12. It all came true: Isaac was born to Abraham, over 600,000 men exited Egypt on foot, all from Abraham's line, and the Savior of the world was born to Abraham's descendants, as Matthew 1 indicates; for all God's words have the force of an oath. Whatever He says is true and certain. On this we may live confidently and die happily.

Now Moses is very careful to say that Abraham heard this, kept it in his heart, and believed it. In other words, he trusted in his Lord Jesus' assurance of grace, hoped with surest hope that God could and would realize His promise, and in such consolation he was filled with boldness, found contentment, took comfort in it, prayed in it, and dispelled his sadness—and that the Lord Jesus *counted* (or, as the Hebrew allows, "imputed") this faith to him as righteousness.

Here, dear heart, learn what the old catholic, Christian, saving faith is, to wit: Whoever believes in the Lord Jesus is accounted, judged, and declared righteous, and saved by God; whoever believes in Jesus Christ receives the forgiveness of sins and life everlasting, and will endure God's judgment. Thus St. Paul appeals with great force to this mighty and central verse of Genesis, saying, "But the words 'it was counted to him' were not written for his sake alone, but for ours also, to whom it will be counted if we believe in Him who raised from the dead Jesus our Lord, who was delivered up for our trespasses and raised for our justification" (Rom.

4:23–25). Refer also to Hebrews 11:8–9, where it suggests that Abraham and Sarah pleased God by faith alone. The Chaldean Bible says, "He believed the word of the LORD, and it was counted to him as righteousness."[594] We may therefore join the apostles in Acts at the First Council, saying, "We believe that we will be saved through the grace of the Lord Jesus Christ, just as they," our fathers in the Old Testament (Acts 15:11). Behold, dear heart, how perfectly Genesis 15 and Acts 15 fit together, how perfectly the Genesis of the Old Testament and the Genesis of the New Testament agree.[595] So let me say once more with St. Paul, "Therefore we conclude that man is justified by faith alone, apart from the works of the Law" (Rom. 3:28). True, the word "alone" does not appear in the Greek; many have fought over that. But the sense is warranted, and the word was likewise used by Ambrose, Primasius, Hesychius, Augustine, Basil, and Chrysostom. In AD 460, Victor, a rhetorician from Marseilles,[596] put the first nineteen chapters of Genesis into verse, in which he says,

> By faith he believed, which faith, alone and naked,
> Was reckoned a perfect crown of justice and merit."[597]

I have never heard a better verse on this passage in all my days. And of course, St. Paul says, "By grace you have been saved through faith, and that not of yourselves: it is the gift of God, not of works, so that no man may boast" (Eph. 2:8–9).

They are the true children of Abraham, then, who with Abraham believe in Jesus Christ. This Christ explains to the Jews in John 8:39. St. Paul, moreover, clearly testifies, "Just as Abraham believed God and it was counted to him as righteousness…know then that those who are of faith, the same are the children of Abraham" (Gal. 3:6–7). These believing hearts will sit at table with Abraham in the kingdom of God [Matt. 8:11] and with Abraham also be justified and saved.

---

594 "Credidit in verbum Domini, et reputatum est ei ad justitiam."

595 "Genesis Veteris Testamenti et Genesis Novi Testamenti conveniunt."

596 Claudius Marius Victor (fl. 5th c.), *alias* Victorius, -inus, a minor Christian poet from Marseilles, not to be confused with 3rd c. martyr St. Victor of Marseilles.

597 "Credidit, et nudae fidei consensio sola / Plenam ad justitiae et meriti reputata coronam est"; Cl. Mar. Vict. *Alethia* 3.486–488 (Gagneius 443–444).

We furthermore see that Abraham did not doubt this, but believed it most certainly, as Paul says in Romans 4:18, for "faith is a certain assurance of things hoped for, and does not doubt things unseen," as Hebrews 11:1 says. For this reason we should remain firm, certain, and confident in Jesus Christ so that by Him we may find a gracious God. We should not despair, doubt, or waver, but boldly say, "I believe that my sins are forgiven,"[598] and that I have the righteousness that avails before God, and eternal life through Jesus Christ, Amen. This is faithful and true, Amen.

Take note of this, dear heart, for the strengthening of your faith so that you do not go astray when you hear that this comforting teaching was revoked and condemned as heretical at the Council of Trent in 1546.

Accordingly, it is our most beautiful comfort in every tribulation, even in the throes of death, that our righteousness rests not on our good works but on the precious merit and grace imparted by Jesus Christ, to whom we must, like Abraham, cling with true faith. Indeed, if our righteousness before God consisted of our own good works, we would justly despair, for then no one would be able to know whether he had done enough. But since the Lord Jesus Himself is our righteousness, and all those who believe in Jesus shall be declared just before God, we can be bold and confident, for one single drop of Jesus Christ's blood outweighs the sins of the whole world. For this reason it was commanded in the old papal agendas that dying Christian should be told:

> You believe that you cannot not be saved or enter eternal life but by the merit of the suffering of your Lord Jesus Christ. Therefore put all your hope and trust in the suffering and death of Jesus Christ. Commit yourself entirely to this death, not doubting or despairing of the mercifulness of God, for the Lord Jesus Christ suffered and died for you and for us all, that He might save us all.[599]

---

598 "Credo remissionem peccatorum."

599 "Credis non aliter te posse salvari, et nec vitam ingredi, nisi per meritum passionis Domini nostri Jesu Christi. Pone ergo totam spem et fiduciam tuam in eandem acerbissimam passionem et mortem Christi. Huic mortitae totum committe, nil dubitans aut desperans de misericordia Dei, passus et mortuus est enim Dominus Jesus Christus pro te et pro omnibus nobis, ut nos omnes salvos faceret: Et ipse salvabit animam tuam. Amen"; *Sancti Anselmi admonitio morienti.*

And among other questions which were to be asked the dying, St. Anselm added this one to the end:

> If he believes that he is saved by Christ's merit and not by his own works, and answers that he believes: Let it be said finally: If the enemy, the devil, ever encounters you, oppose him on every occasion with the merit of the suffering of Jesus Christ.[600]

Just as by true faith in Jesus Christ one is blessed before God, so in the sight of the world one must prove one's faith with good works so that one may also be declared and regarded just and blessed by the world. Therefore James says, "Faith without works is dead." For when James says that man is justified by works, not faith alone, you must take it as in the sight of the world, for the world cannot see the faith hidden in your heart. There you must confess your faith with your mouth and prove it with your deeds. Paul, however, speaks of the faith that justifies us before God. This is why he says, "If Abraham is justified by works, he has glory, but not before God" (Rom. 4:2). On the other hand, James speaks about how one is to be regarded as just before the world, as he makes clear: "Show me your faith," and then: "But if your brother and sister are unclothed, and lack daily nourishment, and someone should say to them, 'May God help you, make you warm and well fed,' but give them nothing that their body needs, what good is it?"—and whereas James is furthermore not talking about that faith which is a certain, joyful, undoubting assurance of God's grace obtained by Jesus Christ, but only about the simple knowledge and belief of the events of the Gospel—for he even says, "the devils believe it also, and shudder" (Surely no one would say that the devil trusts in God's grace and the merit of Christ)—therefore, James' sermon is not contrary to the teachings of St. Paul or of Moses. For St. Paul speaks of how one may stand before God's judgment, not before the eyes of the world. He teaches us how to be justified and blessed before God, and also speaks of such a faith that happily says, "My faith is firm and certain, and I will die believing that God is gracious to me for the sake of Jesus Christ, and that

---

600 "Si credit se meritis passionis Christi, et non propriis, ad gloriam pervenire, et respondeat: Credo: Ultimo debet dicere: Si occurrit tibi inimicus tuus Diabolus, semper opponas ei merita passionis Jesu Christi"; ibid.

I have been forgiven of my sins by grace, and that through the precious merit of Jesus Christ I have righteousness and eternal life with God.

Therefore, in order for one to be justified and blessed before God, let him believe in Jesus Christ, as St. Paul says. But in order for one to be justified and esteemed blessed in the sight of the world, let him prove his faith with good works, do good to his neighbor, and cultivate all godliness, as St. James says. Oh Lord Jesus, like Abraham I believe in You. You are my comfort and shelter. Through You let me receive the righteousness that avails before God, and thus eternal life. Oh, direct me by Your Holy Spirit, that I may think about all that is honorable and virtuous, serve my neighbor according to my ability, and live according to Your will, and so obtain the righteousness which avails before honorable people and have a testimony of my faith before the world. Then I will live and dwell in Your grace in time and in eternity. Amen.

XXXIII. JESUS
Fills Abraham's Ears with a Comforting Promise and Sets before His Eyes a
Blessed Token of Grace, thus Assuring His Heart by Word and Sacrament
That His Children Shall Inherit the Promised Land (Gen. 15[:7–21]).

The Lord Jesus assured Abraham of the Promised Land a third and fourth time in quick succession, for He was not only concerned for Abraham's soul but also for the needs of his body, such as shelter, food, and clothing. Even after His resurrection He was plainly concerned about such things, as when He said, "Children, have you nothing to eat?" (John 21:5). Oh, sweet Lord Jesus, I commend my soul and body to Your gracious care. Look after my soul with Your comfort and my body with Your blessing, and I will be content.

Second, the Lord Jesus defined the borders of the Jewish kingdom, for Psalm 24:1 does not lie when it says, "The earth is the LORD's, and all that is in it, the ground and that which dwells thereon." The kingdoms of the earth are the Lord's, and He gives them to whom He will,[601] as the king of Sweden says on his coinage. When the devil claimed such power [Matt. 4:9; Luke 4:6], he proved himself a liar. O Lord Jesus, all that we have comes from Your hand. For reasons we cannot fathom, You give much to one and little to another, and yet You are able to nourish all who serve You. He who dwells in a little room often has more than he who boasts many realms in his possession. Grant grace, therefore, that we may look only to Your hands and trust confidently in Your care.

Third, the Lord Jesus foretold how Abraham's children would fare in this country. They would first fall into sorrow and trouble. The worthless, greedy Egyptian birds would peck and pester them, darkness and fear would overtake them, and they would be grieved and afflicted; for all God's works start off with such misery and disdain. Yet

---

601 "Dominus dat, cui vult."

their hardship would not last forever. Because of the promise made to Abraham, those birds would be chased away. After that, as Abraham had heard, things would improve for some four hundred years. Then Abraham's children would enter the Promised Land and take it without hindrance. By a great and unexpected good they would be freed from their adversity, as fulfilled in Deuteronomy 12:29. O dear Lord Jesus, all things are known to You. You know what has been, what is now, and what is to come. I take comfort in Your omniscience. You count the days of our sadness. You count the tears of our misery. Because of this I will thank You forever.

The Lord also prophesied to Abraham that he would reach a ripe old age and be peacefully laid to rest in the earth. O Lord Jesus, You are the length of our life; our days are in Your hands. You also lengthened the life of Hezekiah. Preserve our lives, too, until that blessed hour when we shall pass from this paltry, miserable life to the life of everlasting joy.

Also noteworthy here is that God watched the Amorites in their wickedness, yet did not hasten His punishment upon them in His wrath. This they were to earn abundantly first, filling to the full the measure of their sins. God wished to give them sufficient time for repentance, for He is slow to get in the saddle, but also slow to get out. Oh Lord my God, help us to recognize Your long-suffering nature and so be stirred to repentance, for he who constantly and willfully sins against God's grace will be repaid with eternal disgrace.

> I sadly fear, God's slighted grace
> Which long with scorn they did efface,
> Will scarce upon them linger.[602]

Dear heart, contemplate once more Jesus Christ's special work of grace in His dealings with Abraham here. When our Lord assured Abraham of the land, he began by speaking a plain, clear, comprehensible word, then added to it a lovely sign of grace. For when the sacrifice was divided and laid out, each piece one against another, the Lord passed over

---

602 From the hymn "Kommt her zu mir, spricht Gottes Sohn" (ascr. H. Witzstadt, 1528), st. 10, lines 4–6; cf. Mills 48 (st. 7).

the midst of it in a tongue of fire, just as people used to do long ago when they were making a pact with each other, to testify that they would keep good faith (as seen in Jer. 34:18). Some believe that this tongue of fire also consumed the sacrifice. Thus Abraham had Word and Sacrament side by side; yea, he had both letter and seal of the Promised Land. He heard and saw that this land would belong to his children. O Lord Jesus Christ, such is Your old, gracious way. When You want to fill our heart with comfort and completely convince us that You intend our good, You fill our ears with a clear word of grace, and then fill our eyes with a comforting, visible sign of grace and lovely Sacrament. To make Adam and Eve's hearts certain of Your favor, You proclaimed in their ears the First Gospel, and placed before their eyes lovely lambskins. To assure Abel of Your love, You let him hear those beautiful words that his parents had heard: "The woman's Seed shall trample the serpent's head," and with his eyes let him see his sacrifice consumed with fire from heaven. So that Noah might have no doubts about Your grace, You gave him clear assurance in trustworthy words that You would never again destroy the earth with water, and furthermore caused the beautiful rainbow to shine before his eyes as a testimony of this pledge. Likewise, in order that Abraham should have no doubt about Your grace, You spoke clear words for him to hear, and showed Yourself to his eyes in Your lovely tongue of fire. Later in the same way, he received a new word of grace for his ears and circumcision for his eyes, in order that his heart might take comfort in Your friendship. As You always dealt with those who served You, so You still deal with me and all Christians today. You let my ears hear the beautiful words: "For God so loved the world, that He gave His only-begotten Son, that whoever believes in Him should not perish but have eternal life" (John 3:16), and: "Come to Me, all who are weary and heavy laden; I will refresh you" (Matt. 11:28). Then, giving me Holy Baptism and the Holy Supper for my eyes to see, You assure my heart and give it steadfast confidence in Your unfeigned love. Help me to delight in Your gracious way, to hear Your Word gladly, to cherish the Holy Sacraments, to use them often, and not to despise the tokens of Your grace or weary You with disobedience, as Isaiah said to Ahaz (Is. 7:13). In these I have the promised land of eternal life signed and sealed. My ears have heard it in the Gospel, my eyes have seen it in Holy Baptism and the divine Supper, my heart is assured and firmly believes it. O Lord Jesus, for this comforting guarantee of my salvation I will thank You henceforth and forevermore. Amen.